ALASKA'S PARKLANDS

THE COMPLETE GUIDE

NATIONAL
Parks, Monuments, Preserves, Wildlife Refuges, Forests,
Wild and Scenic Rivers

STATE
Parks, Recreation Areas, Historic Sites, Refuges,
Game Sanctuaries

By Nancy Lange Simmerman

The Mountaineers/Seattle

To my parents and to Alaska

THE MOUNTAINEERS: Organized in 1906
"...to explore, study, preserve, and enjoy
the natural beauty of the Northwest."

First edition: first printing June 1983, second printing June 1984,
third printing November 1985, fourth printing June 1987

Published by The Mountaineers
306 2nd Ave. W., Seattle, Washington 98119

Published simultaneously in Canada by Douglas & McIntyre, Ltd.
1615 Venables Street, Vancouver, British Columbia V5L 2H1

Cover photo: Arrigetch Peaks, Brooks Range, Alaska, in July
Photos by the author unless otherwise indicated
Sketch maps and book design by Marge Mueller

Library of Congress Cataloging in Publication Data

Simmerman, Nancy.
  Alaska's parklands, the complete guide.

  Bibliography: p.
  Includes index.
  1. Alaska—Description and travel—1981- —Guide-
books.   2. Historic sites—Alaska—Guide-books.
3. Parks — Alaska — Guide-books.   I. Title.
F902.3.S58 1983   917.98 '045   83-8055
ISBN 0-89886-053-9

Contents

PART I : TRAVEL IN ALASKA   11

PART II: THE PARKLANDS   66

Exit Glacier, Kenai Fjords National Park. (National Park Service photo by Robert Belous)

Foreword

In December 1980, some nine years after Congress set the scene by passage of the Alaska Native Claims Settlement Act, it completed action on and the President signed the long-debated Alaska National Interest Lands Conservation Act.

The Alaska Lands Act, as most of us call it, profoundly affected the future of Alaska. It set aside over 104 million* acres of the 49th state as parks, refuges, monuments and wild and scenic river areas. It created over 43 million acres of new parks—designating 32.4 million of those acres as wilderness. Overall, the act created 13 major additions to the federal national park system and designated 56 million acres of Alaska as Wilderness.

The bill was controversial; residents of the other 49 states joined Alaskans in a spirited debate over the future of the "Last Frontier." While passage of the bill did not please all Alaskans, it has established the "rules of the game" which allow us to get on with the task of preserving and developing our great expanses.

This book is one of the first of what will likely be many volumes devoted to describing the scenic wonders of the new national conservation areas. It describes the areas' locations, climates, physical descriptions, means of access, available activities, sites to see and precautions to be taken in what, in many cases, are wild, untrammeled locales.

Now that America has taken steps to preserve the integrity of these areas for eternity, it is only fitting that Americans view the scenic wonders protected inside the boundaries of the conservation areas.

The splendor which is Alaska can be shared by all, not confined as the exclusive domain of the wealthy or learned. This book starts the process of increasing awareness and appreciation of the beauty and solitude preserved in the conservation areas.

This is an important and worthy undertaking—something which will benefit all Alaskans—in fact, all Americans—for decades to come.

Jay Hammond
Governor 1975-1982

---

*The figure is constantly changing as lands are surveyed, boundaries stabilized, and state and private lands transferred.

Safety Conditions

Travel in many parts of Alaska entails unavoidable risks that every traveler assumes and must be aware of and respect. The fact that an area is described in this book is not a representation that it will be safe for you. Trips vary greatly in difficulty and in the amount and kind of preparation needed to enjoy them safely. Some routes may have changed, or conditions on them may have deteriorated since this book was written. Also, of course, conditions can change even from day to day, owing to weather and other factors. A trip that is safe in good weather or for a highly conditioned, properly equipped traveler, may be completely unsafe for someone else or unsafe under adverse weather conditions.

You can minimize your risks by being knowledgeable, prepared, and alert. There is not space in this book for a general treatise on wilderness safety, but there are a number of good books and public courses on the subject, and you should take advantage of them to increase your knowledge. Just as important, you should always be aware of your own limitations and conditions existing when and where you are traveling. If conditions are dangerous, or if you are not prepared to deal with them safely, change your plans! It is better to have wasted a few days than to be the subject of a wilderness rescue. These warnings are not intended to keep you out of the back country. Many people enjoy safe trips through the back country every year. However, one element of the beauty, freedom, and excitement of the wilderness is the presence of risks that do not confront us at home. When you travel in Alaska, you assume those risks. They can be met safely, but only if you exercise your own independent judgment and common sense.

The Publisher

Gates of the Arctic National Park.

Preface

"Will it be Fairbanks or Istanbul?" I threw the two teaching contracts onto the table and stomped into the sweltering Ohio summer. The decision had to be made quickly. College graduation had been the previous week and, with the impatience of youth, I didn't know what to do with the rest of my life.

The problem resolved itself. The contract to teach chemistry and physics in Turkey was for three years, the contract with the chemistry department at the University of Alaska for only one. I wasn't ready to commit myself any more than necessary, so Alaska it was.

In the year of Alaska's statehood, 1959, with a loaded station wagon and a six-week-old puppy for company, I drove north to my future. Twenty-four years later, I'm still here. I find this state too fascinating and challenging to leave.

With such scenic beauty everywhere, classrooms and laboratories quickly became restrictive, and I turned to outdoor photography for an excuse to roam the mountains and seashores. I crewed on sailboats plying the waters of the Inside Passage and Prince William Sound, kayaked the coast of Katmai National Park and wandered the Valley of Ten Thousand Smokes. I guided visiting hikers in the Noatak National Preserve, studied animals along the Trans-Alaska pipeline, traveled by dogsled in Denali National Park and skied through the Brooks Range, sleeping in holes in the snow.

Important and far-reaching changes have come to Alaska's wilderness over the years. In the past we could wander, fish and hunt at will, largely unrestricted. With the transfer of large amounts of land by the state to private individuals and by the federal government to Alaska natives, and with much land made into parks and refuges, boundaries and regulations proliferated. Long-time Alaskans became perplexed by the new regulations and grumbled about the lack of traditional freedoms, while newcomers faced a complicated wilderness with no signs, boundary markers or fences to identify rivers, mountain peaks or private property.

As confused as everyone else, I began to dig for information. I spent innumerable hours talking with land management personnel and reading a six-foot-high stack of reports. Little had been published about a large number of Alaska's wild places. Finally a book about the state's vast and far-ranging public lands began to take shape.

If this book helps you to appreciate this unique state and travel in it, my efforts will have been worthwhile. The likes of Alaska's colorful history, spectacular scenery and bountiful wildlife cannot be found anywhere else on earth.

N.L.S.
Girdwood, 1983

Acknowledgments

This book would not have been possible without the valuable assistance of more than 100 staff members associated with the Alaska Department of Fish and Game, the Alaska Division of Parks, the Bureau of Land Management, the National Park Service, the U.S. Fish and Wildlife Service and the U.S. Forest Service, who helped find obscure information and who read each description for accuracy.

Special thanks are due James C. Allen of the Alaska Department of Environmental Conservation and James A. Wilkerson, M.D., for reviewing the sections on water

Kenibuna Lake and Shamrock Glacier, Lake Clark National Park. (National Park Service photo by M. Woodbridge Williams)

pollution and treatment; Ron Costello, air taxi operator, for reviewing the section on air taxis; the late Tom Ellis, mountain rescue and emergency medicine instructor, for reviewing the sections on hypothermia, cold-water drowning and frostbite; Douglas S. Fesler, Alaska Division of Parks, and Edward R. LaChapelle, Professor of Geophysics and Atmospheric Sciences, University of Washington, for reviewing the section on avalanches; Louisa Nishitani, fisheries biologist, University of Washington, for reviewing the section on paralytic shellfish poisoning; and James Wise of the Climate Center, Arctic Environmental Information and Data Center, University of Alaska, for his assistance in locating weather records.

Very special thanks are due Betsy Bayes Preis, who helped type the manuscript and unflinchingly met all deadlines, to Alice Copp Smith and Ann Cleeland for their skillful editing of these pages, and to Donna DeShazo for supervising the production of the book.

Introduction

Alaska is a big land, with rivers, lakes and mountains to match. Its portion of the mighty Yukon River winds for 1400 mi (2300 km). Its largest lake, Iliamna, has a surface area of 1000 square miles (2600 square kilometers). It boasts North America's highest peak, 20,320-ft (6194-m) Mount McKinley. Its largest glacier, the Malaspina, is 50% larger than the state of Delaware. Its coastline is longer than those of all the other U.S. maritime states put together.

Across a map of this vast state, a bewildering array of national and state parks, monuments, preserves, refuges, forests and rivers interlock like pieces of an unfinished jigsaw puzzle. This book describes all of these areas, which we'll call "parklands," and provides information about their recreational use, history, geography, wildlife, weather, facilities and access.

Part I of the book is a guide to getting around in Alaska, from the highway and state ferry systems to the most remote wilderness. There are sections on camping, backpacking, boating, village life in the Bush and observing wildlife. Part II consists of individual descriptions of the parklands and Wild Rivers, arranged alphabetically. An accompanying color map helps you locate each wild area described while small maps in the book provide detail.

The Appendix contains useful information to help you plan your trip: locations of public campgrounds, addresses and phone numbers of land managers, information sources, access and services for each village, uses of each parkland, and booklets you can write for.

Selected readings are given within each parkland description. More general readings about Alaska are listed at the end of the book.

If you've never traveled in Alaska before, you'll find it an exciting experience. Basic backpacking skills will stand you in good stead. Beyond these, this book will help you learn about the things unique to Alaska: how to cope with its wildlife, from mosquitoes to bears; how to keep warm in the snow; why many Alaskans think winter is the best season; where you'll find the world's largest concentration of brown bears; which wilderness rivers are seldom visited.

Whether you are an experienced Alaskan exploring further afield, a new resident just learning about your adopted state, or a visitor from the Lower 48 or another country experiencing Alaska for the first time, you can use this book to decide where to go and how to get there.

Backpacking in Denali National Wilderness.

PART I: TRAVEL IN ALASKA

GETTING AROUND

Automobile Travel

Most of Alaska's parklands are far from the road system or have only minimal road access, but 40 areas accessible by automobile, including some uncrowded wildernesses, are described in this book. Relative to its size Alaska contains very few miles of public highway, and most of them are concentrated near the major population centers. Some roads, however, notably the Dalton Highway (the North Slope Haul Road), traverse isolated wild lands. Since roads and highways are occasionally closed by break-up (that springtime phenomenon of slush and knee-deep mud), weather conditions, floods or avalanches, check with the Alaska Department of Transportation or the State Troopers for current information (phone numbers in Information Sources, Appendix).

Although major highways are paved, many of the state's most interesting road miles are not. Good quality, relatively new tires are recommended for all highways, with an extra spare tire for extensive traveling on gravel back roads. Always carry enough fuel, extra engine oil, transmission and brake fluid, extra fan belts, a good jack, a tow chain, a basic tool set, battery jumper cables, road flares, wire, rags and a flashlight with strong batteries. If you are likely to encounter snow, ice and low temperatures, be sure your car is protected with adequate antifreeze, light-weight transmission fluid and proper lubrication. Use studded snow tires and carry tire chains, a shovel that can move large quantities of snow, a sack of sand, sawdust or cat litter for emergency traction, a windshield scraper, sleeping bags or blankets for all passengers, extra warm clothing, matches, a small stove and a saucepan for melting snow and a supply of high-calorie food that can be eaten cold, such as nuts, cookies or fruitcake. To start a fire in an emergency without matches, move the automobile's battery a safe distance from the vehicle and touch the ends of the cables together to produce a spark, letting it fall on a gasoline-dampened rag.

Services on Alaskan highways are limited and often scattered. Major repairs and parts are not usually available in remote areas and small towns, so have your vehicle thoroughly serviced and checked before beginning a trip. Sanitary dump stations for self-contained camper vehicles are found in the major cities but are virtually non-existent elsewhere. It is illegal to dump holding tanks at unauthorized locations.

All road travelers should have one of the published mile-by-mile road guides. The most comprehensive are *The Milepost* (Anchorage: Alaska Northwest Publishing Co., revised annually) and *Alaska Travel Guide* (Larry Lake, P.O. Box 21038, Salt Lake City, Utah 84121, revised annually).

Rental automobiles are available in Anchorage, Bethel, Cordova, Fairbanks, Haines, Homer, Juneau, Kenai, Ketchikan, Kodiak, Seward, Sitka, Skagway, Valdez and Yakutat. Firms in Anchorage and Fairbanks rent motor homes.

Guided Tours and Sightseeing Packages

Many of the parklands described in this book can be visited as part of a tour, either with a group or an independent package-tour plan. A wide range of services exist, from luxury cruise ships leisurely sailing the Inside Passage to bus tours up the Alaska Highway, from posh wilderness lodges to strenuous backpacking trips, from wilderness sailboat charters to guided climbs up Mount McKinley.

Table 2, Appendix, shows which parklands are visited by commercial tours or

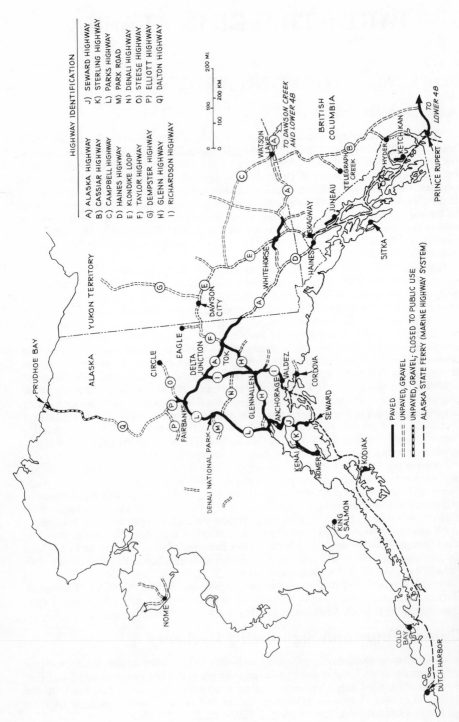

Figure 1. Highways and roads.

guided trips. A list of tour companies, guide services and wilderness lodges is updated annually in the Alaska Division of Tourism's free publication, "Alaska Travel Directory." The Division's address is in Information Sources, Appendix.

Public Transportation

Considering the distances and the logistics involved, Alaska has a fairly good public transportation network of commercial buslines, ferries, railroads and airlines. To reach areas not readily accessible by scheduled public transportation, air taxis (Alaska's term for chartered small planes) and charter boats are readily available. "Alaska Travel Directory" contains a list of land, air and water carriers. See Figure 2 for an idea of how all these transportation forms tie together.

Buses. Most major highways, including the Alaska Highway through Canada, are traveled by commercial buslines. See Tables 1 and 2, Appendix, for communities and parklands accessible by bus. In Information Sources, the Appendix lists buslines serving Alaska and the Alaska Highway. Some of the larger communities have local city bus service, and most have taxicabs.

State ferries. The Alaska Marine Highway System consists of two separate units. The Southeastern system serves Panhandle cities and communities from Haines and Skagway south through the Inside Passage to Prince Rupert, British Columbia, and on to Seattle; the Southwestern system serves Southcentral Alaska from Cordova and Valdez west to Kodiak and Cold Bay. The two units *do not* connect across the Gulf of Alaska.

Any vehicle that may be legally taken on a state highway can be transported on the ferries. A limited number of staterooms are available for overnight travelers, but many passengers choose to sleep in the reclining salon chairs, while others throw sleeping bags on deck for the night. Passengers may not sleep in vehicles on the car deck. Reservations are necessary for all travelers and vehicles.

Alaska State ferry M.V. Bartlett, *Prince William Sound, Chugach National Forest.*

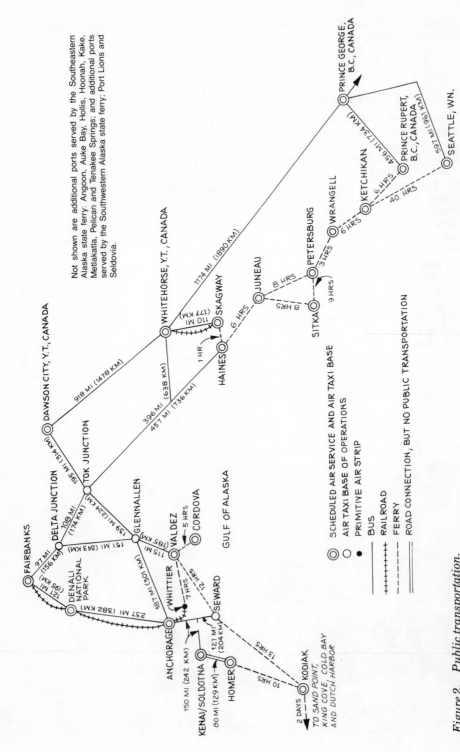

Figure 2. Public transportation.

Railroads. Two railroads have been operating in Alaska, the Alaska Railroad in Southcentral and the White Pass & Yukon Route in Southeastern.

The Alaska Railroad carries passengers between Anchorage, Denali National Park and Fairbanks. During the summer, two types of service are in effect. The Denali Express offers daily express service between Anchorage and Fairbanks with one stop at Denali National Park. The "Local," operating northbound and southbound twice a week, makes local stops and can be flagged at any point along most of the route — ideal for fishermen, backpackers and railbelt cabin owners. The winter schedule is in effect from mid-September to mid-May, when the service is cut to a once-a-week "Local" traveling from Anchorage to Fairbanks on Saturdays, returning to Anchorage on Sundays.

The Alaska Railroad also runs the Whittier Shuttle, transporting passengers and vehicles between Portage and Whittier, a port of call for the Southwestern state ferry. The two communities have no highway link. The Shuttle makes two or three round trips daily between the two communities, but begins and ends the day in Anchorage. In winter, the Whittier Shuttle makes a round trip from Anchorage on Wednesdays, Fridays and Sundays.

Reservations are required for the Denali Express, but none are needed for the "Local" or the Whittier Shuttle unless groups number more than 30. Vehicles having ferry reservations to or from Whittier are given boarding priority on the Whittier Shuttle.

The White Pass & Yukon Route, which carried passengers and vehicles between Skagway, Lake Bennett and Whitehorse, was suspended at press time. It had been operating daily in the summer, with winter service, from mid-September to mid-May, on weekdays only. Reservations were required for both passengers and vehicles, although walk-on passengers were accepted on a space-available basis. These services may be resumed, so check before making your travel plans.

Airlines. This is the most efficient way to get around Alaska due to the great distances involved — if the weather permits. Most major cities and towns are served by daily scheduled jet-liner service. Nearly all other communities not on the road system have air service at least once a week. Many tiny communities not listed in the *Official Airlines Guide* schedule book have weekly or bi-weekly mail planes which will carry passengers on a space-available basis, although the mail takes priority.

Air Taxis

When the airline's schedule is inconvenient, or when you want to land on a wilderness lake or river bar, a chartered plane is the answer. For most economical chartering, plan to travel by public transportation or automobile to a settlement as near your destination as possible that has an air taxi operation. Many other villages will have an agent who can arrange air taxi pickup by radio, but you will probably be charged for all air time accrued by the airplane.

Since travel by air is a way of life in the North, many Alaskans fly their own planes much as you and I drive automobiles. Some are excellent and responsible pilots; some are not. If you consider traveling with a non-certified pilot, ask questions *before* you fly. Choose your pilot carefully. A list of certified air taxi operations is available from the Federal Aviation Administration, Flight Standards Division in Anchorage (address in Information Sources, Appendix).

Whenever you plan to fly by air taxi, make reservations by phone or mail as far ahead as possible. Many air taxi operators are booked months in advance during summer and autumn. Without reservations, you may have to wait several days for available time.

Even if you have reservations, be aware that weather conditions along your route may preclude your leaving on schedule. In such a case, the pilot will take you at the

Snowmobile hauling load on dogsled, Ambler.

first break in the weather, but meanwhile he will be flying other clients. Arrange your personal schedule and food supply to permit several days' leeway if your pickup is delayed by weather conditions. For added safety and your peace of mind, be sure someone other than the pilot knows where you are going and when you should be back.

Most air taxi operations are quite small, often flying one or two planes. They will be landing on wheels, floats, skis or a combination. When you make your reservations, be sure the airplanes have the proper landing gear for your needs. A pilot operating on wheels from his home strip cannot land on a wilderness lake.

White gas and similar camping-stove fuels are not permitted on scheduled commercial airliners but can be carried on air taxi flights. If you travel part of the way by scheduled airline, check on the local availability of your specific fuel when you make air taxi reservations. Most villages have a limited supply of common fuels. Take along your own empty containers to fill from the bulk supply.

If you arrange with a pilot to pick up your party on a certain date, be ready to load at the specified location early in the morning. Better yet, camp there the night before. Air taxi pilots normally have extremely busy schedules and won't wait for you to arrive. If you miss your pickup date, the pilot will return for you later, but at his convenience, and you may be charged for all air travel time involved. Enjoy your pickup day—plan to read, write or take *very short* walks. If weather or mosquito conditions are unpleasant, leave the tent up, but have everything else packed.

During summers in the Arctic, air taxi pilots sometimes work in full daylight until midnight or later to take advantage of good flying weather. If your pilot does not arrive on the scheduled day, double-check your calculations to be sure you haven't missed a day, then relax. Weather conditions at his end could prevent his arrival for several days—or even a week or more in some areas.

Bush pilots are some of the most colorful and responsible people you'll ever meet. They have incredible logistical problems to contend with just getting fuel, parts and periodic aircraft check-ups. Don't fret at delays. Once you put yourself in their hands, sit back, relax and flow with their schedules.

Charter Boats

Most coastal communities have commercial charter boat operations. Where none exist, and in small inland communities along the river systems, an informal charter can often be arranged with a local boat owner.

Off-Road Vehicles

Many Alaskan residents, particularly in remote areas, own swamp buggies, snowmobiles and other vehicles capable of traveling cross-country. When land-use regulations permit, you can sometimes arrange transportation to a specific area.

If you are considering using your own off-road vehicle (ORV), check the regulations for your entire route. Trail bikes, swamp buggies, snowmobiles, four-wheeled drive vehicles—in short, any motorized vehicles traveling off the road system—are classed as ORVs. Hovercraft are classed as ORVs when on land and as powerboats when on water.

For regulatory purposes, snowmobiles and other vehicles operating on snow are usually treated separately. Since they travel on a snowpack and in winter, they have far less impact on vegetation and wildlife than do ORVs used in summer. Many parklands permit the recreational use of snowmobiles when snowcover is sufficient to protect the vegetation. Due to the snowmobile's conflicts with the wilderness values of skiers, snowshoers and dog mushers, many parklands have designated certain areas closed to these vehicles and some prohibit their use altogether. However, more protected land is open to them than is closed.

Off-road vehicles used in the summer affect vegetation and wildlife significantly and, for the most part, are not permitted off established roads and trails in parklands.

See Table 2, Appendix, for information on recreational use of ORVs in parklands. Contact the parkland manager for more specific information. The Alaska Department of Fish and Game restricts ORV crossings of anadromous fish streams. Some areas restrict the use of snowmobiles and ORVs for hunting.

Traveling on an ORV? Let someone know where you are going and how long you plan to be gone. Don't go alone—two machines are safer than one. Take plenty of warm clothing, rain gear, maps, compass, first aid kit, matches, signaling flares and mosquito repellent. Don't forget repair tools and spare parts. And, please, use a good muffler; the noise affects both animals and other people using the area.

A little courtesy doesn't hurt either. Travel beside ski trails and dog sled trails, not on them. Carry out all your garbage; cover any oil or fuel spills. Avoid contaminating streams or ponds, and don't drive over especially sensitive lands where you will leave lasting scars. You will often share the same space with hikers, horseback riders, hunters, fishermen, skiers, snowshoers and dog mushers. They appreciate your courtesy and consideration.

Suggested reading: David Sheridan, *Off-Road Vehicles on Public Land*, Council on Environmental Quality (Washington, D.C.: U.S. Government Printing Office, 1979).

Studying the topographic map, Denali National Wilderness.

Time Zones

For years Alaska has been divided into four time zones, resulting in Juneau, the capital, operating on Pacific Standard Time while Anchorage, the business center of the state, was two hours later. In an attempt to improve communications between the two cities and the rest of the state, beginning in October 1983, Alaska will have only two time zones. Anchorage, Fairbanks, Juneau and most of the state will operate on Yukon Standard Time, one hour later than Seattle. The western coast and the Aleutian Islands will be one hour later than the rest of Alaska.

Maps

Alaska must have been a tough country to explore back in the "old days" before maps were available. The unknown—the incredible distances, the rugged coastline, the endless mountains and swift rivers—would have discouraged most of us. Today, we can preview where we are going, thanks to the U.S. Geological Survey and the National Ocean Survey. Their maps are some of the best bargains to be found in these parts. Map-hounds use them for bedtime "reading" or paper the kitchen walls with them, planning next summer's trips while washing dishes.

Don't set foot in Alaska's back country without a good supply of maps or charts—and know how to read them. Small boaters in Alaska should carry USGS maps as well as marine charts, since maps offer more detailed and accurate information about coastal features. For map sources, see Information Sources, Appendix.

IF YOU'RE FROM OUTSIDE...

...or if you're just starting out to explore this state you've been living in for several years, Alaska has treasures to share that you won't find back home. The abundant wildlife, the rich scenery, the uncrowded wilderness will delight you. But Mother Nature has a few other cards up her sleeve, too. With a little information and some care on your part, even these can enrich your Alaskan experience.

Cameras

If you don't bring a camera to Alaska, you'll soon wish you had. The scenery, the animals and even the people are "picturesque."

Most communities have at least one store that carries film in popular sizes and types. Larger cities have camera stores and several have repair shops. But if the shop must order an item for you, expect a wait of two weeks to two months.

You'll need to protect your delicate equipment from some of Alaska's special hazards. Dust can be a severe problem on unpaved roads and on braided glacial riverbeds during windstorms. Back-country travelers will want plenty of plastic or coated-nylon bags to protect photo gear from rain, during river crossings or while boating. For the best protection, use float bags or put the camera and lenses into two bags, one inside the other, roll the package into the middle of your sleeping bag and put the sleeping bag into a waterproof stuff sack or plastic garbage bag.

When you are photographing outdoors in winter, letting the camera reach air temperature is more convenient than trying to keep it warm inside a coat, where it will collect condensation. Before entering a warm building, place the cold camera and lenses in a plastic bag and tie securely. Condensation will form on the bag, not on and in the camera. When the camera reaches room temperature, it can be removed from the bag. Protection from condensation and subsequent rust is particularly important for cameras containing printed electronic circuitry.

Should disaster strike and your camera end up in the drink, cross your fingers and get busy. If you can, place the camera in fresh water and rush it to a repair shop. Otherwise, first aid goes something like this: If the camera is in fresh water, wind the film back into the cassette and open the camera. If the cassette is wet, put it into the film can and fill with water. (Label the can to warn the processor that the contents are submerged, or they won't appreciate your business.) Your film should be no worse for wear as long as it doesn't dry out.

Leave the camera back open, take off the lens and anything else easily removable and let the pieces dry in the air or in a warm oven. While the camera is drying, manipulate all its functions until it is totally dry.

If the camera ends up in salt water, rinse it thoroughly in fresh water many times. A slight bit of salt water in the mechanism can do far more harm than lots of fresh water. Either dry the camera as described or keep it totally submerged in fresh water until you can get it to a repair shop. If you should drop a camera or lens into silty glacial water, bury it with a ceremony and tears. The face-powder-fine grit won't rinse out.

Gold Panning

Want to find "color"? Gold panning and other recreational mining are permitted on most public lands and in rivers classified as Wild, but private mining claims do exist within some parklands. Respect "private property" signs and be sure you are not trespassing on someone's unmarked claim. Ask locally for information, or contact the parkland manager.

Gold panning in Crow Creek, Chugach National Forest.

Legally, holders of mining claims cannot prohibit public travel across their lands. You may not, however, collect rocks or minerals, enter private structures or interfere with mining operations. Ask permission, if possible, before crossing a claim. For additional information, contact the Land Office of the Bureau of Land Management in Anchorage (see Land Managers, Appendix.)

For your own safety, remember that old mines and abandoned dredges can be dangerous. Timbers on old dredges are often rotten; mine openings are subject to cave-ins; mines often contain stagnant air that can kill you.

Firearms

Unless specifically regulated by a parkland, a municipality or similar authority, rifles, shotguns and handguns may be carried openly in Alaska. Concealed weapons are illegal. It is unlawful to shoot from, on or across a highway or road. Consult specific parkland regulations concerning firearms. One of the following conditions will generally apply: Firearms must be surrendered or made inoperative upon entering the parkland (some national parks and Canada); possession of firearms is permitted, but discharge is prohibited except for self-defense (some state parks); or firearms may be openly carried and used according to safe gun-handling standards and State of Alaska laws. In Canada, handguns are prohibited by law. Contact Canadian customs for more specific information concerning other firearms.

Artifacts and Relics

Many areas of Alaska contain artifacts and relics. The unauthorized collection, theft or destruction of these cultural resources on federal or state land is prohibited by the Antiquities Act of 1906, the Archaeological Resources Protection Act of 1979 and the Alaska Historic Preservation Act. Since these artifacts and relics, once destroyed, can never be replaced, persons caught violating the acts face heavy fines and possible imprisonment.

If you find an artifact or relic, never pick it up, remove or alter it. When the original position of the "find" is lost, much information is destroyed. You can provide a valuable service for Alaska if you make notes about the artifact or relic. Describe your find, make rough sketches or maps and take photographs. Include any significant features such as hearths, arrowhead caches and log construction. Describe the location of the find, with latitude and longitude, if possible. Submit all data to the Bureau of Land Management, Alaska State Office Archaeologist in Anchorage, who will enter the information on BLM inventory forms. The information will also be entered in the State of Alaska's centralized data bank for cultural resources.

Icebergs and Glaciers

Mother Nature's ability as a sculptor is at its finest when she carves icebergs. Life-sized white shimmering castles with turrets, delicate spires and blue walls with windows for peeping through entice people to climb on the bergs, but *don't do it*. Icebergs are floating, even in winter when they seem to be locked in the ice and you can walk right up to them. All the while, however, the submerged portion is being eaten away by water, and when enough is gone, the iceberg is top-heavy. Without warning, it rolls to a new position. If you are standing on the berg or near it on lake ice, or floating nearby in a boat, you could be in serious trouble.

Glaciers, too, are "alive." Ice faces frequently crumble or shed large blocks of ice. Summer or winter, keep your distance from walls of ice, whether on land or in a boat. Tidewater glacier faces "calve" large icebergs and drop others into the water from great heights. The big waves this generates can capsize floating boats and sweep away beached boats or camps placed too near the water.

Travel on glaciers only if you have proper training and equipment. Crevasses are extremely dangerous, and they are often hidden under snow bridges. Some stagnant bodies of glacier ice can be crossed safely, with caution, but stay on bare ice to avoid hidden crevasses and mill holes, the vertical holes by which surface streams enter glaciers.

Tide Flats

Be cautious when walking on tidelands wherever glacial silt is deposited. Although the fine-grained mud appears firm as you walk on it, if you stand in one spot for a short time your feet can become locked in the dense sticky silt. If you cannot step out of your boots easily or you don't have a companion to pull you out, you could be held prisoner, a potentially fatal situation if the tide is coming in.

Avoid walking on beaches where water appears to spring mud or sand, areas of potential quicksand. If you find yourself sinking, attempt to run lightly out of it. If that doesn't work, drop to the surface and crawl, thus spreading your weight over a greater area. For safety's sake, if you venture onto the mudflats, travel with a companion and watch for bore tides, (described in the Boating section of this book).

Mosquitoes

While Alaskan bird life may rejoice at the abundance of mosquitoes and other biting insects, the human population does not. Modern Alaskans have great admira-

Camper wearing mosquito head net while preparing dinner, Katmai National Park.

tion for the earlier residents who worked and traveled in clouds of the hungry insects without benefit of modern repellents.

Common throughout the state, mosquitoes are particularly numerous in the Interior, where summers are warm. Coastal areas with wet, cool summers have fewer mosquitoes than inland areas. Mid-summer through mid-September, other biting insects appear: no-see-ums, white-socks, black flies and moose flies. With proper preparation, though, travel and camping can still be pleasant.

Foremost is Attitude. Accept the fact that mosquitoes will bite you occasionally, that they'll fall into your food, that you'll need to spend a few minutes each night chasing them out of the tent. Without mosquitoes and nine months of winter, Alaska would be as populated as California.

While camping in the Interior, plan to use a minimum of one 1-oz (28-g) container of repellent lotion per week for face and hands alone, and carry a can of spray repellent for clothing and tent netting. Choose brands with a high percentage of DEET (diethyltoluamide), the active ingredient.

The solvent used in most repellents also dissolves many plastics, including the imitation-leather covering on most cameras and binoculars. Repellent in stick form is easy to apply to the face and the back of the hands without leaving traces on the fingertips.

If you expect to be in prime mosquito country, spray or soak a vest or over-shirt well with the most concentrated form of DEET you can find. Store the garment in a plastic bag when you are not wearing it. Be prepared to button your shirt tightly at the neck, sew shut the slit at the sleeve cuffs and pull your socks over the outside of your trousers. Wear clothing made of dense cloth such as thick new denim, canvas or tightly woven wool. Summer temperatures, even in the Brooks Range, can climb above 90°F (32°C), but insects can keep you from shedding clothes. Wear a mosquito-proof hat (smooth fabrics are best). Many people prefer to use head nets, but in the hot weather of the Interior, these can be extremely uncomfortable.

Be sure your mosquito netting and your tent are in good shape. Carry a strip of Velcro or similar fastener long enough to repair a broken tent zipper. Then relax and enjoy yourself.

WILDLIFE

One of the great rewards of wandering through Alaska is seeing its abundant animal life. Large portions of the state have been designated as parks, refuges, monuments and preserves to protect wildlife populations by preserving habitat. Many of these areas are open to recreational hunting and trapping; almost all are open to recreational fishing. Non-consumptive uses and activities that do not disturb wildlife or habitat are permitted nearly everywhere.

For centuries, native Alaskans have used the meat and skins of wild animals for their very survival. To continue this important cultural heritage and lifestyle, many of the parks and refuges established in 1980 permit the subsistence use of animals and plants by local residents, native and non-native. Respect this tradition, and do not tamper with fish wheels, nets, traps, snares or blinds.

Code of Ethics for the Photographer or Wildlife Observer

All observers of wildlife have certain responsibilities, a few designated by law, toward the welfare of animals and their habitats. Please observe the following and encourage others to do so as well.

Avoid startling wildlife. Since most wild residents will flee if you surprise them, you'll have more fun and learn more if the animal is unaware of your presence. If the animal sees you but continues about its normal activities unafraid, consider yourself privileged and do not disturb it. If it is upset by your presence, leave the area or move to a more distant observation point.

It is against the law to deliberately feed bears, wolves, foxes or wolverines or to deliberately leave human food or garbage so that it attracts the animals. Don't harass, molest or impede the natural movement of wild animals, including fish. Unless you have a permit from the Alaska Department of Fish and Game, it is against the law to import, release, handle or capture any live wild animal. If you think an animal has been hurt or abandoned, contact the nearest Alaska Department of Public Safety, Division of Fish and Wildlife Protection office.

Be familiar with the behavior and needs of the animal you are photographing or studying to avoid accidentally damaging it or its environment. If, for example, you tie branches back from the entrance to a den or nest to get a clearer picture, release them before leaving. If the animal is rare or particularly sensitive to disturbance, keep its location secret. Avoid attracting the attention of hunters or trappers through your actions in the field or when setting up blinds for photography.

As of June 1979, 386 species of resident and migratory birds have been identified in Alaska. Coming from as far away as Argentina, Tasmania, Cape Horn and Antarctica, migratory birds rear their young in Alaska, then fly south in the autumn over glaciers, mountain passes, plains and endless miles of ocean to their wintering grounds.

The life cycles of millions of migratory birds depend upon the existence of suitable nesting habitats on Alaska's islands, coastal plains and river valleys. To protect these lands, numerous refuges have been established. Particularly important are the extensive sea-cliff nesting habitats of the Alaska Maritime National Wildlife Refuge and the refuges in the wetlands of the Alaska Peninsula and the Yukon, Kuskokwim and Kobuk river valleys.

If a bird flushes from its nest as you approach, take a quick look if you wish, then immediately leave the area. The bird should return to the nest quickly. Avoid purposely flushing an adult from the nest during cold, rainy or extremely hot weather, thus endangering the eggs or young.

Seabirds are particularly sensitive to disturbance by hikers, airplanes or boats. Both gulls and ravens patrol seabird colonies in search of unattended eggs and chicks. During panic departure adults can break eggs or kick eggs and chicks from nests. Larger chicks may run off and get lost.

Several species of seabirds nest in burrows dug into the ground. Avoid walking in these burrow areas, since they easily collapse under the weight of a person.

At the seashore, catch or dig only what you will eat. Be careful to collect only seashore life which is abundant. When you turn over a rock, move it gently to prevent crushing nearby animals. Replace the rock as you found it when you are finished looking. If you briefly take specimens from the beach, keep them in cool sea water in an uncrowded aquarium and return them to the proper seashore environment while they are still healthy.

Wherever you are, be familiar with the local regulations concerning collection or removal of plant life.

Sport Fishing, Hunting and Trapping

Unless more restrictive sport fishing, hunting or trapping regulations are set by a particular parkland, the regulations established by the Alaska Department of Fish and Game apply. Copies of the current sport fishing, hunting and trapping regulations are available by mail from the Alaska Department of Fish and Game, (address in Land Managers, Appendix) and from agents in most communities. Some state parks and recreation areas which do not permit the discharge of firearms are open to hunting by other means, such as bow and arrow. Marine mammal hunting is

Photographer being attacked near long-tailed jaeger's nest, Trans-Alaska Pipeline Utility Corridor. (Photo by Michael Polzin)

controlled by the federal government; contact the U.S. Fish and Wildlife Service for information.

All residents 16 years of age and older, and all non-residents regardless of age, must have a valid fishing or hunting license and tags while taking or attempting to take fish or game. Special visitor's sport fishing licenses are available for one- and ten-day periods as well as for the standard full year.

In dire emergency, fish or game may be taken without a fishing or hunting license or during a closed season. A "dire emergency" is defined as one in which a person in a remote area, involuntarily without food and without the possibility of obtaining food, would be unable to avoid death or serious and permanent health problems unless the game were taken. All edible portions of the meat must be salvaged and all portions remaining after the emergency has passed must be surrendered to the state.

You may also kill animals in defense of life or property if the situation was not brought about by harassment, by an unreasonable invasion of the animal's habitat or by the improper disposal of garbage or a similar attraction. You must have tried all other practicable means to protect life and property before killing the animal. The carcass is the property of the state. You are required to salvage, immediately, the meat or, if a black bear, wolf, wolverine or coyote, the hide or, if a brown (grizzly) or polar bear, the hide and skull. The Alaska Department of Fish and Game must be notified immediately about the incident and must receive a written report within 15 days.

CAMPING

Summer camping in Alaska can be much like camping elsewhere, especially in Alaska parklands that have developed campgrounds with picnic tables, fire pits, water and toilets. Use a sleeping bag adequate to 20°F (−7°C) or wear additional clothing in a lighter bag at low temperatures. Since you will probably encounter warm nights too, a bag with a full-length two-way zipper can keep your feet cool or can be opened out and used as a blanket.

In severe conditions, your survival may depend upon the warmth of your bag. Down filling, when wet, provides little insulation. For extended backpacking or for use near freezing and below, spun artificial fibers or vapor-barrier bags with fully protected down filling are better choices. Avoid waterproof covers, which invariably cause serious condensation just under the waterproof layer.

Alaskan ground temperatures are cold, particularly in the northern portion of the state, where you'll be sleeping just a few inches above frozen ground. An insulated air mattress or foam pad cuts the ground chill, evident on even the hottest of nights. Never cut boughs from live trees, especially in these northern forests where vegetation grows so slowly.

Tents should have a sewn-in waterproof floor and well-secured mosquito netting. They should be waterproof or have a rain fly. In the Arctic, a rain fly provides a second important type of protection: without something to shield the tent from the intense summer midnight sun, the interior becomes unbearably hot, even at 3 a.m.

River bars are often the only reasonable places to camp in Alaska. Patches of sand are more pleasant to sleep on than tussock grass, the drainage is excellent, the mosquito populations are smaller, water is nearby and presence or absence of animal tracks will alert you to the type of neighbors to expect. River bars, too, are the safest place to build campfires, and driftwood is usually handy. High water the next spring will erase the fire scar. Take pride in keeping your campsite and surrounding area clean; leave no trace of your presence except footprints. Be sure to dig your toilet holes far from the river bar.

Canyon City camp, Chilkoot Trail, Klondike Gold Rush National Historical Park.

Avoid camping on lichen fields or other fragile vegetation that will not repair itself in one growing season. Wherever you camp, pick a site with good natural drainage. Don't ditch around your shelter—it damages vegetation, leaves a scar that will be visible for many years and may start serious erosion.

Set up camp near a source of fresh water, but avoid salmon streams during the spawning season. They will contain smelly dead and dying fish, and you'll likely end up with patrolling bears as neighbors. If you see snails in the lake waters, don't swim. Snails can be host to the parasite that causes "swimmer's itch."

For the most pleasant camping in the wettest areas of Alaska—the coastal rain forests—look for dry ridges or protected beaches with a southern exposure to give the most sun and best drying conditions. Inviting open spaces in the forest, euphemistically called "meadows," are covered with soggy ankle-deep sphagnum moss. Unfortunately, campsites may be difficult to find elsewhere if you are camping along the coast during a period of extreme high tides.

Tidal fluctuations along much of the coastline are large, up to 30 ft (9 m) in some places. Check the tide tables carefully, noting that morning and afternoon tides reach different levels. The lowest ridge of seaweed and other debris on the beach will indicate where the most recent tide has peaked.

Rainy days are a way of life in most coastal areas. Take a large sheet of plastic to hang as a rain and wind shield for cooking, lounging and storage of gear. Take another sheet of plastic to cover the rain fly of your tent. Good drying-out days may occur only once every week or so, and you won't want to spend a sunny day doing camp maintenance. Take along a handful of large plastic garbage bags, too. You'll find uses for them you never imagined.

Carry matches in waterproof cases or well wrapped in plastic bags. Distribute them throughout your gear to ensure that some will stay dry. A camping stove or fire starter for wet wood also makes life more pleasant during long rainy spells.

Choose wool or synthetic pile clothing, which stays warm even when damp. A good pair of rubber boots is more comfortable in coastal rain forests than soggy leather boots.

Many Alaskans look forward to freeze-up, when ice forms on lakes, rivers and wetlands and snow blankets the landscape. No longer is surface travel limited to boating on winding rivers or to circuitous footpaths. On a packed ski, sled or snowmobile trail, the miles slip quickly by. Snow camping can be enjoyable, safe and quite comfortable. Although the short hours of daylight limit wilderness travel from November through January, by March those skilled in winter travel are enjoying freedoms and scenery unknown to summer travelers.

Anyone living or traveling in snow country should know the basics of winter camping and survival for personal safety. If your automobile stalls on an isolated road at −40°F (−40°C), or even at 30°F (−1°C), you might need to know more emergency survival skills than a wilderness traveler equipped with full winter camping gear. Take one of the courses in winter survival and camping taught in many of the larger Alaskan communities. Study books on winter wilderness skills, and learn by traveling with skilled companions. Don't travel alone in winter. Avoid inlets and outlets of lakes, where ice is frequently thin and new snow can obscure the danger. Watch for snow bridges or cornices that might collapse, and be alert for avalanche danger.

Before attempting a wilderness trip in winter, practice your skills and try out your equipment close to a heated retreat. The price of poor judgment, poor equipment or poor planning in the winter can be serious injury, frostbite, hypothermia or death.

Campfires

Be careful with fires in Alaska, particularly in the Interior. Forest and tundra fires burn hundreds of thousands of acres nearly every summer. In the peaty soil that covers much of the state, fires can burn underground the entire winter, only to blaze again when dry summer weather arrives.

Build campfires only on gravel, sand or clay, with a water source nearby. Do not build fires on moss or tundra, areas which are underlain by peat. Stay well away from overhanging branches, downed timber or the root systems of trees.

Burn only downed or dead wood. "Squaw wood," dead small trees and branches easily gathered by hand, can provide all the wood you'll need except in treeless coastal areas where you'll find only large driftwood logs. A collapsible bow saw can cut most firewood. In most parklands cutting live trees and branches for any purpose is prohibited. A few parks prohibit back-country campfires, permitting fires only in developed campground fire pits. During extended dry periods, open fires may be banned in other parklands and areas of Alaska as well.

On the treeless Aleutian Islands, on arctic and alpine tundra and in the Brooks Range, burnable wood grows so slowly that camping stoves are preferred. Any available wood should be saved for emergency use or allowed to return to the soil in its natural cycle.

For convenience as well as ecological reasons, more and more back-country travelers are choosing to carry small lightweight camping stoves that burn white gas, propane, kerosene or alcohol. In the back country, wood is often scarce or wet. Gathering wood, building the fire and cooking over it can be time-consuming, unpleasant or almost impossible in heavy rain, high winds or snowstorms. And then the campfire-blackened cooking pots have to be packed.

Drinking Water

Many of us have drunk sweet and not-so-sweet wilderness water straight from Alaska's streams and lakes for years without ill effects. Lately, however, an extremely unpleasant illness caused by the microorganism *Giardia lamblia* has reached epidemic proportions in Alaska as well as in the Lower 48 states. The spread of "beaver fever" may be due to increased human and dog traffic in the back country. Found in the feces of mammals, *Giardia* cysts are readily transmitted between humans and other animals and, unfortunately for Alaskans, they survive best in cold water. They may be found in any surface water, whether it looks and tastes good or not; water in and below beaver ponds is particularly suspect.

Giardiasis won't kill you—but you might wish it had. Symptoms are painful and incapacitating, usually including diarrhea, abdominal cramps, bloating and loss of appetite and weight. Some victims have lost 30 pounds (14 kg).

Since symptoms appear one to four weeks after infestation, many people become ill only after they have returned home. The symptoms can last up to six weeks. If giardiasis is not treated, it can disappear, only to recur later, and may also be transmitted to others. With proper medication, it can be cured.

Proper sanitation in the wilderness is extremely important. If you are not willing to dispose of your dog's feces as carefully as your own, consider leaving the dog at home. For your safety and that of others, use the following safe disposal methods.

On snow-free terrain: Select a dry spot at least 100 ft (30 m) from any open water. Using a small digging tool, remove a section of tundra or topsoil about 9 inches (23 cm) in diameter. Try to keep the tundra intact so it will continue to grow after you replace it. Dig a hole no deeper than 8 inches (20 cm). The top 6 to 8 inches (15 to 20 cm) of soil contains organisms that decompose organic material, although the process is extremely slow in cold Alaskan soils. After using the hole, fill it with loose soil, replace the tundra mat or topsoil and press firmly into place. Digging a new hole for each use is better for nature's decomposition system than creating a large community hole.

On snow: Select a spot as far away as possible from a stream, river or lake. Bury your waste in the snow and burn all toilet paper. (Snow makes a satisfactory substitute.)

On glacier ice: Collect feces in plastic bags and dump them into a deep crevasse.

Bathing and dishwashing: Carry water in a container to a spot where the used water will sink into the soil, not drain directly into a lake, stream or river. Use biodegradable soap and shampoo. If you wish to swim, sponge off your grime and mosquito repellent well away from the lake or stream first.

Special note to hunters: Bury the animal guts left after field-cleaning the animal; they can contain *Giardia*.

Water treatment. To destroy *Giardia* cysts in stream, lake or snow water, recent research indicates that simply bringing the water to a boil is sufficient. If you suspect other contaminating organisms might be present, boil the water for 20 minutes at sea level, longer at higher elevations. (Boiling water is often inconvenient, however, and little is known about how well it works at higher elevations.)

The two widely-used chemical disinfectants that contain chlorine—Halazone tablets and household bleach—are unsatisfactory for wilderness use because both deteriorate rapidly on exposure to air or warm temperatures.

Iodine is the only reliable chemical agent for producing safe drinking water in the wilderness. Tetraglycine hydroperiodide tablets (Globaline, Potable-Aqua) are convenient, and highly effective as long as they are fresh. Keep them in a tightly closed container and replace them yearly. One tablet per quart or liter of water is adequate, two if the water is colored by leaching. Allow the water to stand for 10 minutes at 68°F (20°C) or for 20 minutes at 32°-41°F (0°-5°C) before drinking. A 2% tincture of iodine may also be used (10 drops per quart/liter), but its strong taste is objectionable to many people. Solutions made from crystalline iodine or potassium iodide are less unpalatable. (Carrying the crystals themselves is not recommended because of the danger of small children's consuming them.) If you add any of the powdered fruit flavorings to the water to mask the iodine taste, be sure that you add it only *after* the required time for purification has elasped; these flavorings usually contain ascorbic acid, which neutralizes the iodine's effect.

Any filtration system that will remove *Giardia* cysts must have a pore size of less than two micrometers. Those available at present which meet this requirement are bulky and expensive. Filtered water, furthermore, must still be chemically treated or boiled to kill viruses.

Bears and Other Large Mammals

Bears roam freely throughout most of Alaska. If you are going to enjoy yourself, you must learn to camp and travel safely, without fear, but with a healthy respect and appreciation for the bear and its environment. Statistically your chances of meeting a bear in Alaska are low, and lower still if you learn where and how to travel. Fear of bears is mostly a fear of the unknown. Adventure stories often exaggerate the danger; stories are seldom written about peaceful encounters or the hundreds of thousands of miles traveled in the back country without meeting bears.

As a visitor to the wilderness, you have an advantage. You anticipate that bears may be nearby and watch for them. The animals are not expecting you, so if you are alert you can normally avoid a meeting. Bears are not waiting to ambush you — they have far more important things to do with their time and energy. Statistics are no consolation, however, when you and a bear are facing each other. This section is designed to help you avoid problems with bears.

Never forget that bears are unpredictable and can inflict serious injury. In Alaska, a bear may be shot at any time of the year in defense of life or property, but a reasonable effort must have been made to protect life or property by other means. If you decide to use a firearm, shoot to kill; a wounded angry bear is dangerous.

Three species of bears inhabit Alaska. Black bears occur in most forested areas. (A brown color phase of the black bear is also found, as is a blue phase, the "glacier bear.") Brown bears, often referred to as "grizzlies" in Interior Alaska, are found throughout the entire state except along Alaska's western coast and on islands in the Aleutians and the Bering Sea. Polar bears, which wander the Arctic coast and pack ice in the Arctic Ocean as far south as St. Lawrence Island, are seldom seen.

Wherever you are, study the landscape around you to determine if bears are likely to be present. Black bears prefer heavily wooded areas; brown bears are most often seen on river bars, near timberline and on the open tundra. When entering a new drainage, especially if you are on foot, find a spot where you have a good view of the countryside and river bed. With binoculars, "glass" the region carefully for all visible wildlife, looking particularly for bears that might be sleeping or quietly feeding.

Watch, too, for bear signs: fresh tracks, bear trails, scats (droppings) or freshly dug areas. Look for bear tracks in muddy spots and on snow patches. Grizzly claw marks are normally well defined; black bear claw marks less so.

Many sections of Alaska contain so many bears that they create, through usage, well-defined trails. Some are as obvious as well-used human foot trails; others are a series of staggered "footprints," well worn because bears commonly step in the same places on the trail.

Expect to find bear trails along lake shores, streams and rivers in which salmon spawn. Trails made by moose, Dall sheep and mountain goats are also common in the vicinity of mineral licks; they may parallel streams in brushy areas and often follow certain topographic features such as ridges or approaches to mountain passes. In country that has few trails maintained by humans, animal trails are a boon to the wilderness traveler, but use them cautiously.

Bears leave massive droppings that may resemble large human feces or merely be large amorphous piles. During berry season, the scats may be blue-black from blueberries or contain numerous whole bright-red high-bush cranberries. A steaming pile indicates a bear not long gone; a pile warm to the touch is only slightly reassuring.

In their search for food, bears, particularly brownies, dig, turning over large areas of tundra while hunting ground squirrels and roots. Although excavations may not be fresh, their frequency gives an idea of how much the area is used by bears at some times of the year.

While traveling in bear country, stay alert and think ahead. Plan your route to avoid blind corners and large areas of brush. Bears are generally considered to have poor vision, but their senses of smell and hearing are excellent. Warn them of your presence in dense brush or forested areas by making noise: talk, sing, rattle rocks in a can, ring bells. Don't whistle, though. You could sound like a ground squirrel or marmot, a favorite food. Near running water or in the wind, a bear might not hear the noise you make.

If possible, walk with your back to the wind, entering thickets from upwind so your drifting scent will warn of your presence. Then give bears enough time to avoid you by moving away. They are just as reluctant to meet you as you are them. At night, use a flashlight.

According to U.S. Forest Service personnel, of the 150 bear maulings in the past 80 years, 69% occurred to people traveling or camping alone. Parties of two accounted for 27% and parties of three, 5%. Always travel with one or more companions in bear country.

Taking your dog into bear country is asking for trouble. After attracting the bear's attention, most likely the dog will come running back to you for protection, with an angry bear close on its heels. If a bear approaches while you are fishing, leave the area quietly and slowly, donating any fish you have caught for the bear's breakfast.

Don't approach a bear's food cache. At the first odor of decomposing meat, retreat quietly. A feeding bear will defend a carcass violently once your presence is known. When a bear temporarily leaves a carcass, it normally covers it with leaves, dirt and branches. The bear is likely to be sleeping nearby.

Avoid approaching a sow bear with cubs. Sows are very protectve and will feel your presence as a threat to their young. Curious cubs, seemingly abandoned, probably have an anxious mother nearby who will charge without warning when she discovers you. Whatever the situation, remember that from a bear's point of view, you are an intruder.

For bear-free camping, choose your campsite carefully. Avoid camping in thick brush, on bear trails or next to water or food sources, especially salmon spawning streams. If you can camp where climbable trees are available, plan on using them in an emergency.

Cache your food at least 100 yd (90 m) from your tents. Hang the food bags from trees, strong tall willow bushes or ropes strung high above the ground between trees. Adult brown bears can easily reach 10 ft (3 m) up a tree, although they normally don't climb. Black bears are excellent tree climbers. Treeless tundra country presents a creative challenge. Consider putting the food bags on top of large boulders or in brushy thickets well off any possible trail.

Losing part of your food supply to a bear not only inconveniences you, but trains

Scientist extracts tooth for study from tranquilized brown (grizzly) bear. (U.S. Fish and Wildlife Service photo)

the bear to look for other food caches. A growing body of evidence indicates that tying a small net bag containing three or four mothballs on the outside of each cached food bag provides significant additional protection from bears, squirrels and other interested wildlife if they haven't yet discovered where to find "people" food. The added weight of a few ounces of mothballs per person is worthwhile insurance. A party of four persons on a two-week trip under hot Interior Alaska summer conditions will use about one-half pound of mothballs. Transport them in a vapor-proof container.

Never sleep in a tent with food or anything carrying food odors. This includes cooking pots, knives, cups and silverware. And it could include your shirt, if food has spilled on it. Carry a bandana to use as a napkin, and store it with the cached food at night. Take a few extra minutes after supper to wash your hands and face and brush your teeth. You might want to hang a bag of mothballs from the tent. The practice of urinating in a perimeter around the camp to "establish territory" has had mixed results. Some bears have been reported to react aggressively to the scent.

Careful food planning will also help minimize bear problems. Never carry peanut butter, smoked fish or bacon. Wrap hard sausages, cheeses and similar foods well to contain odors. Spend an extra hour before leaving home to package food properly.

Plan each group meal as a unit, putting the required portions and accessories (paper towel, small piece of scouring pad, after-dinner mints, etc.) into a strong new plastic bag. Label each bag carefully, tie it securely and put it into a second plastic bag, again tying well. Pack the meals into several sturdy, clean waterproof cloth bags which, with the mothballs, will be hung from trees. Using a number of food-cache bags reduces the likelihood that your entire food supply might be destroyed. Be sure to count the number of bags cached each night and collect them all in the morning.

Before a trip into bear country, wash your backpack thoroughly. On the trip, cache the packframe and bag outside the tent in a large plastic garbage bag with some mothballs on top of it.

In bear country never cook in or near the tent, but plan to cook at least 100 yd (90 m) away. If the local bear population seems large or likely to wander into camp, stop along the trail to cook supper, then travel another hour before camping for the night.

Always keep a clean camp, caching food carefully, disposing of garbage immediately and keeping utensils washed. In Alaska, feeding wild animals or leaving food or garbage in such a manner that it attracts them can bring a penalty of up to six months in jail and a $1000 fine. Burn all packaging material and leftover food or securely wrap the scraps in a plastic bag and store them with the cached food until garbage can be burned or carried out. Always stir campfire ashes, collecting unburned bits of foil and scorched cans and compressing them in one of the plastic bags. The charred remains will weigh surprisingly little and should be packed out with you. If for some reason you must leave the garbage after burning, bury it.

As more and more people venture into the back country, bears learn quickly where to find easy food. If you plan to camp or hike in a heavily used recreation area, ask about the presence of "problem bears"—those that search out campsites and other food sources. Don't endanger the supplies or lives of the next campers by letting bears find food at your campsite and turning them into "problem bears."

These bears will soon be dead bears. Alaska Fish and Game personnel have found that moving a bear to a new environment does not solve the problem. The bear either returns to its original area or continues its destructive habits in its new home. In the Chugach National Forest, "problem bears" are caught in live traps and shot; their hides are sold at state auction and the meat given to charitable institutions. Shooting the bears is preferable to allowing them to maul or kill a human. People who have fed such animals or have allowed them to find food are ultimately responsible for the death of the unfortunate animals.

All bears, like other animals, have a "critical space." By entering into that space either accidentally or intentionally, you are asking for trouble. If you encounter a bear busily picking berries, ripping up the tundra or fishing, and the bear hasn't seen you, stand quietly until it begins feeding again, then move away inconspicuously, preferably downwind and out of sight.

If the bear has seen you, walk slowly backward, all the while facing the bear. *Do not run*; the bear might feel compelled to give chase. You can't outrun a bear; grizzlies can reach 40 mph (64 kph) for short distances.

If you meet a bear on the trail in the woods, step slowly to the side and out of sight, giving it plenty of room to continue. Avoid putting the bear in a situation in which it might feel cornered. Often, once it can no longer see you, a bear will forget you are nearby.

Bears communicate with sounds and body postures, so it helps to understand their language. A pamphlet entitled "The bears and you, or how to become a bear-wise sourdough in ten minutes," by Dave Hardy and Dave Kellyhouse, from which the quotations below are drawn, is highly recommended. It is available from the State-Federal Visitor Center, Anchorage (address in Information Sources, Appendix).

"When approached by humans at distances of 50 yards [46 m] or more, a bear often will stand on its hind legs and swing its head to and fro. When bears do this, they are trying to get a better idea of what you are. Help them! Wave your arms over your head and holler. Often the bears will move off once your identity is known to them. Many a 'charging' bear has been shot as it dropped from this posture to all fours and moved closer to get a better look at a silent human intruder.

"Bears often make a whoosh (woof!) as they turn to run when startled. As long as the bear runs, don't be alarmed. However, if a bear stands its ground and begins a series of woofs (like air being forced out of a bellows), or pops its teeth together, or both, then this is *your* invitation to leave, *slowly*, facing the bear. DON'T TURN AND RUN FROM A BEAR; it may invite pursuit. Bears woof in the same context as a dog growls. This behavior is often followed by a charge or false charge. If a bear turns sideways to you and seems to be ignoring you by looking off into space, this is also an invitation for you to leave. Bears do this to show an adversary how big they are—like a muscleman flexing his biceps. If a bear follows you, drop or toss an article of clothing such as a hat for it to smell. Whatever you do, DON'T IMITATE A BEAR'S SOUNDS OR POSITIONS, even if they sound 'funny' to you the first time."

Bears sometimes make a threatening charge, veering away at the last moment from actual contact. If you are surprised and caught in such a situation, do not retreat. Stand your ground, facing the bear squarely. Hold up your arms to increase your apparent size and talk to the bear in a firm, calm (!) non-threatening voice. Faced with a creature who neither runs nor attacks, the bear might decide not to chance an investigation and continue running.

Most bear charges are bluffs, but if physical contact seems certain, drop to the ground and "play dead." Make no noise. Your vital organs are best protected if you lie on your stomach in the fetal position with your hands clasped over the back of your neck. Like a cat, a bear apparently isn't interested in its victim once it has "killed." Remain motionless until the bear is safely out of sight and sound. Of people injured in bear attacks, 75% have survived.

Hardy and Kellyhouse say, "Most experienced Alaskans carry a firearm with which to protect themselves from bears when they go afield.... If you choose to use a firearm, you have the responsibility to learn to handle it safely and to shoot it accurately.... If you choose not to carry a firearm in bear country, you should carry SOMETHING with which to fend off the pesky campground bear as he comes across the picnic table to get your lunch or as he enters your tent while you are sleeping. You can use noise makers (firecrackers, air horns, shriek alarms, sticks and cooking pots) but the most effective is something to spray at the bear, like a spray can of insect repellent, paint, WD-40, hair spray or dog repellent. A dog repellent product called Halt is effective against bears.... Don't try to use Mace or 'teargas.' They are made for humans and are not considered effective against animals, especially in outdoor situations."

The standard highway flare carried by motorists has also successfully discouraged bears. Both flares and chemical sprays are most useful within tents, vehicles and cabins where the use of firearms is difficult or dangerous. When a party travels with one firearm for the group, the weapon typically accompanies persons leaving camp to fish, hunt or hike. Chemical sprays and flares offer some protection to those left in camp and to those unable or unwilling to use a gun.

Another large mammal deserves a short comment. Moose, found in large numbers throughout Alaska in both wilderness and populated areas, normally coexist peaceably with people. Statistically, the most common danger from moose is an automobile-moose collision, which can severely damage both parties. A cow moose with a calf, however, can be extremely aggressive and charge without warning. Her protectiveness rivals that of a sow bear with cubs, and her flying hooves can inflict serious injury. Since calves are often hidden in the brush out of sight, treat all moose with distant respect.

BACKPACKING AND HIKING

Whatever your degree of hiking skill and stamina, rewarding trips in Alaska await you. Some of the more accessible parklands have marked trails that can be ends in themselves or serve as access to the wilderness beyond. Other parklands are so remote that getting there is an adventure in itself.

Take a few trips suggested in Alaskan guidebooks before striking out cross-country. Be competent at hiking, camping and survival skills before attempting a wilderness trip. If you are new to hiking or backpacking, read some basic manuals and guidebooks and talk to people who have had extensive experience. Better yet, travel with an experienced person in your party or join one of the many commercial guided wilderness trips. The latter can be as strenuous as you wish, from gentle day hikes and float trips to three-week wilderness backpacking sojourns, demanding white-water kayaking or grueling climbs on precipitous mountain peaks.

On tundra and most trails, and when carrying overnight camping gear, most people find that traveling 6 to 10 mi (10 to 16 km) a day on foot is enough. Through brushy, forested or mountainous country, foot travel can be extremely difficult or relatively easy, depending upon the terrain, the density of the ground cover, the difficulty of stream crossings and whether or not good animal trails are available. Look for animal trails along lake shores, streams or river banks, up ridges, approaching mountain passes or near mineral licks. In many cases, a slightly longer route via animal trails will be faster than bushwhacking through difficult terrain. Allow plenty of time for your trip and spend extra time relaxing or exploring from camp.

Study the vegetation as you travel to find out which plant communities are easiest to travel through and learn to identify them from afar. Then, when you reach a viewpoint, you can intelligently study the country ahead to choose a route.

Adequate rain gear is essential to prevent hypothermia. Carry rain pants or rain chaps as well as a rain parka or poncho, since vegetation retains water droplets long after rain has quit. Wear sun glasses on snow and glaciers to prevent snowblindness and carry a small tube of sun cream. Don't forget lots of mosquito repellent.

Unless your route takes you over extensive rock or requires technical climbing skills and heavy climbing boots, you'll be more comfortable traveling in medium-weight hiking boots with lug soles. Many wilderness hikers prefer rubber-footed "shoe pac" boots with leather uppers. Whatever your footgear, be sure it is comfortable and gives you adequate foot and ankle support.

If your feet don't get soaked at some point, it's an unusual backpacking trip in Alaska. Rain, stream crossings, soggy tundra or long sections of tussock grass and bogs will soak even the best-greased leather boot in time. A good pair of gaiters helps, but expect to get wet feet. Take along boot grease and extra socks. Whenever your boots are dry enough, grease them well to protect the leather and to keep it supple. Stiff dried-out leather can start blisters, even from previously comfortable boots.

Take the most detailed topographic maps available for the area you'll be in, and include maps for surrounding areas in the event that you might have to change your route plans. A compass need not be fancy, since most of your navigation will be from topographic maps in large drainages, but always carry one. Know how to allow for magnetic declination, which varies from 27° to 37° east in Alaska. Before taking off on any trip, whether for a few hours or several weeks, leave your route plan and schedule with a responsible person.

One of the delights of traveling the north country in summer is the nearly unlimited daylight. You can determine the amount of daylight for the time of year and the area you'll be in (from the graph in the Appendix.) Add another hour or two of twilight on either end. If this adds up to 24 hours, you'll have no use for a flashlight, but always carry one at other times, especially on fall and winter trips, even short ones.

Crossing Rivers

If you spend much time wandering the back country, you'll be faced with the problem of crossing large streams and rivers. Take your time and plan carefully. Practice crossing rivers in "civilization" before taking off for the wilderness. Alaska Division of Parks or U.S. Forest Service personnel occasionally give one-day river-crossing seminars.

Alaska has two basic types of rivers and streams, those of glacial origin and those not of glacial origin. (The latter are often called "clearwater" regardless of their color.) The water in streams originating from glaciers is gray and opaque from suspended glacier-ground rock "flour," which can deposit in your clothing, greatly increasing your weight and making it difficult to stay afloat if you fall. The murky water obscures the stream bed, making it impossible to gauge the depth visually. Currents are generally swift and the water numbingly cold.

Glacial river beds are frequently a half mile (1 km) or more wide, with the river meandering over only a small portion in a many-braided course. Pick a section of the river that has numerous braids; many small streams are easier to cross than one big one. Cross at the top of the islands, where the river splits and flows in shallower riffles.

Water levels are most likely to be lowest in the morning, especially after a cold night. Levels will be highest when hot sun or heavy rains have accelerated the rate of melting of snowfields and glacier ice. The stream which was a "pussycat" at breakfast could be a raging lion by suppertime. Plan your route accordingly, or camp and wait for low water rather than risk a dangerous crossing.

Clearwater streams are fed from springs, snowmelt and rain. The water may be crystal clear, muddy from recent rains or dark brown from tannin leached from muskeg vegetation. Mountain streams generally flow over rocky or gravel surfaces, but footing is likely to be slippery from algae growth on logs and rocks. Cross where the river is broad, but in an area of shallow riffles.

In the lowlands, small sluggish streams flow through the muskeg in deep channels with nearly vertical banks and few shallows. The stream bed is often of sticky mud or unconsolidated muck. Crossing can be very difficult, despite the narrow width. Look for a log or rocks to cross on or a section of swift shallower water. Larger rivers in the lowlands have typical gravel bars and cut banks, but most of them are too deep to cross by wading unless you can find an area where the river flows over riffles.

Learn to "read" the surface of any river or stream. Drop your pack on the bank and take a half-hour walk up and down the river, studying the water and the terrain. Don't attempt a hasty crossing of a dangerous stream. Avoid crossing at a bend; although the inside may have a gently sloping gravel beach, the current along the outside will be deep and swift, and the bank will most likely be steep and unstable.

On the surface, waves made by the current as it flows over submerged obstacles indicate what is underneath. A large "V" pointing downstream usually shows that the water is flowing through a deep channel. A "V" pointing upstream is probably caused by the water splitting around a submerged rock or snag. A hump in the water, known as a standing wave or haystack, indicates a hole in the river bed just above it. Haystacks and holes are also found downstream from large submerged boulders. The turbulence found in large holes can pull a person under. The size and depth of the submerged object determine the amount of surface disturbance: Smaller or deeper obstructions create less surface turbulence.

Never cross a river or stream barefoot. Cold water quickly numbs bare feet, and you won't feel sharp rocks or rolling boulders. An injured foot could create an emergency situation in the wilderness; at the very least, it is an unnecessary and avoidable irritation.

Many hikers carry a pair of lightweight shoes just for stream crossing. Others

Family crossing small stream uses pole for stability. (Anchorage Times photo by Mark Skok)

wear hiking boots for more secure footing but remove their socks, wiping the boots and their feet afterward and then putting their socks back on.

When the route requires frequent wading, you may prefer to wade, socks and all, wringing your socks out for long dry sections of the trail. Always have a dry pair of socks tucked away to change into when you make camp. In the morning, if stream crossings are again on the schedule, groan loudly and put on the cold, wet socks—they'll warm up shortly. Wearing light nylon or acrylic undersocks will decrease your chances of getting blisters.

Remove your pants before making crossings that will wet you above the knees. Wear rain pants or chaps to break the cold water, but don't tie the legs at the ankle; if you should fall, they could fill with water and drag you under.

Any stream deeper than a "splash-through" should be crossed with caution. The current will almost always be stronger than you expect. Unfasten backpack chest and waist straps before entering the water so you can immediately release the pack if you fall. You may want to tether the pack to you with a lightweight line that is easily releasable.

Either work your way diagonally downstream, moving with the current or, facing upstream, shuffle sideways, probing the bottom contour ahead with a long sturdy stick for a "third leg" and keeping your feet pointed directly upstream. When footing is treacherous, cross in pairs, holding hands, each person carrying a probing stick. Only one person should move at a time. If the party includes older children or timid members, interlock arms and grip a large stick horizontally at breast height, with the heaviest or most experienced party member at the upstream end.

When traveling with children, think carefully before undertaking any but the easiest stream crossings. To cross a stream with a young child, tie the youngster to you, either piggy-back style or on your chest facing you; never carry the child on your shoulders. Don't carry both the child and your pack, at the same time; make two trips.

For very dangerous crossings, use a rope belay from as far upstream as possible, keeping the rope slack at all times. If the person crossing falls, play out the rope fast enough to avoid holding that individual under water. When a number of people will cross and the rope is long enough, rig a fixed line, then belay the last person from the far bank. If the river is too deep to ford safely, change your route.

If you should fall while crossing, immediately get out of your pack. If you are swept downstream, float on your back, feet first so your feet will take the impact of any rocks, until you reach a section of the river that will allow you to work your way to shore.

Mountaineering

"The whole state's nothing but mountains!" one visitor exclaimed after arriving in Anchorage by air on a clear day. His observation was not exactly correct, but Alaska does have a lot of mountains. Of the 20 highest in North America, 11 are in Alaska. Nineteen peaks are over 14,000 ft (4300 m).

Climbing the higher peaks in Alaska is far more dangerous and difficult than climbing high peaks in more temperate regions. Most of the routes are on snow and ice, and climbers must often cross extensive glaciers and snowfields. Severe arctic

Crossing swift, deep stream using a fixed cable, Chugach National Forest.

38

weather conditions prevail at high altitudes. Superior mountaineering skill, stamina and conditioning, sturdy equipment and the ability to survive long periods of cold and wind are essential. Most attractive climbing areas are extremely remote. A party must be self-sufficient and realize that any rescue attempts might be "too little, too late." Unfortunately, many people have died climbing in Alaska.

Getting to the base of the mountain is often an expedition in itself. Alaska's lack of an extensive road system can require a long wilderness hike over rugged terrain, often with vast swamplands, major rivers to be crossed and miles of glacial moraine. Most expeditions choose to charter an air taxi, a power boat, horses or even dogsleds to reach a convenient starting point.

Denali National Park personnel distribute a packet of information intended for mountaineers planning to climb high peaks in the park, but the recommendations apply to climbing any of Alaska's higher mountains. For a listing of mountain and wilderness guide services, consult the current edition of the Alaska Division of Tourism's publication "Alaska Travel Directory." The Alaska Association of Mountain and Wilderness Guides sets professional standards for all recreational guides. The Mountaineering Club of Alaska (Anchorage) sponsors climbs and hikes for club members and their guests and can put you in contact with mountaineering clubs in other parts of the state. Addresses are in Information Sources, Appendix.

Emergencies

Should an emergency occur along the highway system or in a city or village, telephone the nearest Alaska State Troopers' office. In more isolated locations, many private citizens living in the Bush have two-way radios and will be willing to help contact the proper authority.

Most major communities have hospital facilities. Other communities have well-staffed and equipped clinics able to treat many serious medical emergencies, while smaller settlements have village health nurses, trained and experienced in handling Bush medical problems. Through radio contact with physicians at Alaska's hospitals, the health nurse is supported by an extensive medical network and can arrange air evacuation if the situation is critical.

If you are ill, injured or lost in the wilderness, do not fight the conditions. Conserve your energy and body heat. If you are near a water supply, stay there. You can live for days with only water and warmth. Most large rivers in the state are major transportation routes, summer or winter, so you'll have a better chance of being discovered if you travel or camp near one. Stay calm, plan carefully and use the resources of the land for your survival. Eskimos and Indians have done it for centuries.

When traveling in remote areas, consider carrying a small two-way radio for emergency use. An alternative is an emergency locator transmitter (ELT), a small radio transmitter designed for emergency use, which when activated sends a distress signal on a frequency monitored by aircraft. However, this transmitter does not allow you to speak to the pilot. Aircraft traffic varies with your location and the season, of course, but a light plane will cruise through the more popular remote drainages at least once every day or two in the summer, generally more often.

To attract the attention of a passing aircraft without using a radio or a locator transmitter is more difficult, but not impossible. Always carry a signal mirror or some item with a flat, shiny surface capable of reflecting the sun, and learn to use it before going into the wilderness. If possible, build a smoky campfire to help the pilot locate you, or lay out a brightly colored tent or tarp.

Other standard signals for help are: three sounds of any kind repeated at intervals; three fires set in a triangle; green branches on a hot fire, producing white smoke; rubber or plastic on a hot fire, producing black smoke.

Message	Code Symbol
Require assistance	**V**
Require medical assistance	**X**
No or negative	**N**
Yes or affirmative	**Y**
Proceeding in this direction	↑

Figure 3.   Ground-air visual signal codes for communication with aircraft.

To communicate with the pilot of an aircraft once you are spotted, use "SOS" or the following signals adopted in 1982 by the Convention on International Civil Aviation. Make a copy of this page and stick it in your pack.

Obviously, the best situation is to have no emergencies. That's the sign of a well-planned trip—or luck. Expect the unexpected, travel cautiously and be as self-sufficient as possible.

BOATING

Float trips down rivers and along the coast are an ideal way to visit Alaska's back country. The miles slip by quickly with minimal effect on either you or the land, and you are traveling in a time-honored fashion. The Russian fur traders, in the mid-1700s, arrived by ship; but long before Outsiders bumped into these shores, the original people—the Eskimos, Aleuts and Indians—were floating the rivers and coastal waters in their small but seaworthy craft.

Today excellent maps and charts of the state's waters and shorelines are available. Most small boaters prefer to carry USGS maps, the 1:250,000 scale quadrangles for an overview of the route and the surrounding terrain and the 1:63,360 scale for detailed information. Be sure to protect maps well against water and weather. If the area is particularly remote and your party consists of two or more boats, two sets of maps are good insurance. No signposts exist in the wilderness. Contact the manager of the specific wild river or parkland for current information on water levels, hazards and access.

If your route takes you into Canada at any point, you are entering a foreign country and must clear customs. Contact both the Canadian and U.S. customs for instructions before starting your trip. They understand the logistical problems of crossing the border in wilderness areas and will help find a satisfactory solution to the legal requirements. Addresses for both Canadian and U.S. customs offices are listed in Information Sources, Appendix.

Use clothing and sleeping bags that function well when wet. Rain or drizzle can fall for a week at a time. A thunder shower or a capsize can drench your gear unexpectedly, and cool air slows drying time. Keep all equipment dry and in good repair, be able to get out of your craft or your heavy footgear in the event of capsizing, and know how to treat hypothermia and give cardiopulmonary resuscitation (CPR). Whenever capsizing is even a remote possibility, dress warmly regardless of the air temperature. More and more boaters are wearing wet suits to ward off the water's chill, which can range from about 60°F (16°C) to near freezing.

Be particularly cautious on large inland lakes, in coastal fjords, especially in the vicinity of glaciers, and on some mountain-rimmed sections of the Yukon River. Williwaws—sudden violent winds—can strike without warning, building large breaking waves capable of capsizing small boats. A number of lives have been lost in Skilak Lake on the Kenai Peninsula under such conditions. The waters are extremely cold, producing hypothermia or unconsciousness within a short time. Always wear a life jacket.

River Running

Since access to most rivers in Alaska is by air, collapsible kayaks and inflatable boats are popular. A few air taxi pilots will transport canoes or other rigid craft strapped to the struts of a float plane, but FAA regulations generally prohibit transporting passengers at the same time, thus increasing the number of trips required and the expense. Contact the air taxi service well in advance if you plan to use a rigid boat. Such boats are also expensive to ship by air freight. On the other hand, rental boats are hard to find in Alaska; collapsible boats for rent may not exist. Check with sporting goods stores and rental shops in the larger cities, outfitters and wilderness lodges.

For safety, always travel with two or more boats, preferably three. Small groups are also likely to be more welcome than large ones at small villages en route.

Most boaters average five or six hours a day of actual travel on the water. The distance covered per day will, of course, depend upon the weather, the speed of the water (rapid in the mountains, much slower in the flatlands), the number of portages or route inspections required, whether you "float" or actively paddle and the amount of time spent in rest stops, hiking, etc. Assume you'll average the following speeds while actually traveling: lakes, 2 mph (3 kph); clearwater rivers, 3 to 4 mph (5 to 6 kph); glacial rivers, 5 to 7 mph (8 to 11 kph).

For both safety and your enjoyment of the trip, allow plenty of time. Figure on at least one day for sitting out bad weather, resting or exploring for every five or six days of travel.

Alaskan waterways are transportation and freight routes today, just as they have been for centuries, for natives, explorers and prospectors. Log cabins and abandoned villages sit on river banks. Many of the cabins are in use today, private retreats on private land; others are relics located on federal land and protected by law. Look at these decaying ruins, fantasize about the people who once lived there, but leave the artifacts intact. Gather your firewood from the forest, not from Alaska's historic structures. The removal or destruction of any historic object on federal or state land is punishable by fine or imprisonment.

Much of the land selected by Alaska natives under the 1971 Alaska Native Claims Settlement Act lies along rivers and streams. Unless you are sure that the land bordering the river or stream is open to the public, assume it is privately owned, especially in the vicinity of any settlement or village. Ask before you camp.

Do not disturb food or firewood caches. The owner may be depending upon the supplies for survival. Only if your life is truly in danger should you touch the supplies; then replace them as soon as possible or reimburse the owner.

Several Alaskan wilderness rivers heavily used by boaters have become unsightly garbage dumps. Be sure to carry out all of your litter, and if you have space in your boat, pack out some of the non-biodegradable garbage you find.

Kayaker navigating around a snag, Chugach National Forest.

Proper disposal of human waste is a serious problem in Alaska, especially near waterways. Some villages obtain their drinking water directly from rivers and streams. Unless you can find a spring, purify your drinking water, preferably by boiling. Giardiasis has become rampant in Alaska, even in the most remote regions. Help control the problem by being particularly careful with personal hygiene.

Pack all equipment in watertight bags and tie them to the boat. (After a capsize, the boat can normally be found and equipment salvaged, even if the craft is damaged beyond repair, but floating or sunken bags are generally lost for good.) Carry adequate survival equipment, extra paddles, boat-repair materials, a 50-to-100 ft (15-to-30-m) rope and a first-aid kit. Attach a knife, mosquito repellent and waterproof matches to your person so they cannot be lost. Always wear a life vest. Wet suits are recommended in white water and in silty waters.

Be sure your craft will float even when full of water. If you capsize, stay with the boat and work it to shore to prevent damage to the boat or losing it entirely. In most remote areas, you will be in serious trouble without a boat for transportation. Long distances, rivers to be crossed and miles of swamp and muskeg make walking out impractical.

If you feel you must abandon your boat, consider your situation before you decide to travel. If you don't know where you are or are not sure of a safe route to your destination, don't travel. Stay with your boat if someone will be looking for you. From the air, searchers are more likely to see a boat than one or two people.

If you decide to abandon the boat, leave the following information in a conspicuous place near or on the boat: when you left, where you are going, your route, your physical condition, and the supplies you are carrying. Make a continuous map of your route as you go, showing enough detail to enable you to retrace your steps if necessary.

River ratings. River difficulty ratings can change with water levels, depending upon how the water flows over and around obstructions. High water has the added hazard of floating logs, trees and other debris. Always walk the river bank to preview any sections that could cause problems.

Be cautious in how you interpret the International Whitewater Scale. Even within the Lower 48, there are some regional differences; a river rated as WW3 on the East Coast might not be classified as WW3 in the Northwest. Classification of Alaska's rivers is still in its infancy. But, whereas in the Lower 48 you'd probably be able to walk out to the nearest highway if you should lose your boat, in remote wilderness areas of Alaska, all river classifications should be upgraded due to the difficulty of rescue.

There is some overlap, in terms of difficulty, between the flat-water and whitewater classifications. Be sure you understand the differences before attempting these trips.

The following river classification system has been used in this book:

FLAT WATER

FWA (Class A) Easy. Lakes and standing water or very slow-flowing streams. Tidal currents less than 2 mph (3 kph). Little wind or wave activity expected. Sheltered and accessible location.

FWB (Class B) Moderate. Rivers and streams with currents that can be overcome by backpaddling. Tidal currents 2 to 4 mph (3 to 6 kph). Moderate wind and wave action. Rounding headlands or crossing open bays or channels of 3 to 5 mi (5 to 8 km) probable.

FWC (Class C) More difficult. Rivers, streams and tidal currents faster than can be overcome easily by backpaddling. Some skill necessary for sharp bends and back eddies in rivers. Landings and launchings require care, some maneuvering skill required. Storm winds and wave action possible. Extended duration of trip or remote wilderness locations.

WHITE WATER

WW1 (Class I) Easy. Moving water with small regular waves, riffles and sandbanks. Few or no obstructions.

WW2 (Class II) Medium. Rapids with waves up to 3 ft (1 m) and wide, obvious, clear channels. Some maneuvering is required.

WW3 (Class III) Difficult. Rapids with numerous high, irregular waves capable of swamping an open canoe. A splash cover is necessary. Narrow passages require complex maneuvering. Scouting the route from shore is recommended.

WW4 (Class IV) Very difficult. Rapids with turbulent waters, rocks and dangerous eddies. Constricted passages require powerful precise maneuvering and inspection of the route is mandatory. This water is normally too difficult for experts in open canoes. Boaters in covered canoes and kayaks should be able to Eskimo roll. Crash helmets and positive flotation in the boats are mandatory. For highly skilled boaters.

WW5 (Class V) Extremely difficult. Long violent rapids with rocks, big ledges, a very steep gradient and other serious obstacles in the route. Scouting the route from shore is required for safety. Rescue could be difficult, and a significant hazard to life exists in event of mishap. The ability to Eskimo roll under adverse conditions is essential. For a team of experts.

WW6 (Class VI) Extraordinarily difficult. Nearly impossible and very dangerous waters; for teams of expert kayakers and rafters only, with experienced rescue teams and equipment on the banks. Cannot be attempted without risk of life.

Much of the land above the 58th parallel is underlain by permafrost (permanently frozen ground). Surface water from spring snow-melt runoff or summer rains cannot percolate through this frozen layer, and runs immediately into the streams. Water levels in small rivers can rise as much as 3 to 4 ft (1 m) in a few hours. Always store your boat well up on the bank, well tied. Conversely, water levels can drop rapidly during dry periods.

Most river and stream channels are given little or no maintenance. In forested areas, sweepers (horizontal low-hanging trees) and logjams are frequent.

Another hazard, an interesting characteristic of the northland with its cold winters, is overflow ice or "aufeis." (See photograph in Sheenjek National Wild River description.) In an area of low gradient, many arctic and subarctic rivers freeze solid, leaving no channel for water coming from upstream. The trapped water breaks through to the surface repeatedly during the winter, forming extensive and deep fields of ice on river floodplains that often last throughout much of the summer. Check the river channel through the ice for a safe passage before running it.

Blue Water

Traveling by small boat on salt water is one of the finest ways to experience Alaska's mountains, forest and fjords. Before starting a trip, though, ask about local conditions. Many coastal waters have extreme tidal fluctuations, strong currents, uncharted rocks and frequent high winds and waves. The tidal rise and fall can be extremely large in shallow narrowing fjords. Upper Cook Inlet, for example, has a maximum daily range of 38.9 ft (11.9 m) during spring tides.

A few bays go nearly dry at low tides. During periods of large tidal fluctuation, the incoming tide in some of these areas can move as a bore—a swift noisy wall of churning water that can capsize small boats. Bore tides are frequent in Turnagain Arm and Knik Arm in the Anchorage area.

Be especially careful in narrow channels where riptides, whirlpools and standing waves can form. Consult tide tables to determine times of slack water, when you can safely paddle waters that normally have fierce tidal currents. Time your departures to use tidal currents to your advantage, speeding you on your way—a treat in flatwater paddling. Be alert for williwaws; since they tend to recur in the same areas, ask locally for information.

As with river running, always travel in a group of two or more boats. Plan your route so that it parallels shorelines, crossing large bodies of water only during calm seas. Consider a wet suit a necessity if you are kayaking or canoeing. An extended dunking in coastal waters, which average 40° to 55°F (4° to 13°C) in summer, can be fatal; survival time at 40°F (4°C) with light clothing and a life vest is less than two hours.

Rain is a fact of life in coastal Alaska. Expect long periods of fog or low visibility. Avoid major shipping lanes; your small craft probably won't be visible to large vessels, even on sunny days. To increase your chances of being spotted, use brightly colored clothing and boats. (On rainy days, the colors will make you feel better and liven up your photographs.)

One of the delights of blue-water boating is watching seals, sea lions, sea otters and whales. Be cautious, though, when among the large mammals—their actions are unpredictable. The appearance of a killer whale can panic a 2000-lb (900-kg) sea lion into trying to board your small boat.

Give actively feeding whales, too, a wide berth. They normally create no significant danger for the boater, but if a whale surfaces nearby, move slowly out of the area or drift quietly until the animal has moved away. Physical contact with a whale could result in a capsized boat and possibly death to you and your companions. At the very

Bore tide, Turnagain Arm.

least, you will have disturbed an animal extremely sensitive to your presence.

Power and sailboat skippers new to northern waters should contact the U.S. Coast Guard and Coast Guard Auxiliary for information about boating in Alaska's waters. Fuel docks are few and far between; the Coast Guard recommends using no more than one-third of your fuel to travel outward and one-third to get back, reserving one-third for emergencies.

No visual weather warnings are displayed by the U.S. Coast Guard in Alaska. Marine weather forecasts are given by radio or telephone only, using the following terms:

Small craft advisory—sustained weather or sea conditions of more than two hours duration, either present or forecast, which might be hazardous to small boats. Mariners must decide as to the severity of the weather, based upon experience and size and type of boat. Winds of more than 25 knots or hazardous wave conditions are indicated.

Gale warning—winds from 35 to 50 knots are forecast.

Storm warning—winds greater than 50 knots are forecast.

Local AM and FM radio stations broadcast marine weather in Anchorage, Bethel, Cordova, Dillingham, Glennallen, Juneau, Ketchikan, Kodiak, Kotzebue, Nome, Seward, Sitka and Soldotna. Marine and aviation weather is also broadcast weeknights on the "Aviation Weather" program on Alaskan PBS television stations. The National Weather Service gives marine forecasts by telephone in Anchorage, Annette, Cold Bay, Cordova, Juneau, King Salmon, Kodiak, Kotzebue, Nome, Petersburg, Sitka, Valdez, Wrangell and Yakutat.

For written information concerning Alaskan waters, consult the following National Ocean Survey publications: *United States Coast Pilot 8: Pacific Coast, Alaska, Dixon Entrance to Cape Spencer; United States Coast Pilot 9: Pacific and Arctic Coasts, Alaska, Cape Spencer to Beaufort Sea*; and *Tidal Current Tables: Pacific Coast of North America and Asia.*

The unwritten law of the sea requires that you come to the aid of another mariner in distress. If you see a distress signal, notify immediately the nearest Coast Guard station or other authority by radio (channel 9 on CB; channel 16, 156.8 MHz on VHF marine radio). If you can assist the stricken vessel or its passengers without endangering yourself or your craft, do so. Be sure that your own boat has adequate visual distress signals aboard.

Cold Water

When a person is immersed in cold water, the skin and nearby tissues cool rapidly, but it may take 10 to 15 minutes before the temperature of the heart and brain starts to drop. When the body core temperature reaches 90°F (32°C), unconsciousness occurs; when the core temperature drops to 85°F (29°C), the heart usually fails. Drowning in cold water normally occurs, however, because the victim becomes hypothermic and cannot use his arms and legs.

Survival in cold water depends upon many factors: the temperature of the water, body size, fat, and the amount of activity in the water. By swimming or treading water, one loses body heat 35% faster than by floating quietly. An average person wearing light clothing and a life vest can survive for two to three hours in 50°F (10°C) water by remaining still. Alaska's large lakes and coastal waters are generally colder than this. To increase your survival time by conserving body heat, draw your knees up into a fetal position and clasp your arms to your chest; keep your head and neck out of the water. If several people are in the water, huddle closely in a circle.

Water conducts heat from the body many times faster than does air. Since most boats will float even when capsized or swamped, climb onto or into the boat and remain as far out of the water as possible. Always wear an approved life vest; it will keep you afloat even if you are unconscious.

Whether or not to swim for shore is a difficult decision. Some good swimmers have been able to swim 0.8 mi (1.3 km) in 50°F (10°C) water before being overcome by hypothermia. Others have not been able to swim 100 yd (90 m). Since distances on the water are deceptive, stay with the boat if there is any chance whatever of rescue. A capsized boat is far easier for a rescuer to see than a person in the water. Swim for shore (wearing your flotation device) *only* if there is no chance of rescue and you are certain you can make it.

Cold-water drowning. Sudden face contact with cold water (below 70°F, 21°C) touches off a primitive response called the mammalian diving reflex. This complex series of body responses shuts off blood circulation to most parts of the body except the heart, lungs and brain. The oxygen remaining in the blood is transported to the brain, which when cooled requires much less oxygen than usual.

Children and young people are the most frequent drowning victims, but they are also good candidates for resuscitation since they have a more pronounced diving reflex. In research at the University of Michigan Hospital, two-thirds of the cold-water drowning victims who were successfully resuscitated were 3½ years old or younger. The colder the water and the younger the victim, the better the chance for survival. However, an 18-year-old male who was revived after 38 minutes in icy water, 2 hours of resuscitation and 13 hours of medical respiratory support sustained no apparent brain damage.

In a cold-water drowning emergency: 1) Immediately clear the air passage and begin mouth-to-mouth rescue breathing and external heart massage. Do not worry about getting water out of the victim's lungs; the body will absorb it quickly. 2) Prevent the victim from losing more body heat but *do not* rewarm the victim. 3) Quickly transport the victim to the nearest medical facility. Continue CPR without interruption until the victim is under the care of competent medical personnel. 4) Do not give up. Cold-water drowning victims appear dead. Their skin is blue and cold to the touch. Their eyes are fixed and dilated, and there is no detectable heartbeat or breathing. In spite of all this, they may still have a good chance of survival.

BEATING THE COLD AND SNOW

Although the temperature at Fort Yukon, above the Arctic Circle, has hit 100°F (38°C), Alaska isn't exactly Hawaii. A bit of preparation and know-how will keep the chills away, summer or winter, and allow you to have a fine outdoor experience.

Summer shivers are every bit as real as winter shakes. If your feet are cold, put on a hat or parka hood. At 40°F (4°C), half your body's heat production is lost through an unprotected head. Conserve body heat by staying out of the wind or by wearing windproof clothing; drink warm liquids and eat high-calorie foods. In cold weather, fats are the most efficient body fuel, but at high altitudes carbohydrates are frequently more digestible.

Choose clothing that is warm even when wet. Wool, acrylic-type pile or spun artificial fibers are best; avoid cotton or down. Wear enough clothes to be comfortable, but don't overheat to the point of sweating. Waterproof fabrics, even the Gore-Tex type, trap moisture if the temperature is below freezing. Mittens keep hands warmer than gloves.

Boots should be large enough for a felt insole or for several layers of socks. If your feet are cold, *take off* a layer to permit better blood circulation. Ever wonder why the traditional Eskimo mukluk is soft and roomy like a slipper? For extended periods in severe cold, don't wear leather hiking or ski boots unless you use an insulated cover or overboot. Better yet, wear specialized cold-weather boots. Powder snow around your feet on a clear, windless, sunny day can be 20°F (−7°C) colder than the air around your head. Exchanging perspiration-damp socks for dry ones helps to warm the feet, too. Dry the damp ones next to your body in the sleeping bag at night.

If you're having trouble staying warm, "pre-warm" air by breathing through a scarf or fur ruff or forming a parka-hood tunnel. At night put a handkerchief over the breathing hole of a drawn-together sleeping bag hood. Inhaling cold air and exhaling warm air causes significant body heat loss.

Avoid exhausting yourself. If you can't see where you are going, don't travel. Prepare a shelter and wait out the darkness or weather.

The Eskimos have known for centuries that snow makes an excellent shelter, and many winter back-country travelers use snow shelters in preference to tents. If the snow is deep enough, dig a snow cave with a shovel or an automobile hubcap. Since heat rises, make the entrance to the finished cave lower than the cave chamber. Protect the entrance from wind with snow blocks, but don't let it seal shut with blowing snow; maintain adequate ventilation at all times. Enough air will normally pass through most snowpacks, but if the walls and ceiling of your cave become glazed with a light layer of ice from the heat of your occupancy, you could run low on oxygen.

If there is too little snow to construct a cave, dig a trench and cover the top with a tarp. Dead tree branches, grass or sticks laid on the snow floor of your emergency shelter will keep you off the cold snow itself.

Summer or winter, start your bivouac early, well before daylight fades. If this is your first experience, you'll easily spend two to three hours preparing a shelter and gathering firewood. Try to camp near a water source or plan to melt snow for water. Although snow can safely be eaten for moisture, it will rob the body of valuable heat. By drinking water, even if it is cold, you lose far less body heat.

Be alert to the danger of carbon monoxide when fire is used in poorly ventilated shelters, including tents. Unconsciousness can occur without warning. If you feel pressure at your temples, headache, pounding pulse, drowsiness or nausea, breathe fresh air immediately.

Hypothermia

Whenever you and your companions are exposed to windy, cold or wet weather, watch for the symptoms of hypothermia: uncontrollable and continued fits of shivering, vague slow slurred speech, memory lapses and incoherence, fumbling hands, frequent stumbling and drowsiness. A hypothermic person is often unable to get up after a rest stop and acts exhausted. Since many cases of hypothermia develop from being wet in relatively warm air temperatures, from 30° to 50°F (−1° to +10°C), or from simply falling into cold water, the danger is easily underestimated.

First aid for hypothermia: Don't let a hypothermic person exercise, walk or struggle—the activity increases the flow of cold blood from the arms and legs back to the heart. Move the person gently—heartbeat irregularities can result from rough handling. Don't rub or massage any part of the body. Get the person into dry clothes or a warm sleeping bag. If no dry clothing or other covers are available, wring out wet clothes and put them back on, placing the person in rain gear or plastic to slow down heat loss from evaporation and protect from wind.

Don't give a severely hypothermic person hot liquids to drink. A pharyngeal reflex increases the blood flow to the skin and the extremities, bringing cold blood back to the trunk. If the person is only chilled, drinking hot liquids is probably safe.

Rewarm the victim slowly by applying heat from hot-water containers or wrapped hot stones to the areas of the body that transfer heat to the body core most efficiently—the groin, the sides of the chest, the head and the neck. Rewarm cautiously—people have been severely burned from over-enthusiastic warming. While rewarming, insulate the entire body to prevent further heat losses.

Less effective, but often the only choice, is to cover the victim entirely with heated clothing and sleeping bags or provide heat with your body, removing your clothing and the victim's and lying skin-to-skin in a sleeping bag. Two warm bodies with the victim between are even better. An open fire can provide heat, too, but guard against "backside" chill by putting a reflector behind the victim. Get medical help as soon as possible. Complications such as pneumonia or heart problems can occur later in severe cases.

Frostbite

Another danger associated with cold weather is frostbite, the damage resulting from freezing body tissues. Hands, feet, face and ears are the most likely to become frostbitten. Wind chill on exposed flesh speeds freezing; so does direct contact with cold metals and other highly conductive materials. If you must work bare-handed for dexterity, wear thin "thermal" gloves when handling cameras or ski bindings or making equipment repairs.

At low air temperatures, with or without wind, check each other's faces and ears frequently for white patches. Make a mental check of yourself to be sure you can feel sensation in every part of your body, and train yourself to snap to alertness when pain or feeling stop.

Anything which reduces the heat-producing capacity of the body (inactivity, fatigue, hypothermia, shock, or low caloric intake) or which robs the body of heat (inadequate or wet clothing, severe cold, wind or alcohol) contributes to frostbite. An injury, combined with shock, inactivity and anxiety, sets the stage for serious frostbite. Do not apply traction to arm or leg fractures in cold temperatures; splint the fracture "as it lays" and watch the victim carefully for signs of frostbite. In such cases, it can develop rapidly and is often severe.

First-aid treatment for frostbite is complicated and must be done correctly to prevent permanent damage to tissues or joints. Before you travel in Alaska in winter, study the procedures for treating frostbite in a good mountaineering first-aid book (see Additional Reading about Alaska, Appendix).

Extremely light frostbite, often called "frost nip," should be treated immediately. Cover a white patch on the face with a warm hand to return the flesh to a rosy glow. Hold frost-nipped fingers or toes (without boots) in a warm armpit. Never rub a frostbitten area with anything, especially snow.

Treat the frostbitten person for hypothermia, and check other areas—particularly ears, hands, wrists, ankles and feet—for further frostbite. Loosen any tight clothing, but don't ask the person to flex any frozen joints. Get the person to medical help for rewarming as soon as is safely possible.

Begin rewarming the frozen tissue yourself only if the person is in a permanent location and can be completely protected from the cold. If at all possible, don't begin rewarming at high altitudes. The person must not, under any circumstances, use a rewarmed frostbitten part of the body. Walking out on frozen feet will cause far less damage than walking on rewarmed feet.

Avalanches

More than 30% of Alaska is subject to avalanche activity for up to nine months a year. Although most avalanches fall in uninhabited areas without endangering human life or property, between the years of 1970 and 1979, 24 people died in avalanches in the state.

Anyone living in or visiting Alaska, particularly in winter, should know about avalanches: skiers, snowshoers, dog mushers and snowmobilers. So should motorists; the Seward, Richardson, Glenn and Haines highways and the Hope Road

Avalanche path, Chugach State Park.

are a few of the public roads that cross dangerous avalanche paths. Do not rely on state highway precautionary road closures for your safety. Learn to identify hazardous conditions and limit your travel at those times. In summer, mountaineers, hikers—anyone traveling on snow in the mountains—can also face avalanche hazard.

Your best insurance for trouble-free snow-country travel is educating yourself. Study the publications listed in the Appendix and attend one of the many avalanche education seminars given in the state or in the Lower 48 annually. Many sessions are free or have only a nominal fee. Contact the Alaska Division of Parks or the U.S. Forest Service for information. Before starting a winter trip, call the parkland manager; in Southcentral Alaska, check the Avalanche and Mountain Weather Forecast phone recording in Anchorage. In Southeastern, call the Juneau number (listed in Information Sources, Appendix).

Make sure that all party members understand avalanche rescue techniques thoroughly. Throughout Alaska, rescue assistance is generally a day or more away, while minutes often mean the difference between survival and death.

All members of a party venturing into hazardous areas should wear avalanche-victim locator beacons (electronic transceivers). Three popular compatible brands are the PIEPS, SKADI and Echo.

Each transceiver, worn like a necklace, is set to transmit continuously. If a companion is buried, searchers switch their units to receive the "beep-beep" signal of the buried beacon, the signal becoming stronger the closer a searcher is to the buried unit. Be sure batteries are strong and fully charged before each trip.

Once the locator beacon has been found, probing with a long stick accurately identifies the exact location of the victim. Some sort of probe should be carried. The standard avalanche probe is a rigid tube about 10 ft (3 m) long, with most models breaking into sections for easy transporting. Ski poles are available which convert into avalanche probes by joining the pole sections after the handles and baskets have been removed.

At least one Alaskan directly owes his life to the locator beacon and to his companions who efficiently located and uncovered the little box. The victim was encased in hard dense snow, 6 ft (2 m) deep, for 30 minutes before the shovelers freed him. The victim's locator beacon, his good health and his prepared companions were more than luck. Obviously, each person in the party should carry a shovel. Statistically a person buried for 30 minutes has a 50% chance of being found alive. For burial deeper than 6 ft (2 m), survival is not likely.

The use of avalanche cords has been popular for many years. The cord, a long trailing brightly colored nylon line, is supposed to "float" on the surface of the avalanche leading rescuers to the victim, but often the cord is buried deeper than the victim. Rescue by locator beacon is faster and more effective.

Party members should have training in first aid, especially in cardiopulmonary resuscitation (CPR). Courses are taught frequently in most communities. Five percent of avalanche victims have broken bones; eighty percent of avalanche deaths are caused by suffocation.

If you are caught in an avalanche, fight for your life! Yell immediately to attract attention—let your companions know you are being carried away. If you are on skis or a snowmobile, try to run out of the avalanche to safety. If outrunning it fails, get rid of any equipment like skis or poles that might pull you under or hurt you. Make a vigorous effort to swim. It can help you stay on top of the snow or bring you to the surface. If you have control, try to descend feet first to fend off rocks or trees.

As the snow slows, give an extra kick for the surface. Before the snow stops moving, protect your face with one arm, trying to make an air space. With the other, reach for the surface. Your companions will find you easily if even your fingers show. If you can dig yourself out, do so. Your companions may need help. If you are trapped, stay calm to conserve air and strength. Meditate, relax, avoid panic. Don't shout excessively or struggle. Your rescuers probably won't be able to hear you even if they seem to be standing on your head. If you feel that you might pass out, let it happen. Your body needs less air when you are unconscious.

If a companion is caught in an avalanche and you are not, don't panic. Check first for further avalanche danger. A second slide from a tributary drainage might follow the first. Station an observer in a safe place to watch for further avalanches and establish a safe escape route for all searchers.

Mark the spot where the person was last seen and search downhill, following the flow lines of the avalanche. Work silently, listening for possible cries from the victim. Look particularly wherever snow debris accumulates—in front of trees, on the outside of a turn in the avalanche path, at the foot of the avalanche. Leave any of the victim's possessions in the place where you find them, sticking up in the snow, to help establish the direction the victim was carried. Make probes from whatever is handy—ski poles, tree branches, anything. You are the victim's only hope. Continue probing, digging and marking the searched areas until you have exhausted all possibilities. Search at least two hours before giving up. Be sure, however, that you, the survivors, don't endanger your own lives through exhaustion and hypothermia. If the victim is found alive, give CPR immediately if necessary, and treat for shock and hypothermia.

Lest you begin to feel that Alaska presents only challenges beyond the ability of an average person—it isn't so. Few Alaskans have experienced hypothermia, frostbite or avalanches. Nevertheless, such hazards do exist. If you are out in the back country on your own, you should understand them.

VILLAGES AND THE BUSH

For decades, to Outsiders, the romance of Alaska has been the cozy snow-laden log cabin and the stilt-legged cache in the forest, snowshoes crossed over the door, smoke curling from the chimney, the northern lights dancing above and wolves howling in the night air.

Many Alaskans still live in the Bush, but few cabins are as picturesque as those painted on Alaska souvenirs, nor are the people as isolated from society as the early sourdoughs or the nomadic native Alaskans once were. The heartbeat of rural Alaska today lies primarily within the villages, where schools, supplies, transportation, medical help and jobs are available. Television received from satellite signals and movies provide entertainment. Most houses are of frame construction, complete with electricity and running water. A snowmobile sits outside the front door.

You'll find that rural villages of fewer than 400 people have limited services. Most have active community organizations, a church and perhaps an air taxi operation. Local power boats might be available for charter. The village store carries basic food and merchandise suited to the local lifestyle, but if a shipment is late, the shelves can be quite empty. Generally, however, fresh fruits and frozen meats are stocked, along with standard canned and packaged foods, white gas and kerosene. Shopping at village stores can be a pleasant and interesting experience.

In many villages, visitors are not frequent, you may be the subject of a lot of curiosity and gossip. Small villages are much like extended families. Enjoy your stay, but be unobtrusive, friendly and courteous.

Ask before you camp, bathe in the river, or build a fire. You might be tenting in someone's back yard, washing off your accumulated grime upstream from the village water supply or burning a personal wood supply. Assume that all land in the vicinity of a village is privately owned and you won't be far wrong. Many villages have designated areas for visitors to camp and to use for personal hygiene, so ask. Ask, too, about the village social schedule. You might have arrived in time for movie night or some other special occasion that you may be invited to attend.

Many villages have voted themselves "dry," prohibiting the importation or sale of alcoholic beverages. If your baggage includes alcohol, avoid displaying or consuming it in public until you are aware of local regulations.

A few villages have indicated that they prefer not to have visitors or tourists in their settlements. (See Table 1, Access and Services, Villages and Cities, in Appendix.) Please respect their request for privacy and, if your route passes through these villages, be friendly but do not linger. Many Alaskans strongly value their quiet isolated lifestyle and are justifiably upset when the uninvited world beats a path to their doors.

To appreciate village life, an understanding of the heritage of Alaska's first people is essential. The books by Robert Arnold and Lael Morgan, listed in "Alaska's history and people" section of Additional Reading about Alaska in the Appendix, are good starting points.

Telephones in the Bush

For years, two-way radios were the standard communication in both isolated households and villages. They are still in use, but the more convenient telephone, using a satellite-bounced signal, now connects almost all Alaskan communities. Many small villages have just one community telephone, however, often located in a private home.

To reach an individual or business in a village with a community phone, obtain the village phone number from Directory Assistance and call, either leaving a message

Eskimo children, Ambler.

or making arrangements to speak directly to the desired person at some time in the future. Many community phones are available for village use only during certain hours. Arrange to be available for a return call from your party at one of the village phone-use times or ask to have your party waiting at the phone for your call. Remember that your party may have to travel a mile or more by foot, boat, snowmobile or dogsled to reach the telephone. Similarly, the person answering the telephone might have difficulty getting a message to your party.

Private Lands

As a result of the 1971 Alaska Native Claims Settlement Act, one-ninth of Alaska's acreage is being transferred to private ownership, most of it in the rural areas, some contained within parks and refuges. The national forests, the Yukon Delta, Yukon Flats and Selawik national wildlife refuges and the Wrangell–St. Elias National Preserve contain significant amounts of private acreage, but you can assume that most of the lands and waterways are open to public travel.

Public access marker.

Outside parklands, you must assume land is privately held if it is easily accessible from the road system, a village or a river, or if it contains any type of structure, from a cabin to a fish drying rack or a permanent campsite. If you wish to cross or camp on private land, ask permission before doing so. Be a courteous guest, protect the vegetation from serious damage, cut no live trees, leave no garbage and do not hunt.

Before beginning a wilderness trip, contact the appropriate native corporation (see Figure 4) for information regarding native land holdings, sending a sketch of your route and a self-addressed stamped envelope. Addresses are in the Information Sources, Appendix. Guidelines are still being worked out, so expect inconsistencies and delays.

The whole concept of public vs. private lands throughout the state and their use has been a highly controversial issue in Alaska and will continue to be so for some time, so don't be upset by an occasional angry Alaskan. Use all of your diplomatic skills and you'll both be happier.

Land beneath navigable lakes, rivers and streams is regulated by the state. It is therefore considered public land below mean high water and is open to public travel. (This in no way guarantees public access across private lands to reach the lake, river or stream.) Those who defined navigability for the Lower 48 many years ago did not

Figure 4. *Alaska native corporation regions. (From Anchorage Daily News)*

foresee the use of float planes or the importance of small river boats, Hovercraft, canoes, kayaks and rafts in Alaska. Nor does it address the use of frozen waterways as transportation corridors—a major use of the river and stream systems in much of Alaska for more than six months each year.

Your help is needed. The State of Alaska is gathering information to substantiate claims regarding the navigability, historical use and economic importance of *any* body of water in the state. The intent is to establish legal guidelines for public use of Alaska's waterways that will be binding upon future generations. Contact the Navigability Project, Division of Research and Development, Alaska Department of Natural Resources (address in Information Sources, Appendix) to report your use of a water course for foot travel, dogsled travel, rafting, float plane landing, etc.

For information regarding the status of a specific piece of land, contact the Land Office, Bureau of Land Management (address in Land Managers, Appendix). Because of the continuing transfer of lands from the public domain to private ownership, no current map exists showing land ownership. BLM coordinates information about all lands within the state, stores it on microfiche and makes it available to the public.

WILD FOODS

To many Alaskans, May and June mean more than spring flowers. Tender young plants lift their leaves toward the warm sun—salads waiting to be gathered. Fish swim the cool stream waters, clams spout on the beaches and, by August, berry bushes hang heavy with plump fruit. In autumn, hunters stalk the hills for game.

Alaska's bounty awaits you, but be aware of state and parkland restrictions. The harvesting of animal life, including some shellfish, is controlled by the Alaska Department of Fish and Game unless otherwise restricted by parkland regulations. Hunting, fishing and trapping are discussed in the section about wildlife.

Plants and Mushrooms

Wild plants and berries for personal use may be gathered on most state and federal lands, although some areas do not permit digging the roots. The Cooperative Extension Service (address in Information Sources, Appendix) has an excellent illustrated booklet, "Wild Edible and Poisonous Plants of Alaska," by Christine A. Heller. Mushroom hunting is also popular in Alaska. Check the Cooperative Extension Service booklet, "Know Alaska's Mushrooms," by Virginia L. Wells and Phyllis E. Kempton, or *The Alaskan Mushroom Hunter's Guide* by Ben Guild (Anchorage: Alaska Northwest Publishing Co., 1977). Be sure you can recognize both poisonous plants and poisonous mushrooms.

Paralytic Shellfish Poisoning

At unpredictable times and places, "red tides" occur along the coast, evidence of dense populations of dinoflagellates, a marine protozoan. Certain species of dinoflagellates can produce potent neurotoxins that can cause death within 2 to 12 hours. Numerous fatalities throughout the history of the Pacific coast have been attributed to paralytic shellfish poisoning. Not all red tides produce toxin. In Alaska toxic dinoflagellates rarely form visible red tides; toxic shellfish usually occur when the water is not discolored.

Shellfish most likely to concentrate the toxin by consuming the dinoflagellates are clams, mussels, cockles, scallops, rock scallops and oysters. Crabs, shrimp and abalone are not known to cause paralytic shellfish poisoning. Most shellfish lose their toxicity within several weeks after exposure, but butter clams can retain the toxin for as long as two years. Poisonous shellfish cannot be distinguished by sight, taste or smell. Isolated pockets of toxic shellfish can occur in an area of non-toxic ones.

Only Alaska's commercial razor clam beaches are monitored for the toxin and bacteria levels on a regular basis by the State of Alaska. If toxin is discovered, an announcement is made through local news media. Monitoring on a few other beaches occurs on an informal unscheduled basis. Since most of Alaska's clam beaches will probably continue to be unmonitored, treat all clams, mussels, cockles, rock scallops and oysters as potentially toxic. For current information on toxicity levels, contact the local Alaska Department of Health and Social Services, Division of Public Health or the Alaska Department of Fish and Game. Remember, however, that the beach that is safe today may be contaminated tomorrow.

Reaction to the toxin may be more severe if the shellfish are consumed with an alcoholic beverage. Some evidence also exists that adaptation to shellfish toxin can occur in people who eat shellfish regularly.

Although some toxin can be removed by discarding the dark digestive gland, gills, the nectar in which the shellfish are cooked, and the siphons of butter clams, there could be enough toxin left in the shellfish to cause illness or even death. The toxin is unaffected by cooking, canning, freezing, pickling or drying the seafood.

No antidotes exist for paralytic shellfish poisoning. Swallowing even a small amount of toxic meat or nectar can be fatal. Symptoms of paralytic shellfish poisoning are a tingling or numbness of lips, face and neck and prickliness in fingers and toes. Headache, dizziness and nausea may follow. In severe cases, speech becomes incoherent and the victim has a general feeling of weakness and lightness, the pulse is rapid and breathing is difficult. Death occurs by respiratory paralysis and cardiovascular collapse.

First aid for paralytic shellfish poisoning: Induce vomiting; give a rapid-acting laxative. Treat for shock; use CPR—mouth-to-mouth resuscitation and closed-cardiac massage—if necessary. Do not give alcohol, digitalis or stimulants. Get the victim to a doctor immediately. If the victim survives longer than 12 hours, chances of recovery are good. Suggested reading: D. B. Quayle, *Paralytic Shellfish Poisoning in British Columbia* (Ottawa, Canada: Fisheries Research Board of Canada, 1969).

Other types of poisoning can occur from eating shellfish. Those contaminated by raw human sewage can cause nausea, vomiting, diarrhea and abdominal pain that strikes about ten hours after ingestion and usually subsides rapidly. Severe contamination can cause hepatitis, which takes much longer to develop and recover from. Erythematous shellfish poisoning, an allergic reaction to shellfish, produces swelling, itching and redness affecting the face and neck, and sometimes the whole body.

THE LAND—ITS FORMS AND ITS WEATHER

Bordered on three sides by oceans and on the fourth by continental North America, the land masses of Alaska are affected by arctic, continental and maritime air masses. The result is a number of climate patterns, with complex transitions between them. Topography has such a significant effect on weather, climate and plant life that climatic and vegetation zones can best be described by major topographic regions (see Figure 5).

Two large mountain belts—the Alaska Range paralleling the southern coast and the Brooks Range in the northern part of the state—separate the lowlands and rolling hills of the Interior from the rest of the state.

North of the Brooks Range, the land slopes gently from the base of the mountains to the Arctic Ocean, forming the "North Slope." Along the western Gulf of Alaska, the southwestern extension of the Alaska Range becomes the Aleutian Range and the Aleutian Islands, while along the east Gulf Coast, the range becomes the St. Elias Mountains and the Coast Mountains. A spur of the Alaska Range, the Kenai and the Chugach Mountains, drops steeply to tidewater along the north Gulf of Alaska coast.

Extensive glaciation has occurred across Alaska. Today, many of its mountainous areas contain massive icefields and piedmont and valley glaciers, remnants of the latest glacial advance.

Much of Alaska's landmass is underlain by permafrost. Only the Aleutian Islands and the lands adjacent to the Gulf of Alaska do not contain significant amounts of permanently frozen ground (see Figure 6).

The North Slope, western Alaska, the Alaska Peninsula and the Aleutian Islands are almost entirely treeless. Forests cover only about 30% of the state's surface area (see Figure 7). The distribution of many animal species correlates closely with the existence or absence of forests.

Thirty-three species of trees are native to the state, the fewest number of species found in any of the 50 states. Only 12 species can be classed as large trees, more than 70 ft (20 m) high. Nine of these species are found only in the coastal forests of

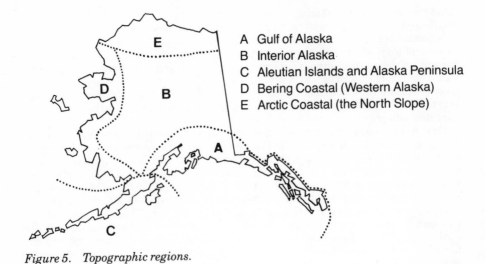

A Gulf of Alaska
B Interior Alaska
C Aleutian Islands and Alaska Peninsula
D Bering Coastal (Western Alaska)
E Arctic Coastal (the North Slope)

Figure 5. Topographic regions.

Southeastern Alaska; Sitka spruce and western hemlock predominate. Interior Alaskan boreal forest (taiga) contains three species of large trees: white spruce, paper birch and balsam poplar.

The Topographic Regions

The Gulf of Alaska region. The Alaska Range and the Gulf of Alaska coast from the base of the Alaska Peninsula to the southern tip of the Southeast Panhandle are strongly influenced by air masses flowing from the Gulf of Alaska. Summers are mild, with frequent rains and long periods of overcast; winters are also mild, with temperatures above or near freezing along the outer coast, becoming colder in protected interior regions south of the Alaska Range. Where Gulf of Alaska weather influences prevail, salt water is ice-free in the winter.

Local topography largely determines the amount of precipitation, with the greatest amount on south-facing slopes and coastlines. In general, precipitation is heavy, ranging from 30 inches (76 cm) to an estimated 400 inches (1000 cm) annually. October is consistently the wettest month. Clear days occur most frequently from February through June. Fog occurs the entire year, but is most likely in late summer and early winter. Snow often falls wet and heavy, sometimes light and powdery only to turn heavy as temperatures rise. Winds are generally light in protected valleys, but almost constant and often strong along the coast and at high elevations.

Long summer days accompany short twilight nights in June and July in the northern part of the region. The Panhandle experiences short dark nights in June and has longer winter days than the Anchorage area.

Dense coniferous forests occur in coastal areas of high precipitation from Southeastern Alaska north around the Gulf of Alaska to Kodiak Island. Boreal forests cover the drier regions of the Kenai Peninsula and northern Cook Inlet. The topography is generally steep and mountainous; timberline ranges from 2000 to 3000 ft (600 to 900 m).

Extensive alder thickets crowd the mountainsides from sea level to the alpine tundra meadows, filling forest openings not occupied by bogs and choking most

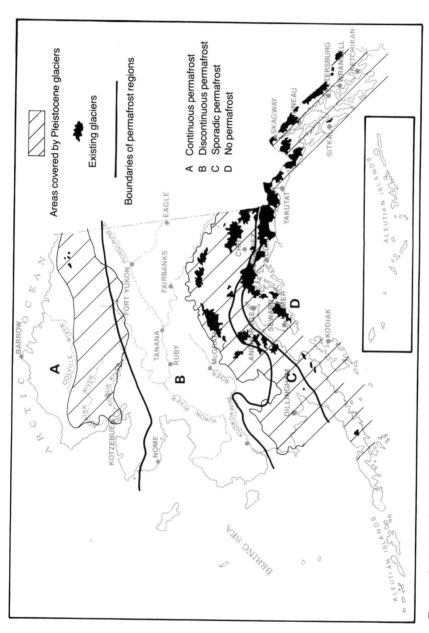

Figure 6. Extent of existing glaciers, Pleistocene glaciers and permafrost regions. (Modified from Clyde Wahrhaftig, Physiographic Divisions of Alaska, U.S. Geological Survey Professional Paper No. 482. Washington, D.C.: U.S. Government Printing Office, 1965.)

avalanche paths, stream beds and river banks. Ferns and spiny devil's club grow among the alders.

Muskeg, a ground cover of thick sphagnum moss, sedges, rushes, low shrubs and fruticose lichens, forms where drainage is poor in flat areas, in depressions and on slopes with abundant water. Beneath its surface a thick layer of peat has built up, and ponds frequently lie terraced in the peat.

On mountain slopes and ridges above timberline not covered by permanent snowfields or glaciers and wherever winter snows linger late into the spring, alpine tundra, a tenacious low mat of herbaceous and shrubby plants, is found.

The Interior Alaska region. The large area of plains, hills and low mountains lying between the Brooks Range and the Alaska Range experiences sunny, sometimes hot, summers from late May to late August. Winters are long and cold; occasional "chinooks" (warm southerly winds) can bring above-freezing temperatures, but at other times, temperatures can drop to −50° or −60°F (−46° or −51°C).

Precipitation is greater than on the Arctic Slope, but is still considered light, 12 to 20 inches (30 to 50 cm) a year. In summer, rain may fall either as periods of drizzle or as heavy showers, often accompanied by thunder and lightning. The greatest number of clear days occurs in winter, although in populated areas ice fog—formed when moisture in the air crystallizes and remains suspended as fine ice particles—blocks the sun for weeks at a time. Winds are generally light.

The long summer days of May, June and July end in a brief colorful twilight nominally designated as "night." Winter days are short, with an hour or two of twilight before darkness falls and before sunrise.

Boreal forest, or taiga, grows in this area of light precipitation and extreme climatic conditions. On north-facing slopes and moist lowlands, particularly in areas underlain by an impervious permafrost layer, a slow-growing scrawny black spruce forest with a thick moss ground cover usually forms. Trees 2 inches (5 cm) in diameter can be over 100 years old.

In swales and flat areas too wet for tree growth, there are bogs of sphagnum mosses, grasses and sedges. Most bogs occur where old river terraces, flood and outwash plains, old river deltas, sloughs and ponds have filled with vegetation.

Willow and alder thickets are found near treeline, often dense, sometimes growing open and well spaced on alpine tundra. Alders predominate in the wetter areas. On newly formed alluvial deposits on braided river floodplains, willow thickets dominate.

The Aleutian region. The Alaska Peninsula, the Aleutian Islands, Kodiak and Afognak islands and the islands of the Bering Sea are under a strong maritime influence and rarely receive whole days of sunshine. Clouds, fog, heavy precipitation, high winds, an annual temperature range of 30° to 55°F (−1° to +13°C) and high humidities make this one of the most uncomfortable regions in the world. In the Aleutians, for example, expect cloudiness 90% of the time in the summer, 50% of the time in the winter. During the summer months, cloud-ceiling heights are below 1000 ft (300 m) about 50% of the time. Seas are ice-free in winter.

Steep pressure gradients between the air masses of the Bering Sea and the north Pacific cause frequent gale-force winds and williwaws (sudden strong winds created by mountain topography) with gusts of over 70 knots (36 m per second).

This region is almost treeless. Vegetation is primarily cottongrass tussocks, with occasional low, dense heath shrubs and meadows of tall grasses. Much of western Kodiak Island is covered by thick brush; the eastern portion of the island and Afognak Island contain coastal rain forest.

The Bering Coastal region. The flat, treeless plain bordering the Bering Sea north of the Alaska Peninsula and continuing northward to Point Hope on the Chukchi Sea has a climate controlled by the nearness of open ocean. Throughout most of the year, maritime influences create cool summers, with considerable cloudi-

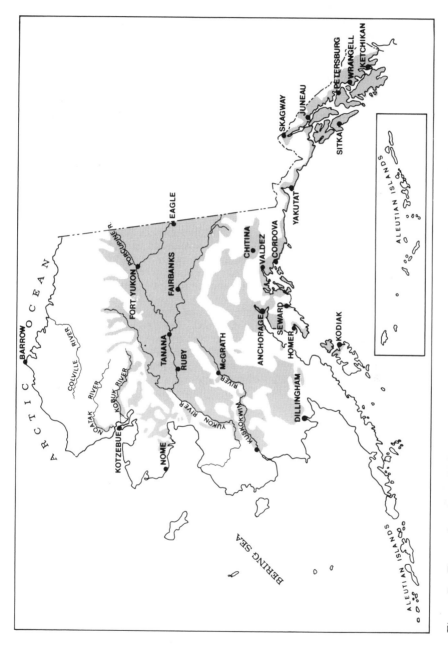

Figure 7. Forested regions. (U.S. Department of the Interior, Fish and Wildlife Service, Circular 211)

61

ness, fog and drizzle near the coast. At increasing distances from the coast, continental masses begin to dominate the weather. Winter temperatures vary between 0°F (−18°C) and freezing so long as open water remains offshore; lower temperatures occur once the ocean has frozen in January. Seas in the southern extent of the region are normally blocked by significant ice formation from December through April; in the north, ice stops shipping from October through June.

Despite extensive overcast, precipitation is light. Summer showers bring the largest amount; snow, sometimes wet and heavy, falls from late September to May. Winds blow moderately and steadily along the coast, frequently reaching gale force.

Much of the area is covered by moist tundra. Cottongrass tussocks predominate, with pockets of dwarf shrubs or alder-willow thickets. Where the land is flat with much underlying permafrost and standing water, many shallow lakes dot the wetlands, particularly in the Yukon-Kuskokwim delta. Here the vegetation is primarily a sedge-cottongrass mat, but with few tussocks.

The Arctic Coastal region. The North Slope and the north side of the Brooks Range are normally influenced by arctic air masses, resulting in a cold climate throughout the year. Although temperatures are normally comfortable from June through mid-August, freezing temperatures can occur even in summer. Winter lasts nine months and temperatures are low. Coastal waters contain large masses of ice even in summer.

Precipitation is light throughout the year, appearing in the summer as drizzle and fog. Snow, generally powdery and wind-drifted, covers the ground from September through May. The greatest number of clear days occur in February and March; cloudiness is most likely July through September. Winds frequently reach gale force and blow more or less continually. Summer days are 24 hours long; winter days consist of a few hours of twilight.

Except for a few isolated stands of trees on river gravel floodplains, the area is treeless. Willow bushes grow profusely in river beds. The flat northern coastal areas, underlain by continuous permafrost, are covered by wet tundra with many north/south-oriented shallow lakes. One can frequently observe "patterned ground"— irregular polygon-shaped patterns on the soil, varying from 3 to 90 ft (1 to 27 m) in diameter, formed by repeated freeze-thaw cycles.

Weather Data

Over the years, weather records have been kept for most settlements in Alaska— some sketchily for only a few years, some faithfully for decades. Even the most incomplete records are of interest to visitors, since they give some indication of the temperatures and precipitation to be expected for the area.

Because most parklands are some distance from a weather station, you are encouraged to study topographic maps and extrapolate, from the Weather Tables in the Appendix, probable temperature and precipitation differences for the area you'll visit. Figures 8, 9 and 10 will also help.

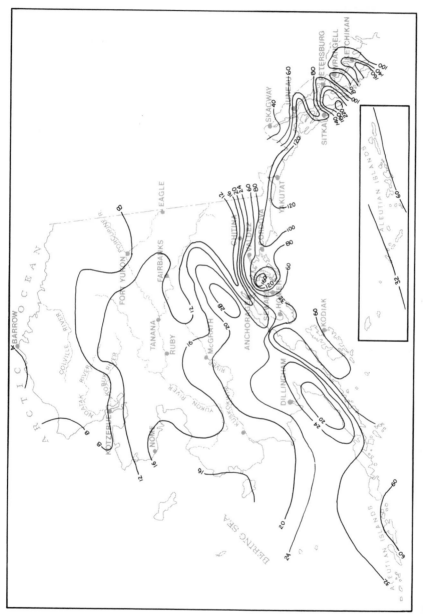

Figure 8. Average annual precipitation in inches. (From Clyde Wahrhaftig, Physiographic Divisions of Alaska)

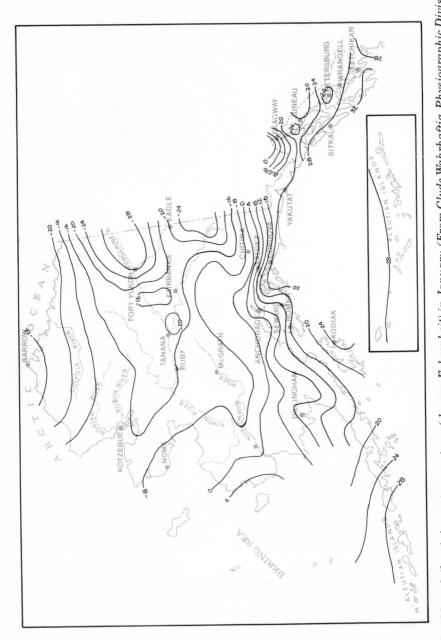

Figure 9. *Mean daily minimum temperatures (degrees Fahrenheit) in January. (From Clyde Wahrhaftig, Physiographic Divisions of Alaska)*

Figure 10. Mean daily maximum temperatures (degrees Fahrenheit) in July. (From Clyde Wahrhaftig, Physiographic Divisions of Alaska)

PART II: THE PARKLANDS

ABOUT THE PARKLAND DESCRIPTIONS

Parkland name. The official name at press time is given. Local usage often lags behind official name changes. The Alaska National Interest Lands Conservation Act of 1980 changed the name or designation of a number of existing parklands. For example, Mount McKinley National Park became Denali National Park and Preserve.

The two accepted spellings "fjord" and "fiord" have created an unavoidable inconsistency in this book. The National Park Service uses the former spelling, as we do; the U.S. Forest Service uses the latter.

Location. Parkland locations are described first with respect to the divisions of the state in Figure 11. A more precise location is given next, referring to a nearby major town, natural feature or parkland. Map coordinates are given for a representative point within the parkland.

Size. The acreage listed is the best available at press time. Boundaries are occasionally changed through additions, deletions or land exchanges. In more re-

Rocky shore, Kenai Fjords National Park. (U.S. Fish and Wildlife Service photo by Jo Keller)

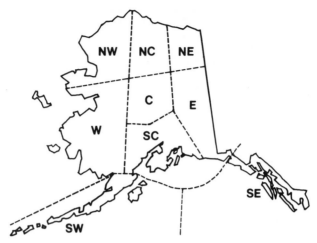

Figure 11. Divisions of the state for locating parklands.

cently designated parklands, sizes have been estimated until detailed surveys can be made.

High point/low point. Comparison of these figures help describe the terrain of the parkland, whether it has high or low relief, an alpine or low-elevation environment.

River rating. Wild Rivers and other floatable streams are rated according to a standard system, described in Part I. Since the rivers were rated by those who happened to run them, at water levels which may or may not have been typical, ratings should be used as a general guide only. A few rivers are seldom visited; information given for the more popular ones is more dependable, but remember that the challenge of a stream can change greatly with different water levels. Classification varies with the remoteness of the region; for a cautionary note, see "River Running," Part I.

Popular trip length. Although the Wild River designation generally starts at the headwaters of a river, the upper reaches will not have sufficient water to float a canoe, kayak or raft. Since this book is oriented toward the recreational visitor, distances are calculated between points used by boaters and are expressed in estimated river miles and kilometers, not straight-line distances. Because some rivers flow in a relatively straight channel while others meander in closely packed loops, the maps accompanying the Wild River descriptions include a "meander factor." Multiplying the apparent map length of a river by the meander factor gives a more accurate estimate of the distance a boat will travel. A factor of 1.2 indicates a relatively straight channel, while a factor of 2 indicates wide meanders.

Annual high water. High water levels can generally be expected at certain times of the year due to snow-melt run-off or normal seasonal rain. Some streams can be run only at high water, while others are hazardous at high water and are better run at lower water levels. Each year is different, and unseasonable precipitation or drought will affect the navigability of a particular stream.

Best time of year. Although some activities can be pursued through the greater part of the year, a few months are normally the most pleasant for a given activity. (Bear in mind, of course, that unusual weather conditions can change everything.) Optimum times for summer travel are indicated by "foot," and for winter travel, by "ski."

USGS maps. Two topographic map scales are most useful for travelers, the 1:250,000 scale, in which 1 inch equals 3.9 mi (1 cm equals 2.5 km) and the 1:63,360 scale, in which 1 inch equals 1 mi (1 cm equals 0.63 km). The maps listed for a parkland are those that most reasonably show the entire unit. To describe the extensive Yukon Delta National Wildlife Refuge requires 14 1:250,000-scale maps; most of the refuge is also mapped in the 1:63,360 scale. Tiny Sitka National Historical Park, on the other hand, is best described by "Sitka A-4," a 1:63,360-scale map; but the traveler might also wish to refer to the 1:250,000-scale map to understand the relationship of the park to surrounding lands.

Maps of land units are listed in alphabetical order. Wild River maps are listed in the order of use while floating downstream. See also the section about maps in Part I of this book.

Established or designated as Wild River. The year in which the land or river unit was officially set aside as a protected area is given. Name-change dates are noted in the text.

Managed by. Six government agencies—four federal and two state—manage Alaska's public lands. Addresses and phone numbers are listed in the Appendix.

Parkland descriptions include points of interest and history, wildlife, general recreational information, facilities available, boating information, weather, prominent peaks (not necessarily the highest), access information and suggested reading. Parkland regulations are current at press time, but are subject to change. Looking over some of the literature available about the parklands is an excellent way to understand more about the land, its significance and special features. Alaska-oriented publications of a more general nature are included in the Appendix.

Whenever a parkland is too small to be shown on the color USGS map inserted into this book, a sketch map is included with the parkland description. A sketch map is included for each Wild River, showing major features of interest to boaters. *Do not attempt to float a river using this map*; carry the most detailed USGS maps you can find.

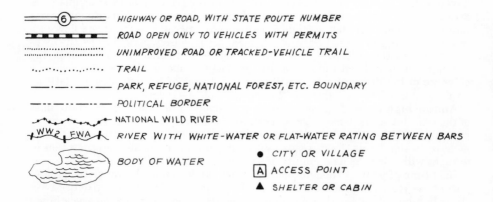

Figure 12. Sketch map legend.

THE 111 NATIONAL AND STATE PARKLANDS

Key to location of parklands in Figure 13:

1. Admiralty Island National Monument, Tongass National Forest
2. Alagnak National Wild River
3. Alaska Chilkat Bald Eagle Preserve
4. Alaska Maritime National Wildlife Refuge
5. Alaska Peninsula National Wildlife Refuge
6. Alatna National Wild River
7. Aleutian Islands Refuge, Alaska Maritime National Wildlife Refuge
8. Andreafsky National Wilderness and Wild River
9. Aniakchak National Monument, Preserve and Wild River
10. Ann Stevens–Cape Lisburne Refuge, Alaska Maritime National Wildlife Refuge
11. Arctic National Wildlife Refuge and Wilderness
12. Baranof Castle Hill State Historic Site
13. Beaver Creek National Wild River
14. Becharof National Wildlife Refuge and Wilderness
15. Bering Land Bridge National Preserve
16. Bering Sea Refuge, Alaska Maritime National Wildlife Refuge
17. Birch Creek National Wild River
18. Bogoslof Refuge, Alaska Maritime National Wildlife Refuge
19. Caines Head State Recreation Area
20. Cape Krusenstern National Monument
21. Captain Cook State Recreation Area
22. Chamisso Refuge, Alaska Maritime National Wildlife Refuge
23. Chena River State Recreation Area
24. Chilikadrotna National Wild River
25. Chilkat State Park
26. Chugach National Forest
27. Chugach State Park
28. Coronation Island Wilderness, Tongass National Forest
29. Creamer's Field Migratory Waterfowl Refuge
30. Delta National Wild and Scenic River
31. Denali National Park and Preserve
32. Denali State Park
33. Endicott River Wilderness, Tongass National Forest
34. Forrester Island Refuge, Alaska Maritime National Wildlife Refuge
35. Fort Abercrombie State Historic Park
36. Fortymile National Wild, Scenic and Recreational River
37. Gates of the Arctic National Park and Preserve
38. Glacier Bay National Park and Preserve
39. Goose Bay State Game Refuge
40. Gulkana National Wild River
41. Harding Lake State Recreation Area
42. Hazy Islands Refuge, Alaska Maritime National Wildlife Refuge
43. Iditarod National Historic Trail
44. Independence Mine State Historic Park
45. Innoko National Wildlife Refuge and Wilderness
46. Ivishak National Wild River
47. Izembek National Wildlife Refuge and Wilderness
48. John National Wild River
49. Kachemak Bay State Park
50. Kanuti National Wildlife Refuge
51. Katmai National Park and Preserve
52. Kenai Fjords National Park

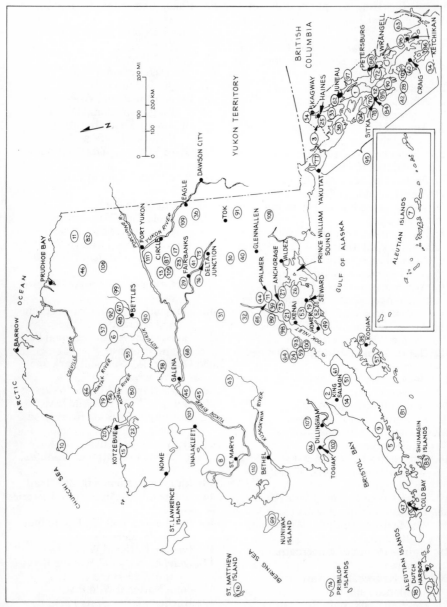

Figure 13.   Location of parklands.

53. Kenai National Wildlife Refuge and Wilderness
54. Klondike Gold Rush National Historical Park
55. Kobuk National Wild River
56. Kobuk Valley National Park
57. Kodiak National Wildlife Refuge
58. Koyukuk National Wildlife Refuge and Wilderness
59. Lake Clark National Park and Preserve
60. Maurelle Islands Wilderness, Tongass National Forest
61. McNeil River State Game Sanctuary
62. Mendenhall Wetlands State Game Refuge
63. Misty Fiords National Monument, Tongass National Forest
64. Mulchatna National Wild River
65. Nancy Lake State Recreation Area
66. Noatak National Preserve and Wild River
67. North Fork, Koyukuk National Wild River
68. Nowitna National Wildlife Refuge and Wild River
69. Nunivak National Wildlife Refuge and Wilderness
70. Old Sitka State Historic Site
71. Palmer Hay Flats State Game Refuge
72. Petersburg Creek–Duncan Salt Chuck Wilderness, Tongass National Forest
73. Potter Point State Game Refuge
74. Pribilof Islands
75. Quartz Lake State Recreation Area
76. Rika's Landing State Historic Site
77. Russell Fiord Wilderness, Tongass National Forest
78. St. Lazaria Refuge, Alaska Maritime National Wildlife Refuge
79. Salmon National Wild River
80. Selawik National Wildlife Refuge, Wilderness and Wild River

81. Semidi Refuge, Alaska Maritime National Wildlife Refuge
82. Sheenjek National Wild River
83. Simeonof Refuge, Alaska Maritime National Wildlife Refuge
84. Sitka National Historical Park
85. South Baranof Wilderness, Tongass National Forest
86. South Prince of Wales Wilderness
87. Steese National Conservation Area
88. Stikine–LeConte Wilderness, Tongass National Forest
89. Susitna Flats State Game Refuge
90. Tebenkof Bay Wilderness, Tongass National Forest
91. Tetlin National Wildlife Refuge
92. Tinayguk National Wild River
93. Tlikakila National Wild River
94. Togiak National Wildlife Refuge and Wilderness
95. Tongass National Forest
96. Totem Bight State Historic Park
97. Tracy Arm–Fords Terror Wilderness, Tongass National Forest
98. Trading Bay State Game Refuge
99. Trans-Alaska Pipeline Utility Corridor
100. Tuxedni Refuge, Alaska Maritime National Wildlife Refuge
101. Unalakleet National Wild River
102. Walrus Islands State Game Sanctuary
103. Warren Island Wilderness, Tongass National Forest
104. West Chichagof–Yakobi Wilderness, Tongass National Forest
105. White Mountains National Recreation Area
106. Wind National Wild River
107. Wood–Tikchik State Park
108. Wrangell–St. Elias National Park and Preserve
109. Yukon–Charley Rivers National Preserve
110. Yukon Delta National Wildlife Refuge
111. Yukon Flats National Wildlife Refuge

Admiralty Island National Monument, Tongass National Forest

1

Location: Southeastern Alaska, south of Juneau; 57°30'N 134°20'W
Size: 957,587 acres (387 530 hectares)
High point: 4650 ft (1420 m)
Low point: Sea level

Best time of year: Foot, June–October; boat, June–October; ski, January–March
USGS maps: Juneau, Sitka, Sumdum
Established: 1980
Managed by: U.S. Forest Service

The rugged spine of a partially submerged mountain range with many bays and inlets, Admiralty Island Monument has the greatest known concentration of nesting bald eagles in the world, averaging more than one nest per mile (1.6 km) of coastline in Seymour Canal—and one brown (grizzly) bear for every two eagles. Dense spruce-hemlock rain forests rise to about 1500 ft (460 m) on the mountainsides, dotted with muskeg meadows. Above treeline, rock outcroppings thrust above alpine meadows and isolated snowfields.

For centuries, Tlingit Indians have lived and hunted on the island, known to them as *Xootsnoowu*, "the fortress of the bears." Travel gently, without interrupting the personal rhythms and privacy of Angoon residents. Learn about the Tlingit culture before you come. Admiralty Island was first visited by explorers—the Vancouver party—in the 18th century; it contains ruins of more recent occupations of whalers, canneries and mining operations.

Trumpeter swans, whistling swans and other migrating waterfowl stop on the island. Chatham Strait is a major flyway. Watch also for Sitka blacktail deer, beavers and furbearers and, offshore, seals, sea lions and whales. Humpback whales winter in the canal; sea lions haul out on East Brother and West Brother islands.

The Forest Service maintains 12 public-use recreational cabins (reservations required, fee), 9 Adirondack-style open shelters and an information office in Angoon. Marked trails include 19 mi (31 km) for hiking and a canoe route with 19 mi (31 km) of water travel and 7 mi (11 km) of portages. Prepare for long periods of rain. Camping in the back country is unrestricted; campfires are permitted, but expect wood to be wet. Camp and travel to avoid confrontations with the large numbers of bears. (See Part I of this book for suggestions.) Fishing, hunting, firearms and fixed-wing aircraft are all permitted; snowmobiles and off-road vehicles are not. Outboard motors of 10 hp or less are permitted on most lakes. Be aware that private lands exist within the Monument boundary.

Boat travel: Admiralty Island Canoe Traverse, FWA, Mole Harbor on Seymour Canal to Angoon at Mitchell Bay, with portages, 26 mi (42 km). Swift tidal currents in restricted bays and inlets can make boating hazardous. Plan travel in these areas during slack water.

The maritime climate brings cool, wet overcast summers and mild, wet overcast winters. (See the Angoon weather table.) Winds are variable. Daylight on June 21 is 18 hours, on December 22, 6½ hours. Prominent peak: Eagle Peak, elevation 4650 ft (1417 m).

The Monument is accessible only by boat or float plane. Nearby Angoon is a port of call for the Southeastern Alaska state ferry. Services available in Angoon include air taxis, scheduled air service and food. Lodging and boat charters are available, but should be scheduled in advance.

Admiralty Island. (National Park Service photo by M. Malik)

The island was named in 1794 by Captain George Vancouver for the British Admiralty. The Russian name for the island was *Ostrov Kutsnoi*, which translates as "fear island."

Suggested reading: Alaska Geographic, *Admiralty: Island in Contention* (Anchorage: Alaska Northwest Publishing Co., 1973); Scott Foster, "Around Admiralty Island in 140,000 Strokes" (*Alaska* magazine, July 1981); Lael Morgan, *And the Land Provides: Alaska Natives in a Year of Transition* (New York: Anchor Press, 1974); Margaret Piggott, *Discover Southeast Alaska with Pack and Paddle* (Seattle: The Mountaineers, 1974); O. M. Salisbury, *The Customs and Legends of the Thlinget Indians of Alaska* (New York: Bonanza Books, 1962).

2

Alagnak
National Wild River

Location: Southwestern Alaska, heading in Katmai National Preserve; 59°00′N 155°56′W
River rating: WW3-FWC from Kukaklek Lake, WW1-FWC from Nonvianuk Lake
Popular trip lengths: 60 to 70 mi (100 to 110 km)

Best time of year: June–September
Annual high water: June, August
USGS maps: Iliamna A-7, A-8; Dillingham A-1, A-2, A-3
Designated as Wild River: 1980
Managed by: National Park Service

From the northwestern corner of Katmai National Preserve, the Alagnak flows through gently rolling hills to the wetlands of Kvichak Bay. Scattered stands of spruce dot the open tundra.

The river heads in two separate lakes. From Kukaklek Lake, it flows in white water through a canyon within which dangerous WW3 rapids appear without warning around a blind corner. The rapids are particularly hazardous at high water, and the steep canyon walls do not permit portaging. From Nonvianuk (Nanwhyenuk) Lake, the river takes a more gentle gradient without serious obstacles. The current on the lower part of the river is affected by ocean tides. From Kukaklek Lake (A) to Hallersville (C) is about 70 mi (110 km); from Nonvianuk Lake (B) to Hallersville, about 60 mi (100 km). (Hallersville, abandoned, exists in name only.)

The open country traversed by the river is excellent for spotting moose, brown (grizzly) bears, red foxes, wolves and wolverines. Watch also for raptors, beavers, mink, muskrats, porcupines and migratory waterfowl. The lakes and rivers support rainbow trout, grayling, lake trout, red salmon and king salmon. Several commercial fishing lodges operate on nearby private lands within the Park and Preserve and along the river downstream.

Camping is unrestricted and good in the upper river area; few dry campsites exist in the wetlands. Carry a camping stove, since deadwood is sparse on the upper river and is probably wet lower down. Contact the National Park Service at King Salmon, Brooks Camp or Nonvianuk for the required back-country use permit. Within Katmai National Preserve, fishing, hunting, firearms, powerboats and fixed-wing aircraft are permitted.

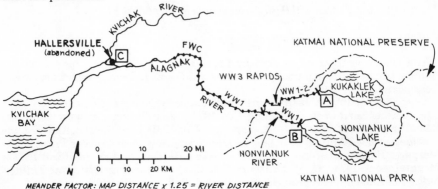

MEANDER FACTOR: MAP DISTANCE x 1.25 = RIVER DISTANCE

Alagnak National Wild River. (National Park Service photo)

Expect cool, wet summers with frequent overcast in this maritime climate. (See the King Salmon weather table.) Winds are generally moderate and frequently strong. Daylight on June 21 is 18½ hours, on December 22, 6 hours.

To reach the river, take a float plane to either Kukaklek Lake (A), elevation 800 ft (240 m), or Nonvianuk Lake (B), elevation 631 ft (192 km). Leave the river by air taxi from the lower Alagnak or the Hallersville area (C), elevation 50 ft (15 m). Air taxis, food and lodging are available at King Salmon, Naknek, Brooks Camp and Kulik Lodge. King Salmon has scheduled air service from Anchorage.

Suggested reading: U.S. Department of the Interior, *Proposed Iliamna National Resource Range*, Final Environmental Impact Statement (Washington, D.C.: U.S. Government Printing Office, 1974).

3  Alaska Chilkat Bald Eagle Preserve

Location: Southeastern Alaska, north of Haines; 59°20′N 135°55′W
Size: 49,000 acres (20 000 hectares)
High point: 250 ft (76 m)
Low point: Sea level

Best time of year: Foot, May–October;
  boat, May–October;
  ski, December–March
USGS maps: Skagway B-2, B-3, C-3
Established: 1982
Managed by: Alaska Division of Parks

Between late October and mid-December each year, as many as 3500 bald eagles from Southeastern Alaska, British Columbia, the Yukon Territory and Washington State feed on spawned-out remains of a late chum salmon run in the Chilkat River. Attracting the largest concentration of bald eagles in the world, warm water from the Tsirku (Big Salmon) River tributary keeps a 2-mi (3-km) stretch of the Chilkat

Bald eagle defending its salmon. (U.S. Fish and Wildlife Service photo by Jo Keller)

River open in the winter, permitting access to the dying salmon after other rivers have frozen. The eagles are easily viewed along Mile 19 to Mile 20 of the Haines Highway, where they congregate in the trees and on the river bars. Smaller numbers of eagles use the area year-round.

Harassing or otherwise disturbing the eagles is prohibited by both state and federal laws. The bald eagle was designated our national emblem in 1782, but long before that it was one of the most important clan totems of the Pacific Northwest Indians.

Primarily a braided river bed, the Chilkat River floodplain supports numerous tall cottonwood trees that provide convenient perches for the eagles. Sitka spruce, western hemlock and lodgepole pine grow on higher ground. Part of the old Dalton Trail, a route to the Klondike gold fields at the turn of the century, passes through the Preserve.

Photographing and observing the eagles are the most popular activities in the Preserve, but for your own comfort, avoid standing under perched eagles—their "aim" is excellent. Fishing and hunting are permitted; snowmobiles and off-road vehicles may be used only in designated areas. The Preserve is undeveloped.

The maritime climate brings cool, wet overcast summers and mild, wet overcast winters. (See the Haines weather table.) Winds are variable and can be strong, with blowing dust on the river bars. Daylight on June 21 is 18½ hours, on December 22, 6 hours.

The Haines Highway, from about Mile 8 to Mile 30, runs adjacent to or within the Preserve, making this an easily accessible area. A port of the Southeastern Alaska state ferry, Haines also has scheduled bus and air service. Rental cars, stores, restaurants, lodging and tours to the Preserve are available in Haines.

Because of the manner in which the eagles perch solemnly in groups on the stately cottonwoods, the area is locally known as the "bald eagle council grounds."

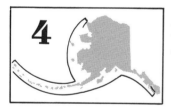

4 Alaska Maritime National Wildlife Refuge

Location: Coastal Alaska, from the Chukchi Sea to Southeastern Alaska
Size: 3,549,000 acres (1 436 000 hectares)
High point: 9372 ft (2857 m), on Shishaldin Volcano in the Aleutian Islands
Low point: Sea level

Best time of year: See individual Refuge descriptions
USGS maps: See individual Refuge descriptions
Established: 1980
Managed by: U.S. Fish and Wildlife Service

A mind-boggling assortment of more than 2400 islands, rocks, spires, reefs and headlands make up this Refuge, established to protect seabirds and marine mammals and their habitats, from farthest north Alaska to the southern tip of the Panhandle. Over 20 million seabirds, about two-thirds of Alaska's total, use the Refuge—more than the sum of all other seabird populations in the Northern Hemisphere. Some of the marine birds are unique to North America, including eight species that breed only in Alaska. Most abundant are murres, auklets, storm-petrels, puffins, kittiwakes, fulmars, gulls, cormorants, murrelets and guillemots. Also

Seabirds on wrecked ship, Middleton Island. (U.S. Fish and Wildlife Service photo by Arthur Sowls)

protected by the Refuge are most of Alaska's sea otters—about 150,000 animals—250,000 sea lions and substantial numbers of walrus, seals and whales.

Ten former refuges, established prior to 1980, are incorporated into the Alaska Maritime National Wildlife Refuge. To indicate the diversity of the Refuge lands, these and one area added in 1980 are treated separately in this book (see Aleutian Islands, Ann Stevens–Cape Lisburne, Bering Sea, Bogoslof, Chamisso, Forrester Island, Hazy Islands, St. Lazaria, Semidi, Simeonof and Tuxedni).

In general, visitors are not encouraged. Human activity is disruptive to bird nesting, breeding and rearing of young. In some areas, visitor restrictions may be in effect. Camping is permitted in most areas, although it is practical only on larger islands and mainland areas. Campfires may be built, but most areas are treeless, wet and windswept.

The Alaska Maritime Refuge is mostly undeveloped with the exception of one public-use recreational cabin on Chisik Island in the Tuxedni Refuge and four on Adak Island in the Aleutian Islands Refuge (reservations required). Since some parts of the Refuge are closed to hunting, powerboats, snowmobiles and fixed-wing aircraft, check with the Refuge Manager before visiting.

Most of the Refuge lands and waters are extremely remote and hard to reach. Frequent violent and long-lasting storms make boating and air travel hazardous; there are few anchorages, protected waters or airfields. Refer to individual Refuge descriptions or contact the Refuge Manager for further access information.

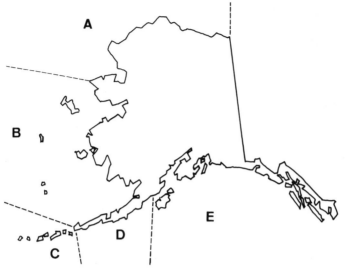

Description of Management Units (north to south):

A. Chukchi Sea Unit
    Ann Stevens–Cape Lisburne
    Cape Thompson
    Chamisso Refuge
B. Bering Sea Unit
    Cape York
    Sledge Island
    Bluff
    Cape Darby
    Cape Denbigh
    Besboro Island
    Bering Sea Refuge (St. Matthew and Hall islands)
    Hagemeister Island
    Pribilof Islands
    All other public lands on islands, islets, rocks, reefs, spires and designated
        capes and headlands in the Bering Sea
C. Aleutian Islands Unit
    Aleutian Islands Refuge
    Bogoslof Refuge
D. Alaska Peninsula Unit
    Puale Bay cliffs
    Semidi Islands Refuge
    Simeonof Refuge
    All other public lands on islands, islets, rocks, reefs, spires and designated
        capes and headlands south of the Alaska Peninsula from Katmai National
        Park to False Pass
E. Gulf of Alaska Unit (west to east)
    Tuxedni Refuge
    Latax Rocks
    Barren Islands
    Pye Islands
    Chiswell Islands and vicinity

Middleton Island
St. Lazaria Refuge
Hazy Island Refuge
Forrester Island Refuge
All named and unnamed islands, rocks, reefs, spires remaining in public
  domain around Kodiak and Afognak Islands and elsewhere in the Gulf of
  Alaska

Suggested reading: William R. Hunt, *Arctic Passage: The Turbulent History of the Land and People of the Bering Sea,* 1697-1975 (New York: Charles Scribner's Sons, 1975); Arthur L. Sowls, Scott A. Hatch and Calvin J. Lensink, *Catalog of Alaskan Seabird Colonies* (Fish and Wildlife Service, U.S. Department of the Interior, 1978); U.S. Department of the Interior, *Proposed Alaska Coastal National Wildlife Refuge,* Final Environmental Impact Statement (Washington, D.C.: U.S. Government Printing Office, 1974).

Least auklets and crested auklets. (U.S. Fish and Wildlife Service photo by Glen Elison)

Pavlof Volcano and Pavlof Sister. (U.S. Fish and Wildlife Service photo by Dave Spencer)

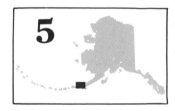

5 Alaska Peninsula National Wildlife Refuge

Location: Southwestern Alaska, on the Alaska Peninsula; 56°N 160°W
Size: 3,500,000 acres (1 400 000 hectares)
High point: 8905 ft (2714 m)
Low point: Sea level
Best time of year:
Foot, May–September;
boat, May–August

USGS maps: Chignik, Cold Bay, False Pass, Port Moller, Stepovak Bay, Sutwik Islands, Ugashik
Established: 1980
Managed by: U.S. Fish and Wildlife Service

In this exceptionally scenic area a long chain of active volcanoes rises from sea level, connected by treeless lowlands, rolling tundra-covered hills, grasslands, lakes, rivers and a long, varied Pacific Ocean coastline. Pavlof Volcano, one of the most active in the world, has erupted at least 30 times in the past 200 years.

Rich in animal life, the Refuge contains major populations of brown (grizzly) bears, caribou, moose, bald eagles, migratory waterfowl and salmon as well as wolves, wolverines, peregrine falcons, seabirds, sea otters, seals and sea lions. Many of the bears den on volcano slopes.

Wildlife observation, fishing, hunting, beachcombing, backpacking and mountaineering attract most visitors to the Refuge. No recreational facilities have been developed, although a few commercial fishing and hunting lodges (reservations required) are on private lands within the Refuge boundaries. Camping is unre-

Devil's Bay, Alaska Peninsula National Wildlife Refuge. (U.S. Fish and Wildlife Service photo by Nina Faust)

stricted on public lands. Respect private property and ask permission before camping or trespassing. Campfires are permitted in the Refuge; the beaches have large quantities of driftwood, but plan to use a camping stove inland. Travel cautiously and avoid attracting the numerous bears when you camp. Mosquitoes and other biting insects may be a problem from June through mid-September; carry head nets and plenty of repellent. Horses, powerboats (except airboats), snowmobiles and aircraft landings are all permitted; aircraft must operate at altitudes and in flight paths that will not disturb wildlife.

Expect cool wet summers and mild wet winters along the Pacific coast, colder winters and less rain all year inland and along Bristol Bay. (See the Cold Bay weather table.) The area experiences strong winds, long periods of rain and frequent storms. Hypothermia is a constant danger. Since weather often delays planned air or water travel, carry extra food. Daylight on June 21 is 18 hours, on December 22, 7 hours. Prominent peaks in the Refuge are Pavlof Volcano, elevation 8905 ft (2714 m) and Mount Veniaminof, elevation 8225 ft (2507 m).

Access to the Refuge is by air or water. Cold Bay, King Cove, King Salmon, Port Heiden and Sand Point have scheduled airline service; the first three towns also have air taxi services. The Southwestern Alaska state ferry docks at Chignik, Cold Bay, King Cove and Sand Point on a limited schedule. Boat charters are available in most communities, sometimes on an informal basis, but caution is advised; frequent strong winds, fog and storms make boating hazardous. Cold Bay, King Salmon and Sand Point provide limited stores, restaurants and lodging.

Suggested reading: Alaska Geographic, *Alaska's Volcanoes: Northern Link in the Ring of Fire* (Anchorage: Alaska Northwest Publishing Co., 1976); Bernard R. Hubbard, S.J., *Mush, You Malemutes!* (New York: American Press, 1932); O. J. Murie, *Fauna of the Aleutian Islands and Alaska Peninsula* (Washington, D.C.: U.S. Fish and Wildlife Service, 1959).

6

Alatna
National Wild River

Location: Northcentral Alaska, Gates of the Arctic National Park; 67°30′N 153°55′W
River rating: WW3-FWB
Popular trip lengths: 74 mi (120 km) to 260 mi (420 km)

Best time of year: July–September
Annual high water: July–August
USGS maps: Survey Pass, Hughes, Bettles
Wild River designation: 1980
Managed by: National Park Service

A clearwater river winding through the heart of the Brooks Range, the Alatna drains south from the treeless Arctic Divide to the Koyukuk River lowlands. Flowing through rugged alpine mountains in its upper reaches, then past quiet lakes, it finally meanders in long swings across the broad forested valley floor. The Arrigetch Peaks area is reached from the Alatna River near Circle Lake or from Takahula Lake.

One of the popular float trips begins near the headwaters at a series of unnamed alpine lakes and ends at the village of Allakaket, about 260 mi (about 420 km) downstream. Shorter sections can also be run, but check with your air taxi pilot for access. Wild River designation extends from the headwater lakes to the Gates of the Arctic National Park boundary, a distance of about 90 mi (140 km). The river presents no serious obstacles to boaters, although the section from the headwater lakes to Unakserak River may require considerable lining.

Watch for Dall sheep, caribou, moose, brown (grizzly) bears, black bears, wolves, wolverines, red foxes, lynx, ptarmigan, hawks, owls and migrating waterfowl.

Excellent hiking terrain is accessible from the upper and middle Alatna. Camping is unrestricted and best on river gravel bars. Since upstream rainstorms can raise river levels several feet in a short time, be sure your campsite and beached boats are safe. Campfires are permitted, but build small ones on river gravel, not on tundra or in the forest. Plant life grows so slowly in the North that camping stoves are

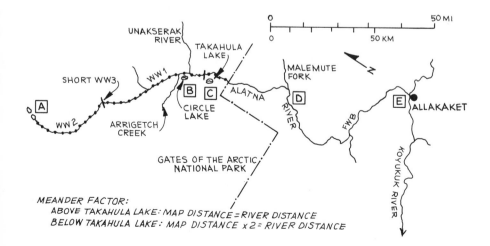

MEANDER FACTOR:
ABOVE TAKAHULA LAKE: MAP DISTANCE = RIVER DISTANCE
BELOW TAKAHULA LAKE: MAP DISTANCE x 2 = RIVER DISTANCE

83

Upper Alatna River. (National Park Service photo)

preferred in alpine areas. There are no visitor facilities or marked trails. Sports fishing is permitted in the Alatna River valley; sports hunting is not. Since the area is also used by local residents for subsistence fishing, hunting and trapping, do not infringe on these traditional rights by disturbing wildlife or equipment. Fixed-wing aircraft landings are permitted. Use of powerboats is restricted to certain areas; off-road vehicle use requires a special permit. Snowmobiles may be used when adequate snow cover exists.

In general, the sub-arctic continental climate brings warm dry summers, although in the mountains temperatures are cooler and there is more rainfall. (See the Wiseman weather table.) Winds are normally light. Daylight on June 21 is 24 hours; on December 22, the sun does not rise above the horizon, but midday brings about five hours of twilight. Expect large populations of mosquitoes and other biting insects from June through August.

To reach the river, take a scheduled air carrier from Fairbanks to Bettles (Evansville), then charter an air taxi to the river. Popular river access points are the unnamed lakes (A), elevation 2800 ft (850 m), at the headwaters of the Alatna River, and Circle Lake (B), elevation about 900 ft (about 300 m), near Arrigetch Creek. Float planes also land on Takahula Lake (C), elevation 810 ft (250 m); a short portage trail leads to the river. Leave the river by air taxi from Malamute Fork (D), elevation 700 ft (200 m), or by scheduled air carrier from Allakaket (E), elevation 400 ft (100 m). Bettles and Allakaket have stores; Bettles has a lodge with food service and showers.

A popular and scenic river ideal for a first wilderness float trip, the Alatna presents no serious obstacles of weather or terrain. Careful planning is necessary, however, since the area is remote.

Suggested reading: Robert Marshall, *Alaska Wilderness: Exploring the Central Brooks Range* (Berkeley: University of California Press, 1970; originally published in 1956 as *Arctic Wilderness*).

7

Aleutian Islands Refuge, Alaska Maritime National Wildlife Refuge

Location: Southwestern Alaska, in the Aleutian Islands; 53°N 173°E to 55°N 163°W
Size: 2,720,400 acres (1 100 900 hectares)
High point: 9372 ft (2857 m), Shishaldin Volcano on Unimak Island
Low point: Sea level
Best time of year: Foot, May–September; boat, June–August; ski (marginal), January–March

USGS maps: (West to east) Attu, Kiska, Rat Islands, Gareloi Island, Adak, Atka, Seguam, Amukta, Samalga Island, Umnak, Unalaska, Unimak, False Pass, Cold Bay
Established: 1913
Managed by: U.S. Fish and Wildlife Service

The Aleutian Islands, a long chain of ocean-bound volcanoes stretching 1100 mi (1800 km) across the North Pacific Ocean toward Russia, contain great numbers of sea otters, seals and sea lions and some of the world's largest seabird rookeries. The largest known fulmar colony, estimated at 450,000 birds, is located on Chagulak Island.

Biologically, the Aleutians are stepping-stones between the Asian and North American continents; the western islands have Asian vegetation features, while the eastern islands have plant life typical of the North American mainland. Of the 227 species of birds recorded on the islands, 79 are of Asian origin.

Large concentrations of waterfowl use the islands, both during migrations and as nesting and wintering grounds. One-half of the world's emperor geese winter here. The Aleutian Canada goose, one of the world's rarest birds, has been exterminated by foxes on all but tiny, remote Buldir and Chagulak islands.

Scientist netting auklets for banding, Buldir Island. (U.S. Fish and Wildlife Service photo by Elaine Rhode)

Harlequin beach, Aleutian Islands coastline. (U.S. Fish and Wildlife Service photo)

When visited by the first Europeans—the Russian Vitus Bering and his crew in 1741—the islands were already home for the gentle Aleuts. Two years later, Russian fur traders swarmed in, plundering from the Aleuts and enslaving them to harvest sea otters. Partly due to newly introduced diseases, the Aleut population dropped from about 20,000 to fewer than 2500 by 1850. The sea otter population was nearly exterminated by 1911 through the efforts of both Russian and U.S. traders. Today the Aleut population is healthy, and the sea otters are increasing in numbers.

Almost all land mammals on the islands have been introduced by man. Commercial fur farming from 1915 into the 1940s brought the arctic fox; now wild, the foxes prey upon the native fauna. Atka supports a herd of 2500 wild reindeer; caribou have been introduced on Adak. Only Unimak Island, a short 0.5 mi (0.8 km) from the mainland, supports naturally-occurring caribou, as well as brown (grizzly) bears, wolves, wolverines, red foxes, arctic foxes and river otters.

Many of the islands contain abandoned military installations and other remnants of World War II battles against Japanese invaders. Today Adak, Shemya and Attu have active military installations but no civilian communities.

Originally known as the Aleutian Islands National Wildlife Refuge, in 1980 the area was redesignated a part of the newly formed Alaska Maritime National Wildlife Refuge. It includes 2,210,000 acres (894 000 hectares) of wilderness.

The North Pacific Ocean and the Bering Sea produce a maritime climate at its foggiest; the Aleutians create a barrier between the frigid Bering Sea and the warm Japanese and California currents arriving from the south. Summers are cool and wet; winters are mild and wet. (See the Atka and Cold Bay weather tables.) Winds are constant and moderate to strong; frequently storm follows storm, accompanied by violent wind squalls. Due to the almost constant wind and rain, hypothermia is an ever-present danger. Daylight on June 21 is 17 hours, on December 22, 7½ hours.

The islands, many with active volcanoes, rise directly from the ocean, skirted with treeless grasslands and tundra-covered slopes; the highest are Shishaldin Volcano, elevation 9372 ft (2857 m) on Unimak Island and Makushin Volcano, elevation 6680 ft (2036 m) on Unalaska Island.

Adak, with a military base, is the only island in the Refuge with recreational facilities, consisting of five cabins (reservations required) and five survival supply barrels. Camping and campfires are permitted throughout the Refuge; plenty of driftwood, often wet, can be found along the coast, but plan to use a camping stove inland. Fishing, hunting and fixed-wing aircraft are permitted generally; some areas are closed to powerboats and snowmobiles. Due to the frequent storms, fog and lack of protected waters, boating is hazardous.

Access to the Refuge is normally by air; allow extra time and food for delays caused by weather. Adak (military clearance required), Akutan, Cold Bay, Dutch Harbor/Unalaska, False Pass, Nikolski and Shemya (military clearance required) have scheduled air service; air taxis are available at Cold Bay and Dutch Harbor. The Southwestern Alaska state ferry visits Cold Bay about three times a summer. Stores or restaurants can be found at Akutan, Nikolski, Cold Bay and Dutch Harbor; the latter two also have lodging.

Because of the distances involved, a visit to the Refuge can be expensive and requires careful preparation. Persevere: Many travelers feel the Aleutians are the most fascinating part of Alaska.

Suggested reading: Alaska Geographic, *Alaska's Volcanoes: Northern Link in the Ring of Fire* (Anchorage: Alaska Northwest Publishing Co., 1976; Stan Cohen, *The Forgotten War: Pictorial History of World War II in Alaska* (Missoula, Mont.: Pictorial Histories Publishing Co., 1981); H.B. Collins, Jr., et al, *The Aleutian Islands: Their People and Natural History* (Washington, D.C.: Smithsonian Institution, 1945); Brian Garfield, *The Thousand-Mile War: World War II in Alaska and the Aleutians* (Garden City, N.Y.: Doubleday and Co., 1969); Lael Morgan, *The Aleutian Islands* (Anchorage: Alaska Northwest Publishing Co., Alaska Geographic, 1980).

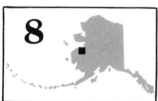

8   Andreafsky National Wilderness and Wild River, Yukon Delta National Wildlife Refuge

Location: Western Alaska, northwest of St. Marys; 63°N 162°W
Wild River rating: Andreafsky, WW2-FWB; East Fork, WW1-2
Popular trip length: 100 mi (160 km)
Wilderness Size: 1,100,000 acres (445 000 hectares)
High point: 3408 ft (1039 m)
Low point: 25 ft (8 m)
Best time of year: Foot, late May–September; boat, late May–September; ski, February–April

USGS maps for Wilderness:
Holy Cross, Kwiguk, St. Michael, Unalakleet
USGS maps for Wild Rivers:
Andreafsky River: Unalakleet A-6; St. Michael A-1; Kwiguk D-1, C-1, C-2, B-2, A-4, A-3. East Fork: Unalakleet A-6; Holy Cross D-6, C-6; Kwiguk C-1, B-1, B-2, A-2, A-3
Established: 1980
Managed by: U.S. Fish and Wildlife Service

A wilderness section of the Yukon Delta National Wildlife Refuge, Andreafsky contains two of the most important salmon spawning streams in the entire Yukon drainage, the Andreafsky and its East Fork. Flowing through parallel valleys, the

Brown (grizzly) bear, Andreafsky River. (National Park Service photo by Jim Morris)

clearwater rivers rise in tundra-covered uplands, to meander through balsam poplar and white spruce forests lower down.

Commercial reindeer herds, once grazed in the area by Eskimos and later abandoned, joined local migrating caribou to interbreed, producing strangely marked wild offspring. The Wilderness supports abundant populations of large mammals, notably brown (grizzly) bears that fish the rivers for salmon in July and August. Watch also for black bears, moose, beavers, arctic foxes, red foxes, lynx, river otters, wolves and wolverines.

An area without recreational development, Andreafsky attracts river runners, fishermen, hunters, backpackers and ski tourers. Fixed-wing aircraft may land within the Wilderness; powerboats and snowmobiles are permitted. Camping is unrestricted, but avoid areas heavily used by bears. Campfires are permitted, but use a camping stove in tundra areas or build fires on river gravel.

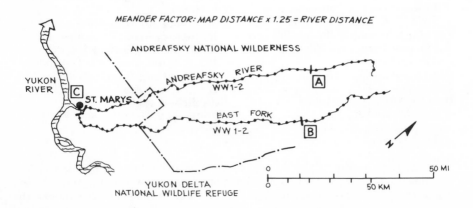

River travel: Andreafsky National Wild River and the East Fork are reached by air taxi to lakes or the river, (A) and (B), at the 500 to 1000 ft (150 to 300 m) elevation. The trip ends at St. Marys (C), at the confluence of the Andreafsky and Yukon rivers, elevation 20 ft (6 m). All but the lower 20 to 30 mi (30 to 50 km) is designated Wild River.

Due to its proximity to salt water, the Wilderness has a subarctic climate that is transitional between maritime and continental. Expect cool summers, with some fog and some warm days; winters are cold, dry and severe. (See the Bethel weather table.) Winds are moderate to light. Daylight on June 21 is 20½ hours, on December 22, 5 hours.

St. Marys, a transportation center for the lower Yukon River area, provides modern visitor facilities, frequent scheduled flights from Anchorage and air taxi service. Other villages in the area with scheduled air service are Mountain Village, St. Michael and Stebbins.

An area not commonly seen by visitors, Andreafsky is a gentle, yet remote, wilderness.

9 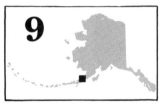 Aniakchak National Monument, Preserve and Wild River

Location: Southwestern Alaska, on the Alaska Peninsula; 56°50′N 158°10′W
River rating: WW1-4
Popular River trip length: 32 mi (52 km)
Monument/Preserve size: 586,000 acres (237 000 hectares)
High point: 4400 ft (1300 m)
Low point: Sea level

Best time of year:
Foot, June–September;
boat, June–September
USGS maps for Monument/Preserve: Bristol Bay, Chignik, Sutwik Island, Ugashik
USGS maps for River: Chignik D-1, Sutwik Island D-6, D-5
Established: 1978
Managed by: National Park Service

A massive, rugged, active volcano rising starkly from lush coastal beaches and grasslands, Aniakchak contains one of the largest calderas in the world, 6 mi (10 km) in diameter. It holds the turquoise waters of Surprise Lake as well as cinder cones, lava plugs and hot springs. Aniakchak last erupted in 1931, in a large explosion that spewed ash over a large area of Alaska. Challenging Aniakchak National Wild River drains Surprise Lake, passing turbulently through "The Gates," a 2000-ft- (600-m-) deep canyon eroded through the caldera rim, to empty into the Pacific Ocean at Aniakchak Bay, a distance of 32 mi (52 km). If the weather is clear, both the Pacific Ocean and the Bering Sea can be seen from the rim of the caldera.

The area is treeless, with rolling grasslands on the Pacific Coast, moist tundra on the Bristol Bay drainage and brushy stream banks in the lowlands. Watch for brown (grizzly) bears, moose, caribou, bald eagles, red foxes, and, offshore, seals, sea lions, sea otters and whales.

Only the strong, fit and well-prepared should undertake a visit to this scenic and exciting volcano. The weather on Aniakchak is severe; life-threatening conditions

Aniakchak River flowing through "The Gates." (National Park Service photo by Keith Trexler)

can develop rapidly. Extremely violent winds in the caldera, particularly near "The Gates," can shred tents and prevent air rescue. To retreat to Meshik, 20 mi (32 km) to the west, requires a climb of 1000 vertical ft (300 m) to the caldera rim, then a 2400-vertical-ft- (730-m-) descent to sea level through wetlands and brush—a superhuman undertaking in stormy weather. Prepare for long periods of cold, rainy, windy weather—hypothermia is a constant danger in this maritime climate where summers are cold and wet and winters mild and wet. (See the Cold Bay weather table.) In contrast to the southeast side of the mountain, where annual precipitation is 128 inches (325 cm) a year, the northwest side has only 15 inches (38 cm) a year. Temperatures on the southeast side range from 60°F to 20°F (16°C to −7°C), while temperatures on the northwest side can range from 80°F to −30°F (27°C to −34°C). Cloud cover at 1500 ft (500 m) on the mountain is normal. Winds average 15 to 20 mph (24 to 32 kph) with storm gusts over 100 mph (160 kph). Daylight on June 21 is 18 hours, on December 22, 6½ hours.

MEANDER FACTOR: MAP DISTANCE x 1.3 = RIVER DISTANCE

Back-country use permits, required for visitors' safety, are obtainable at the King Salmon office. In this undeveloped area, camping is unrestricted. Carry a camping stove; firewood is scarce away from the beaches. Rough seas, fog or storms often delay pickup, so take extra food. Sports hunting is permitted in the Preserve, but not in the Monument. Fishing, firearms, powerboats and fixed-wing aircraft are permitted throughout; snowmobiles are limited to designated areas.

River travel: Rafts are recommended for turbulent Aniakchak National Wild River. To reach the headwaters at Surprise Lake (A), elevation 1055 ft (322 m), take an air taxi from King Salmon, arranging for a pickup from Aniakchak Bay (B) at sea level. Both King Salmon and Port Heiden (Meshik) have scheduled airline service and food; modern lodging is available at King Salmon.

Suggested reading: Alaska Geographic, *Alaska's Volcanoes: Northern Link in the Ring of Fire* (Anchorage: Alaska Northwest Publishing Co., 1976); Bernard R. Hubbard, S.J., "A World Inside a Mountain" (*National Geographic*, Vol. 60[3], 1931), *Cradle of the Storms* (New York: Dodd, Mead and Co., 1935) and *Mush, You Malemutes!* (New York: American Press, 1932); U.S. Department of the Interior, *Proposed Aniakchak National Monument*, Final Environmental Impact Statement (Washington, D.C.: U.S. Government Printing Office, 1974).

10 Ann Stevens –Cape Lisburne Refuge, Alaska Maritime National Wildlife Refuge

Location: Northwestern Alaska, northwest of Kotzebue; 68°50′N 166°10′W
Size: 20,000 acres (8100 hectares)
High point: 2034 ft (620 m)
Low point: Sea level

Best time of year: June–September
USGS map: Point Hope
Established: 1980
Managed by: U.S. Fish and Wildlife Service

The headlands of Cape Lisburne project from the far northwest corner of Alaska into the frigid Chukchi Sea. Precipitous rock cliffs provide no harbors or anchorages in this area of drifting ice and strong ocean currents. More than 170,000 seabirds nest on the cliffs, primarily thick-billed murres, common murres and black-legged kittiwakes. A U.S. Air Force early-warning site perches on the Cape. The Refuge was named in memory of Ann Stevens, wife of one of Alaska's U.S. senators.

At nearby Cape Thompson, early sailors listened for the commotion of cliff-nesting seabirds to help them avoid the headlands in the thick fogs characteristic of the region. In the early 1960s, scientists for the Atomic Energy Commission's Project Chariot extensively studied the flora, fauna, climate and geology of the area to determine the feasibility of excavating a deep-water seaport with nuclear explosions; the harbor was not built.

On the headlands, covered by tundra and dotted with small streams and ponds, the wildlife is typical of the far arctic—caribou, moose, brown (grizzly) bears, wolves, wolverines, arctic foxes, red foxes and musk-oxen. Common sea mammals are seals, walruses and whales.

Cape Lisburne has one airstrip. No recreational facilities have been built, but camping is unrestricted. Campfires are not practical; use a camping stove. Fishing,

Cape Lisburne sea cliffs with icebergs below. (U.S. Fish and Wildlife Service photo by Elaine Rhode)

hunting and snowmobiles are permitted; aircraft may land in the area, but are prohibited near the seabird cliffs during nesting. Take warm, windproof clothes and adequate rain gear. Since fog, storms or winds often delay pickup by air, pack extra supplies.

In this arctic maritime climate, cool, cloudy, foggy summers and cold, dry, severe winters are the rule. (See the Kotzebue weather table.) Winds are usually constant and strong, especially over the cliffs. Daylight on June 21 is 24 hours; on December 22, 0 hours, with 5 hours of twilight.

Access to the area is by air. Cape Lisburne, Kotzebue and Point Hope have scheduled air service; air taxis operate from Kotzebue. Stores, restaurants and lodging are available in Kotzebue and Point Hope.

Suggested reading: Richard K. Nelson, *Hunters of the Northern Ice* (Chicago: University of Chicago Press, 1972); Norman J. Willimovsky, *Environment of the Cape Thompson Region, Alaska* (Washington, D.C.: U.S. Atomic Energy Commission, 1966).

11

Arctic
National Wildlife Refuge and Wilderness

Location: Northeastern Alaska, north of Fort Yukon; 69°N 144°W
Size: 18,054,624 acres (7 306 447 hectares)
High point: 9050 ft (2758 m)
Low point: Sea level
Best time of year: North slope: foot, June–September; boat, late June–August on rivers, mid-July–August along Arctic coast; ski, March–April. South slope: foot, June–September; boat, late May–September; ski, March–April

USGS maps: Arctic, Barter Island, Black River, Chandalar, Christian, Coleen, Demarcation Point, Flaxman Island, Mt. Michelson, Philip Smith Mountains, Sagavanirktok, Table Mountain
Established: 1960
Managed by: U.S. Fish and Wildlife Service

From the barrier islands and saltwater lagoons on the Arctic Ocean coast to the rich boreal forests in valleys of the southern Brooks Range, the Refuge and Wilderness protect a unique cross-section of arctic and subarctic wildlife habitats. Containing the highest peaks of the Brooks Range, the Refuge straddles a 220-mi- (350-km-) long section of the eastern Range and includes large drainages on both sides. Throughout, land surfaces are molded by severe surface freeze-thaw cycles and deeply buried permafrost. Irregular polygon-shaped patterns are particularly conspicuous. Low mounds called pingos, "dripping" shapes produced by sliding surface soil and "drunken forests" may also be seen.

North of the Brooks Range lie the treeless tundra-covered foothills and flatlands of the Arctic coastal plain. On the south, treeless mountain ridges drop to rich conifer-hardwood forests in the river valleys. With its name change in 1980, the former Arctic National Wildlife Range was also enlarged, with most of the original Range becoming an 8,000,000-acre (3 000 000-hectare) Wilderness.

By arctic standards, wildlife is abundant. The 110,000-animal Porcupine (River) caribou herd winters on the south side of the Brooks Range in both Alaska and Yukon Territory; the herd moves north to the coastal plain where cows calve in early June. Except for pregnant females that den ashore in winter, polar bears remain on the offshore ice pack. Moose, brown (grizzly) bears, wolves, wolverines and red foxes are found throughout most of the area, while black bears, coyotes, lynx, porcupines and beavers prefer forest habitats. Dall sheep and marmots like the high mountain country; musk-oxen and arctic foxes roam the northern slope. Offshore in the Arctic Ocean swim ringed seals, bearded seals, bowhead and beluga whales, and occasionally spotted seals, walrus and gray whales. This is fine country for raptors: watch for peregrine falcons, gyrfalcons, rough-legged hawks, golden eagles and snowy owls as they hunt for lemmings, voles, snowshoe hares and ground squirrels. The Refuge's migratory birds travel to all parts of the world, including Antarctica.

Long a mecca for backpackers, river runners, wildlife observers and other wilderness travelers, the Refuge offers excellent hiking terrain for the most part, in mountain valleys with many clear-running streams. Camping is unrestricted in this undeveloped area, and campfires are permitted, but since the existing forests grow so slowly and much of the Refuge is treeless, visitors are asked to use camping stoves.

Grayling and arctic charr from the Kongakut River. (U.S. Fish and Wildlife Service photo by Jo Keller)

Fishing, hunting, powerboats and fixed-wing aircraft are all permitted. Pack lots of mosquito repellent, and perhaps a head net, for summer trips.

Water travel: By late July, the sea ice has usually broken up enough to permit small-boat travel along the coast. Peters and Schrader lakes are usually ice-free by July 20. Extensive overflow ice ("aufeis") accumulates on many of the floodplains and remains much of the summer; float the channels through the ice cautiously. Canning River, WW1-2, from the headwaters area on Marsh Fork to the upper river delta, 100 mi (160 km); Chandalar River, East Fork, WW2-FWA, from Arctic Village to Venetie 170 mi (270 km); Ivishak National Wild River, WW1-FWC, see description; Kongakut River, WW1-2, from the bend turning north (T65, R41E) to the Beaufort Sea, 75 mi (120 km); Porcupine River, WW1-FWB, from upper Porcupine River or Summit Lake on Bell River, Yukon Territory, to Fort Yukon, 300 mi (480 km) (you must contact both U.S. and Canadian customs for clearance prior to your trip—see Information Sources in the Appendix for addresses); Sheenjek National Wild River, WW2-FWB, see description; Wind National Wild River, WW1-3, see description.

The weather north of the Arctic Divide is typical of an arctic maritime climate— cool, dry and often foggy summers; cold, dry, severe winters. Winds are constant and moderate to strong. South of the Arctic Divide, a subarctic continental climate prevails, with warm, dry summers (somewhat cooler in the mountains, with snow possible at any time) and cold, dry, severe winters. Winds, except in exposed mountain areas, are generally light. (See the Wiseman and Galbraith weather tables.) Daylight on June 21 is 24 hours; on December 22, 0 hours, with 5 hours of twilight. Prominent mountain peaks: Mount Isto, elevation 9050 ft (2758 m); Mount Chamberlin, elevation 9020 ft (2749 m); Mount Michelson, elevation 8855 ft (2699 m).

Access to this remote roadless area is normally by air. Air taxis operate from Barter Island (Kaktovik) and Fort Yukon. Scheduled airlines serve Arctic Village, Barter Island, Deadhorse (Prudhoe Bay), Fort Yukon and Venetie, communities which also have small general stores. The Dalton Highway skirts the Refuge, but at press time, travelers on the stretch from Mile 211 north to Prudhoe Bay must have a travel permit. (See the Trans-Alaska Pipeline Utility Corridor description, #99.) Mile 211 is about 40 mi (60 km) south of the nearest Refuge boundary and 155 mi (249 km) north of the Yukon River. Arctic Village, Deadhorse and Fort Yukon have lodging.

Suggested reading: Alaska Geographic, *The Brooks Range: Environmental Watershed* (Anchorage: Alaska Northwest Publishing Co., 1977); Dale Brown, *Wild Alaska* (New York: Time-Life Books, 1972); John P. Milton, *Nameless Valleys, Shining Mountains* (New York: Walker and Co., 1969); Olaus J. Murie, *Journeys to the Far North* (Palo Alto, Calif.: The Wilderness Society and American West Publishing Co., 1973); U.S. Department of the Interior, *Proposed Arctic National Wildlife Refuge* and *Proposed Porcupine National Forest*, Final Environmental Impact Statements (Washington, D.C.: U.S. Government Printing Office, 1974).

12 Baranof Castle Hill State Historic Site

Location: Southeastern Alaska, in Sitka; 57°03′N 135°20′W
Size: 1 acre (0.4 hectare)
High point/low point: 50 ft (15 m)

Best time of year: Any time
USGS map: Sitka A-4
Established: 1968
Managed by: Alaska Division of Parks

On this hill on October 18, 1867, the American flag was first raised over Alaska during the transfer of the territory from Russian rule. Here, too, in 1959, when Alaska was granted full statehood, the 49-star flag first flew.

Extending their control to Southeastern Alaska in 1799, Russian fur traders originally settled at Old Sitka, about 7 mi (11 km) north of this site, but the fort was destroyed in 1802 during a Tlingit Indian attack. Two years later, Alexander Baranof, manager of the Russian-American Company and governor of Alaska until 1818, returned and drove the Tlingits from their village nearby. (See Sitka National Historical Park.)

Baranof built a fortified and finely furnished house on this hill in 1804. Seal-oil lamps in the cupola window served as the first lighthouse for mariners in western North America. Baranof, and succeeding Russian governors who built residences on this same hill, controlled an area stretching from California to Bristol Bay in Southwestern Alaska. The site was added to the National Register of Historic Places in 1962.

From Castle Hill, which commands a magnificent view of Sitka's waterfront, watch for sea mammals—dolphins and porpoises, sea otters, seals, sea lions and

Baranof Castle Hill State Historic Site.

whales. Interpretive plaques, walkways and benches invite a leisurely visit. Children will enjoy "protecting" the fort from "sea attack" using the antique cannons.

Expect a maritime climate with cool, wet summers and mild, wet winters. (See the Sitka weather table.) Winds are generally light. Daylight on June 21 is 18 hours, on December 22, 7 hours.

Access to the Historic Site is by stone steps from the corner of Lincoln and Katlian streets or from a gentle foot trail behind the hill. Overnight camping is not permitted. Stores, restaurants, lodging, taxicabs, rental cars and water and air taxi charters are available in Sitka. The Southeastern Alaska state ferry dock is 7 mi (11 km) north of Sitka, on Halibut Point Road. Sightseeing tours, with schedules coordinated to ferry and cruise ship arrivals and departures, stop at the park and other points of interest. Both the ferry terminal and the airport are serviced by local buses.

Suggested reading: Alaska Geographic, *Sitka and Its Ocean/Island World* (Anchorage: Alaska Northwest Publishing Co., 1982); Hector Chevigny, *Lord of Alaska: Baranov and the Russian Adventure* (Portland, Oreg.: Binford and Mort, Publishers, 1970); *Russian America: The Great Alaskan Venture, 1741-1867* (Portland, Oreg.: Binford and Mort, Publishers, 1979); P.A. Tikhmenev, *A History of the Russian-American Company* (Seattle: University of Washington Press, 1978-1979).

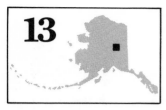

13

Beaver Creek
National Wild River

Location: Eastern Alaska, in the White Mountains National Recreation Area; 65°22′N 147°30′W
River rating: WW1-FWB
Popular trip length: 130 mi (210 km)
Best time of year: May–September

Annual high water: May
USGS maps: Livengood B-1, B-2, C-2, C-1, D-1; Circle C-6, D-6, D-5
Designated as Wild River: 1980
Managed by: Bureau of Land Management

A clear, gentle wilderness stream, the Beaver winds through rich boreal forests in the rounded White Mountains of Interior Alaska. White limestone cliffs and pinnacles line portions of the river. At "Big Bend," warm springs keep the river open all winter, providing good late-season grayling fishing. From Nome Creek to the flats below Victoria Creek is about 130 mi (210 km). To continue on Beaver Creek and down the Yukon River, leaving the Yukon at the Dalton Highway bridge, is another 270 mi (430 km).

The Beaver has no large rapids or serious obstacles, although the upper river flows frequently over exposed bedrock. The current in the lower river below Victoria Creek is extremely slow as it meanders through the Yukon Flats National Wildlife Refuge. Often the water has a harmless brown tint leached from the bog vegetation.

Animals of the boreal forest include moose, black bears, brown (grizzly) bears, caribou, wolves, wolverines, red foxes, coyotes, lynx, porcupines and beavers. Watch

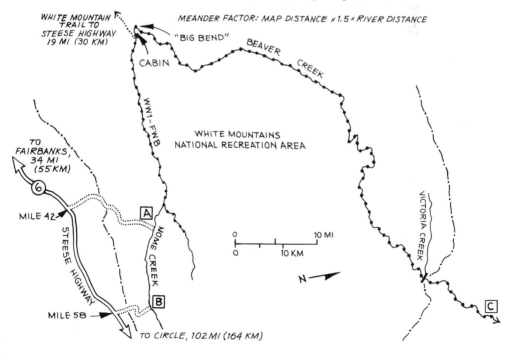

Rafters on Beaver Creek National Wild River. (Bureau of Land Management photo by Rich Tobin)

for Dall sheep on the treeless summits above the river. Grayling inhabit the upper river; below Victoria Creek, you can fish for northern pike and whitefish.

Camping, unrestricted, is best on gravel bars, but be aware that rain storms upriver can raise water levels rapidly without warning. Campfires are permitted. A BLM public-use recreational cabin, the Borealis–LeFevre cabin, sits on the right (northern) bank before "Big Bend." Reservations are required and a fee is charged. Fishing, hunting, firearms, fixed-wing aircraft and powerboats are all permitted. Expect hungry mosquitoes and other biting insects in summer months.

Summer weather is warm and dry, with frequent sunny days, some overcast. Thunderstorms are common in this subarctic continental climate. (See the Fairbanks weather table.) Winds are generally light. Daylight on June 21 is 22 hours, on December 22, 3 hours.

To reach the river, drive to Mile 42 on the Steese Highway north of Fairbanks. A 15-mi (24-km) unimproved gravel miners' road near Belle Creek leads to the Nome Creek tributary (A), elevation 1700 ft (520 m). Upstream an alternate access (B) is at the 2100-ft (640-m) level via a 7-mi (11-km) unimproved road along U.S. Creek from Mile 58, Steese Highway. Leave the river by air taxi, landing on the river or on gravel bars in the flats (C), elevation 700 ft (200 m), below Victoria Creek. Air taxis, rental cars, food and lodging are available at Fairbanks.

Suggested reading: U.S. Department of the Interior, *Proposed Beaver Creek National Wild River*, Final Environmental Impact Statement (Washington, D.C.: U.S. Government Printing Office, 1975.)

14

Becharof
National Wildlife Refuge
and Wilderness

Location: Southwestern Alaska, south
of King Salmon; 58°00′N 156°30′W
Size: 1,200,000 acres (486 000 hectares)
High point: 4835 ft (1474 m)
Low point: Sea level
Best time of year: Foot,
June–September; boat,
June–September; ski,
February–April

USGS maps: Karluk, Mt. Katmai,
Naknek, Ugashik
Established: 1978
Managed by: U.S. Fish and Wildlife
Service

In one of Alaska's finest brown (grizzly) bear habitats, as many as 300 bears congregate in the eastern portion of the Refuge when the abundant red salmon spawn. A large bear may weigh 1400 lb (640 kg) and stand 10 ft (3 m) tall. This area of the Alaska Peninsula is a major spawning ground for the important Bristol Bay salmon fishery.

The Refuge, of which 400,000 acres (160 000 hectares) were designated as Wilderness in 1980, encompasses virtually the entire watershed surrounding Becharof

Becharof Lake shoreline hike. (U.S. Fish and Wildlife Service photo by Jo Keller)

Lake. Becharof is the second largest lake in Alaska; only Iliamna Lake is larger. The rolling tundra-covered hills and lake-dotted wetlands provide excellent habitat for caribou, moose and waterfowl. Numerous bald eagles, nesting on sea cliffs, patrol for carrion and seabirds. Also found in the Refuge are wolves, wolverines, beavers, red foxes, tundra hares, snowshoe hares, muskrats and river otters. Along the seashore, watch for sea otters, seals, sea lions and whales.

Wildlife is the major attraction of the Refuge, bringing photographers, wildlife observers, big-game hunters and fishermen. Powerboats, snowmobiles and fixed-wing aircraft landings are permitted. Boaters on Becharof Lake should stay near shore; without warning, violent winds can whip the lake surface to white water with large waves. Camping is unrestricted, but avoid areas heavily used by bears. Firewood is scarce in this treeless wilderness; plan to use a camping stove. Prepare for long periods of wind and rain. The Refuge has no visitor facilities.

River travel: King Salmon River, WW1, from the largest lake at the headwaters of Gertrude Creek to Egegik, 70 mi (110 km). (Note that another King Salmon River is located southwest of Becharof Lake, draining into Ugashik Bay.)

The Refuge has a maritime climate, with cool, wet summers, mild, wet winters and frequent overcast. (See the King Salmon weather table.) Winds are normally strong. Heavy storms lasting several days, generally accompanied by violent winds, can restrict air travel. Carry extra food in case your air taxi pickup is delayed. Daylight on June 21 is 18½ hours, on December 22, 6½ hours. Prominent peak: Mount Peulik, elevation 4835 ft (1474 m).

The Refuge is most easily reached via air taxi from Egegik, King Salmon or Naknek, the latter two having stores, restaurants and lodging. Scheduled air service lands at King Salmon and Egegik; the community of Egegik prefers not to have visitors.

15

Bering Land Bridge National Preserve

Location: Northwestern Alaska, southwest of Kotzebue; 66°N 164°W
Size: 2,767,520 acres (1 120 000 hectares)
High point: 3380 ft (1030 m)
Low point: Sea level

Best time of year: Foot, June–October; boat, June–September; ski, March–April
USGS maps: Bendeleben, Kotzebue, Shishmaref, Teller
Established: 1980
Managed by: National Park Service

More than 10,000 years ago, humans and many plants and animals are thought to have migrated to North America from Asia across a neck of land now inundated by the Bering Sea. A drop in sea level of only 100 ft (30 m) would re-create a similar "bridge" today connecting Alaska and Russia.

Only 60 mi (100 km) from the Siberian mainland, the Preserve contains sea cliffs, lagoons, clear lakes and streams, granite tors, hot springs, lava beds and significant archaeological sites. Inland, the vast coastal wet-tundra flatlands rise to the rolling treeless uplands of the Bendeleben Mountains. Today local Eskimos use the area

Eskimo woman boiling walrus flippers. (National Park Service photo by Robert Belous)

extensively for subsistence hunting and fishing—a primary reason for establishing this preserve.

Musk-oxen have been reestablished in the area surrounding Ikpek Lagoon. The ecological niche normally occupied by caribou has been filled by Eskimo-owned reindeer, a close relative of the gentle tundra traveler. Watch also for moose, brown (grizzly) bears, wolves, wolverines, arctic foxes, red foxes and, on offshore ice floes, polar bears. Seals, walrus and whales swim the coastal waters. The shoreline is a major migration route for seabirds and migratory waterfowl, many of which nest on the coastal flatlands.

The Preserve contains no roads or recreational development. Camping is unrestricted on public lands. Respect the extensive private landholdings, most of which are along the coast and may not be marked. Do not enter cabins or other private structures. Campfires are technically permitted, but wood is scarce, especially inland. Expect mosquitoes in July and August. Prepare for periods of rain and strong winds; hypothermia is a constant danger. Fog or winds can delay your air pickup, so carry extra food. Hunting, fishing, firearms, fixed-wing aircraft, powerboats and snowmobiles are all permitted.

In this arctic maritime climate, summers can be cool, foggy and overcast, with warmer temperatures and more sun inland. Winters are cold, dry and severe. (See the Kotzebue weather table.) Winds are constant and moderate, frequently strong. Daylight on June 21 is 23 hours, on December 22, 1 hour.

Access to the Preserve is by air taxi from Kotzebue or Nome or by charter boat from Shishmaref or Deering. Scheduled air service lands at Kotzebue, Nome, Shishmaref, Deering and Wales. The villages have small general stores but limited supplies. Restaurants and lodging are available in Kotzebue and Nome.

Suggested reading: Hans-Georg Bandi, *Eskimo Prehistory* (Seattle: University of Washington Press, 1966); Jeffrey Goodman, *American Genesis* (New York: Summit Books, 1981); David M. Hopkins, *The Bering Land Bridge* (Stanford, Calif.: Stanford University Press, 1967); U.S. Department of the Interior, *Proposed Bering Land Bridge National Monument* and *Proposed Chukchi-Imuruk National Reserve*, Final Environmental Impact Statements (Washington, D.C.: U.S. Government Printing Office, 1974).

16 Bering Sea Refuge, Alaska Maritime National Wildlife Refuge

Location: Western Alaska, in the Bering Sea; 60°25′N 172°50′W
Size: 81,340 acres (32 920 hectares)
High point: 1505 ft (459 m) on St. Matthew Island
Low point: Sea level

Best time of year: June–September
USGS map: St. Matthew
Established: 1909
Managed by: U.S. Fish and Wildlife Service

These three extremely remote islands in the Bering Sea—St. Matthew, Hall and Pinnacle—are used by marine mammals and large numbers of seabirds, primarily cormorants, murres, puffins, auklets, gulls, common eiders and oldsquaw ducks. The islands are also the major U.S. nesting grounds for the McKay's bunting.

Walrus Tusk Beach, St. Matthew Island. (U.S. Fish and Wildlife Service photo by Anthony DeGange)

The islands originally supported a dense polar bear population, but by 1899 hunters had eradicated the animals. Bering Sea National Wildlife Refuge was established to preserve the remaining wildlife. In 1980, the Refuge was designated a part of the Alaska Maritime National Wildlife Refuge.

During World War II, reindeer were introduced onto St. Matthew Island as an emergency food supply for resident military personnel who manned weather stations and navigational equipment. Left alone after the war, the reindeer overpopulated the island, stripping the vegetation, until a sudden die-off occurred in 1964, reducing the population to less than 100.

Restrictions may be in effect; contact the Refuge Manager before going to the islands. Hunting is not permitted. No development exists other than an abandoned military airstrip. The islands have no good anchorages. Frequent and long-lasting storms and fog make flying and boating hazardous.

The subarctic maritime climate brings cool, foggy summers and cold, dry winters. (See the Nunivak Island weather table.) Winds are strong. The Bering Sea is ice-free by June. Daylight on June 21 is 19 hours, on December 22, 6 hours.

Suggested reading: Anthony R. DeGange and Arthur L. Sowls, *A Faunal Reconnaissance of the Bering Sea National Wildlife Refuge* (Anchorage: U.S. Fish and Wildlife Service Field Report No. 77-039, 1978).

Birch Creek
National Wild River

17

Location: Eastern Alaska, in the
  Steese National Conservation Area;
  65°15′N 145°30′W
River rating: WW1-3
Popular trip length: 125 mi (200 km)
Best time of year: May–July

Annual high water: July
USGS maps: Circle B-4, B-3, B-2, B-1,
  C-1
Designated as Wild River: 1980
Managed by: Bureau of Land
  Management

With its headwaters near timberline in the rolling Yukon-Tanana uplands, Birch Creek winds through boreal-forested valleys to emerge eventually in the wetlands of the Yukon River valley in the Yukon Flats National Wildlife Refuge. Although it flows through uninhabited wilderness, the creek is often extremely muddy from placer gold mining in its headwaters and tributaries. Near and below the Steese Highway bridge at Mile 147, which marks the end of the Wild River designation, Birch Creek is a slow meandering stream, with occasional sloughs and old river channels obscuring the main channel. About 150 mi (240 km) below the bridge, the river divides into two channels which enter the Yukon River 20 mi (32 km) apart. The distance from the access at Mile 94, Steese Highway, to the take-out at Mile 147, Steese Highway at the bridge is about 125 mi (200 km). Continuing down Birch Creek and the Yukon River to the Dalton Highway bridge adds another 300 mi (480 km).

During periods of low water, the upper 8 mi (13 km) of the river may require lining and extensive dragging, particularly in late summer. The WW3 rapids about 6 mi (10

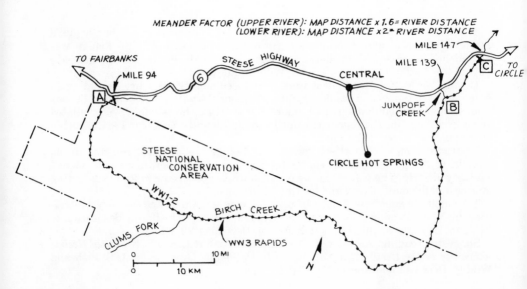

Birch Creek. (Bureau of Land Management photo by Rich Tobin)

km) below Clums (Coulombes) Fork can be dangerous and should be lined or portaged. Numerous sweepers hang from the banks.

Watch for moose, caribou, black bears, brown (grizzly) bears, wolves, coyotes, red foxes, lynx, wolverines, porcupines and beavers, and fish for grayling and northern pike.

Camping is unrestricted and best on gravel bars. Be aware that rainstorms upstream can raise the water level several feet without warning. Campfires, fishing, hunting, firearms, fixed-wing aircraft and powerboats are all permitted. Expect large numbers of mosquitoes and other biting insects from June through August.

In a subarctic continental climate, the area normally has warm, dry summers with occasional thundershowers. (See the Fairbanks weather table.) Winds are generally light. Daylight on June 21 is 22 hours, on December 22, 3 hours.

To reach the river, drive the Steese Highway north of Fairbanks to Mile 94, where a short side road leads to a parking area. Line boats 0.25 mi (0.4 km) down the tributary to Birch Creek (A), elevation 2000 ft (600 m). Take out at Jumpoff Creek (B), Mile 139, Steese Highway, or at the Steese Highway bridge over Birch Creek at Mile 147 (C), elevation 600 ft (200 m). Food and lodging are available at Central and Circle Hot Springs.

Suggested reading: U.S. Department of the Interior, *Proposed Birch Creek National Wild River*, Final Environmental Impact Statement (Washington, D.C.: U.S. Government Printing Office, 1975).

Bogoslof Refuge, Alaska Maritime National Wildlife Refuge

18

Location: Southwestern Alaska, in the Aleutian Islands north of Umnak Island; 53°56′N 168°02′W
Size: 175 acres (71 hectares)
High point: 360 ft (110 m), on Bogoslof Island

Low point: Sea level
Best time of year: May–September
USGS map: Umnak
Established: 1909
Managed by: U.S. Fish and Wildlife Service

"Bogoslof! Bogoslof!" ("God's voice!") shouted the Aleuts as the island rose from the sea during a fiery eruption. Bogoslof Island, formed in 1796, and Fire Island, formed in 1883, are of particular interest to biologists because they have come into existence within recent historic time. Today these two remote, rocky islands contain 90,000 seabirds—primarily murres, puffins, kittiwakes and gulls—and 5000 Steller's sea lions.

Sea lions on the beach, Bogoslof Refuge. (U.S. Fish and Wildlife Service photo)

Treeless Bogoslof consists of a vegetated lava dome with the one rugged spire of Castle Rock, black lava cliffs and sandy bouldered beaches. Fire Island is a single, barren pinnacle rising 40 ft (12 m) above the sea. During World War II, a military outpost was established on Bogoslof. Designated a National Wildlife Refuge early in the century, Bogoslof became a part of the Alaska Maritime National Wildlife Refuge in 1980.

Visits to this undisturbed sanctuary are limited to those with scientific or educational purposes. Hunting, firearms and aircraft are not permitted. Contact the Refuge Manager before planning a trip.

The islands are isolated and hard to reach. Frequent, violent and long-lasting storms make boating and flying dangerous. There are no anchorages, airstrips or development. Dutch Harbor/Unalaska is the nearest community that has scheduled air service, air taxis, stores, restaurants and lodging.

The weather is typical of a maritime climate: cool, wet, foggy summers and mild, wet, foggy winters. (See the Cold Bay weather table.) Here the Bering Sea is ice-free the entire year. Winds are usually constant and strong, and severe storms are frequent.

Suggested reading: Alaska Geographic, *Alaska's Volcanoes: Northern Link in the Ring of Fire* (Anchorage: Alaska Northwest Publishing Co., 1976); G.V. Byrd *et al.*, "Changes in Marine Bird and Mammal Population on an Active Volcano in Alaska" (*The Murrelet*, vol. 61 [1980], 50-62); Bernard R. Hubbard, S.J., *Mush, You Malemutes!* (New York: American Press, 1932).

19  Caines Head State Recreation Area

Location: Southcentral Alaska, south of Seward; 59°59′N 149°25′W
Size: 5961 acres (2412 hectares)
High point: 3380 ft (1030 m)
Low point: Sea level
Best time of year: Foot, May–September; boat, May–September; ski, February–April

USGS maps: Blying Sound D-7; Seward A-7
Established: 1971
Managed by: Alaska Division of Parks

In the waters of Resurrection Bay, pilings of an old military dock stand as quiet sentinels. An old road about 2 mi (3 km) long, overgrown by alders, climbs from tidewater to an exposed point on the towering shale cliffs of Caines Head. Here cling bunkers and other remnants of Fort McGilvray, part of Alaska's World War II coastal defense system.

Completely undeveloped, the Recreation Area appeals to boaters who enjoy primitive camping, hiking and beachcombing. The terrain is steep, with numerous creeks and ponds dotting the dense coastal forest. Camping is unrestricted; campfires, fishing and hunting are permitted.

Watch the ocean for sea mammals—dolphins, porpoises, seals, sea lions, sea otters and whales. On land expect moose, black bears, brown (grizzly) bears, mountain goats, wolves and bald eagles.

The maritime climate brings cool, wet overcast summers and mild, wet overcast winters. (See the Seward weather table.) Winds are moderate, frequently strong. Daylight on June 21 is 19 hours, on December 22, 6 hours.

Access to Caines Head is by boat or float plane. Air taxis, charter boats, stores, restaurants and lodging are available in Seward, 8 mi (13 km) from the Recreation Area. Be cautious on Resurrection Bay; its waters can be treacherous during periods of high winds, and strong tidal currents can make landing difficult.

Suggested reading: Stan Cohen, *The Forgotten War: Pictorial History of World War II In Alaska*) Missoula, Mont.: Pictorial Histories Publishing Co., 1981); Brian Garfield, *The Thousand-Mile War: World War II in Alaska and the Aleutians* (Garden City, N.Y.: Doubleday and Co., 1969); Major George L. Hall, *Sometime Again* (Seattle: Superior Publishing Co., 1945); Emmanuel R. Lewis, *Seacoast Fortification of the United States: An Introductory History* (Washington, D.C.: Smithsonian Institution, 1970).

Military dock at Pier Cove. (Photo by Pete Martin)

Cape Krusenstern. (National Park Service photo by M. Woodbridge Williams)

20 · Cape Krusenstern National Monument

Location: Northwestern Alaska,
northwest of Kotzebue; 67°30'N
163°30'W
Size: 540,000 acres (219 000 hectares)
High point: 2285 ft (696 m)
Low point: Sea level

Best time of year: Foot,
June–September; boat,
June–August; ski, March–April
USGS maps: Kotzebue, Noatak
Established: 1978
Managed by: National Park Service

Curving in graceful arcs parallel to the Chukchi Sea shore, 114 beach-sand ridges, deposited by the ocean over time, hide an unusual archaeological site in the far Arctic. The ridges contain artifacts from every known Eskimo occupation of North America in chronological order, dating from 6000 B.C. Some of the artifacts relate to cultures never before described. (Collecting artifacts or bones is prohibited.) Beach ridges continue to form today, mainly at Sheshalik Spit, where local Eskimos fish and hunt marine mammals much as their ancestors did.

Five large lagoons and many small lakes dot the wide coastal plain of wet tundra. Further inland, rolling hills topped by dry tundra are connected by large areas of tussock grass, discouraging all but the hardiest foot traveler. Permafrost underlies the area, and only the top 20 inches (50 cm) of soil thaws each year. (During the Pleistocene epoch, when the Cape was part of the Bering Land Bridge, the seas and land are thought to have been ice-free.)

Musk-oxen, earlier exterminated, have been reestablished in the Mulgrave Hills, joining other mammals of the tundra: caribou, moose, brown (grizzly) bears, red foxes, arctic foxes, wolverines and wolves. Watch for Dall sheep in the Igichuk Hills and, offshore, polar bears, seals, walrus and whales.

Eskimos hauling an oogruk (bearded seal) aboard. (National Park Service photo by Robert Belous)

The area is without recreational development. Camping is unrestricted on public lands except in archaeological zones. Respect private lands (extensive along the coast, particularly on the Spit) and any structures or possessions that might be on them. Ask locally before selecting a campsite. Drinking water is hard to find near the ocean, since the lagoons are brackish and may contain rotting fish. A few small lakes are fresh enough to drink from. Plan to use a camping stove; strong winds and the scarcity of firewood can make campfires impractical. If you build a fire, do so on beach sand, not on tundra or other areas underlain with peat. Fishing, firearms, fixed-wing aircraft, powerboats and snowmobiles are permitted within the Monument; sports hunting is not, although the area is used by the local people for subsistence food gathering. Hypothermia is a constant danger—prepare for long periods of rain and strong winds. Since fog or winds can delay a planned air or water pickup, carry extra food. Those inexperienced in the Arctic should not plan winter visits.

Summers are cool, cloudy and often foggy, with more sun and warmer temperatures inland. Winters are cold, dry and severe. (See the Kotzebue weather table.) Winds are constant and moderately strong most of the time, very strong during storms. Daylight on June 21 is 24 hours, on December 22, 0 hours, with 6 hours of twilight.

Access to the Monument is by light plane or boat, both of which can be chartered in Kotzebue. If you cross from Kotzebue in your own hand-powered boat, be extremely cautious on this frigid, hazardous water. Scheduled air service is available to Kotzebue, Kivalina and Noatak, all of which have food supplies. Lodging is available at Kotzebue.

Suggested reading: Alaska Geographic, *The Kotzebue Basin* (Anchorage: Alaska Northwest Publishing Co., 1981); J. L. Giddings, *Ancient Men of the Arctic* (New York: Alfred A. Knopf, 1967); Richard K. Nelson, *Hunters of the Northern Ice* (Chicago: University of Chicago Press, 1972); William and Carrie Uhl, *Tagiumsinaaqmiit, Ocean Beach Dwellers of Cape Krusenstern Area: Subsistence Patterns* (Fairbanks: University of Alaska, 1977); U.S. Department of the Interior, *Proposed Cape Krusenstern National Monument*, Final Environmental Impact Statement (Washington, D.C.: U.S. Government Printing Office, 1974).

21   Captain Cook State Recreation Area

Location: Southcentral Alaska, north of the city of Kenai; 60°47′N 151°03′W
Size: 3257 acres (1318 hectares)
High point: 125 ft (38 m)
Low point: Sea level

Best time of year: Foot, May–October; boat, May–October; ski, February–April
USGS map: Kenai D-3
Established: 1970
Managed by: Alaska Division of Parks

In 1778 English explorer Captain James Cook sailed into Cook Inlet, searching unsuccessfully for a "northwest passage" through North America. According to his log, he sent a boat ashore to bury a marker at Point Possession northeast of here, claiming the land for King George III, although the marker has never been found.

Cook Inlet and Mount Spurr from Captain Cook State Recreation Area.

In this area of gently rolling wooded knolls and lakes, watch for moose, black bears, brown (grizzly) bears, beaver, wolves, coyotes, red foxes, porcupines, bald eagles and migratory waterfowl. Whales travel the waters of Cook Inlet.

Captain Cook State Recreation Area is a developed, but uncrowded, park on the shores of Cook Inlet, an excellent destination for families with children. Facilities include picnic shelters, three campgrounds (79 units) including a remote boat-in campsite on Stormy Lake, water, toilets and a boat launch on Stormy Lake. A cross-country ski trail, 2 mi (3 km) long, starts at Bishop Creek Campground. Back-country camping is permitted.

Build campfires in campground firepits only; use a camping stove elsewhere. Picnicking, beachcombing, hiking, boating, fishing, swimming, snowmobiling, ski touring and ice-fishing are popular activities. Powerboats are permitted; horses, fixed-wing aircraft, snowmobiles and off-road vehicles are not. The discharge of firearms is prohibited. Swimming and boating are not recommended in Cook Inlet; the incoming tide can be swift and dangerous. Drive with care on the saltwater beaches; the sand is frequently too soft to support standard tires.

Expect cool, overcast summers and cold, overcast winters. The maritime climate is strongly influenced by continental land masses that bring in subarctic winter cold. (See the Kenai weather table.) Winds are constant and moderate along the beaches of Cook Inlet, lighter inland. Daylight on June 21 is 19½ hours, on December 22, 5½ hours.

The entrance to the Recreation Area at Mile 36, North Kenai Road, is 25 mi (40 km) north of the city of Kenai, which has car rentals, taxicabs, scheduled bus and air service from Anchorage, stores, restaurants and lodging. The Recreation Area is also the terminus of the Swanson River Canoe Trail (see Kenai National Wildlife Refuge).

Suggested reading: John Cawte Beaglehole, *The Life of Captain James Cook* (Stanford, Calif.: Stanford University Press, 1974); Alan Villiers, *Captain James Cook* (New York: Charles Scribner's Sons, 1967).

22
Chamisso Refuge, Alaska Maritime National Wildlife Refuge

Location: Northwestern Alaska, southeast of Kotzebue; 66°13′N 161°52′W
Size: 455 acres (184 hectares)
High point: 246 ft (75 m) on Chamisso Island

Low point: Sea level
Best time of year: June–September
USGS maps: Selawik A-6, B-6
Established: 1912
Managed by: U.S. Fish and Wildlife Service

Established as a refuge to protect seabird nesting sites, Chamisso and Puffin islands and nearby islets are used by large populations of horned puffins, thick-billed murres and black-legged kittiwakes. Most of the nesting sites are on Puffin Island, which drops steeply to tidewater; the cliffs have long been a source of murre and kittiwake eggs for local Eskimos, who are permitted to continue gathering them for subsistence. Horned puffins normally nest in rock crevices and boulder piles, but on Puffin Island they have dug underground burrows similar to those of tufted puffins.

With a large sandspit and a low shoreline, tundra-covered Chamisso Island has fewer nesting seabirds. Chamisso, the larger island, was named for Adelbert von Chamisso, botanist on the Russian ship *Rurik*, which first visited the islands in 1815 under the command of Otto von Kotzebue.

The waters of Spafarief Bay contain walrus, seals, porpoises and whales; in winter an occasional arctic fox may trot across the frozen bay from the mainland. Originally designated a National Wildlife Refuge, Chamisso became a part of the Alaska Maritime National Wildlife Refuge in 1980.

Horned puffins. (U.S. Fish and Wildlife Service photo by Anthony DeGange)

Human visitors are not encouraged on the Refuge during nesting season. Contact the Refuge Manager before planning a trip, since visitor restrictions may be in effect. The Refuge is undeveloped.

In this arctic maritime climate, cool, cloudy, foggy summers and dry, cold, severe winters are the norm. (See the Kotzebue weather table.) With the frequent fog and strong winds, hypothermia is a danger. Long-lasting storms make boating hazardous, and there are no good anchorages. Daylight on June 21 is 24 hours; on December 22, 3 hours.

Kotzebue is the closest major settlement, with stores, restaurants, lodging, scheduled air service and air taxis. Deering, a small village southwest of the Refuge, has a store and scheduled air service.

Suggested reading: Alaska Geographic, *The Kotzebue Basin* (Anchorage: Alaska Northwest Publishing Co., 1981); Anthony R. DeGange and Arthur L. Sowls, *A Survey of the Chamisso Island National Wildlife Refuge* (Anchorage: U.S. Fish and Wildlife Service Field Report No. 77-040, 1978).

23 Chena River State Recreation Area

Location: Eastern Alaska, east of Fairbanks; 64°55'N 146°25'W
Size: 254,080 acres (102 823 hectares)
High point: 4421 ft (1348 m)
Low point: 700 ft (210 m)

Best time of year: Foot, May–October; boat, May–September; ski, February–April
USGS maps: Big Delta D-5, D-6; Circle A-5, A-6
Established: 1967
Managed by: Alaska Division of Parks

A section of the Chena River floodplain, with its sloughs, marshes and the surrounding rolling hills, forms the Chena River State Recreation Area. Float the river as it winds through the forests of spruce, aspen and birch; or climb to the tors, large vertical outcroppings of quartz diorite and granite on the hills south of the Chena River, some standing 200 ft (60 m) high.

Wildlife is typical of Interior Alaska — moose, black bears, brown (grizzly) bears, caribou, wolves, wolverines, coyotes, red foxes, beavers, river otters, porcupines, grouse, ptarmigan, hawks and golden eagles.

The easily accessible Recreation Area is popular with Fairbanks residents for hiking, rock-climbing, horseback riding, fishing, hunting, river running, ski touring, dog mushing and snowmobiling. Sections are closed to horses and snowmobiles. Facilities include campgrounds, picnic areas, toilets and 35 mi (56 km) of marked trails. Camping and campfires are permitted in the back country.

River travel: Chena River, WW1-FWB, from Mile 39.6, Chena Hot Springs Road, to Fairbanks, 70 mi (113 km). This is one of the finest canoe rivers in the Fairbanks area, but watch for sweepers and logjams.

Expect warm, dry summers with occasional thundershowers and some cool, rainy days in this subarctic continental climate; winters are cold, dry and severe. (See the Fairbanks weather table.) Winds are generally light, but may be strong on hilltops. Daylight on June 21 is 22 hours, on December 22, 3½ hours. The terrain is primarily

Granite Tors. (Photo by Sandy Rabinowitch)

rolling boreal-forested uplands with alpine tundra above 2800 ft (850 m). Prominent peak: Chena Dome, elevation 4421 ft (1348 m).

The Recreation Area is accessible by automobile from Mile 26 through Mile 53, Chena Hot Springs Road, which bisects the park. Restaurants and lodging are available within the park, in Chena Hot Springs (Mile 58) and in Fairbanks, 30 mi (50 km) away. Fairbanks also has auto rentals.

24  Chilikadrotna National Wild River

Location: Southcentral Alaska, in Lake Clark National Park and Preserve; 60°40′N 154°10′W
River rating: WW3-FWB
Popular trip length: 70 to 200 mi (110 to 320 km)

Best time of year: June–September
Annual high water: June, August
USGS maps: Lake Clark C-3, C-4, C-5, C-6, C-7.
Designated as Wild River: 1980
Managed by: National Park Service

Flowing down the west side of the Alaska Range through gentle upland forests of spruce, birch and aspen, the Chilikadrotna is a swift, twisting, narrow river, most suitable for rafts or kayaks; canoeists attempting it should be very experienced. Although only the first 10 mi (16 km) from its source in Twin Lakes is designated as Wild River, the remainder to its confluence with the Mulchatna is *de facto* wilderness. The Twin Lakes area has good hiking terrain. Combine the Chilikadrotna with the Mulchatna and the Nushagak (see Mulchatna National Wild River description) for a float trip of about 200 mi (320 km) to New Stuyahok.

Rafters on Chilikadrotna River. (National Park Service photo by Pat Pourchot)

Expect a series of WW2-3 rapids the first 5 mi (8 km) below Twin Lakes and again about 5 mi (8 km) below Little Mulchatna River. Numerous sweepers overhang the river after the first 8 mi (13 km). Be alert for logjams.

Excellent fishing is reported for lake trout in Twin Lakes and for salmon, rainbow trout, Dolly Varden, grayling and pike in the rivers. Moose, black bears, brown (grizzly) bears, wolves, wolverines, red foxes and porcupines wander the rolling hills and forested lowlands. Caribou calve in the Twin Lakes area.

Campsites and firewood are plentiful along the river; camping is best on gravel bars. Fishing, firearms, powerboats and fixed-wing aircraft are permitted. Sports hunting is allowed in the Preserve but not in the Park. No recreational facilities are available.

The climate is transitional between subarctic continental and maritime; expect cool summers with frequent overcast. (See the Port Alsworth weather table.) Winds are light to moderate. Daylight on June 21 is 19½ hours, on December 22, 5½ hours.

To reach the river, take an air taxi to Twin Lakes (A), elevation 1979 ft (603 m). End the trip by taking an air taxi from the Dummy Creek area of the Mulchatna (B), elevation 600 ft (200 m), or continue to New Stuyahok on the Nushagak River, elevation 100 ft (30 m). New Stuyahok has scheduled air service and a general store. Air taxis are available from Anchorage, Dillingham, Homer, Iliamna, Kenai and Port Alsworth.

Suggested reading: Richard Proenneke with Sam Keith, *One Man's Wilderness: An Alaskan Odyssey* (Anchorage: Alaska Northwest Publishing Co., 1973); James Van Stone, *Eskimos of the Nushagak River: An Ethnographic History* (Seattle: University of Washington Press, 1967).

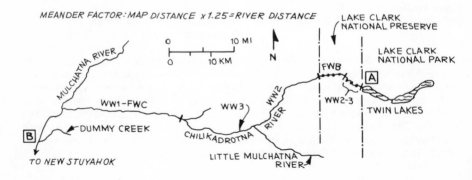

Chilkat State Park

25

Location: Southeastern Alaska, south
  of Haines; 59°10′N 135°17′W
Size: 6045 acres (2446 hectares)
High point: 1741 ft (531 m)
Low point: Sea level

Best time of year: Foot, May–October;
  boat, May–October; ski,
  December–March
USGS maps: Skagway A-1, A-2
Established: 1975
Managed by: Alaska Division of Parks

For years the Chilkat Indians guarded the access to mountain passes into Interior
Alaska from the Chilkat Peninsula, thus controlling trade between the Russians and
the Interior Indians. Early Chilkat Indians dried halibut on what is now known as
Battery Point, but after a large group of them died in nearby Lynn Canal, the
survivors placed dog-shaped rocks as memorials and abandoned the area. In 1891,
the U.S. Coast and Geodetic Survey named it Battery Point because of its resemblance to earthwork fortifications.

*Chilkat State Park (upper left) along Chilkat Inlet, with Haines and Port Chilkoot in
foreground. (Photo by Pete Martin)*

The two sections of Chilkat State Park include the former Battery Point State Recreation Area and the entire lower end of the Chilkat Peninsula. The area is tranquil, with spectacular views of Davidson and Rainbow glaciers across Chilkat Inlet.

Watch for moose, brown (grizzly) bears, black bears, deer and bald eagles in the Park; whales, seals and sea otters in Lynn Canal and Chilkat Inlet; and mountain goats on the mountainsides beyond.

Popular activities in the Park include beachcombing, fishing, picnicking and camping in a dense coastal conifer forest or on the beach. Campfires are permitted in campground firepits or at established trailside tent sites only. In addition to the two campgrounds (37 units), facilities include picnic tables and shelters, toilets, a boat launch and 10 mi (16 km) of marked trails. Hunting and snowmobiles are restricted to specific areas; off-road vehicles are not permitted. Do not discharge firearms near campgrounds, roads or trails.

Expect a maritime climate with cool, wet summers and mild, wet winters. (See the Haines weather table.) Winds are generally moderate and constant on exposed headlands. Sudden severe winds and waves on Lynn Canal can capsize small boats; there are uncharted rocks. Daylight on June 21 is 18 hours, on December 22, 6 hours.

Chilkat State Park is an excellent destination for families with children and for those who want developed campground facilities. It is accessible by automobile; take Mud Bay Road south from Haines for 7 mi (11 km), then the 2-mi (3-km) side road that leads to the Park. Battery Point is reached via a 2.4-mi (3.9-km) trail from the end of Beach Road, about 2 mi (3 km) from downtown Haines. Rental cars, stores, restaurants and lodging are available in Haines, a highway access point to the Southeastern Alaska state ferry system. The town also has scheduled bus and air service.

Suggested reading: Elizabeth Hakkinen, *The Song of the Chilkat People* (Haines, Alaska: Lynn Canal Publishing Co., 1970); Hjalmar Rutzebeck, *Alaska Man's Luck* (New York: Boni and Liveright, 1920) and *My Alaska Idyll* (New York: Boni and Liveright, 1922).

26   Chugach National Forest

Location: Southcentral Alaska, southeast of Anchorage; 61°15′N 149°20′W

Size: 5,940,000 acres (2 404 000 hectares)

High point: 13,176 ft (4016 m)

Low point: Sea level

Best time of year: Foot, May–October; boat, May–October; ski, January–March

USGS maps: Anchorage, Bering Glacier, Blying Sound, Cordova, Middleton Island, Seward, Valdez

Established: 1907

Managed by: U.S. Forest Service

A magnificent area of forests, mountains, glaciers, lakes, rivers, fjords and seashores, Chugach National Forest includes 41-mi- (66-km-) long Columbia Glacier and the Sargent Icefield. Prince William Sound, a large island-protected sea with fjords and tidewater glaciers, is surrounded by high heavily glaciated mountains. Along the western boundary, on the Kenai Peninsula, the Seward Highway winds

Ski touring, Center Creek, Kenai Peninsula.

through once-glaciated mountains and beside large lakes. Dense conifer forests rise to about 1000 ft (300 m). Higher, a band of nearly impenetrable brush finally yields to alpine tundra.

The region had long been occupied by Chugach Eskimos and Eyak Indians when Captain James Cook explored Prince William Sound and Turnagain Arm in 1778. A gold rush began to the Kenai Peninsula in 1888; later copper mines were established on Latouche Island and at Ellamar in Prince William Sound. Canneries and salteries scattered throughout the Sound processed the abundant fish harvest, and fur farmers raised blue foxes on small islands. By 1930, major mining activity had ceased; in the 1960s the last of the remote canneries shut down. Today the Sound is fished commercially for crab, halibut, salmon, herring and herring roe. Tankers carrying North Slope oil from Valdez travel through eastern Prince William Sound en route to the Lower 48.

The epicenter of the destructive 1964 earthquake (8.4 on the Richter scale) was near Miner's Lake, west of Columbia Glacier; land to the west sank a maximum of 8 ft (2.4 m), while land to the southeast rose as much as 35 ft (11 m).

Wildlife is abundant in the National Forest and in the waters of Prince William Sound. Moose are particularly abundant on the Kenai Peninsula, north of Turnagain and on the Copper River delta. The bountiful delta, nesting grounds and staging area for more than two million migratory waterfowl and 40 million shorebirds, was made a Critical Habitat Area within the National Forest in 1978. About 40,000 ducks nest here. Dall sheep are found primarily in the mountains on the western side of the National Forest, while mountain goats range over most of the Forest's uplands. Caribou have been reestablished on the Kenai Peninsula, with a small band in the vicinity of Resurrection Creek and American Pass. Sitka blacktail deer are found

Dilapidated mine buildings, Kenai Peninsula.

primarily on Montague and Hinchenbrook islands. Other wildlife includes brown (grizzly) bears, black bears, wolves, wolverines, coyotes, beavers, red foxes, snowshoe hares, lynx, marmots, marten, mink, muskrats, river otters, porcupines, pikas, arctic ground squirrels, red squirrels, bald eagles and about 250 other species of birds. Offshore, in Prince William Sound, watch for seals, sea lions, sea otters, dolphins, porpoises and whales.

The entire National Forest is a popular recreation area for both Alaska residents and visitors. Most people stay near the road system for picnicking, berry-picking and camping. Mount Alyeska, Alaska's largest ski resort and a popular summer tourist attraction, is located at Girdwood, southeast of Anchorage. Much-photographed Portage Glacier and Portage Lake, with a visitors' center and interpretive programs, lie at the head of Turnagain Arm. The National Forest maintains 16 campgrounds (433 units, fee), 35 public-use recreational cabins (reservations by lottery, fee), 9 boat ramps and almost 200 mi (320 km) of marked trails. Back-country camping is unrestricted. Campfires in campgrounds are permitted in existing firepits only; in the back country, fires are permitted except during periods of extreme fire danger. Firewood may be cut for personal use from dead or downed trees only, 200 ft (60 m) or more from main roads, campgrounds or trails. Gold panning on public lands is permitted, but other recreational mining equipment may be restricted.

Popular off-road activities include hiking and backpacking, river running, beachcombing and ski touring. The National Forest is also extensively used for fishing, hunting and snowmobiling and, to a lesser extent, for horseback riding, powerboating and off-road vehicle travel, all of which are subject to restricted periods or places of use. During the red salmon runs of July and August, the Russian River is the most intensively used fishery in the state, with fishermen standing elbow-to-elbow. Firearms are permitted, but may not be used near campgrounds, roads or

Spawning pink salmon, Prince William Sound.

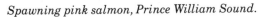

The village of Tatitlek, Prince William Sound.

trails. Fixed-wing aircraft are permitted by the Forest Service, although State of Alaska and FAA restrictions may be in effect.

Since large numbers of bears live in the National Forest, travel and camp to avoid contact with them (see Part I for suggestions). Severe avalanche hazard can exist in winter and spring; fatalities have occurred. And last, but extremely important, do not climb on icebergs or approach glacier faces at any time, winter or summer.

Large portions of eastern Prince William Sound have been selected by various native corporations under the Alaska Native Claims Settlement Act of 1971. Ask for permission at Tatitlek, Cordova or the office of the Chugach Natives, Inc., in Anchorage before camping or hunting in their areas. Numerous private landholdings and mining claims exist elsewhere within the National Forest; respect private property and do not enter buildings or disturb claim markers and equipment.

River travel: Alaganik Slough, FWA-B, Mile 22.3, Copper River Highway bridge to the boat ramp at the end of the 3-mi (5-km) side road from Mile 17, Copper River Highway, 4.5 mi (7 km). Strong winds or adverse tidal conditions can prevent your return to the boat ramp from downstream. Granite Creek/East Fork, WW1-2, Mile 65.5, Seward Highway (Bertha Creek Campground) to Mile 60, Seward Highway (just below the Silvertip Highway Maintenance Camp), 9 mi (14 km). Beyond this point are WW3-5 rapids. East Fork/Sixmile River, WW2-5, Mile 60, Seward Highway to Sunrise, 11 mi (18 m). Upper Kenai River, WW1-2, Mile 47.8, Sterling Highway (at the Kenai River bridge) to Mile 0.2, Skilak Lake Loop Road (Jean Creek Campground), 15 mi (24 m). Portage Creek, WW1, outlet of Portage Lake to Mile 79, Seward Highway, 6 mi (10 km). The waters of the rivers and lakes of the National Forest and Prince William Sound are extremely cold; wetsuits and adequate flotation equipment are mandatory.

Two climate patterns prevail in the National Forest. Inland, Kenai Peninsula has cool, often overcast, summers; winters are crisp and cold. (See the Moose Pass weather table.) Winds are light to moderate. Prince William Sound, on the other hand, has a typical maritime climate, with cool, wet summers and mild, wet winters. (See the North Dutch Group weather table.) The Sound stays ice-free all winter except where bays receive large amounts of fresh water from rivers and streams. Winds are light to moderate, with severe storms in autumn. Daylight on June 21 is 19½ hours, on December 22, 5½ hours. Prominent peaks: Mount Marcus Baker, elevation 13,176 ft (4016 m); Mount Valhalla, elevation 12,135 ft (3699 m); Mount Witherspoon, elevation 12,012 ft (3661 m).

The western portion of the National Forest on the Kenai Peninsula is easily accessible by automobile via the Seward and Sterling highways. Automobiles can be rented in Anchorage and Seward, while scheduled buses travel both highways. Sightseeing tours regularly visit Mount Alyeska and Portage Glacier. The Alaska Railroad makes daily runs in the summer from Anchorage to Portage and Whittier, with a less frequent schedule in winter.

Sightseers at Portage Glacier.

Sailors on Prince William Sound.

The Prince William Sound region has only two highway portals: the vehicle-carrying Alaska Railroad from Portage to Whittier and the Richardson Highway to Valdez. The Southwestern Alaska state ferry connects the ports of Whittier, Valdez, Cordova, the San Juan fish hatchery and Seward. From Cordova, the Copper River Highway leads through the delta to the river, but is not connected to the state highway system. Automobiles can be rented in Seward, Valdez and Cordova. Sightseeing tours and cruise boats travel in summer between Whittier and Valdez, with a stop to view Columbia Glacier.

Scheduled air service is available between Anchorage, Cordova and Valdez; air taxis are based at Anchorage, Cooper Landing, Cordova, Moose Pass, Seward and Valdez. Sailboats may be chartered in Seward, Valdez and Whittier, while powerboat charters operate from Cooper Landing, Cordova, Seward, Valdez and Whittier. All communities have stores and restaurants. Lodging is available at roadside motels, wilderness lodges, Cooper Landing, Cordova, Girdwood/Alyeska, Moose Pass, Seward, Valdez and Whittier.

Suggested reading: Alaska Geographic, *Cook Inlet Country* (Anchorage: Alaska Northwest Publishing Co., 1977); Alaska Geographic, *Prince William Sound* (Anchorage: Alaska Northwest Publishing Co., 1975); Mary J. Barry, *A History of Mining on the Kenai Peninsula* (Anchorage: Alaska Northwest Publishing Co., 1973); Lone E. Janson, *The Copper Spike* (Anchorage: Alaska Northwest Publishing Co., 1975); Helen Nienhueser and Nancy Simmerman, *55 Ways to the Wilderness in Southcentral Alaska* (Seattle: The Mountaineers, 1978); Lawrence Rakestraw, *A History of the United States Forest Service in Alaska* (Anchorage: Alaska Historical Commission and the U.S. Forest Service, Department of Agriculture, 1981); U.S. Geological Survey, *The Alaska Earthquake: March 27, 1964*, Geological Survey Professional Papers 542-545 (Washington, D.C.: U.S. Government Printing Office, 1966).

Chugach State Park

Location: Southcentral Alaska, east of Anchorage; 61°20′N 149°20′W
Size: 490,000 acres (198 000 hectares)
High point: 8005 ft (2440 m)
Low point: Sea level

Best time of year: Foot, June–October; boat, June–October; ski, February–April
USGS maps: Anchorage, Seward
Established: 1970
Managed by: Alaska Division of Parks

An impressive glaciated landscape of forested and alpine valleys, sharp ridges, lakes, meadows and craggy summits, Chugach State Park presses against the Municipality of Anchorage to create a stunning backdrop for the city. In the eastern section of the Park, the pastoral beauty gives way to a wild white symphony of snaking glaciers, perennial snows and shining peaks.

Turnagain Arm, a fjord along the southern boundary of the Park, has one of the highest tidal variations in the world, more than 32 ft (10 m). Tidal bores, turbulent incoming tides with a breaking wave in the lead, are frequently seen from the Seward Highway.

Wildlife includes moose, black bears, brown (grizzly) bears, mountain goats, Dall sheep, wolves, wolverines, coyotes, red foxes, porcupines, hawks and bald eagles. In May, when the "hooligan" (smelt) migrate through Turnagain Arm to their river spawning areas, white beluga whales and eagles come in to feed on the tasty fish.

A popular recreation area at Anchorage's doorstep, Chugach State Park has room for picnickers, hikers, campers, backpackers, rock climbers, mountaineers, boaters, river runners, hang gliders, ski tourers, dog mushers, snowmobilers, fishermen and hunters. Firearms, hunting, horses, aircraft landings, powerboats, snowmobiles and all-terrain vehicles are permitted in specific areas only. Hikers should practice crossing glacial streams before attempting Eagle River. Boaters on Eklutna Lake need to watch for sudden strong winds that can capsize small boats. Quicksand-like mud makes the tide flats of Turnagain Arm unsafe.

Highway waysides, picnic areas and shelters, campgrounds (78 units), and a visitors' center at Mile 12, Eagle River Road, are some of the facilities. Park rangers schedule programs about wilderness survival and avalanche awareness as well as interpretive lectures and guided hikes. The Park contains 50 mi (80 km) of marked hiking trails, 20 mi (32 km) of marked ski trails and 10 mi (16 km) of marked snowmobile trails. Back-country camping is unrestricted, but groups must be no larger than 20. In summer, campfires may be built only in campground firepits; use camping stoves elsewhere.

River travel: Upper Eagle River, WW1-3, from Mile 9, Eagle River Road to Eagle River Campground area, 13 mi (21 km). Below the campground, Eagle River becomes severely turbulent—for experts only.

Although the Park's climate is transitional between subarctic maritime and continental, local topography and elevation largely determine its weather. In general, summers are mild, winters can be either mild or cold. (See the Anchorage weather table.) The maritime influence increases from west to east, causing cooler summers, warmer winters and increased precipitation in the eastern section. Anchorage averages 15 inches (38 cm) of precipitation a year, while Girdwood/Alyeska, only 30 mi (50 km) away, receives 70 inches (180 cm). Winds are generally light in the valleys, frequently severe in the mountains. Daylight on June 21 is 19½ hours, on December 22, 5½ hours. Prominent peaks: Bashful Peak, elevation 8005 ft (2440 m); Baleful Peak, elevation 7900 ft (2400 m); Bellicose Peak, elevation 7640 ft (2329 m). Treeline is about 2000 ft (600 m); some areas have a band of dense brush above the trees before giving way to alpine tundra. Many cliffs and peaks contain "rotten" rock unsafe for climbing. In winter, spring and early summer, avalanche danger can be severe throughout the Park.

Chugach State Park has many road access points from the Seward Highway, the Hillside area of Anchorage and the Glenn Highway. Contact Park personnel for a brochure and map. Rental cars, taxicabs and air taxis are available in Anchorage. The Anchorage municipal "People Mover" bus has routes to the Hillside area; intercity buses travel the Seward and Glenn highways. Lodging, stores and restaurants are found in Anchorage, Bird Creek, Eagle River, Eklutna, Girdwood/Alyeska, Indian and Peters Creek.

Suggested reading: Helen Nienhueser and Nancy Simmerman, *55 Ways to the Wilderness in Southcentral Alaska* (Seattle: The Mountaineers, 1978.)

Hikers in Chugach State Park.

Helm Point. (U.S. Forest Service photo)

28 Coronation Island Wilderness, Tongass National Forest

Location: Southeastern Alaska, south of Sitka; 55°53′N 134°15′W
Size: 19,232 acres (7783 hectares)
High point: 1960 ft (600 m)
Low point: Sea level

Best time of year: April–August
USGS maps: Craig D-7, D-8
Established: 1980
Managed by: U.S. Forest Service

The steep, protruding summit of a partially submerged mountain, Coronation Island is covered by a dense spruce-hemlock rain forest. It has windswept beaches, precipitous cliffs and a few protected coves, all surrounded by rocky shoals. An important seabird nesting and perching area, the island is also used by bald eagles, black bears, Sitka blacktail deer and wolves. Offshore swim seals, sea lions, sea otters and whales, with large numbers of harbor seals congregating in the bay near Helm Point.

The island is undeveloped. Camping, campfires, fishing, hunting and firearms are permitted. Since firewood is normally wet and winds strong, camping stoves are recommended. Prepare for long periods of rain. Prolonged storms can delay scheduled pickup and make boating hazardous. Only experienced boaters should attempt to visit the island.

In this maritime climate, summers are cool, wet and overcast, winters mild, wet and overcast. (See the Sitka weather table.) Winds are constant and moderate to strong, becoming especially severe during autumn storms. Daylight on June 21 is 17½ hours, on December 22, 7 hours. Prominent peaks: Needle Peak, elevation 1960 ft (600 m); Windy Peak, elevation 1765 ft (538 m).

Access to the island is by float plane or boat. Air taxis operate from Ketchikan, Petersburg, Sitka and Wrangell; boat charters are available at most coastal communities. Food and lodging are available at Craig, Ketchikan, Klawock, Petersburg, Sitka and Wrangell.

Captain George Vancouver named the island as he sailed past it on September 22, 1793, the anniversary of the coronation of George III of England.

29 Creamer's Field Migratory Waterfowl Refuge

Location: Eastern Alaska, in
  Fairbanks; 64°52′N 147°45′W
Size: 1788 acres (724 hectares)
High point: 500 ft (150 m)
Low point: 450 ft (140 m)

Best time of year:
  Foot, April–October;
  ski, December–March
USGS map: Fairbanks D-2
Established: 1968
Managed by: Alaska Department of
  Fish and Game

Creamer's Dairy, once the nation's northernmost milk producer, is situated on a major waterfowl migration route. In 1903 C.T. Hinckley began a dairy farm in the Alaskan wilderness; 25 years later he sold it to Charlie and Anna Creamer. With its grazing cows and rippling hayfields, Creamer's farm brought a touch of nostalgia to

Canada geese at Creamer's Field. (Alaska Department of Fish and Game photo)

Alaskans transplanted from the Lower 48. The fallow hayfields emerging from winter snows attracted thousands of hungry traveling birds and numerous resident birdwatchers.

When the Creamers retired from farming in the mid-1960s, Fairbanks area residents thwarted efforts to turn the fields into housing subdivisions, leading to the establishment of a wildlife observation and environmental education area. The dairy was placed on the National Register of Historic Places in 1977.

The Refuge, with interpretive signs, observation platforms and a 2-mi (3-km) self-guiding nature trail, is open to visitors year-round. Waterfowl populations are greatest from late April through May and again in August. The east field is closed to entry during the spring migration period. Horses may use the area but are not permitted on the nature trail. Camping is not permitted. Frequent winter sights are dog mushers, cross-country skiers and snowmobilers.

Fairbanks, with its subarctic continental climate, enjoys warm, dry summers and endures cold, dry, severe winters. (See the Fairbanks weather table.) Winds are normally light. Daylight on June 21 is 22 hours, on December 22, 3½ hours.

Creamer's Field is located at 1300 College Road, between the Fairbanks city center and the University of Alaska. Rental cars and taxicabs are available in Fairbanks; city buses travel College Road and stop at the Refuge. Stores, restaurants and lodging are available in Fairbanks and College.

The buildings of Creamer's Dairy provide an historic and photogenic background to a long-standing Fairbanks wildlife attraction. Don't miss this charming refuge.

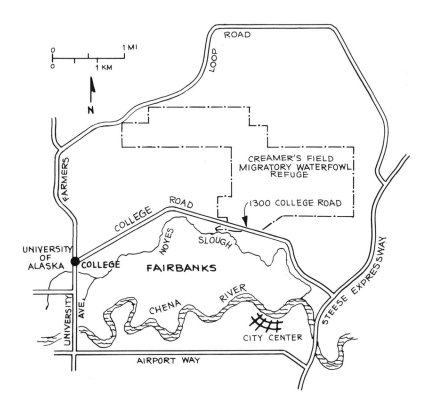

30

Delta National Wild and Scenic River

Location: Eastern Alaska, south of
 Delta Junction; 63°10′N 145°50′W
River rating: WW1-3 with WW5 rapids
 (portage possible)
Popular trip length: 35 mi (56 km)
Best time of year: June–September
Annual high water: June

USGS maps: Mt. Hayes A-4, B-4,
 (WW5 and beyond) C-4, D-4; Big
 Delta A-4
**Designated as Wild and Scenic
 River**: 1980
Managed by: Bureau of Land
 Management

Flowing north literally through the snow-capped Alaska Range, the Delta is an anomaly in the world of mountain rivers. Rising in the tranquil alpine Tangle Lakes in the southern foothills, it meanders cold and clear. Entering the Range, it picks up icy, gray silty water from four major glaciers and myriad smaller ones. Becoming braided and violent in the heart of the mountains, it is suitable only for expert boaters below Mile 212.5, Richardson Highway.

Soon the river flows past the chaotic moraine of Black Rapids Glacier (more easily viewed from the highway). In 1937, the 20-mi- (30-km-) long glacier surged more than 4 mi (6 km), advancing up to 200 ft (60 m) a day, stopping just short of the highway and historic Black Rapids Roadhouse. Beyond the glacier, the river becomes more gentle again.

A popular recreational river, the Delta is accessible from the highway system. From Tangle Lakes to the first take-out is 35 mi (56 km) and to Delta Junction another 55 mi (89 km).

Two mi (3 km) below Tangle Lakes, waterfalls mark the river's crossing of the Denali Fault, one of the longest fault zones in Alaska, which extends westward through the summit of Mount McKinley. A 0.25-mi (0.4-km) two-section portage follows a well-defined trail. Below the falls, 2 mi (3 km) of WW3 can be run along the left side or lined from the right bank. Requiring skillful handling around rocks, this section takes its toll of canoes each year. WW2 continues to the first highway contact. Beyond the take-out, the next 30 mi (50 km) should be run only by experienced boaters in rafts or kayaks.

MEANDER FACTOR: MAP DISTANCE x 1.3 = RIVER DISTANCE

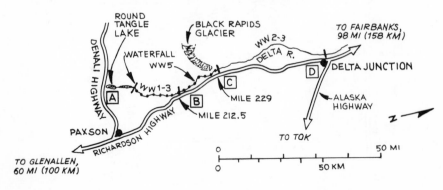

Waterfall below Tangle Lakes. (National Park Service photo)

Wildlife includes moose, caribou, brown (grizzly) bears, black bears, coyotes, red foxes, wolves, wolverines, lynx and beavers. Watch for bison (introduced in the 1950s) along the lower river. Approach no closer than 300 ft (90 m) to eagles' nests.

Camping is unrestricted and campfires are allowed. Since wood may be scarce on the upper river, use a camping stove. The lower river banks are forested. Fishing, hunting, firearms, fixed-wing aircraft and powerboats are all permitted. Expect mosquitoes and other biting insects in summer.

In this subarctic continental mountain climate, summers are cool, moist and often overcast. (See Denali National Park weather table.) Winds are moderate to strong. Daylight on June 21 is 21½ hours, on December 22, 4½ hours.

The headwaters of the river are at Round Tangle Lake (A), elevation 2791 ft (851 m), accessible from the Tangle Lakes Campground, Mile 22, Denali Highway. The first take-out (B), elevation 2600 ft (800 m), is at Mile 212.5, Richardson Highway, where the river parallels the road. Below Black Rapids Glacier, an access (C), elevation 2200 ft (670 m), is at Mile 229, Richardson Highway, near Onemile Creek. You can also leave the river at Delta Junction (D), elevation 1100 ft (340 m).

Scheduled buses travel the Richardson Highway. Food and lodging are available at roadside businesses, Delta Junction and Paxson.

Ski tourers meet dog musher, Mount McKinley in background.

31  Denali National Park and Preserve

Location: Central Alaska, north of Anchorage; 63°N 150°W
Size: 6,000,000 acres (2 430 000 hectares)
High point: 20,320 ft (6194 m)
Low point: 525 ft (160 m)
Best time of year: Foot, June–September; boat, June–September; ski, February–April

Maps: USGS, Healy, Kantishna River, Mt. McKinley, Talkeetna; Special maps, USGS, Mount McKinley National Park (the original park on one map for convenience); Bradford Washburn, "A Map of Mount McKinley, Alaska" (the mountain and its immediate vicinity in excellent detail)
Established: 1917
Managed by: National Park Service

With towering granite spires and snowy summits lost in the clouds, Denali National Park and Preserve straddles a 160-mi (260-km) section of the Alaska Range. Dominating the skyline, Mount McKinley is North America's highest mountain.

The long-standing name "Mount McKinley National Park" was changed in 1980. Most Alaskans prefer "Denali"—the Athabascan Indian name for the mountain, meaning "the high one." At the same time the name was changed, an additional 3,756,000 acres (1 520 000 hectares) were added to include, finally, the southern flanks of the Alaska Range, with its immense glaciers draining from the McKinley-Foraker massif, and the spectacular Cathedral Spires to the southwest. Mount McKinley towers at 20,320 ft. (6194 m); Mount Foraker, known by local Indians as *Menlale* ("Denali's Wife"), is 17,395 ft (5302 m). Also added were boreal-forested flatlands and the rolling Kantishna Hills to the north to complete the habitat protection for caribou, moose, bears and wolves of the Park. Except for a strip of land containing the Park Road, the original Park was designated as Wilderness and retains the original management restrictions.

Long famous for its abundant and visible large mammals, Denali National Park is on the "must-see" list of more visitors to Alaska than any other attraction. Paralleling the Alaska Range and traversing rolling open tundraland, the Park Road provides ideal viewing for wide-eyed wildlife enthusiasts. They can watch wolves stalk caribou and see brown (grizzly) bears feed from a moose carcass or scratch their backs on road signs. Dall sheep graze on slopes nearby, red foxes play with kits and, for the lucky viewer, a wolverine lopes beside a braided glacial stream.

The open tundra of the park seems to have been created for the foot traveler—no trails are needed along the mountain streams and over the rolling hills. Marked trails are found primarily in the forested areas at Park Headquarters and near Wonder Lake. Backpacking, hiking and camping are so popular that the National Park Service has had to develop a quota system for back-country use to protect the fragile tundra and provide an uncrowded wilderness experience for each user. Per-

Dall sheep.

Wonder Lake Campground, Denali National Park with Mount McKinley in background.

mits for back-country travel and for campground use are available at the Riley Creek Information Center on a first-come basis. There are no restrictions on day hiking except in several small closed areas. Park Service personnel encourage back-country users to consider trips in the north and south additions and in nearby Denali State Park.

With the increase in off-road foot travelers comes a serious problem: grizzlies can become "park bears," animals that search out visitors and their campsites, hoping for tasty handouts. Camp and travel carefully, and check with the Park Service before traveling anywhere on foot, to avoid the territories of "problem bears." In the Wilderness, campfires are permitted in campground fire pits only; use camping stoves in the back country. In the remainder of the Park and in the Preserve, campfires are permitted.

Read about crossing rivers before trying your first one; Park rivers are swift, braided glacial streams. Prepare for mosquitoes in June and July. Fishing is permitted throughout; hunting is allowed only in the Preserve. Park regulations prohibit pets, firearms, horses, fixed-wing aircraft, powerboats and snowmobiles in the Wilderness, but all are permitted in the remainder of the Park and in the Preserve. Non-motorized uses of the Wilderness in winter are encouraged, particularly ski touring and dog mushing. Registration at Park Headquarters is required for climbing on Mount McKinley or Mount Foraker.

Visitors' facilities include seven campgrounds (225 units, first-come basis, registration required at the Riley Creek Information Center). Campgrounds are open from approximately May 15 to September 15, except the two at Park Headquarters are open year-round. Also at Park Headquarters are a hotel, dining room, bar, gift shop, telephone, post office, service station, grocery store, railroad depot and an airstrip. Interpretive programs are given daily in the summer.

A concessioner's wildlife bus tour (fee) leaves the hotel daily in season. Free shuttle buses travel the Park Road regularly during daylight hours, connecting Riley Creek and the hotel area with Eielson Visitors' Center, Wonder Lake and points between, a round trip of up to 172 mi (270 km). Popular with hikers, photographers and animal watchers, the buses can be left or boarded at any point along the Park Road. Private automobiles are permitted only as far as Mile 14, Savage River area, except when used for access directly to a reserved campground unit. After Labor Day, private vehicles may drive the entire road until snow closes it.

River travel and boating: Kantishna River, FWA, from Lake Minchumina to Manley Hot Springs on the Tanana River, 250 mi (400 km); Nenana River, WW1-5,

Caribou.

from the Denali Highway to Healy, 40 mi (60 km); Wonder Lake, FWA, hand-powered or sail boats only.

Summer weather can be cool, often with long periods of overcast or drizzle, despite the Park's interior Alaska location. Temperatures in winter are cold with little precipitation, but warmer with more snow south of the Range. (See the Denali National Park weather table.) Winds are generally light in the lowlands, often severe on mountain peaks. Daylight on June 21 is 21½ hours, on December 22, 4½ hours. Other prominent peaks: Mount Hunter, elevation 14,580 ft (4444 m); Mount Silverthrone, elevation 13,220 ft (4029 m); Mount Crosson, elevation 12,775 ft (3894 m); Mount Carpe, elevation 12,550 ft (3825 m); Mount Huntington, elevation 12,240 ft (3731 m).

For automobile travelers, the park entrance is at Mile 237, Parks Highway, 237 mi (381 km) north of Anchorage. The area is also served by scheduled buses between Anchorage and Fairbanks, the Alaska Railroad and scheduled air service. Air taxis operate from Denali National Park, Cantwell and Talkeetna. The Park Road winds 87 mi (140 km) through the park and continues a short distance to a dead end in the Kantishna area of the north addition. The area south of the Alaska Range is most accessible by air taxi from Talkeetna or by foot from the end of the Petersville Road, an unsurfaced 33-mi (53-km) homestead and mining access road leaving Mile 115, Parks Highway, at Trapper Creek. Inquire locally about the condition of the road. Food and lodging are available at numerous roadside businesses and at Denali National Park, Healy, Cantwell and Talkeetna.

Suggested reading: Belmore Browne, *The Conquest of Mount McKinley* (1915; reprint ed., New York: Houghton Mifflin, 1956); Steve Buskirk, *Mount McKinley, Story Behind the Scenery* (Las Vegas: KC Publications, 1978); Art Davidson, *Minus 148°: The Winter Ascent of Mt. McKinley* (New York: W.W. Norton and Co., 1969); James Greiner, *Wager With the Wind: The Don Sheldon Story* (New York: Rand McNally and Co., 1974); Terris Moore, *Mt. McKinley: The Pioneer Climbs* (Seattle: The Mountaineers, 1981; originally published in 1967); Adolph Murie, *A Naturalist in Alaska* (New York: Devin-Adair Co., 1961).

32 Denali State Park

Location: Southcentral Alaska, north of Anchorage; 62°45′N 150°05′W
Size: 324,240 acres (131 215 hectares)
High point: 4558 ft (1389 m)
Low point: 500 ft (150 m)

Best time of year: Foot, June–September; boat, June–September; ski, February–April
USGS maps: Talkeetna, Talkeetna Mountains
Established: 1970
Managed by: Alaska Division of Parks

Straddling the Parks Highway, the southern foothills of the Alaska Range provide panoramic views of Mount McKinley, 35 mi (56 km) away, Mount Hunter, Mount Silverthrone, the Moose's Tooth, Tokosha Spires and Ruth, Buckskin and Eldridge glaciers. Ruth Glacier Overlook, Mile 135 on the Parks Highway, is just 5 mi (8 km) from the glacier's terminus. The view of Mount McKinley and the Alaska Range

Mount McKinley from Parks Highway, Denali State Park.

from Curry Ridge was a popular goal for passengers on the early Alaska Railroad, when Curry was a regular overnight stop on the two-day trip between Anchorage and Fairbanks. Sydney Laurence, renowned pioneer Alaskan artist, frequently painted Mount McKinley from a vantage point in the Peters Hills, the western end of the Park.

Watch for moose, black bears, brown (grizzly) bears, Dall sheep, caribou, red foxes, coyotes, wolves, wolverines, lynx, golden eagles, bald eagles, and peregrine falcons.

In this relatively undeveloped park, popular activities are photography, picnicking, swimming, hiking, camping, boating on Byers Lake, fishing, river running, ski touring and wilderness travel. Hunting is allowed if firearms are not used. Fixed-wing aircraft and powerboats are restricted to specific areas; horses, snowmobiles and off-road vehicles are not permitted. Facilities include informational exhibits, highway rest areas, picnic sites, a campground at Byers Lake, water and toilets. Campfires are permitted in campground firepits only; use a camping stove elsewhere. Back-country camping is unrestricted. One marked trail, 4 mi (6 km) long, leads from Byers Lake Campground to Curry Ridge; another 40 mi (64 km) of trails are under construction. Another trail climbs from the highway along Little Coal Creek to timberline on Indian Ridge at the northern end of the Park. Once above timberline, about 2000 ft (600 m) elevation, hiking is easy on the alpine tundra. Numerous small lakes dot the landscape.

River travel: Chulitna River, WW3-FWC, from Mile 194.5, Parks Highway to Talkeetna, 98 mi (158 km).

Although the Park's weather is moderated by its proximity to the ocean, many features of a subarctic continental climate prevail. Summer weather is typical of mountainous areas—often cool, with frequent overcast; winters are cold and brisk. (See the Talkeetna weather table.) Daylight on June 21 is 19½ hours, on December 22, 5½ hours.

Paralleling the Chulitna River, the paved George Parks Highway, from Mile 132 to Mile 170, runs north-south through the Park, making it one of the most accessible in

Alaska. Scheduled bus service and sightseeing tours travel the highway daily in summer; rental cars are available in Anchorage. East of the highway, on the other side of Curry and Indian ridges, the Alaska Railroad, from Mile 243.5 to Mile 279, winds through the Park along the Susitna River. Disembark on the west side of the river, just past Gold Creek. The western extent of the Park, in the Peters Hills, is reached from the Petersville Road, which leaves Mile 115, Parks Highway, at Trapper Creek. Inquire locally about the current condition of the unsurfaced homestead and mining road. Air taxi service is available in Talkeetna. Restaurants and lodging can be found at numerous roadside businesses near the Park and at Talkeeta and Cantwell.

Suggesting reading: Jeanne Laurence, *My Life With Sydney Laurence* (Seattle: Superior Publishing Co., 1974).

33 Endicott River Wilderness, Tongass National Forest

Location: Southeastern Alaska, south of Haines; 58°45′N 135°30′W
Size: 98,729 acres (39 954 hectares)
High point: 5805 ft (1769 m)
Low point: 50 ft (15 m)

Best time of year: Foot, May–September; boat, May–September
USGS map: Juneau
Established: 1980
Managed by: U.S. Forest Service

A glacially carved river basin in the Chilkat Range of the St. Elias Mountains, Endicott River Wilderness adjoins the eastern edge of Glacier Bay National Park. The valley heads in snowfields and glaciers. Lower down, there is heavy brush above timberline, changing to rich spruce-hemlock rain forests below. A low pass at the head of the valley leads into Adams Inlet of Glacier Bay National Monument.

Many bald eagles that nest along the banks fish the Endicott River for salmon—as do brown (grizzly) bears and black bears. Moose, wolves, wolverines and mountain goats are all found in the Wilderness.

Undeveloped and seldom visited, the scenic rain-forest Wilderness can be used for back-country camping, backpacking, fishing and hunting. Firearms and fixed-wing aircraft landings are permitted. Campfires may be built, but wood is generally wet. There are long periods of rain and wind, particularly in the autumn, making camping unpleasant and boating on Lynn Canal hazardous, or delaying planned pickup. Severe avalanche hazard can exist.

The maritime climate is often overcast; summers are cool, winters mild. (See the Haines weather table.) Winds are generally light in the lowlands, moderate to strong at high elevations. Daylight on June 21 is 18½ hours, on December 22, 6 hours. Prominent peak: Mount Young, elevation 5805 ft (1769 m).

Access to the Wilderness is commonly by float plane or boat, both available for charter in Haines. Small wheeled planes occasionally land on a small river bar. Haines also offers food, lodging and scheduled air service and is a port of call for the Southeastern Alaska state ferry.

Mountain goats. (U.S. Fish and Wildlife Service photo by Mike Vivion)

34   Forrester Island Refuge, Alaska Maritime National Wildlife Refuge

Location: Southeastern Alaska, southwest of Craig; 54°48′N 133°31′W
Size: 2832 acres (1146 hectares)
High point: 1340 ft (408 m) on Forrester Island

Low point: Sea level
Best time of year: May–September
USGS map: Dixon Entrance D-5
Established: 1912
Managed by: U.S. Fish and Wildlife Service

Three islands, Forrester, Lowrie and Petrel, and numerous offshore rocks make up this remote seabird refuge in the Gulf of Alaska near Dixon Entrance, a critical habitat for more than a million birds. On islands seemingly deserted by day, huge populations of Leach's storm petrels, fork-tailed storm petrels, Cassin's auklets and rhinoceros auklets nest in underground burrows, emerging only after dark to feed in the open ocean. Since nearly all available soil is honeycombed with the burrows,

Tufted puffin. (U.S. Fish and Wildlife Service photo)

which are up to 15 ft (5 m) long, a single person walking on an island collapses many tunnels. Visitor restrictions may be in effect, so contact the Refuge Manager before planning a trip.

Forrester Island, whose mountainous steep slopes are heavily forested, has dense underbrush, many cliffs and few beaches. Petrel Island, 300 ft (100 m) high, is also densely forested atop precipitous sea cliffs. Lowrie Island is 250 ft (75 m) high and essentially flat. The refuge became a part of the Alaska Maritime National Wildlife Refuge in 1980.

The islands have a maritime climate, with cool, wet summers and mild, wet winters. (See the Annette Island weather table.) Winds are variable. Daylight on June 21 is 17½ hours, on December 22, 7 hours. Undeveloped, the islands have no anchorages or airstrips.

Suggested reading: Anthony R. DeGange *et al.*, *The Breeding Biology of Seabirds on the Forrester Island National Wildlife Refuge* (Anchorage: U.S. Fish and Wildlife Service, 1976).

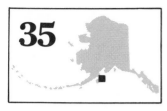

35 | Fort Abercrombie State Historic Park

Location: Southwestern Alaska, near Kodiak on Kodiak Island; 57°50′N 152°25′W
Size: 183 acres (74 hectares)
High point: 100 ft (30 m)
Low point: Sea level

Best time of year: Foot, May–October; boat, May–October; ski, January–March
USGS map: Kodiak D-2
Established: 1969
Managed by: Alaska Division of Parks

An observation post on this forested cliff overlooking Narrow Strait and the Gulf of Alaska was manned 24 hours a day after the attack on Pearl Harbor in December, 1941. Following Japanese attacks on Attu, Kiska and Unalaska in the western Aleutian Islands, the post was fortified and renamed for Lt. Col. William R. Abercrombie, who was instrumental in U.S. Army explorations of Alaska in the late 19th century. From 1942 to 1944, as many as 200 men were stationed here; the fort appears to have been abandoned after 1944. The site was placed on the National Register of Historic Places in 1970. Today the gun mounts and bunkers sit quietly in the wind. In

View from World War II observation post.

an outdoor amphitheater next to the Park, a spectacular drama, "Cry of the Wild Ram," is presented each August.

Keep an eye open in the rain forest for Sitka blacktail deer, red foxes, snowshoe hares, red squirrels and weasels (ermine). Salmonberries are ripe by August. Watch the ocean for porpoises, dolphins, sea otters, seals, sea lions and whales.

The Park has one campground (20 units, some of them walk-in sites), set in tall Sitka spruce trees, a visitor center and a 3-mi (5-km) marked trail. Campfires are permitted only in campground fire pits. Wood is likely to be wet. Keep children away from the sea cliffs. At Lake Gertrude, swim, fish and canoe; beachcomb along the coast. Hunting, use of firearms, horses, powerboats, snowmobiles and off-road vehicles are prohibited.

Expect rain. Kodiak Island's maritime climate is wet, with cool summers and mild winters. (See the Kodiak weather table.) Winds are generally light in the forest, gusty on exposed headlands. Daylight on June 21 is 18 hours, on December 22, 6½ hours.

To reach the Park, follow Rezanoff Road from downtown Kodiak 3.9 mi (6.3 km) to a sign for the Park. A short side road leads to the right. Rental cars, restaurants and lodging are available in Kodiak. A port of call for the Southwestern Alaska state ferry, Kodiak also has scheduled air service.

Suggested reading: Stan Cohen, *The Forgotten War* (Missoula, Mont.: Pictorial Histories Publishing Co., 1981); Brian Garfield, *The Thousand-Mile War: World War II in Alaska and the Aleutians* (New York: Ballantine Books, 1975); Major George L. Hall, *Sometime Again* (Seattle: Superior Publishing Co., 1945); Emmanuel R. Lewis, *Seacoast Fortifications of the United States: An Introductory History* (Washington, D.C.: Smithsonian Institution, 1970).

36 Fortymile National Wild, Scenic and Recreational River

Location: Eastern Alaska, northwest of Tok; 64°18′N 141°30′W
River rating: WW1-2 with WW3-5 rapids (line or portage)
Popular trip lengths: 70 to 170 mi (110 to 270 km)
Best time of year: May–September
Annual high water: May
Maps: USGS, from West/Dennison forks to O'Brien Creek, Tanacross D-3, D-2; Eagle A-2, B-2, B-1. From Middle Fork to O'Brien Creek, Eagle B-5, B-4, B-3, B-2, A-2, B-1. From O'Brien Creek to Eagle, (USGS maps) Eagle B-1, A-1; [Canadian maps (1:50,000 scale), Dawson quad] 116 C/7, 116 C/8, 116 C/9, 116 C/10; (USGS maps) Eagle C-1, D-1.
Designated as Wild, Scenic and Recreational River: 1980
Managed by: Bureau of Land Management

With clear sparkling rapids, quiet pools, forested river banks and white marble bluffs, the Fortymile River flows through gentle, rounded mountains to join the Yukon River. It was named in 1886 because it was 40 mi (64 km) downstream from the Hudson's Bay post Fort Reliance.

Placer and hydraulic gold mining began in the Fortymile country in 1886, ten

Lining "The Kink." (National Park Service photo)

years before the Klondike strike in Canada, and it continues today. Mammoth gold dredges, once operated on Walker and South forks, stand among the fireweed as ghostly relics of the industry of an earlier day.

The river has numerous access points from the gravel-surfaced Taylor Highway as it winds over the Tanana-Yukon uplands to Eagle. The West, Dennison and Mosquito forks are mainly WW1, with some WW2-3 rapids that present no serious obstacles. The Middle Fork, although primarily WW1 with WW2 rapids, has dangerous WW3 at "The Chute," which can be lined on the right bank. A short distance farther, WW5 rapids at "The Kink" must be portaged. Below O'Brien Creek, WW3 "Deadman Riffles" can cause trouble for canoes. Across the Canadian border, the canyon contains a two-part WW4 rapids, separated by calm water. It can be lined; use the north bank at times of high water. Watch for sweepers anywhere.

Distances to O'Brien Creek are, on the South Fork from Mile 49, Taylor Highway, 69 mi (111 km) and from Ketchumstuk on Mosquito Fork, 79 mi (127 km). On the Middle Fork from Joseph to O'Brien Creek is 88 mi (142 km). From O'Brien Creek to Eagle via the Yukon River is about 100 mi (160 km).

Watch for wildlife typical of the boreal forest — moose, black bears, brown (grizzly) bears, wolves, wolverines, coyotes, red foxes, lynx, porcupines, grouse, ptarmigan, grayling, northern pike and sheefish. The Fortymile caribou herd migrates through the area.

Due to heavy use of the river by recreational miners, camping along the river for more than ten days requires a special permit. Rainstorms upriver can raise the water level rapidly; choose campsites carefully and tie boats at night. Campfires are permitted, but build them on river gravel. In 1966, forests of the Middle and Dennison forks burned. Fishing, hunting, firearms, fixed-wing aircraft and powerboats are all permitted. Sporting weapons may be taken into Canada, but handguns are prohibited. Expect hungry mosquitoes and other insects in summer months.

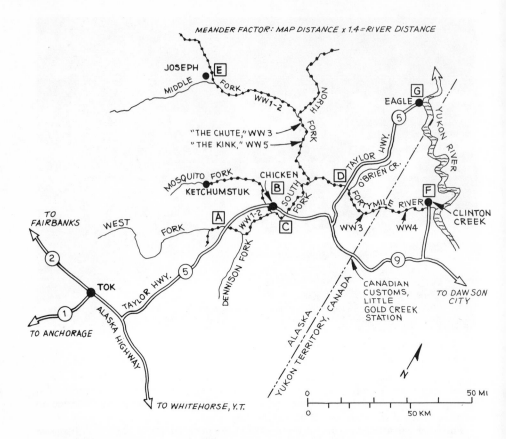

MEANDER FACTOR: MAP DISTANCE x 1.4 = RIVER DISTANCE

The Fortymile flows through many mining claims and other private lands. Do not trespass or enter privately owned structures. Removal of any artifact or object of historic value from federal or state land is prohibited and subject to prosecution.

The Fortymile country has pleasant, warm, dry summers, but prepare for periods of rain and thundershowers in this subarctic continental climate. (See the Eagle weather table.) Winds are normally light. Daylight on June 21 is 21½ hours, on December 22, 4 hours.

Access to the West/Dennison forks is at Mile 49, Taylor Highway, at the West Fork bridge (A), elevation 1850 ft (564 m), floatable at high water only. Other accesses are at Chicken (B), Mile 66, elevation 1550 ft (472 m), and at the South Fork bridge (C), Mile 75, elevation 1500 ft (460 m). Many people pull out at O'Brien Creek (D), Mile 112, elevation 1300 ft (400 m); land on the right bank immediately below the bridge, where an access road leads to the highway. To float the Middle Fork, take an air taxi to the airstrip at Joseph (E), elevation 2300 ft (700 m). Just before the river enters the Yukon, it touches the highway system again at Clinton Creek in Canada (F), elevation 900 ft (300 m), (no services available) or you may continue on the Yukon to Eagle, Alaska (G), elevation 900 ft (300 m), Mile 161, Taylor Highway and the end of the road. Air taxis, food and lodging are available at Eagle and Tok. Eagle also has scheduled air service.

If you travel into Canada, you are required to clear customs. Contact Canadian customs at Dawson City or Whitehorse before starting the float trip. (Addresses and phone numbers are in the Appendix.) Officials are aware of the inconvenience this

Gold dredge in the Fortymile country.

causes for river travelers and make the legal requirements as painless as possible. You may clear Canadian customs in person at Little Gold Creek Station at the Alaska-Yukon border on Alaska Route 5/Yukon Highway 9, 44 mi (71 km) from Chicken. Upon re-entry into the U.S., you must clear customs at Eagle.

Suggested reading: Robert Specht, *Tisha* (New York: St. Martin's Press, 1976); U.S. Department of the Interior, *Proposed Fortymile National Wild River*, Final Environmental Impact Statement, (Washington, D.C.: U.S. Government Printing Office, 1974); David B. Wharton, *The Alaska Gold Rush* (Bloomington: Indiana University Press, 1972).

37 Gates of the Arctic National Park and Preserve

Location: Northcentral Alaska, in the Brooks Range; 68°N 152°W
Size: 8,090,000 acres (3 274 000 hectares)
High point: 8510 ft (2594 m)
Low point: 300 ft (90 m)

Best time of year: Foot, mid-June–September; boat, July–August; ski, March–April
USGS maps: Ambler River, Chandalar, Chandler Lake, Hughes, Killik River, Philip Smith Mountains, Survey Pass, Wiseman
Established: 1980
Managed by: National Park Service

A scenic, remote, undeveloped parkland astride the Arctic Divide in the Brooks Range, Gates of the Arctic is one of the finest large wildernesses remaining in the world. The rugged but not intimidating mountains hold a few glaciers—small by Alaskan standards—clearwater rivers, alpine lakes and mile after mile of inviting

Ski touring party, with Boreal Mountain, part of "The Gates" on the left.

tundra-covered slopes. North of the divide, the area is treeless; the lower valleys on the south side are forested. Six National Wild Rivers lie wholly or partially within the Park: Alatna, John, Kobuk, Noatak, North Fork of the Koyukuk and Tinayguk. Access to the Arrigetch Peaks area is from the Alatna River. Of the parkland's total size, 7,052,000 acres (2 854 000 hectares) are designated as Wilderness.

Robert Marshall first explored the central Brooks Range in 1929 and eloquently described it in his book *Alaska Wilderness*. He romantically designated as the "Gates of the Arctic" the two peaks, Boreal Mountain and Frigid Crags, that stand as sentinels on the North Fork of the Koyukuk River 100 mi (160 km) north of the Arctic Circle.

Wildlife typical of this arctic/subarctic zone includes Dall sheep, caribou, moose, brown (grizzly) bears, black bears, wolves, wolverines, red foxes, coyotes, lynx, beavers, snowshoe hares, hoary marmots, marten, mink, muskrats, river otters, porcupines, arctic ground squirrels, red squirrels and northern flying squirrels. Hawks, owls and ptarmigan are frequently seen. Since vegetation grows so slowly here, the land supports a lower density of animals than is found farther south.

A popular area for hiking, river running and mountaineering, the parkland is getting increasing use in the winter by ski touring parties and dog mushers. Camping is unrestricted, but every effort should be made to avoid destroying the fragile vegetation or leaving any sign of use. Camping stoves are preferred since northern wood grows so slowly. Fishing, firearms, horses, fixed-wing aircraft, powerboats and snowmobiles are permitted throughout; hunting is permitted in the Preserve only, not in the Park. Expect hungry mosquitoes until mid-August. Numerous private landholdings and mining claims exist within the parkland boundaries; respect private property and do not enter cabins. This is a remote area, not suitable for casual visits; plan your trip carefully.

River travel: Alatna National Wild River, WW3-FWB, see description; Ambler River, WW2-3, from the upper river to Ambler, 80 mi (130 km); Anaktuvuk River,

WW3-FWA, from Cache Lake to the Colville River, 120 mi (190 km); Etivluk River, WW2-FWB, Nigtun Lake to Umiat, 160 mi (260 km); John National Wild River, WW1-3, see description; Killik River, WW1-3, from lake at headwaters of Easter Creek to Umiat, 120 mi (190 km); Kobuk National Wild River, WW1-FWB, see description; Koyukuk River, Middle Fork, WW1-FWA, from Wiseman to Bettles (Evansville), 90 mi (145 km); Nigu River, WW3-FWB, from lake in pass drained by Nigu and Alatna rivers to Umiat, 220 mi (350 km); Noatak National Wild River, WW1-2, see description; North Fork of the Koyukuk National Wild River, WW1-2, see description; Tinayguk National Wild River, WW2, see description.

Weather in the parkland varies significantly with location. South of the Arctic Divide and below 2500 ft (760 m) elevation, a subarctic continental climate prevails: summers are warm and dry in the lowlands, cooler with more precipitation in the mountains. Winters are cold, dry and severe, and warmer in the mountains than in the lowlands. (See the Wiseman weather table.) Winds are generally light. Drainages north of the Arctic Divide, below 2500 ft (760 m) elevation, have an arctic climate, with cool, dry summers and cold, dry, severe winters. (See the Galbraith weather table.) Winds are light to moderate and frequent. In the higher mountains, above 2500 ft (760 m), summers are normally cool, with frequent overcast. Winters are cold and dry, and while temperatures are not so severe as in the southern lowlands, winds can be moderate to strong. Daylight on June 21 is 24 hours, on December 22, 0 hours, with 5 hours of twilight. Prominent peaks are: Mount Igikpak,

Air taxi, Circle Lake, Alatna River Valley.

Ski planes land on Lake Takahula to pick up ski touring party.

elevation 8510 ft (2594 m); Mount Doonerak, elevation 7457 ft (2273 m); Cockedhat Mountain, elevation 7610 ft (2320 m); Boreal Mountain, elevation 6666 ft (2032 m); Frigid Crags, elevation 5550 ft (1692 m); Arrigetch Peaks, elevation 7500 ft (2300 m).

The parkland is commonly reached by air taxi from Bettles (Evansville) although the village of Anaktuvuk Pass, lying within the Park, is served by scheduled airline. Motorists on the rigorous Dalton Highway (North Slope Haul Road) can reach the Park from Wiseman and points north along the Dietrich River. (See the Trans-Alaska Pipeline Utility Corridor description.) Wiseman, Ambler and Kobuk have scheduled air service; Ambler also has an air taxi. Bettles has lodging and a dining room; all of the villages except Wiseman have general stores.

Suggested reading: Alaska Geographic, *The Brooks Range: Environmental Watershed* (Anchorage: Alaska Northwest Publishing Co., 1977); Lois Crisler, *Arctic Wild* (New York: Harper and Row, 1973); Robert Marshall, *Alaska Wilderness: Exploring the Central Brooks Range* (Berkeley: University of California Press, 1970; originally published in 1956 as *Arctic Wilderness*); Gilbert and Vivian Staender, *Adventures with Arctic Wildlife* (Caldwell, Idaho: Caxton Printers, 1970); U.S. Department of the Interior, *Proposed Gates of the Arctic National Park*, Final Environmental Impact Statement (Washington, D.C.: U.S. Government Printing Office, 1974).

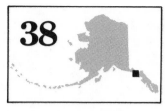

38

Glacier Bay National Park and Preserve

Location: Southeastern Alaska, west of Juneau; 59°N 136°W
Size: 3,280,000 acres (1 327 000 hectares)
High point: 15,300 ft (4663 m)
Low point: Sea level

Best time of year:
Foot, June–September; boat, May–October; ski (marginal), January–March
USGS maps: Juneau, Mt. Fairweather, Skagway, Yakutat
Established: 1925
Managed by: National Park Service

Massive tidewater glaciers, lofty mountain peaks, ice-sculptured fjords, saltwater beaches and scoured rock emerging from an ice age—Glacier Bay in the St. Elias Mountains is John Muir country. Some of the glaciers are retreating, some advancing and some holding their own. By walking from the base of a retreating river of ice along its earlier path, you can follow a wonder of nature: the gradual transformation of barren rock into rich coastal forest. The icy, plankton-rich ocean waters are favorite feeding areas for humpback, killer and other whales, porpoises, sea lions and seals.

The summit of Mount Fairweather, 15,300 ft (4663 m), stands less than 15 mi (24 m) from tidewater. Nearby, in an indentation of the Gulf of Alaska coast, lies Lituya Bay where, in 1958, a mammoth earthquake-triggered rock and ice slide crashed

Nature walk with interpreter. (National Park Service photo by Robert Belous)

Grand Plateau Glacier. (National Park Service photo by Robert Belous)

into the waters of the bay. The resulting wave scoured timber from the bay's hillsides to a height of 1720 ft (524 m).

In addition to marine mammals, Glacier Bay protects a large bear population, both brown (grizzly) and black. A rare color phase of the black bear, the "blue" glacier bear, is occasionally sighted. Watch also for moose, wolves, wolverines, Sitka black-tail deer, mountain goats and bald eagles. The coastline of the Gulf of Alaska is a major migratory bird route. North and South Marble Islands, which contain the largest seabird colonies in the Park, are closed to foot traffic during nesting season, from May 1 to September 1. Other bird colonies are similarly protected.

The tidewater glaciers and ice-choked fjords are one of the most popular destinations for visitors to Alaska. Most cruise ships plying the Inside Passage cruise the bay but do not stop. Park facilities include a lodge, dining room, gift shop, ranger station, fuel dock for boats, a campground (35 units) and 3 mi (5 km) of marked trails. Some drainages offer excellent wilderness hiking; other valleys are choked by thick brush or blocked by raging streams.

Back-country camping and mountaineering are not restricted but, for your own safety, check out and in with the Park Service at Bartlett Cove. Since firewood is frequently wet or unavailable, use a camping stove. Fishing is permitted, but hunting and the carrying of firearms are permitted only in the Preserve. Float-plane landings are permitted on all salt water except Adams Inlet. North of Sea Otter Creek (north of Cape Fairweather), planes may land on fresh water and on the beach below mean high tide.

Boat travel: Seeing the Park by water is an ideal way to avoid the brush and glacial streams, but be conservative in the icy waters of the fjords, whether in a tiny kayak or a large powerboat. Keep your distance from icebergs and glacier faces. Boating permits are required from June 1 through August 31. Check with park rangers regarding restrictions in waters where humpback whales feed. River travel: Alsek River, WW2-4, from Haines Junction to Dry Bay, 230 mi (370 km).

Glacier Bay has a maritime climate, with cool, wet summers and mild, wet winters. Overcast conditions are normal. (See the Glacier Bay weather table.) Winds are variable and calm to strong. At high elevations, severe arctic conditions prevail. Daylight on June 21 is 18½ hours, on December 22, 6 hours. In addition to Mount Fairweather, prominent peaks include Mount Quincy Adams, elevation 13,650 ft (4161 m) and Mount Crillon, 12,726 ft (3879 m).

Wherever you travel, prepare for long periods of rain and strong winds—hypothermia is a real danger. Because fog, storms and winds often affect schedules, plan extra food whether you are traveling on foot or boating.

Access to the park is by air or water. Scheduled air service serves Gustavus and Yakutat. A short bus route connects Gustavus and park headquarters at Bartlett Cove, but the local road system cannot be reached via the contiguous state highway system or from the state ferry. Sightseeing boats leave from Bartlett Cove, Gustavus and Juneau. The park concessioner's boat, offering daily trips from Bartlett Cove to Muir Inlet, regularly drops off and picks up backpackers and kayakers. Charter boats are available in Gustavus, Haines, Hoonah, Juneau and Skagway. Air taxis operate from Gustavus, Haines, Juneau, Skagway and Yakutat. Food and lodging are found at the Glacier Bay Lodge at Bartlett Cove and in Gustavus.

Suggested reading: William Boehm, *Glacier Bay: Old Ice, New Land* (Anchorage: Alaska Geographic, Alaska Northwest Publishing Co., 1975); Dave Bohn, *Glacier Bay: The Land and the Silence* (Anchorage: Alaska Natural History Association, 1977); Dale Brown, *Wild Alaska* (New York: Time-Life Books, 1972); John Muir, *Travels in Alaska* (1915; reprint ed., New York: AMS Press, 1978); U.S. Department of the Interior, *Proposed Glacier Bay National Monument Additions*, Final Environmental Impact Statement (Washington, D.C.: U.S. Government Printing Office, 1974).

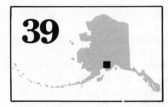

39

Goose Bay
State Game Refuge

Location: Southcentral Alaska, north
  of Anchorage; 61°22′N 149°55′W
Size: 13,262 acres (5367 hectares)
High point: 250 ft (76 m)
Low point: Sea level

Best time of year: Foot,
  April–October; boat, April–October;
  ski, January–March
USGS map: Anchorage B-6
Established: 1975
Managed by: Alaska Department of
  Fish and Game

Only 12 mi (19 km) by air from downtown Anchorage, Goose Bay Refuge is of special interest to waterfowl lovers. It includes the marshlands and mud flats of lower Goose Creek and the surrounding lowlands. Canada geese, pintails, green-winged teal and mallards are the most common species that nest here and use the area as a resting ground during spring and fall migrations.

Birdwatchers and photographers are the chief visitors during late April and early May, while waterfowl hunters appear in September and October. The scattered hunting shacks, in existence before the establishment of the Refuge, are private property and should not be disturbed.

Undeveloped for recreational use, the Refuge sports a usable abandoned airstrip at the southern end of the Knik-Goose Bay Road. Camping on public land is unrestricted; campfires are permitted, but little wood is available. Firearms, horses, powerboats, off-road vehicles, snowmobiles and fixed-wing aircraft landings are all permitted. Caution: incoming tides can be swift, with frequent large tidal bores. Tideflats mud is soft and treacherous.

Located at tidewater, the Refuge has a subarctic maritime climate. (See the Anchorage weather table.) Winds are generally moderate to strong. Daylight on June 21 is 19½ hours, on December 22, 5½ hours.

The Refuge is most easily reached by air taxi from Anchorage, Eagle River, Palmer or Wasilla, or by automobile via the mostly paved Knik-Goose Bay Road from Wasilla, a distance of 22 mi (35 km). The nearest stores, restaurants and lodging are in Wasilla.

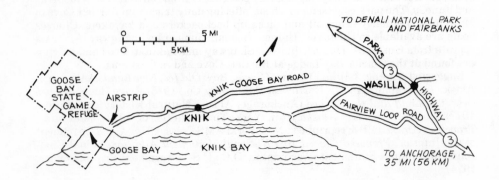

Swans and ducks, Goose Bay Refuge. (U.S. Fish and Wildlife Service photo)

40 Gulkana National Wild River

Location: Eastern Alaska, north of
Glennallen; 62°35′N 145°40′W
River rating: Main river and Middle
Fork, WW4-FWA; West Fork,
WW2-FWA
Popular trip lengths: 35 to 119 mi (56
to 191 km)
Best time of year: August–September
Annual high water: June

USGS maps: Paxson Lake to
Sourdough: Gulkana D-4, C-4; Middle
Fork to Sourdough via Tangle Lakes:
Mt. Hayes A-5; Gulkana D-5, D-4,
C-4; West Fork to Sourdough:
Gulkana D-6, C-6, C-5, C-4.
Sourdough to Gulkana: Gulkana C-4,
B-4, B-3
Designated as Wild River: 1980
Managed by: Bureau of Land
Management (above Sourdough)

Flowing southward through the forested foothills of the Alaska Range, the Gulkana is a heavily traveled, moderately difficult white-water river with three floatable branches. Most boaters begin at Paxson Lake, easily accessible by automobile. There are two sets of rapids, WW3 for 3 mi (5 km) below Paxson Lake and the Canyon

Rapids, with a 0.25 mi (0.40 km) portage, then WW3-4 for 8 mi (13 km) around boulders and logs. The remainder of the river to Sourdough, where the Trans-Alaska oil pipeline crosses overhead, is WW1-2. From Sourdough (which has the oldest operating roadhouse in Alaska, still in its original picturesque log cabin) to the village of Gulkana, the river is WW2, with a short stretch of WW3. From Paxson Lake access to Sourdough is 45 mi (72 km) and to Gulkana, another 35 mi (56 km). Below Sourdough, the river flows through native lands of Ahtna, Inc.

The Middle Fork begins at Dickey Lake, accessible by portages from Tangle Lakes, which have a highway access. The longest portage is 1.3 mi (2.1 km). The upper river is shallow, swift and rocky, requiring frequent lining; sweepers and logjams can be a problem until the Middle Fork joins the main Gulkana below Paxson Lake. From Tangle Lake to Sourdough is 84 mi (135 km).

The West Fork is a relaxed meandering stream, but watch for sweepers and logjams. From the headwaters to Sourdough is about 100 mi (160 km).

Wildlife is typical of the boreal forest—moose, black bears, brown (grizzly) bears, wolves, wolverines, coyotes, red foxes, lynx, and beavers. Caribou, during their spring and fall migrations, cross the river between Paxson and Glennallen. Approach eagles' nests no closer than 300 ft (90 m). Red salmon spawn in the headwaters; rainbow trout, whitefish and grayling are also found.

Once an attractive and lightly traveled wilderness river, the Gulkana is showing the effects of use by numerous boaters. Leave a clean campsite, use existing fire pits and dispose of human waste properly. Be sure to carry drinking water in, or boil all water taken from the river and its tributaries. Above Sourdough, camping is unrestricted and campfires are permitted, but boaters are encouraged to use camping stoves to reduce the impact on the forests. Cache food high in trees at night to avoid attracting bears. Expect large populations of mosquitoes and other biting insects from June through August. Fishing, hunting, firearms, fixed-wing aircraft and powerboats are all permitted on public lands. Below Sourdough, those fishing from shore must have an access permit (fee), available at the Ahta Lodge in Glennallen.

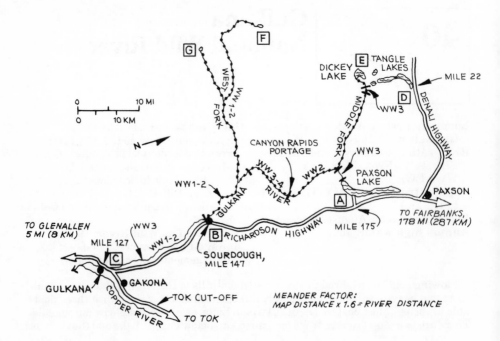

Canoeists coming around a logjam, Middle Fork, Gulkana River. (National Park Service photo by Pat Pourchot)

The climate is subarctic continental mountain; summers are cool, often drizzly and overcast. (See the Denali National Park weather table.) Winds are normally light. Daylight on June 21 is 20 hours, on December 22, 5 hours.

Access to Paxson Lake (A), elevation 2553 ft (778 m), is at Paxson Lake Campground, Mile 175, Richardson Highway. A 500-ft (150-m) boardwalk leads to the lake. Up the lake 4 mi (6 km), automobiles can drive to the water's edge at a state wayside. The Sourdough access (B), elevation 1900 ft (580 m), is at Sourdough Creek Campground, Mile 147, Richardson Highway. The Gulkana public take-out (C), elevation 1400 ft (330 m), is on native land on the west (right) bank near the bridge, Mile 127, Richardson Highway. The boat ramp on the east bank is a commercial facility.

Middle Fork access starts at the Tangle River Campground (D), elevation 3000 ft (900 m), Mile 22, Denali Highway, or you can take an air taxi to Dickey Lake (E), elevation 2870 ft (875 m). To reach the West Fork, fly to lakes (F) or (G), elevation 2700 ft (820 m), at the headwaters.

Scheduled buses travel the Richardson Highway; air taxis operate from Gakona, Glennallen and Paxson. Food and lodging are readily available at roadside businesses and at Gakona, Glennallen and Paxson.

41 Harding Lake State Recreation Area

Location: Eastern Alaska, southeast of Fairbanks; 64°25′N 146°50′W
Size: 95 acres (38 hectares)
High point/low point: 720 ft (220 m)

Best time of year; Foot, May–October; boat, June–September; ski, February–April
USGS map: Big Delta B-6
Established: 1980
Managed by: Alaska Division of Parks

Harding Lake.

A large lake surrounded by rolling hills of spruce, birch and aspen, Harding is one of the few large Interior Alaska lakes accessible from the road system. The highly developed Recreation Area is excellent for families with small children. The water level in the lake has dropped significantly, creating a shoreline with a very shallow gradient. Deep water is at least 0.25 mi (0.4 km) from the water's edge, so the warm lake waters are a safe place for family play.

Numerous birds nest along the shores and in the surrounding boreal forest. Watch for muskrats in the lake and for forest animals—moose, black bears, red foxes, snowshoe hares, lynx, porcupines, grouse, flying squirrels and red squirrels.

Harding Lake has picnic tables, a shelter, a boat ramp, drinking water, toilets and an RV waste dump. Horseshoes, volleyballs, nets and baseballs can be checked out at the ranger station. Swimming, fishing, ice fishing, hiking, cross-country skiing and snowshoeing are popular activities. Camping is permitted only in the campground (89 units) and at a walk-in campsite; campfires are restricted to campground fire pits. Snowmobiles (when there is sufficient snow cover) and powerboats are permitted; hunting, trapping, firearms, horses, off-road vehicles and aircraft are prohibited.

The warm, dry summers of the subarctic continental climate make this a popular playground for Fairbanks and Delta Junction residents. Winters are cold, dry and severe. (See the Fairbanks weather table.) Winds are normally light. Daylight on June 21 is 21½ hours, on December 22, 4½ hours.

Since this is Interior Alaska, expect large populations of mosquitoes and other biting insects in June and July. As the lake waters warm, swimmers may contract "swimmer's itch."

The Recreation Area, 42 mi (68 km) southeast of Fairbanks, is reached from Mile 321.5, Richardson Highway, between Fairbanks and Delta Junction, by a 1.4-mi (2.3-km) side road leading from the highway. (Don't be confused by Harding Lake Road, an access to summer homes near Mile 320.) Scheduled buses travel between Fairbanks and Delta Junction; automobiles can be rented in Fairbanks. Roadside businesses provide food and lodging, as do Fairbanks and Delta Junction.

Hazy Islands Refuge, Alaska Maritime National Wildlife Refuge

42

Location: Southeastern Alaska, south of Sitka; 55°54′N 134°36′W
Size: 32 acres (13 hectares)
High point: Estimated 500 ft (150 m)
Low point: Sea level

Best time of year: May–September
USGS map: Craig
Established: 1912
Managed by: U.S. Fish and Wildlife Service

Far offshore in the Gulf of Alaska, this refuge consists only of four or five exposed rocks with little vegetation, but it provides a predator-free nesting area for large numbers of common murres, glaucous-winged gulls, pigeon guillemots, tufted puffins and horned puffins. Brandt's cormorants, which nest on only one other island in Alaska, are also found here.

The rocks, 10 mi (16 km) west of Coronation Island Wilderness, are isolated, without landing or camping sites, shelter or water. Frequent storms and violent wind

Big Hazy Island. (U.S. Fish and Wildlife Service photo by Arthur Sowls)

squalls make boating hazardous. Visitors are not encouraged; restrictions may be in effect, so contact the Refuge Manager before planning a trip. Originally a separate refuge, the islands became a part of the Alaska Maritime National Wildlife Refuge in 1980.

The maritime climate brings cool, wet summers and mild, wet winters. (See Sitka weather table.) Winds are moderate to strong. Daylight on June 21 is 17½ hours, on December 22, 7 hours.

The Hazy Islands are extremely remote and hard to reach. Air taxis operate from Ketchikan, Petersburg, Sitka and Wrangell; boat charters are available at most coastal communities. Food and lodging are found at Craig, Ketchikan, Klawock, Petersburg, Sitka and Wrangell.

43 Iditarod National Historic Trail

Location: Southcentral, Central and Western Alaska, from Seward to Nome

National Historic Trail System: 2264 mi (3645 km)

High point: 3400 ft (1000 m)

Low point: Sea level

Best time of year: Foot, June–September (Seward–Anchorage area); winter travel, February–March

USGS maps: (East to west) Seward, Anchorage, Tyonek, Talkeetna, Lime Hills, McGrath, Medfra, Iditarod, Ophir, Ruby, Nulato, Unalakleet, Norton Bay, Solomon, Nome

Established as National Historic Trail: 1978

Coordinators: Alaska Division of Parks and Bureau of Land Management

Mail carrier on Iditarod Trail, taken between 1915 and 1925. (Photo courtesy of the Anchorage Historical and Fine Arts Museum)

Although portions of the Iditarod route have been used for centuries by Eskimos and Athabascan Indians, it was thousands of Outsiders, attracted by gold strikes at the turn of the century, who created a major winter trail network connecting Seward and Nome. The first substantial gold strike, on the north shore of the Kenai Peninsula in 1889, attracted large numbers of prospectors who soon stamped out trails in the valleys. Ten years later, the famous gold-bearing sands of Nome's beaches started another stampede. With land and waters locked in snow and ice for eight months of the year, an alternative to summer river travel was necessary, and the winter trail was born. Eventually the trail took the name of the active Iditarod mining district. The southern portion of the trail, near Seward, was first marked about 1890, the remainder surveyed and marked after 1907.

Soon roadhouses sprang up, spaced about 20 mi (30 km) apart along the trail—about the distance that could be traveled in a winter's day by dogsled. From 1914 to 1921, the trail was also used by mushers who contracted to carry the U.S. mail. The Iditarod had a final surge of glory in the winter of 1924-25, when a relay of 20 dog mushers rushed serum from Nenana to diphtheria-stricken Nome, 674 mi (1085 km), in a record 127½ hours. After 1925, when air travel reached Alaska, freighting and extensive travel over the trail nearly ceased.

Of this trail network, 2264 mi (3645 km) have been designated as a National Historic Trail. The primary route from Seward to Nome is 938 mi (1510 km) long. Popular uses of the trail system today include hiking, skiing, dog mushing and snowmobiling. Since much of the route winds west of Anchorage through uninhabited river valleys, vast wetlands and coastal flatlands, winter travel is the most appropriate. Some sections of the trail, not yet included in the National Trail system, cross private lands or mining claims. Trail easements exist in most of these areas,

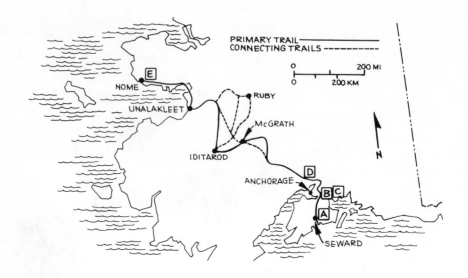

but travelers and campers must remain on the easements. Campfires are generally permitted on public lands, but are specifically prohibited in Chugach State Park. Severe avalanche hazard exists along mountainous portions of the trail. Prepare carefully for winter travel; temperatures can drop well below −40°F (−40°C) between Anchorage and Nome. (Since the trail crosses several climatic regions, refer to the descriptions of nearby parklands and the weather tables for weather information.)

A few small sections of the trail south of Anchorage are popular summer hiking trails. Much of the remainder of the southern part of the historic route is part of the state highway system. Villagers along the northern half use the trail for winter travel between villages.

A major segment of the trail, with a length officially designated as 1049 mi (1688 km), has been used since 1973 for the annual Iditarod Trail Sled Dog Race from Anchorage to Nome. The mushers vie for $100,000 in prize money, with the first-place musher receiving $24,000. The record time stands at 12 days, 8 hours, 45 minutes and 2 seconds, set by Rick Swenson in 1981.

Marked portions of the Iditarod Trail accessible from the road system are: (A) Johnson Pass Trail, Chugach National Forest, a 21-mi (34-km) hiking trail with trailheads at Mile 32.5 and Mile 63.8, Seward Highway. (B) Crow Pass/Eagle River Trail, Chugach National Forest and Chugach State Park, a 20-mi (32-km) hiking trail with trailheads at Mile 5.5, Crow Pass Road (from Girdwood) and Mile 12, Eagle River Road (from Eagle River). The U.S. Forest Service maintains a public-use recreational cabin at Crow Pass (reservations rquired, fee). The Chugach State Park visitors' center is at the Eagle River trailhead. (C) Indian Pass/Ship Creek Trail, Chugach State Park, a 21-mi (34-km) hiking or ski touring trail with trailheads accessible from Mile 103, Seward Highway (a 1-mi [2-km] side road leads north to the trailhead) and Mile 5, Glenn Highway (follow the Arctic Valley Ski Bowl Road 6 mi [10 km] to the trailhead). (D) Knik/Finger Lake Trail, a 100-mi (160-km) dog mushing or ski touring trail starting from Mile 13.5, Knik-Goose Bay Road (from Wasilla). The Nome to Council Road (E) parallels the Iditarod Trail for 33 mi (53 km) between Nome and Solomon.

Suggested reading: Tim Jones, *The Last Great Race* (Seattle: Madrona Publishers, Inc., 1982).

44 Independence Mine State Historic Park

Location: Southcentral Alaska, northwest of Palmer; 61°47′N 149°17′W
Size: 272 acres (110 hectares)
High point: 3400 ft (1000 m)
Low point: 3200 ft (980 m)

Best time of year: Foot, June–September; ski, October–April
USGS map: Anchorage D-7
Established: 1979
Managed by: Alaska Division of Parks

Weather-bleached frame buildings stand ghost-like on the foggy tundra, surrounded by the craggy Talkeetna Mountains; at the mine shafts, high on perpendicular cliffs, more buildings cling to imperceptible niches. Originally staked in 1907 by the Alaska Gold Quartz Mining Company, the claims, known as the Independence

Abandoned buildings at Independence Mine, 1970.

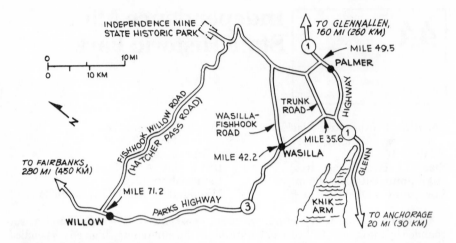

Mines, were transferred to the Alaska-Pacific Consolidated Mining Company in 1933. From then to 1943, they yielded more than 10,300 lb (4670 kg) of gold, making them the second largest lode-gold producer in Alaska (the Alaska-Juneau Gold Mining Company was larger). Wartime priorities closed the mines during World War II, and later attempts to re-open them failed. The mine buildings were placed on the National Register of Historic Places in 1974.

Entirely above treeline and sitting in a bowl-shaped valley at the headwaters of Fishhook Creek, the Independence Mine area is renowned for having the earliest and lightest accessible powder snow in the area, attracting cross-country skiers from all over Southcentral Alaska. (Caution: Avalanches can occur.) Although the Park occupies only a small area, the entire valley is popular with summer visitors for picnicking, berry-picking, hiking and hang gliding. Tundra wildflowers are at their best in late June and early July. Wildlife is rather sparse, but watch for marmots, mountain goats and Dall sheep, brown (grizzly) bears, caribou, wolves and wolverines.

Facilities include a visitors' center and museum. Until restoration is complete, visitors are not permitted to wander within the buildings. Camping is permitted, although campfires are not; use a camping stove. Hunting, horses, snowmobiles and off-road vehicles are prohibited. Numerous mining claims and private lands exist in the area, so ask before picking up rocks or panning for gold; obey "No Trespassing" signs.

Astride the transition from a subarctic maritime to a subarctic continental climate, the mine area has cool, frequently overcast, summers and cold, clear winters. (See the Anchorage weather table.) Winds are normally light. Daylight on June 21 is 20 hours, on December 22, 5 hours.

The Park is accessible by automobile from the Fishhook-Willow Road (Hatcher Pass Road), which can be reached from four state highway points: (1) Mile 49.5, Glenn Highway, intersection with the Fishhook-Willow Road, 1 mi (2 km) north of Palmer; the Park is 18 mi (29 km) away. (2) Mile 35.6, Parks Highway, intersection with Trunk Road, 0.3 mi (0.5 km) north of the junction of the Parks and Glenn highways. Follow Trunk Road 6.6 mi (10.6 km) to its intersection with Fishhook-Willow Road. (3) Mile 42.2, Parks Highway, intersection with Wasilla-Fishhook Road (Wasilla's Main Street). Follow it north 10.5 mi (17 km) to the Fishhook-Willow Road. (4) Mile 71.2, Parks Highway at Willow, intersection with the west end of the Fishhook-Willow Road (Hatcher Pass Road); the park is about 32 mi (51 km) away. Not maintained in winter, the road over Hatcher Pass from Willow is normally plowed for only the first 17 mi (27 km). By mid-June, the full length is open. The other accesses are open year-round.

Rental cars are available in Anchorage; groceries, gas, restaurants and lodging are found at roadside businesses along the highways and in Palmer, Wasilla and Willow. One or two lodges operate near Independence Mine.

Suggested reading: Claus M. Naske, "Transition: Economic to Recreational Resource II, Hatcher Pass" (*Northern Engineer*, vol. 10 [4], pp. 16-25); David and Brenda Stone, *Hard Rock Gold* (Juneau: City of Juneau, 1980); U.S. Geological Survey, *Geology and Ore Deposits of the Willow Creek Mining District, Alaska*, USGS Bulletin No. 1004 (Washington, D.C.: U.S. Government Printing Office, 1954).

45 Innoko National Wildlife Refuge and Wilderness

Location: Western Alaska, east of Unalakleet; 63°N 158°W
Size: 3,850,000 acres (1 558 000 hectares)
High point: 1330 ft (400 m)
Low point: 50 ft (15 m)

Best time of year: Foot, June–September; boat, June–September; ski, March–April
USGS maps: Holy Cross, Iditarod, Nulato, Ophir, Unalakleet
Established: 1980
Managed by: U.S. Fish and Wildlife Service

Lying in two parts along the east bank of the Yukon River, the Refuge is 80% wetlands, with muskeg, islands of black spruce, lakes and meandering rivers and streams. Rolling hills border the river. In the southeastern corner of the Refuge, 1,240,000 acres (502 000 hectares) are designated as Wilderness. The lands, transitional between the open tundra of western Alaska and the boreal forest of interior

Innoko River. (U.S. Fish and Wildlife Service photo by Jo Keller)

Alaska, are used by locals for subsistence food and supplies. Russian fur traders set up a post at Nulato in 1838, but long before that, local Indians traded fine beaver pelts with coastal Eskimos. Yukon River salmon continues to be a staple food for both humans and dogs.

A major nesting area for waterfowl, the Refuge harbors more than 380,000 ducks and 65,000 geese each summer; of the 338 species of birds found in Alaska, 140 can be found in the Refuge. Most abundant species are pintails, widgeon, scaup, white-fronted geese and Canada geese. In addition to the 20,000 beavers, other furbearers thrive in this wet refuge, as do moose and black bear. Found here also are caribou, brown (grizzly) bears, coyotes, red foxes, lynx, wolves and wolverines. So are large numbers of another choice Alaskan wildlife species — mosquitoes.

The Refuge is roadless and undeveloped. Camping is unrestricted on public lands, although dry campsites may be difficult to find; campfires are permitted. Numerous private lands exist within the boundaries — do not disturb buildings, fish camps or equipment. Hunting, fishing, powerboats, snowmobiles and fixed-wing aircraft landings are permitted.

River travel: Yukon River, FWB within the Refuge; Innoko River, FWB within the Refuge.

Expect warm, dry summers and cold, dry, severe winters in this subarctic continental climate. (See the Galena weather table.) Winds are normally light. Daylight on June 21 is 24 hours, on December 22, 0 hours with about 6 hours of twilight.

Access to the Refuge is by air taxi from Galena or Grayling or by charter boat, available informally at most villages in the area. Scheduled air service is available to Anvik, Flat, Galena, Grayling, Kaltag, Koyukuk and Nulato, all of which have general stores. Galena has lodging; Koyukuk and Nulato prefer not to have tourists.

Suggested reading: William Loyens, *The Changing Culture of the Nulato Koyukon* (Madison: University of Wisconsin Press, 1970); Lael Morgan, *And the Land Provides: Alaska Natives in a Year of Transition* (New York: Anchor Press, 1974); U.S. Department of the Interior, *Proposed Koyukuk National Wildlife Refuge*, Final Environmental Impact Statement (Washington, D.C.: U.S. Government Printing Office, 1974; includes Innoko).

Mosquitoes on tent — waiting. (National Park Service photo by Jim Morris)

Ivishak River. (National Park Service photo)

46 Ivishak National Wild River

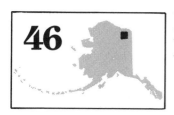

Location: Northeastern Alaska, in the Arctic National Wildlife Refuge; 69°05′N 147°30′W
River rating: WW1-FWC
Popular trip lengths: 95 to 150 mi (150 to 240 km)
Best time of year: July
Annual high water: June

USGS maps: Arctic D-5; Philip Smith Mountains D-1; Sagavanirktok A-1, A-2, B-2, B-3, (Sagavanirktok River continuation) C-3, D-3; Beechy Point A-3
Designated as Wild River: 1980
Managed by: U.S. Fish and Wildlife Service

A float down the Ivishak provides an intimate view of Alaska's famous North Slope. A highly braided swift river on the treeless arctic tundra, the Ivishak flows north toward the Arctic Ocean. During periods of low water, lining may be necessary from Porcupine Lake at the headwaters to the main river, as well as on portions of the main river itself. By continuing down the Sagavanirktok River, the boater traverses a cross-section of Alaska's North Slope, from the crest of the Brooks Range north to the Arctic Ocean. From Porcupine Lake (A) to the Sagavanirktok River (B) is 95 mi

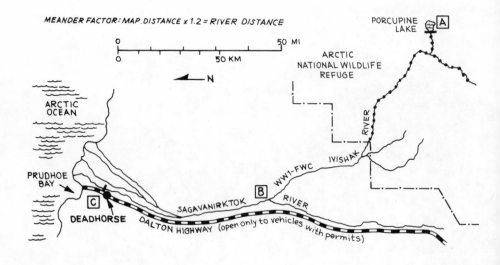

(150 km); to Deadhorse (C) another 55 mi (88 km). "Ivishak" means "red earth"; "Sagavanirktok" means "swift current."

The upper half of the Ivishak flows through tundra-covered mountains with excellent hiking terrain. The lower river and the Sagavanirktok cross a broad open floodplain with scrub willow. Extensive overflow ice accumulates on the floodplain and remains much of the summer. Scout the channel before running it to be sure it doesn't disappear under the ice shelf. Wild River designation extends for the first 45 mi (72 km).

The open vistas are excellent for spotting caribou as well as the numerous raptors that search endlessly for lemmings, voles and ground squirrels. Moose and willow ptarmigan usually stay in river willow thickets. Watch also for brown (grizzly) bears, arctic foxes, red foxes, Dall sheep, wolves and wolverine—and perhaps musk-oxen. The waters support arctic char, grayling and burbot.

Camping is unrestricted; the area is treeless, so carry a camping stove. Fishing, hunting, snowmobiles and fixed-wing aircraft landings are permitted. The North Slope can be mosquitoville, so pack lots of repellent and a head net.

Because of the pack ice in the Arctic Ocean to the north, a pervading coolness affects even the warmest summer sun. The arctic climate is transitional between continental and maritime: summers are cool and dry, with frequent fog near the coast. (See the Galbraith weather table.) Winds are generally light to moderate in the mountains and often strong near the coast. Daylight on June 21 is 24 hours, on December 22, 0 hours, but with several hours of twilight.

To reach the river, take an air taxi to Porcupine Lake (A), elevation 3000 ft (910 m). Leave the river by air taxi from lakes or gravel bars on the lower Ivishak (B), elevation 600 ft (180 m), or, if regulations permit, by automobile from the Dalton Highway, just north of Pump Station 2, at about Mile 370, where the Sagavanirktok River closely parallels the road. As of 1983, this rigorous unpaved highway, originally known as the North Slope Haul Road, is closed to the public northbound at Mile 211, 155 mi (249 km) north of the Yukon River. An alternative take-out point is 55 mi (89 km) downstream at Deadhorse (C), elevation 43 ft (13 m), the airport and commercial center for the Prudhoe Bay oilfield development. Scheduled air service, food and lodging are available at Deadhorse, Fort Yukon and Barter Island (Kaktovik). Air taxis operate from Barter Island and Fort Yukon.

47

Izembek
National Wildlife Refuge
and Wilderness

Location: Southwestern Alaska, on the Alaska Peninsula; 55°N 163°W
Size: 320,893 acres (129 861 hectares)
High point: 5784 ft (1763 m)
Low point: Sea level

Best time of year: Foot, May–September; boat, May–September; ski, January–March
USGS map: Cold Bay
Established: 1960
Managed by: U.S. Fish and Wildlife Service

Hugging the north shore of the tip of the Alaska Peninsula, the largest eelgrass beds in the world supply food for nearly the entire North American population of migrating black brant. From mid-April until about May 20 and again from August to early November, these geese, up to 200,000 strong, feed in the Refuge on the way to and from their northern nesting grounds. Large concentrations of other waterfowl and shorebirds also use the large saltwater lagoons, notably emperor geese, Taverner's Canada geese, cackling Canada geese, bald eagles, pintails, mallards, oldsquaws, harlequin ducks and rock sandpipers, as well as a non-migratory population of about 600 whistling swans. Steller's eiders are the most abundant wintering duck.

Aghileen Pinnacles. (U.S. Fish and Wildlife Service photo)

Harbor seals search the lagoons, brown (grizzly) bears patrol the beaches and streams for spawning salmon and caribou roam the treeless uplands. Watch also for wolves, wolverines, red foxes, land otters, porcupines and arctic hares. Offshore look for sea otters, porpoises, sea lions and whales, especially gray whales.

The lagoon was named for Karl Izembek, surgeon aboard the Russian sloop *Moller*. Russian ships wintered in nearby Bechevin Bay in the early 1800s, and their encampment site is still visible inside Hook Bay. Residents trapped furbearers extensively in the area until World War II, when the military moved into the area; quonset huts and scattered fuel barrels now rust in the sea air.

In this area of rolling tundra-covered hills rising on the northeast to the spectacular volcanic Aghileen Pinnacles, a sub-arctic maritime climate prevails, with cool, overcast summers, and cold, dry, severe winters. (See the Cold Bay weather table.) Winds are constant and moderate to strong, with frequent storms or fog often delaying air travel. Violent wind squalls can make the lagoons treacherous for small boats. Daylight on June 21 is 17½ hours, on December 22, 7 hours. Prominent peaks: Frosty Peak, elevation 5784 ft (1763 m); Mount Dutton, elevation 4834 ft (1473 m); Aghileen Pinnacles, elevation 4800 ft (1500 m).

Camping and campfires are unrestricted. Driftwood is available on beaches, but use camping stoves inland. Camp and travel to avoid the many brown bears. Fishing, hunting and horses are permitted. Snowmobiles and any other vehicles are restricted to designated roads. Aircraft may land only below mean high tide, which is outside the Refuge boundary. Motorboats are allowed on the Refuge, but jetboats are not.

Refuge headquarters are in the nearby town of Cold Bay. A 10-mi (16-km) road from town provides access to Izembek Lagoon; travel to other parts of the Refuge is limited to foot and boat. Both Cold Bay and King Cove have scheduled air service and are visited on a limited schedule by the Southwestern Alaska state ferry. A store, a restaurant, lodging and one air taxi are available in Cold Bay.

Suggested reading: Arthur S. Einarsen, *Black Brant: Sea Goose of the Pacific Coast* (Seattle: University of Washington Press, 1965).

48 John National Wild River

Location: Northcentral Alaska, in Gates of the Arctic National Park; 67°30′N 152°20′W
River rating: WW1-3 from Anaktuvuk Pass; WW1-2 from Hunt Fork
Popular trip length: 100 mi (160 km)

Best time of year: July–September
Annual high water: July–August
USGS maps: Chandler Lake, Wiseman D-5, C-5, B-5, B-4, A-4; Bettles D-4
Designated as Wild River: 1980
Managed by: National Park Service

A scenic clearwater river winding from a remote rugged mountain wilderness, the John drops gently from treeless alpine headwaters to richly forested lowlands. The valley is narrow enough to bring the mountains close to the river. Hiking is excellent in the upper river area. From Hunt Fork to Bettles (Evansville) is about 100 mi (160

John River valley. (National Park Service photo by Pat Pourchot)

km). Since the John enters the Koyukuk about 5 mi (8 km) downstream from Bettles, allow a day to line upriver.

Above Hunt Fork, water levels are normally too low to float, although some boaters have portaged and lined from Anaktuvuk Pass. Expect some WW3 rapids, for experienced boaters only. A strenuous but rewarding alternative is to hike the 40 mi (64 km) from Anaktuvuk Pass, arriving in time to meet the boats when they are flown into "Hunt Fork" lake. Expect some difficult stream crossings.

The name "Anaktuvuk" is said to come from the Eskimo word *anaqtoq*, ("dung"), referring to the presence of caribou. Not surprisingly, the John River valley is a major migration route between their summer and winter ranges. Watch also for moose, brown (grizzly) bears, black bears, Dall sheep, wolves, coyotes, wolverines, red foxes and lynx.

Camping along the river is generally best on river bars. Build campfires on river gravel, not on tundra; better still, carry a camping stove and save the slow-growing northern wood. Since rainstorms upstream can quickly raise river levels several feet, be careful where you set up camp and store gear. Expect hungry mosquitoes until

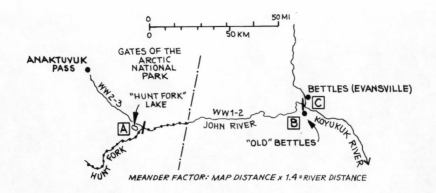

MEANDER FACTOR: MAP DISTANCE x 1.4 = RIVER DISTANCE

mid-August. Fishing, firearms, fixed-wing aircraft and powerboats are permitted; hunting is not.

Summers in the mountains can be cool and overcast, becoming warmer and drier toward the lowlands. (See the Wiseman weather table.) Winds are generally light. Daylight on June 21 is 24 hours, on December 22, 0 hours, with 5 hours of twilight.

To reach the river, take an air taxi from Bettles (Evansville) (C) to "Hunt Fork" lake (A), elevation 1149 ft (350 m). Leave the river by air taxi from "old" Bettles (B), elevation 600 ft (200 m), at the mouth of the John, or line upstream to Bettles (Evansville) (C). Bettles (Evansville) and Anaktuvuk Pass have scheduled air service and general stores; the former also has lodging and a dining room.

Suggested reading: Robert Marshall, *Alaska Wilderness: Exploring the Central Brooks Range* (Berkeley: University of California Press, 1970; originally published in 1956 as *Arctic Wilderness*).

49 Kachemak Bay State Park

Location: Southcentral Alaska, southern tip of the Kenai Peninsula; 59°25′N 151°15′W
Size: 350,000 acres (142 000 hectares)
High point: 4233 ft (1290 m)
Low point: Sea level

Best time of year: Foot, May–October; boat, April–October; ski, February–March
USGS map: Seldovia
Established: 1970
Managed by: Alaska Division of Parks

With noisy seabird and seal rookeries, spawning streams and important saltwater nurseries, this park protects a wide variety of wildlife habitats. Precipitous peaks, immense glaciers and the Harding Icefield make for spectacular scenery.

The region appears to have been occupied by Eskimos in the eighth century B.C. In 1778, Captain James Cook explored Kachemak Bay; in 1795, Russians established a sawmill here. The community of Halibut Cove, center of a thriving fishing industry from 1911 to 1928, is today home for some of Alaska's finest artists and craftspersons.

Sailing on Kachemak Bay, Kachemak Bay State Park and Grewingk Glacier in background.

Watch for moose, black bears, brown (grizzly) bears, mountain goats, wolves, bald eagles, seabirds, dolphins, porpoises, seals, sea lions and whales. Avoid disturbing the seabird and seal rookeries.

Except for a primitive campground (5 units) with pit toilets and 6 mi (10 km) of marked trail from Glacier Spit to near Grewingk Glacier, no visitors' facilities have been developed. Beachcomb, hike to the glaciers, climb the mountains or ski tour— this is some of the finest wilderness available in Southcentral Alaska. Back-country camping is unrestricted; campfires are permitted. Avoid trespassing on the numerous private landholdings scattered along the Kachemak Bay shoreline. Fishing and hunting are permitted; the use of horses, snowmobiles and off-road vehicles and the landing of fixed-wing aircraft are not. A few areas are closed to powerboats. Use caution crossing Kachemak Bay in small boats; winds can build large waves in a short time. Williwaws can occur in Sadie Cove and Tutka Bay. Expect tidal fluctuations of up to 28 ft (8.5 m). Much of the mountainous area is subject to avalanches.

Weather is controlled by the maritime climate; expect cool, overcast summers and mild, overcast winters. (See the Homer weather table.) Winds are light to moderate at low elevations, often strong on the peaks. Daylight on June 21 is 18½ hours, on December 22, 6 hours. In the rugged maritime mountain range, the densely forested slopes extend to about 1000 ft (300 m); brush continues to 2500 ft (800 m).

Air taxis, charter boats and excursion boats transport visitors to the Park from Homer and Seldovia. Popular access points are: Glacier Spit; Halibut Cove, from which a 2-mi (3-km) trail leads to Grewingk Glacier; Sadie Cove; Tutka Bay; and a road from Seldovia to Rocky Bay on the Gulf of Alaska coast via Jakolof Bay. Jakolof Bay has a public dock. Both Homer and Seldovia have stores, restaurants and lodging. A number of attractive wilderness lodges lie within or near the Park.

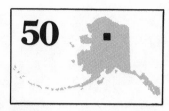

50 Kanuti
National Wildlife Refuge

Location: Central Alaska, south of
 Bettles; 66°30′N 151°30′W
Size: 1,430,000 acres (579 000 hectares)
High point: 3536 ft (1078 m)
Low point: 350 ft (110 m)

Best time of year: Foot,
 June–September; boat,
 June–September; ski, March–April
USGS map: Bettles
Established: 1980
Managed by: U.S. Fish and Wildlife
 Service

In a refuge on the rolling partly forested plain of the Kanuti and Koyukuk rivers, the lakes, ponds and marshes provide nesting habitats for large populations of migratory waterfowl. Alaska's greatest nesting density of white-fronted geese is found here. On the river terraces roam moose, black bears, brown (grizzly) bears, coyotes, red foxes, lynx, wolves and wolverines. Beavers, marten, mink and muskrats

White-fronted goose. (U.S. Fish and Wildlife Service photo by Jo Keller)

live in the wetlands. The Western Arctic caribou herd comes into the area in the winter.

Sithylemenkat Lake, in the southeastern corner of the Refuge, is thought by some scientists to be an ancient meteorite crater.

Camping and campfires are permitted in this undeveloped, roadless refuge. Fishing is permitted throughout; hunting, powerboats, snowmobiles and fixed-wing aircraft are subject to certain restrictions; off-road vehicles are not permitted. The area is extensively used by locals for subsistence hunting and fishing; respect private lands and equipment within the Refuge. Expect large populations of mosquitoes and other biting insects in summer.

River travel: Jim River, WW2, from the Dalton Highway to Allakaket, 130 mi (210 km); Kanuti River, WW1-FWB, from the Dalton Highway to Hughes, 240 mi (390 km); South Fork of the Koyukuk River, WW1 through the Refuge; Fish Creek, WW2, from the Dalton Highway to Allakaket, 130 mi (210 km).

The Refuge has a subarctic continental climate with warm, dry summers and cold, dry, severe winters. (See the Bettles weather table.) Winds are normally light. Daylight on June 21 is 24 hours, on December 22, 2½ hours.

The Refuge can be reached by foot, air or boat. Skirting the eastern boundary, from Mile 123 to Mile 135, the Dalton Highway (North Slope Haul Road) crosses several rivers that flow west through the Refuge. Scheduled air service is available to Allakaket, Bettles (Evansville) and Hughes; air taxis are based at Bettles. Both Allakaket and Bettles have general stores; the latter has a lodge. The village of Hughes prefers not to have tourists.

Katmai National Park and Preserve

Location: Southwestern Alaska, northwest of Kodiak Island; 58°30′N 155°W

Size: 3,955,000 acres (1 601 000 hectares)

High point: 7606 ft (2318 m)

Low point: Sea level

Best time of year: Foot, June–September; boat, June–September; ski (marginal), February–April

USGS maps: Afognak, Iliamna, Karluk, Mt. Katmai, Naknek

Established: 1918

Managed by: National Park Service

Katmai is a land of contrasts: the "moonscape" barrens of the volcanically formed Valley of Ten Thousand Smokes, dense forests with lakes and streams where brown bears fish for salmon, Pacific Ocean shores where eagles soar, spacious rolling tundra lands and snow-capped summits of steaming volcanoes.

In June 1912 Mount Katmai volcano and nearby Novarupta erupted in an incandescent lava flow, burying an entire 20-mi (32-km) valley under ash and pumice. After Mount Katmai collapsed, forming a caldera, a glacier formed within—the only glacier in the world whose date of origin is known.

Archaeological excavations indicate that the area has been occupied by native cultures for at least 4500 years. Originally established as a National Monument,

Waterfall at tidewater, Kukak Bay.

Katmai has received additional lands four times. In 1980, 3,473,000 acres (1 405 000 hectares) of its land were designated as Wilderness.

The largest sanctuary for brown (grizzly) bears in the U.S., Katmai owes its fame to the major red salmon runs in the Naknek River drainage that attract the bears. Most of the bears weigh from 400 to 800 lb (180 to 360 kg). Excellent sportfishing for salmon, rainbow trout, lake trout, northern pike and grayling in the rivers and lakes attracts fishermen from all over the world. The rich forest and tundra lands abound in moose, caribou, red foxes, wolves, wolverines, lynx, river otters, mink, marten, beavers, migratory waterfowl and shorebirds. Bald eagles nest throughout—near lakes and streams inland and on rock spires along the Pacific coast—while offshore swim seals, sea lions, sea otters and whales.

Essentially a roadless wilderness, the Park offers good hiking on volcanic tuff in the Valley of Ten Thousand Smokes; no trails are needed. A 6-mi (10-km) marked trail climbs Dumpling Mountain near Brooks Camp. Wherever salmon are found, bears create well-traveled trails parallel to river and lake shores. The trails make excellent human walking too, but use them cautiously; the bears regard them as their own property and demand right-of-way.

Recreational facilities are concentrated on the lakes west of the Aleutian Range. Concessioner-operated Brooks Camp, Grosvenor Camp and Kulik Lodge each have a lodge, cabins, and a dining room; Brooks Camp also has a convenience store and rents canoes, fishing equipment and guide-operated boats. In addition, at Brooks Camp are a ranger station, interpretive programs and a campground (30 tent spaces) with cooking shelters, fire pits and two caches for food storage. The concessioner rents tents and camping stoves; limited fuel is available. Van tours to the Valley of Ten Thousand Smokes visitors' center leave the Brooks Camp area daily (charge).

Back-country camping and mountaineering in the Park and Preserve are unrestricted, although back-country use permits are required (available from the Brooks Camp ranger station or the King Salmon headquarters). No wood is available in the Valley of Ten Thousand Smokes; since wood in forests may be wet, carry a camping stove. Hunting, firearms and off-road vehicles are not permitted within the Park; powerboats, fixed-wing aircraft and snowmobiles are zoned. In the Preserve, hunting is permitted.

Boating and river travel: Kayaking and canoeing are popular sports on the inland lakes and rivers and on the scenic Pacific coast bays. Stay near shore on the large lakes; sudden winds can whip lake surfaces to white water. Bay of Islands lake trip: FWA, from Brooks Camp to the Bay of Islands in Naknek Lake and return, 40 mi (64 km); "Savonoski Loop," WW2-FWA, from Brooks Camp to Grosvenor Lake, down Savonoski River and return to Brooks Camp on Naknek Lake, 72 mi (116 km) with a 1-mi (1.6-km) portage; Alagnak National Wild River, WW3-FWC, see description.

The maritime climate brings cool rainy summers with warmer, somewhat drier weather inland. Winters are mild and wet near the coast, cooler and drier inland. (See the King Salmon weather table.) Winds are frequently strong, with heavy storms lasting several days accompanied by violent winds; anticipate delays if you travel by air taxi. Daylight on June 21 is 18½ hours, on December 22, 6 hours. Prominent peaks: Mount Denison, elevation 7606 ft (2318 m); Mount Griggs (Knife Peak), elevation 7600 ft (2300 m); Mount Mageik, elevation 7250 ft (2210 m); Mount Katmai, elevation 6715 ft (2047 m).

Most common access to Katmai is by air from King Salmon, which has daily scheduled air service from Anchorage. Frequent amphibious flights connect to Brooks Camp. Air taxis based at King Salmon, Naknek, Kulik Lodge or Kodiak can give scenic tours or transport visitors to drop-off points throughout the Park. A 10-mi (16-km) gravel road connects King Salmon with Lake Camp, on Naknek Lake just inside the western boundary at the head of Naknek River, but it is not connected with the contiguous state highway system. Both King Salmon and Naknek provide food

Brown (grizzly) bear, Brooks River.

and lodging. Several small fishing lodges on private lands within the Preserve also provide accommodations (reservations required).

Suggested reading: Dave Bohn, *Rambles Through an Alaskan Wild: Katmai and the Valley of the Smokes* (Santa Barbara, Calif.: Capra Press, 1979); Dale Brown, *Wild Alaska* (New York: Time-Life Books, 1972); Robert F. Griggs, *The Valley of Ten Thousand Smokes* (Washington, D.C.: The National Geographic Society, 1922); John A. Hussey, *Embattled Katmai: A History of Katmai National Monument* (San Francisco: National Park Service, U.S. Department of the Interior, 1971); Susan Hackley Johnson, *Exploring Katmai National Monument and the Valley of Ten Thousand Smokes* (Anchorage: Alaska Travel Publications, 1976).

52  Kenai Fjords National Park

Location: Southcentral Alaska, southwest of Seward; 60°N 150°W
Size: 587,000 acres (238 000 hectares)
High point: 6340 ft (1932 m)
Low point: Sea level

Best time of year: Foot, mid-June–August; boat, late April–early August; ski, February–April
USGS maps: Blying Sound, Kenai, Seldovia, Seward
Established: 1980
Managed by: National Park Service

176

Boasting snowy peaks with glaciers grinding to the sea, steep-walled fjords and the massive Harding Icefield, the Kenai Fjords is one of Alaska's most scenic—and treacherous—parklands. The Kenai Mountains, pressed toward the ocean by tectonic forces, front on the stormy Gulf of Alaska.

Many of the Park's glaciers are rapidly retreating. McCarty Glacier has receded more than 20 mi (32 km) since 1910. Starting at one of the glaciers, follow the colonization of plant life on the barren moraine, from the first tenuous lichens near the ice masses to the full climactic richness of the stately coastal forests.

Mountain goats feed on the crags. In the lowlands roam moose, black bears, coyotes, wolverines and red foxes. Brown (grizzly) bears are found in the Resurrection River valley and on hillsides bordering Resurrection Bay. Bald eagles are widespread, while tufted puffins, horned puffins, kittiwakes, murres and auklets nest abundantly in Aialik and Harris bays. Harbor seals congregate at the heads of most fjords, while sea lions breed on offshore islands. Watch the coastal waters for sea otters and whales.

Camping and campfires are permitted throughout. Expect wet weather and strong winds, especially along the coast; hypothermia is a constant danger. Hiking, except in the Resurrection River valley, is difficult because of the steep terrain; mountaineering is unrestricted. In winter, heavy snows or rain often produce severe avalanche hazard. Boaters will find few beaches or well-protected bays. Fishing, firearms, horses, powerboats, fixed-wing aircraft and snowmobiles are all permitted; hunting and off-road vehicles are not.

Exit Glacier.

Harbor seals lounging on iceberg, Kenai Fjords. (National Park Service photo by M. Woodbridge Williams)

The maritime climate brings cool, wet summers and mild, wet winters. (See the Seward weather table.) Winds are light in protected areas, moderate to strong on exposed headlands, ridges and peaks. Extensive storm systems isolate the fjords after late August. Daylight on June 21 is 19 hours, on December 22, 6 hours.

The Park is accessible from an 8-mi (13-km) road up the Resurrection River valley from Mile 3, Seward Highway. A bridge over the river provides access to Exit Glacier and the nearby ranger station. The fjords themselves are hazardous; all front on the unpredictable Gulf of Alaska and have strong tidal currents, poorly charted bays and uncharted rocks. Only experienced boaters should attempt to visit these waters. If you depend on an air taxi or charter boat, weather and high seas can delay your pickup for days or even weeks.

An hour or two of "flight-seeing" from Seward or Homer or a day-long charter cruise are the most popular ways to view the outer coast. The Southwestern Alaska state ferry between Seward and Kodiak provides views of the Park but does not stop. Stores, restaurants and modern lodgings are available in Seward and Homer.

Suggested reading: Edgar P. Bailey, "Distribution and Abundance of Marine Birds and Mammals along the South Side of the Kenai Peninsula, Alaska" (*The Murrelet*, Vol. 59 [1978], 82-91); U.S. Department of the Interior, *Proposed Harding Icefield–Kenai Fjords National Monument*, Final Environmental Impact Statement (Washington, D.C.; U.S. Government Printing Office, 1974).

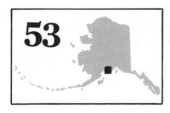

53

Kenai
National Wildlife Refuge
and Wilderness

Location: Southcentral Alaska, Kenai
   Peninsula; 60°30′N 150°10′W
Size: 1,970,000 acres (797 000 hectares)
High point: 6612 ft (2015 m)
Low point: Sea level

Best time of year: Foot, May–October;
   boat, June–September; ski,
   February–April
USGS maps: Kenai, Seldovia, Seward
Established: 1941
Managed by: U.S. Fish and Wildlife
   Service

Covering a long, broad swath of the western Kenai Peninsula, the Refuge was originally known as the Kenai National Moose Range. Its name was changed in 1980, when 240,000 acres (97 100 hectares) of land were added; 1,350,000 acres (546 300 hectares) of the combined lands were designated as wilderness. A vast system of mountains, forests, rolling hills, wetlands, rivers, streams and lakes supports several large fish and wildlife populations, particularly salmon and moose. Large areas

Swan Lake Canoe Route.

of the Refuge have burned, the two most recent large fires occurring in 1947 and 1969. While fires destroy much of value, moose benefit, since the new growth of willow, aspen and birch appeals to their taste. Moose are most likely to be seen along the road system in winter and spring, when snow drives them to the lowlands. Eighty percent of North America's trumpeter swan population nests in Alaska, with 25 to 30 pairs nesting on the shallow lakes of the Refuge each year. Watch also for Dall sheep, mountain goats, caribou, black bears, brown (grizzly) bears, wolves, wolverines, beavers, bald eagles, loons, ptarmigan and grouse. The Swanson River area contains producing oil wells, the first to supply oil in Alaska in commercial quantities.

A popular recreation area for Cook Inlet area residents and visitors, Kenai offers picnicking, berry-picking, fishing, hunting, hiking, backpacking, camping, boating, river running, ski touring, snowmobiling and mountaineering. Particularly popular are the Swan Lake and Swanson River canoe routes, chains of more than 40 lakes, two rivers and numerous wetlands in the northern part of the Refuge; these are gentle waters for novice boaters. Horses are permitted throughout; off-road vehicles are prohibited. Use of powerboats, snowmobiles and aircraft is restricted in some areas. In mountainous regions, winter travelers may encounter severe avalanche hazard.

Facilities include 18 picnic sites, 7 campgrounds (264 units), 10 boat ramps, a visitors' center in Soldotna, interpretive displays and more than 200 mi (300 km) of marked trails. Additional camping space is available at commercial roadside campgrounds; back-country camping is unrestricted. Campfires are permitted except when forest fire danger is high.

Boating and river travel: Kenai River, WW3-FWA, from Kenai Lake to the city of Kenai, 90 mi (145 km); Swan Lake Canoe Route, FWA, numerous routes up to 60 mi (97 km) long; Swanson River Canoe Route, FWA, numerous routes up to 80 mi (129 km) long. On Skilak and Tustumena Lakes, boaters should stay near shore; several lives have been lost in the large waves and white water generated by sudden violent winds.

Weather patterns in the Refuge are typical of a subarctic maritime climate: cool summers and frequent overcast near the coast and mountains, warmer and sunnier inland on the rolling hills. Winters are cold, especially inland. (See the Kenai weather table.) Winds are generally light in the mountain valleys (but with the possibility of williwaws) and moderate to strong near the coast and on mountain peaks. Daylight on June 21 is 19 hours, on December 22, 6 hours. The highest peak within the Refuge is Truuli Peak, elevation 6612 ft (2015 m), in the heavily glaciated backbone of the Kenai Mountains along the southeastern boundary of the Refuge; here, too, is the massive Harding Icefield.

The paved Sterling Highway, from Mile 54.7 to Mile 76, about 120 mi (190 km) from Anchorage, runs through the heart of the Refuge. Major side roads, mostly unpaved, are: Skilak Lake Loop Road, 18 mi (29 km); Swanson River and Swanson Lake roads, a total of 35 mi (56 km); North Kenai Road (see Captain Cook State Recreation Area); Tustumena Lake Road, from the Kasilof area, 6 mi (10 km) long. Scheduled buses travel the Sterling Highway from Anchorage to Soldotna and Kenai; scheduled air service is available to Homer, Kenai and Soldotna. Air taxis are based at Cooper Landing, Homer, Kenai, Seward and Soldotna; charter boats at Homer, Soldotna and Sterling. A small passenger ferry, primarily used by sport fishermen, crosses the Kenai River from Mile 55, Sterling Highway to the mouth of the Russian River. Rental cars are available in Anchorage and Kenai; restaurants and lodging are found at numerous roadside businesses and in Homer, Kenai, Soldotna and Sterling.

Suggested reading: Alaska Geographic, *Cook Inlet Country* (Anchorage: Alaska Northwest Publishing Co., 1977); Helen Nienhueser and Nancy Simmerman, *55 Ways to the Wilderness in Southcentral Alaska* (Seattle: The Mountaineers, 1978); Cornelius Osgood, *The Ethnography of the Tanaina* (New Haven: Yale University Press, 1966).

54 Klondike Gold Rush National Historical Park

Location: Southeastern Alaska, at Skagway; 59°30′N 135°20′W and Seattle, Washington
Size: 13,000 acres (5300 hectares)
High point: 3500 ft (1100 m)
Low point: Sea level

Best time of year: Skagway and Seattle, any time; Chilkoot Trail, late June–early September
Maps: USGS, Skagway B-1, C-1; Canadian maps (1:50,000 scale), Skagway 104 M/11 East, 104 M/14 East
Established: 1980
Managed by: National Park Service

Four far-flung parks in one, this living memorial to the frenzied Gold Rush of 1898 stretches from Seattle to rugged mountains on the Alaska–British Columbia border. Here are the famous town of Skagway, the townsite of Dyea and the rigorous Chilkoot Trail and White Pass, all of which have been placed on the National Register of Historic Landmarks.

Shelter cabin, Canyon City, Chilkoot Trail.

It all started with a note in the Seattle *Post-Intelligencer* on July 17, 1897: "The steamer Portland, headed for Seattle out of St. Michael, Alaska, steamed down to Seattle this morning with a ton of gold aboard." In Seattle, where the word "Gold!" reached the outside world and the rush to the Klondike gold fields began, a visitors' center in Pioneer Square now presents interpretive displays, films and advice.

Up north, Skagway was the end of the line for steamships laden with gold-seekers from Seattle. A boisterous city in its heyday, today Skagway is a viable Alaskan town with many of its original buildings—some with false fronts—boardwalks, dirt streets, a Gold Rush Cemetery, a railroad station, a marina, a museum, a campground and a National Park Service visitors' center. Walking and bus tours of the historic town are available.

Travel over the strenuous and dangerous Chilkoot Trail all but ceased when the White Pass and Yukon Railroad was completed in 1900. Until autumn 1982, the historic narrow-gauge railroad hauled passengers, freight and vehicles between Skagway, Alaska, and Whitehorse in Canada. Economic conditions forced a temporary, perhaps permanent, closure of the line; at press time, the future of the railroad is uncertain. Contact the Park headquarters or the Alaska Division of Tourism for current information.

Klondike Highway 2, 78 years younger than the railroad, also crosses White Pass, paralleling the tracks as it winds up the Skagway River to the 2890-ft (881-m) pass. Canadian customs are near the border 22 mi (35 km) from Skagway; a U.S. customs office is 6 mi (10 km) north of Skagway. The Skagway-Carcross section has not been maintained in winter.

The townsite of Dyea, at tidewater 9 mi (14 km) northwest of Skagway, is the beginning of the Chilkoot Trail. Other than Slide Cemetery, the resting place for more than 60 men and women buried in 1898 by an avalanche on the Chilkoot Pass, few relics remain of the busy frontier town. National Park Service facilities include a ranger information station, campground and parking area.

The Chilkoot Trail climbs over Chilkoot Pass in the rugged Coast Mountains. Beginning at Dyea in a coastal rain forest, the trail snakes upward, gradually steepening, through a rocky, brushy canyon to the foot of barren Chilkoot Pass. The final ascent to the pass, elevation 3739 ft (1140 m), is extremely steep and filled with unstable boulders—a slope more easily climbed than descended.

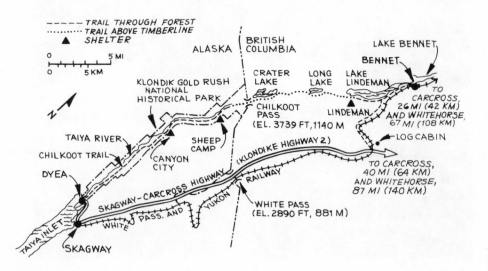

Abandoned boiler, Chilkoot Trail.

You'll cross into Canada at the summit. Within a few miles the summit snow gives way to spacious meadows of alpine tundra, inviting off-trail exploration. The gentle pleasant downgrade continues to Lake Lindeman and Lake Bennett, elevation 2153 ft (656 m). Since you'll be crossing the U.S.-Canadian border, you must clear customs. Check with the Park Service for current regulations concerning hikers on the Chilkoot Trail.

If the railroad is operating, buy your ticket before hiking the trail (none are sold at Lake Bennett, nor are there commercial facilities for hikers) and return to Skagway in scenic comfort. Hikers can also board or get off the train at Carcross and Whitehorse.

To exit via Klondike Highway 2, turn right where the north end of the Chilkoot Trail reaches the railroad and follow the tracks south about 5 mi (8 km) to the highway crossing at Log Cabin, near Kilometer Post 45, 27 mi (43 km) from Skagway. Check the bus schedule or arrange a pickup before starting your hike.

Allow three to four days for the 33-mi (53-km) hike. In summer the trail is crowded. Weather is normally wet and foggy, but the trip is worth every hardship. (See the Skagway weather table.) The maritime climate changes to a drier, warmer subarctic continental climate in Canada. Daylight on June 21 is 18½ hours, on December 22, 6 hours.

Strong winds at the pass can be dangerous. Driving rain, thick fog, deep mud and slick rocks are normal, so prepare for them. Hypothermia is a constant danger. Large residual snowfields at the pass persist into late summer; be sure to wear sunglasses if skies are clear to prevent snowblindness, and use extreme caution if the pass is icy. Despite the large numbers of people hiking the trail, conditions are rugged and can be life-threatening. Feel the presence of the '98ers—they labored under similar conditions with a year's supply of grub and equipment, but you'll have the benefit of today's lightweight equipment and freeze-dried food. Write for National Park Service literature (Skagway office) before tackling the pass. Do not attempt the trip in winter; avalanche hazard can be severe.

Trailside facilities include three drying-out log-cabin shelters with wood stoves. Camp only at one of the 10 designated camping areas (fire rings and pit toilets) or more than 100 ft (30 m) off the trail. Campfires are permitted only at the designated camping areas; otherwise use a camping stove.

All artifacts in the U.S. and Canada are protected; do not collect or damage them. Firearms may not legally be taken into Canada; check guns with the Skagway Police Department or the Royal Canadian Mounted Police before the hike. Hunting, horses and motorized vehicles are prohibited. Dogs must be kept on a leash at all times.

Skagway, Whitehorse and Carcross are on the highway system and have scheduled bus and train service, food and lodging; the first two also have campgrounds, scheduled air service and air taxis. Taxicabs in Skagway can take hikers to the Dyea trailhead. Skagway is a port of call for the Southeastern Alaska state ferry.

Suggested reading: Pierre Berton, *The Klondike Fever, The Life and Death of the Last Great Gold Rush* (New York: Alfred A. Knopf, 1958); Norm Bolotin, *Klondike Lost: A Decade of Photographs by Kinsey & Kinsey* (Anchorage: Alaska Northwest Publishing Co., Alaska Geographic, 1980); Howard Clifford, *The Skagway Story* (Anchorage: Alaska Northwest Publishing Co., 1975); Archie Satterfield, *Chilkoot Pass: The Most Famous Trail in the North* (Anchorage: Alaska Northwest Publishing Co., 1980); David B. Wharton, *The Alaska Gold Rush* (Bloomington: Indiana University Press, 1972).

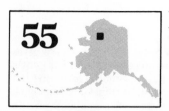

55

Kobuk
National Wild River

Location: Northcentral Alaska, in Gates of the Arctic National Park and Preserve; 66°50′N 154°40′W
River rating: WW1-FWB with portage
Popular trip length: 140 mi (225 km)
Best time of year: July–September

Annual high water: July–August
USGS maps: Survey Pass, Hughes, Shungnak, Shungnak D-2
Designated Wild River: 1980
Managed by: National Park Service

A gentle woodland river draining mountain-rimmed Walker Lake, the Kobuk flows through two scenic canyons in the southern Brooks Range foothills to meander across a broad wetland valley near Kobuk village. The upper reaches offer excellent walking and good mountain vistas, but extensive low-elevation hiking is difficult because of forest underbrush and tussock grass. From Walker Lake to Kobuk village is 140 mi (225 km).

Eskimos fishing for whitefish, Kobuk River. (National Park Service photo by Robert Belous)

185

Canoeing on the Kobuk River. (National Park Service photo by Pat Pourchot)

Just downstream from Walker Lake, a short stretch of WW3-4 white water can be lined or portaged on the east bank. The Lower Kobuk Canyon, with 1 mi (2 km) of WW2-3 rapids, can be lined along the west bank. Below Pah River, local villagers use the river, winter and summer, for travel between villages and for access to fishing and hunting grounds. Numerous private lands, which may not be posted, line the Kobuk; travel quietly and courteously and respect private property.

Watch for woodland animals of the river valley—moose, caribou, black bears, wolves, wolverines, coyotes, beavers, red foxes, lynx, snowshoe hares, northern flying squirrels, red squirrels, porcupines, beavers, marten, mink, muskrats and river otters. Below the Lower Canyon, brown (grizzly) bears fish the river during salmon season.

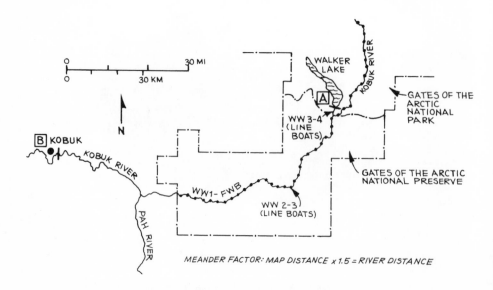

Camping is best on river bars. Expect mosquitoes and other biting insects in summer months. Hunting is permitted in the Preserve but not in the Park. Fishing, firearms, fixed-wing aircraft and powerboats are allowed in both.

The subarctic continental climate brings warm dry summers in the river lowlands, but cooler weather, with more rain, in the mountains. (See the Kotzebue weather table.) Winds are normally light. Daylight on June 21 is 24 hours, on December 22, 2 hours.

To reach the river, take an air taxi from Bettles (Evansville) or Ambler to Walker Lake (A), elevation 637 ft (194 m). Float to Kobuk village (B), elevation 175 ft (53 m), or villages downstream. Scheduled air service serves Bettles, Kobuk, Shungnak, Ambler and most villages beyond, all of which have general stores. Bettles has lodging as well.

Suggested reading: Alaska Geographic, *The Kotzebue Basin* (Anchorage: Alaska Northwest Publishing Co., 1981); J. L. Giddings, *The Arctic Woodland Culture of the Kobuk River* (Philadelphia: University of Philadelphia Museum, 1952) and *Kobuk River People* (College, Alaska: University of Alaska Press and University of Washington, 1961).

56  Kobuk Valley National Park

Location: Northwestern Alaska, east of Kotzebue; 67°30′N 159°30′W
Size: 1,702,000 acres (688 800 hectares)
High point: 4760 ft (1450 m)
Low point: 50 ft (15 m)

Best time of year: Foot, June–September; boat, June–September; ski, March–April
USGS maps: Ambler River, Baird Mountains, Selawik, Shungnak
Established: 1978
Managed by: National Park Service

Nestled at the southern base of the gentle western Brooks Range, the Kobuk River meanders quietly through a broad forested valley that harbors an amazing treasure: sand dunes. The largest group of barchans—shifting, crescent-shaped dunes—covers 25 square miles (65 square kilometers). In this little Sahara in the Arctic, summer air temperatures can soar to more than 100°F (38°C). Today's dunes are an exposed portion of a much larger dune field formed by glaciers to the north during the last Ice Age and now stabilized by subarctic vegetation.

The Kobuk valley region remained ice-free during the glaciation and supported an arctic steppe environment, with grasslands that attracted the large mammals of the Pleistocene. While the animals have vanished, several plants of that epoch have survived on the dunes.

The Kobuk valley has been used by people for subsistence needs and transportation corridors since the Pleistocene. Onion Portage, a short-cut across a sweeping loop in the Kobuk River channel, is one of North America's most important archaeological sites, containing more than 30 layers of artifacts dating as far back as 12,000 years and correlating closely with the beach-ridge artifacts found at Cape Krusenstern National Monument.

Brown (grizzly) bear tracks along Ahnewetut Creek, Kobuk Sand Dunes. (National Park Service photo by Robert Belous)

The Park sits astride the transition between boreal forest and the treeless arctic tundra that extends westward to the Chukchi Sea. The Salmon National Wild River drains southward from the Baird Mountains into the Kobuk River.

Used by the western Arctic caribou herd both summer and winter, the valley is also a major junction of the Asiatic and North American migratory bird flyways. Other animals of the Park include moose, brown (grizzly) bears, black bears, Dall sheep, wolves, wolverines and lynx.

In this undeveloped park, camping is not restricted except in sensitive archaeological areas and on native lands; campfires are permitted. Numerous private lands exist within the boundaries, especially along the river; please respect them. Expect large numbers of mosquitoes and other biting insects in summer months. Fishing, firearms, fixed-wing aircraft, powerboats and snowmobiles are all permitted; sports hunting is not. Good hiking terrain is found in the sand dunes and in the Baird and Waring mountains.

River travel: Kobuk River, FWA within the Park; Salmon National Wild River, WW1, see description.

A subarctic continental climate brings summers that are often warm and dry, winters that are cold, dry and severe. (See the Kotzebue weather table.) Strong winds can make float travel difficult. Daylight on June 21 is 24 hours, on December 22, 1 hour.

A roadless area, the Park is reached by air taxi or boat. Ambler, Kiana and Kotzebue all have air taxis, charter boats, scheduled air service and food; all but Ambler have lodging.

Suggested reading: Alaska Geographic, *The Kotzebue Basin* (Anchorage: Alaska Northwest Publishing Co., 1981); J. L. Giddings, *The Arctic Woodland Culture of the Kobuk River* (Philadelphia: University of Philadelphia Museum, 1952), *Kobuk River People* (College, Alaska: University of Alaska Press and University of Washington, 1961) and *Ancient Men of the Arctic* (New York: Alfred A. Knopf, 1967); U.S. Department of the Interior, *Proposed Kobuk Valley National Monument*, Final Environmental Impact Statement, (Washington, D.C.: U.S. Government Printing Office, 1974).

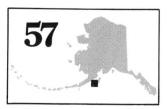

57 Kodiak National Wildlife Refuge

Location: Southwestern Alaska, portions of Kodiak, Afognak and Uganik islands; 57°N 154°W
Size: 1,865,000 acres (754 700 hectares)
High point: 4470 ft (1362 m)
Low point: Sea level

Best time of year: Foot, May–August; boat, May–August; ski (marginal), January–March
USGS maps: Afognak, Kaguyak, Karluk, Kodiak, Trinity islands
Established: 1941
Managed by: U.S. Fish and Wildlife Service

Protecting one of the chief strongholds of the Alaska brown (grizzly) bear, the Refuge is a spine of once-glaciated mountains and rolling tundra uplands. Steep-walled fjords create 800 mi (1300 km) of coastline. An estimated 2400 bears—one of the world's highest densities—fed by the abundant spawning salmon, inhabit the

Rafters on Terror Bay. (U.S. Fish and Wildlife Service photo by M. Nowak)

Refuge. The brown bear is the largest living terrestrial carnivore, with males weighing up to 1200 lb (540 kg) and females to 700 lb (300 kg).

Other wildlife found in the Refuge includes bald eagles, Sitka blacktail deer, feral reindeer, mountain goats, red foxes, river otters, ptarmigan and colonies of tufted puffins and cormorants; numerous waterfowl winter in the Refuge. The Afognak Island section of the Refuge contains introduced Roosevelt elk. Watch the ocean and bays for seals, sea lions, sea otters and whales.

Most visitors come to the Refuge to fish, hunt, beachcomb or boat. Cross-country hiking can be extremely difficult due to thick brush. Any trails on the island were created by the bears, who regard them and the salmon streams as their property; be careful where and how you hike and camp. Horses, powerboats and float planes are permitted; off-road vehicles are not. In this windy, rainy area, hypothermia is a constant danger. Since scheduled air or water pickup can be delayed, carry extra food. Expect large populations of mosquitoes and other biting insects from June through September.

Camping is unrestricted and campfires are permitted, but wood may be wet or scarce. Refuge facilities consist of a visitor center near Kodiak City and 11 public-use recreational cabins, all accessible by seaplane; four are also accessible by ocean-going boat. Cabin reservations are selected by lottery from applications received prior to one of the four appropriate drawing dates. Contact the Refuge Manager for information. Cabins not reserved during the drawing are available on a "first-come" basis. Respect private lands within the Refuge boundaries.

River travel: Karluk River, FWB, from Karluk Lake to Karluk Village, 25 mi (40 km).

The maritime climate brings cool wet summers and mild wet winters. Expect intense autumn storms with prolonged rain. (See the Kodiak weather table.) Rainfall varies greatly, dependent upon topography, with the northwestern coast receiving half the precipitation of the southeastern coast and Kodiak. Winds are constant and moderate, generally severe during storms. The Afognak part of the Refuge is forested with Sitka spruce; most of the western section is treeless, except for large cottonwoods in the valleys, and covered by thick grasses and brush. Prominent peaks: Koniag Peak, elevation 4470 ft (1362 m); Mount Glottof, elevation 4405 ft (1343 m).

The only practical means of access to the Refuge is by air taxi from Kodiak or Larsen Bay or by charter boat from Kodiak, both expensive. Mail planes with limited passenger space service Akhiok, Alitak, Amook, Karluk, Larsen Bay, Old Harbor, Olga Bay, Vilage Islands and Parks, but access into the Refuge overland is impractical. Lodging may be available at commercial hunting lodges (reservations required). Kodiak, a port of call for the Southwestern Alaska state ferry, has charter boats, stores, restaurants, lodging, rental cars and taxicabs. Frequent scheduled airline service connects Kodiak with Anchorage and Seattle.

Suggested reading: Nancy Freeman, *Kodiak: Island of Change* (Anchorage: Alaska Northwest Publishing Co., Alaska Geographic, 1977); International Conference on Bear Research and Management, *Bears—Their Biology and Management, Vol. IV* (Washington, D.C.: U.S. Government Printing Office, 1980); Ales Hrdlicka, *The Anthropology of Kodiak Island* (Philadelphia: Wistar Institute of Anatomy and Biology, 1944); Thor N. V. Karlstrom and George E. Ball, *The Kodiak Island Refugium: Its Geology, Flora, Fauna and History* (Toronto: University of Alberta, 1969).

58 Koyukuk National Wildlife Refuge and Wilderness

Location: Western Alaska, north of
Galena; 65°40′N 156°20′W
Size: 3,550,000 acres (1 437 000
hectares)
High point: 3200 ft (980 m)
Low point: 125 ft (38 m)

Best time of year: Foot,
June–September; boat,
June–September; ski, March–April
USGS maps: Hughes, Kateel,
Melozitna, Nulato, Shungnak
Established: 1980
Managed by: U.S. Fish and Wildlife
Service

A classic river floodplain with oxbow lakes and scroll meanders surrounding the village of Huslia, the Refuge area is of great importance to the local people. Because it was not covered by glaciers in the last Ice Age, the region is thought to have been a refuge for humans and wildlife, who have used the area ever since. Primarily wetlands, with sloughs, lakes, muskeg and boreal-forested lowlands, the river basin is surrounded by high rolling hills along the Refuge boundaries. Treeline is about 3000 ft (900 m). The unexpected Nogahabara Sand Dunes lie west of Huslia in a 400,000-acre (162 000-hectare) wilderness.

Waterfowl, Koyukuk Refuge. (U.S. Fish and Wildlife Service photo)

The Refuge includes prime habitat for large populations of moose, furbearers, particularly beavers, and for nesting waterfowl, primarily pintails, mallards, green-winged teal, widgeons, canvasbacks, scaups, scoters, white-fronted geese and Canada geese. The Koyukuk River basin appears to be the northwestern nesting limit of the trumpeter swan. Watch also for black bears, brown (grizzly) bears, coyotes, red foxes, lynx, wolves and wolverines. Portions of the Western Arctic caribou herd winter here.

The area is remote and roadless, with no recreational development. Camping and campfires are permitted on public lands. Numerous private lands exist within the Refuge, particularly along navigable streams. The people of the area do not encourage tourists and other visitors; please respect their property and privacy. Fishing is permitted; with certain restrictions, so are hunting, powerboats, snowmobiles and fixed-wing aircraft. Expect large populations of mosquitoes and other biting insects during summer months.

River travel: Koyukuk River, FWA within the Refuge.

In this subarctic continental climate, summers are warm and dry, winters are cold, dry and severe. (See the Galena weather table.) Winds are normally light. Daylight on June 21 is 24 hours, on December 22, 3 hours.

Access to the Refuge is by air or boat. Galena, Hughes, Huslia and Koyukuk have scheduled air service and general stores; Galena has lodging and air taxis.

Suggested reading: James Huntington, *On the Edge of Nowhere* (New York: Crown Publishers, 1966); William Loyens, *The Changing Culture of the Nulato Koyukon* (Madison: University of Wisconsin Press, 1970); Lael Morgan, *And The Land Provides: Alaska Natives in a Year of Transition* (New York: Anchor Press, 1974); Hudson Stuck, *Ten Thousand Miles With a Dogsled* (New York: Scribners, 1914); U.S. Department of the Interior, *Proposed Koyukuk National Wildlife Refuge*, Final Environmental Impact Statement (Washington, D.C.: U.S. Government Printing Office, 1974).

59 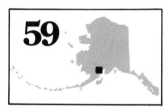 Lake Clark National Park and Preserve

Location: Southcentral Alaska, west of Cook Inlet; 61°N 153°W
Size: 3,655,000 acres (1 479 000 hectares)
High point: 10,197 ft (3108 m)
Low point: Sea level

Best time of year: Foot, June–September; boat, June–September; ski, February–April
USGS maps: Iliamna, Kenai, Lake Clark, Lime Hills, Seldovia, Tyonek
Established: 1978
Managed by: National Park Service

Turquoise lakes, glaciers, steaming volcanoes, precipitous granite spires, thundering waterfalls and wave-washed seashores are all here. A rugged wilderness not yet well known, the Lake Clark area holds some of Alaska's finest scenery. Moist coastal forests beside Cook Inlet give way inland to alpine tundra and mountain-rimmed lakes, all rich with wildlife. The Tlikakila River flows through a major earth fault that runs through the area. The Park's two spectacular volcanoes, Mount Iliamna, elevation 10,016 ft (3053 m), and Mount Redoubt, elevation 10,197 ft (3108 m), are easily seen from Anchorage and the Kenai Peninsula. Mount Redoubt erupted in 1966, spewing ash over the Anchorage area. Originally established as a national monument, the area became a park in 1980, with 2,470,000 acres (1 000 000 hectares) designated as Wilderness.

The lakes and numerous rivers, including three designated National Wild Rivers—the Chilikadrotna, the Mulchatna and the Tlikakila—attract boaters and fishermen. Backpackers and mountaineers appreciate the uncrowded wilderness and varied terrain. Winter travelers should be aware of severe avalanche hazard in many areas.

Moose roam throughout, as do brown (grizzly) bears, black bears, wolves, wolverines, and red foxes. Dall sheep live on many of the peaks; caribou are found primarily in the western uplands of the Preserve. The only known inland seal population in the U.S. is in Lake Iliamna, lying just outside the boundary but formed

Camping on Lake Clark.

from headwaters within the Park. This watershed is one of the important producers of red salmon in the world, contributing 33% of the entire U.S. catch and 16% of the world catch.

Other than a ranger station at the settlement of Port Alsworth on Lake Clark, there are no Park Service visitor facilities. Camping is unrestricted; campfires, fishing, firearms, powerboats, fixed-wing aircraft and snowmobiles are permitted. Hunting is permitted in the Preserve but not in the Park. Travel and camp to avoid meeting or attracting bears.

River travel: Chilikadrotna National Wild River, WW3-FWB, see description; Mulchatna National Wild River, WW3-FWC, see description; Necons-Stony rivers, WW2-FWB, from Two Lakes to Stony River village, 150 mi (140 km); Newhalen River, WW1-5, from Sixmile Lake to Newhalen (portage possible), 25 mi (40 km); Telaquana-Stony rivers, WW3-FWB, from Telaquana Lake to Stony River village, 150 mi (240 km); Tlikakila National Wild River, WW1-4, see description. Travel the Park's lakes cautiously—dangerous large waves and strong winds can develop swiftly.

Expect cool summers in the mountains and, with the proximity to salt water, mild winters with frequent overcast. (See the Port Alsworth weather table.) Winds are generally light to moderate. Daylight on June 21 is 19½ hours, on December 22, 5½ hours.

Access to the Park and Preserve is normally by air taxi from Anchorage, Homer, Iliamna, Kenai or Port Alsworth. Iliamna and Stony River have scheduled air service. Frequent, but unscheduled, air service connects Anchorage and Port Alsworth. The only nearby bed-and-board services are at wilderness lodges within and near the Park and Preserve; reservations are generally required.

Suggested reading: Alaska Geographic, *Bristol Bay Basin* (Anchorage: Alaska Northwest Publishing Co., 1978); Richard Proenneke with Sam Keith, *One Man's Wilderness: An Alaskan Odyssey* (Anchorage: Alaska Northwest Publishing Co., 1973); U.S. Department of the Interior, *Proposed Iliamna Natural Resources Range* and *Proposed Lake Clark National Park and Preserve*, Final Environmental Impact Statements (Washington, D.C.: U.S. Government Printing Office, 1974).

60 Maurelle Islands Wilderness, Tongass National Forest

Location: Southeastern Alaska, south of Sitka; 55°40′N 133°40′W
Size: 4937 acres (1998 hectares)
High point: 600 ft (200 m), on Anguilla Island

Low point: Sea level
Best time of year: April–August
USGS maps: Craig C-5, C-6
Established: 1980
Managed by: U.S. Forest Service

An exposed group of about 30 low-relief forested islands, islets and wave-washed rocks, the Maurelles are surrounded by rocky shoals. With their windswept beaches, rocky shorelines and rich spruce-hemlock rain forests, the islands make for interesting saltwater kayaking. They were named for the Spanish navigator Don Francisco

Antonio Maurelle, who surveyed the region from 1775 to 1779 under the command of Don Juan de la Bodega y Quadra.

Sea otters, seals, sea lions and whales use the waters. Seabirds nest and perch ashore. On the larger islands you may see black bears, wolves, Sitka blacktail deer and bald eagles.

The islands have no recreational facilities. Camping, campfires, firearms, fixed-wing aircraft and powerboats are permitted. Carry a camping stove, since wood will probably be wet and winds often too strong to build a fire. Prepare for long periods of rain and strong winds. Carry extra food, since weather can delay planned pickup. The waters can be hazardous; only experienced boaters should attempt to visit the islands.

Cool, wet overcast summers and mild, wet overcast winters are normal for this maritime climate. (See the Sitka weather table.) Winds are constant and often strong, especially during autumn storms. Daylight on June 21 is 17½ hours, on December 22, 7 hours.

The islands are reached by float plane or boat. Air taxis operate from Ketchikan and Wrangell. Craig and Klawock have boat charters, scheduled air service, food and lodging.

Maurelle Islands. (U.S. Forest Service photo)

Photographers at viewing ledge, McNeil Sanctuary. (Photo by Third Eye Photography)

61

McNeil River
State Game Sanctuary

Location: Southcentral Alaska, southwest of Homer; 59°06′N 154°15′W
Size: 85,000 acres (34 000 hectares)
High point: 4672 ft (1424 m)
Low point: Sea level

Best time of year: Foot, May–October; boat, April–October; ski, February–March
USGS map: Iliamna A-4
Established: 1967
Managed by: Alaska Department of Fish and Game

A mecca for wildlife photographers, the Sanctuary was established to protect the numbers of brown bears that congregate at McNeil River falls in July and August to fish for migrating salmon. More than 20 bears at a time may be at the falls or sleeping nearby. Before visitor restrictions were put into effect, the crush of competing photographers caused the bears to leave the falls temporarily. With fewer visitors, restricted to a permanent viewing "cave" (a shallow depression in a gravel bank about 150 ft [46 m] from the main fishing area), the bears tolerate the intrusion and continue their normal activities.

At a rate of 10 per day, permits to visit McNeil River falls between July 1 and August 25 are issued by lottery from applications received by May 1 by Alaska Department of Fish and Game, Anchorage office. Visitors to the falls must remain within the designated area and behave quietly and unobtrusively. Additional restrictions may be put into effect at any time. Firearms are permitted for self-protection, but are not necessary; armed ADF&G personnel accompany visitors each day. Visitors are required to sign a liability waiver, but there have been no cases of human injury from bears at McNeil River and no bears have been destroyed since the permit system was initiated.

In this maritime climate, expect cool, overcast summers and mild, overcast winters. (See the Homer weather table.) Winds are generally moderate, often severe. Daylight on June 21 is 18½ hours, on December 22, 6 hours. The terrain of the Sanctuary consists of tideflats, shrubby lowlands of the McNeil River valley and nearby tundra-covered uplands.

Access to the Sanctuary is by float plane, large-tired beach-landing aircraft or boat. Most visitors arrive by air taxi, timing the arrival to coincide with high tide. Since fog, storms or high winds often delay scheduled pickup, pack extra food. ADF&G will supply a list of licensed air carriers that fly to McNeil River; include a self-addressed stamped envelope. Air taxis, stores, restaurants and lodging are available in Anchorage, Homer, Kenai, King Salmon and Soldotna.

Suggested reading: Wade T. Bledsoe, Jr., "The Social Life of an Unsociable Giant" (*Audubon*, May 1975); Allen L. Egbert and Michael H. Luque, "Might Makes Right Among Alaska's Brown Bears" (*National Geographic*, September 1975); John Ibbotson, "Bear Encounters of a Very Close Kind" (*Adventure Travel*, August 1980); Derek Stonorov, "Protocol at the Annual Brown Bear Fish Feast" (*Natural History*, November 1972).

62 Mendenhall Wetlands State Game Refuge

Location: Southeastern Alaska, in Juneau; 58°20'N 134°35'W
Size: 3800 acres (1500 hectares)
High point: 10 ft (3 m)
Low point: Sea level

Best time of year: Foot, any time
USGS map: Juneau B-2
Established: 1976
Managed by: Alaska Department of Fish and Game

In the heart of Juneau, these tidal marshlands and willow thickets are a staging area for migrating waterfowl and shorebirds in the spring (April and May) and fall (September to November). The Mendenhall is well known for large concentrations of Vancouver Canada geese from late winter through spring; you can observe them easily from the road. The Refuge is also used by other marsh-associated birds, including bald eagles, short-eared owls and marsh hawks, and by furbearers, especially land otters and mink. Year-round residents, Vancouver Canada geese and mallards nest in the area.

Other than an interpretive center at Lemon Creek, the Refuge is undeveloped. Regularly used by joggers and hikers, it also attracts beachcombers, photographers, fishermen and waterfowl hunters. Other hunting is prohibited. No aircraft or motorized vehicles (except boats launched outside the Refuge) are permitted. Use caution when venturing onto the tideflats—wind-blown high tides can catch the unwary.

Juneau's maritime climate brings cool, wet, overcast summers and mild, wet,

Whistling swans, Mendenhall Wetlands. (U.S. Fish and Wildlife Service photo by Jo Keller)

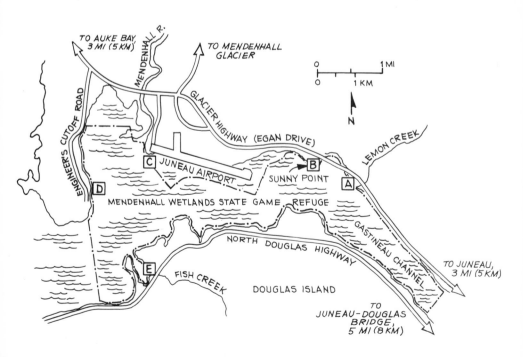

overcast winters. (See the Juneau weather table.) Winds are moderate. Daylight on June 21 is 18½ hours, on December 22, 6 hours.

The Refuge lies beside the Juneau airport and east along Glacier Highway (Egan Drive) from Mile 3.5 to Mile 10 (measured from the Juneau downtown ferry terminal). The most convenient access points to the Refuge's tideflats are at Lemon Creek (A), Mile 5.9; Sunny Point (B) at Mile 7; from the west end of the Juneau airport (C); and from the Engineer's Cutoff Road on the Mendenhall Peninsula (D). On Douglas Island, the North Douglas Highway parallels the Refuge from Mile 4.5 to Mile 9.5; an access is at Fish Creek (E), Mile 8.2.

Rental cars and taxicabs are available at the Juneau airport and in the city of Juneau; scheduled buses travel the Glacier Highway. The Southeastern Alaska state ferry calls at either Juneau or Auke Bay, depending upon the particular routing. Stores, restaurants and lodging are available in Juneau and Auke Bay and along the highway.

63 Misty Fiords National Monument, Tongass National Forest

Location: Southeastern Alaska, east of Ketchikan; 55°30′N 130°30′W
Size: 2,294,343 acres (928 491 hectares)
High point: 7499 ft (2286 m)
Low point: Sea level

Best time of year: Foot, May–October; boat, April–October; ski, January–March
USGS maps: Bradfield Canal, Ketchikan, Prince Rupert
Established: 1980
Managed by: U.S. Forest Service

Sheer granite walls tower thousands of feet into the clouds above narrow glacier-carved fjords and quiet valleys. The Monument lies sandwiched between two impressive fjords, Behm Canal, stretching 117 mi (188 km), and Portland Canal, 72 mi (116 km) long. Two spectacular sights are Punchbowl Cove in Rudyerd Bay and New Eddystone Rock, the latter named in 1793 by Captain George Vancouver because of its resemblance to the lighthouse rock off the coast of Cornwall, England. Although the area is only recently free of major glaciation, vegetation is lush, with dense spruce-hemlock rain forests and inviting muskeg and alpine meadows. Treeline is at about 2000 ft (about 610 m). Unusual for Southeastern Alaska are the periodic lava flows that occur near Blue River. In 1981 the U.S. Borax and Chemical Corporation began efforts to open a molybdenum mine deep within the Monument, with access from the head of Wilson Arm of Smeaton Bay.

Wildlife is abundant and varied, with mountain goats, brown (grizzly) bears, black bears, Sitka blacktail deer, wolverines, wolves, red foxes, beavers, mink, marten, river otters, a few moose and numerous bald eagles. Offshore, watch for seals, sea lions, porpoises, dolphins and whales.

The Forest Service maintains 13 public-use recreational cabins (reservations required, fee), three Adirondack-style open shelters and 15 mi (24 km) of marked trails. Back-country camping is unrestricted and campfires are permitted, but the wood will most likely be wet. Prepare for long periods of rain; prolonged storms can

Sailing on Rudyerd Bay, Misty Fiords National Monument.

delay planned pickup. In winter, avalanche hazard can be severe. Camp and travel to avoid confrontations with the numerous bears. Fishing, hunting, firearms, horses, fixed-wing aircraft and powerboats are permitted; snowmobiles and off-road vehicles are not.

A maritime climate prevails along the coast with cool, wet overcast summers and mild, wet overcast winters. (See the Annette Island weather table.) Inland, weather is more continental, with less rainfall. Winds are light to moderate at low elevations, moderate to severe at high elevations. Daylight on June 21 is 17½ hours, on December 22, 7 hours. Prominent peaks: Mount John Jay, elevation 7499 ft (2286 m); Mount Jefferson Coolidge, elevation 7073 ft (2156 m).

Access to the Monument is normally by air or water. Excursion boats from Ketchikan and cruise ships visit the Fiords. Charter boats are available at Ketchikan; air taxis are based at Ketchikan and at Stewart, B.C. All three communities have food and lodging. Several wilderness lodges operate within the Monument. Scheduled airlines serve Ketchikan and Stewart; Ketchikan is a port of call for the Southeastern Alaska state ferry.

64

Mulchatna
National Wild River

Location: Southcentral Alaska, in
Lake Clark National Park and
Preserve; 60°47′N 154°10′W
River rating: WW3-FWC
Popular trip lengths: 100 to 230 mi
(160 to 370 km)
Best time of year: June–September

Annual high water: June, August
USGS maps: Lake Clark D-3, D-4, C-4,
D-5, D-6, C-6, C-7, B-7, B-8; Taylor
Mountains B-1, A-1, A-2; Dillingham
D-2, D-3, C-3, C-4, B-4
Designated as Wild River: 1980
Managed by: National Park Service

From jewel-like Turquoise Lake nestled at the base of Telaquana Mountain, the Mulchatna flows through the rolling Bonanza Hills in a challenging, shallow, rocky channel, more suitable for rafts and kayaks than canoes. Hiking in the alpine valleys and to the many glaciers is tempting in this open scenic tundraland. West of the Bonanza Hills, about 20 mi (30 km) below Turquoise Lake, the valley broadens; here the river trip is a gentle float through forests of spruce, birch and aspen. From here on, watch for sweepers and logjams. Expect a stretch of fast white water above Bonanza Creek; a portage is possible. After winding through low hills, the river floodplain widens to wetlands and joins the lowlands of the Nushagak. From Turquoise Lake to New Stuyahok on the Nushagak is about 230 mi (370 km). Although only the upper 24 mi (39 km) are designated as Wild River, the watershed remains wild. Private lands border the river in the vicinity of New Stuyahok.

Watch for caribou in the Turquoise Lake area, where they calve in the spring. Keep an eye open, too, for moose, black bears, brown (grizzly) bears, wolves, wolverines, red foxes, beavers, porcupines and waterfowl. Fishing for lake trout, rainbow trout, Dolly Varden, salmon, grayling and pike can be excellent.

Camping and campfires are permitted throughout, with many good campsites the entire length of the river. Fishing, firearms, powerboats and fixed-wing aircraft are all allowed in this undeveloped region. Sports hunting is permitted in the Preserve, but not in the Park.

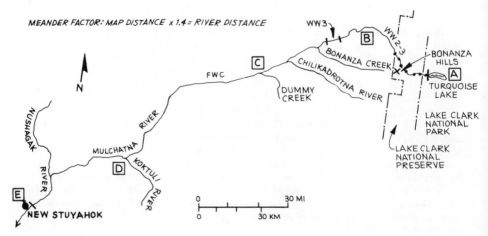

Rafting on the Mulchatna River near Turquoise Lake. (National Park Service photo by Jim Morris)

Expect overcast and cool summers in a subarctic climate transitional between continental and maritime. (See the Port Alsworth weather table.) Winds are generally light to moderate. Daylight on June 21 is 19½ hours, on December 22, 5½ hours.

Reach the river by air taxi to either Turquoise Lake (A), elevation 2504 ft (763 m), or the small lakes (B) below the Bonanza Hills, elevation 1200 ft (370 m). Float planes can land on the river at Dummy Creek (C), elevation 600 ft (200 m), or at the Koktuli River (D), elevation 300 ft (90 m), or boaters can continue to New Stuyahok (E), elevation 100 ft (30 m), and return by scheduled air service. The village has a general store, but few other amenities. Air taxis are available from Anchorage, Dillingham, Homer, Iliamna, Kenai and Port Alsworth.

Suggested reading: James Van Stone, *Eskimos of the Nushagak River: An Ethnographic History* (Seattle: University of Washington Press, 1967).

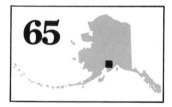

65   Nancy Lake State Recreation Area

Location: Southcentral Alaska, west of
  Wasilla; 61°38′N 150°05′W
Size: 22,685 acres (9180 hectares)
High point: 375 ft (114 m)
Low point: 116 ft (35 m)

Best time of year: Foot, May–October;
  boat, June–October; ski,
  January–March
USGS maps: Anchorage C-8;
  Tyonek C-1
Established: 1966
Managed by: Alaska Division
  of Parks

Nancy Lake State Recreation Area is an excellent, lightly developed playground for families who enjoy water sports and gentle hiking terrain. Now richly forested and studded with more than 130 lakes, the area was once the bed of a giant glacier that scoured out Cook Inlet as it flowed from the Alaska Range south into the Gulf of

South Rolly Lake.

Alaska. After the glacier's retreat, plants and animals returned and the Tanaina Indians established a subsistence culture at Indian Bay on Nancy Lake. Today, the lake's clear waters provide some of the finest recreation in the Cook Inlet area. Amid gently rolling hills known as drumlins, the forests, marshes, streams and lakes are home for numerous animals, birds and fish.

Watch for moose, black bears, brown (grizzly) bears, beavers, lynx, coyotes, wolves, hawks, owls and migrating waterfowl. Red-necked grebes nest here, as do arctic and common loons; sandhill cranes greet spring with their courtship dances en route to nesting grounds.

Popular activities are picnicking, swimming, fishing, boating, hiking, berry-picking, cross-country skiing, snowshoeing, dog mushing, snowmobiling and ice fishing. Portions of the Recreation Area are closed to snowmobiles and powerboats; horses, off-road vehicles and aircraft landings are not permitted. Hunting is allowed, but firearms may not be used. Facilities include picnic tables, boat ramps, water, toilets, a campground (100 units) and 11 primitive campsites on the canoe trails. Thirty additional developed campsites are accessible from the Parks Highway at Nancy Lake Wayside just outside the Recreation Area. Campfires are restricted to campground fireplaces; use camping stoves elsewhere. Back-country camping is permitted. Black bears are common—do not leave food or garbage where it might attract them. Swimmers may contract swimmer's itch in the warmer lakes. Marked trails: 11 mi (18 km) for hikers, including a self-guiding nature trail; 10 mi (16 km) maintained for cross-country skiers. Private lands exist within the Recreation Area boundaries; respect signs and do not disturb buildings.

Boating and river travel: Nancy Lake State Recreation Area canoe lake route, FWA with portages, 16 mi (26 km); Little Susitna River, FWB, from Little Susitna River bridge, Mile 57, Parks Highway, to the portage trail into Nancy Lake SRA canoe trail system, 25 mi (40 km). Do not destroy or change beaver dams; they maintain critical water levels in the lakes.

The subarctic maritime climate is influenced by continental land masses; summers are warm and sunny, winters dry and cold. (See the Talkeetna weather table.) Winds are normally light. Daylight on June 21 is 19½ hours, on December 22, 5½ hours.

Access to the Recreation Area is from Mile 67.2, Parks Highway, 67 mi (108 km) north of Anchorage, between Wasilla and Willow. Automobiles can be rented in Anchorage. Scheduled buses serve the Parks Highway. Visitors may also take the Alaska Railroad, debarking at White's Crossing. Stores, restaurants and lodging are available along the road and at Wasilla.

Suggested reading: Cornelius Osgood, *The Ethnography of the Tanaina* (New Haven: Yale University Press, 1966).

66  Noatak National Preserve and Wild River

Location: Northwestern Alaska, northeast of Kotzebue; 68°N 159°W
Wild River rating: WW1-2
Popular trip length: 350 mi (560 km)
Preserve size: 6,550,000 acres (2 650 000 hectares)
High point: 4915 ft (1498 m)
Low point: 100 ft (30 m)
Best time of year: Foot, mid-June–September; boat, mid-June–August; ski, March–April

USGS maps for Preserve: Ambler River, Baird Mountains, Delong Mountains, Howard Pass, Killik River, Misheguk Mountain, Noatak
USGS maps for Wild River: Survey Pass, Ambler River, Howard Pass, Misheguk Mountain; Misheguk Mountain A-3, A-4, A-5; Baird Mountains D-3, D-4, D-5, D-6; Noatak D-1, D-2, C-2, C-3, B-3, B-2, A-2, A-1
Established: 1978
Managed by: National Park Service

Far above the Arctic Circle, the treeless sweep of gentle mountains emphasizes the moods of the arctic sky. The endless summer days create a tranquil pace of life. The Preserve, along with the western part of Gates of the Arctic National Park, protects almost the entire watershed of the Noatak River, one of the finest large wilderness

Ipnelivik River, Noatak National Preserve.

areas remaining in North America. Except for about 700,000 acres (about 280 000 hectares) near the village of Noatak, the entire Preserve is designated as Wilderness. Originally established as a national monument, the area became a national preserve in 1980.

The Noatak National Wild River drains westward through a broad gently sloping valley in the Brooks Range to empty into the Chukchi Sea near Kotzebue. Numerous tributary valleys, especially along the upper half of the river, beckon the hiker. From its headwaters on glacier-pocked Mount Igikpak in Gates of the Arctic National Park, the river flows through narrow canyons, beside steep-walled peaks, across broad lake-dotted basins and down two canyons to open as a wide braided river on a forested floodplain. The Wild River designation ends at the Kelly River, 33 mi (53 km) above Noatak village. Below Noatak, the river flows through the Igichuk Hills to spread in a wide wetland delta. If you choose to paddle to Kotzebue, be cautious on the delta mudflats and on the frigid hazardous waters of Hotham Inlet. From Lake Matcharak in Gates of the Arctic Park to Noatak village is about 350 mi (560 km). Although remote, the Preserve attracts many boaters and hikers; it is a gentle wilderness in danger of being trampled by those who come to embrace it.

Wildlife, abundant by arctic standards, is limited by the slow-growing northern vegetation. Watch for the western Arctic caribou herd en route between its wintering

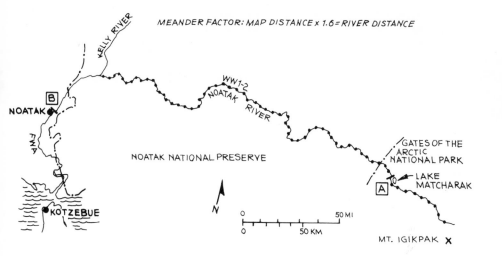

grounds along the Kobuk River and its summer calving areas north of the Brooks Range. Dall sheep graze mountain slopes throughout the Preserve. Look also for moose, brown (grizzly) bears, black bears, wolves, wolverines and red foxes. The vast treeless tundra makes bird-watching especially rewarding.

Summers are often warm and frequently hot in this subarctic solar basin, but prepare also for cold rainy weather with the possibility of light snow. Near the coast, expect a maritime influence with more overcast and fog. Winters are cold, dry and severe. (See the Kotzebue weather table.) Winds are generally light, but can be strong, making float travel difficult when they come from the west. Daylight on June 21 is 24 hours, on December 22, 0 hours, with 5 hours of twilight.

Camping is permitted throughout the Preserve and is best on riverbars and dry tundra knobs. Since northern wood grows so slowly, use a camping stove in this treeless country. If you do build a campfire, build it on river gravel only; tundra wildfires are a serious problem during long hot summer days. Fishing, hunting, firearms, fixed-wing aircraft, powerboats and snowmobiles are all permitted.

Travel with care in this extremely remote area. Take extra food, since fog in Kotzebue or clouds over the mountains toward Bettles can delay air pickup. Large numbers of hungry mosquitoes hatch in summer, so carry head nets and a good supply of repellent. Numerous private lands line the lower Noatak within the Preserve; try not to camp on private property.

Access to this vast roadless area is normally by air taxi from Bettles (Evansville) or Kotzebue, both of which have scheduled air service, food and lodging. Access to float the Noatak River is by air taxi from Bettles or Kotzebue to Lake Matcharak (A), elevation 1600 ft (488 m), to lakes farther upstream or to river bars. Pickup can be made from Kotzebue by light aircraft on lakes near the lower river, on the river itself or on gravel bars—or continue to Noatak village (B), elevation 50 ft. (15 m), which has scheduled air service.

Suggested reading: Alaska Geographic, *The Kotzebue Basin* (Anchorage: Alaska Northwest Publishing Co., 1981); Claire Fejes, *People of the Noatak* (New York: Alfred A. Knopf, 1966); Michael Jenkinson, *Wilderness Rivers of America* (New York: Abrams, 1981); U.S. Department of the Interior, *Proposed Noatak National Preserve*, Final Environmental Impact Statement (Washington, D.C.: U.S. Government Printing Office, 1974).

67

North Fork of the Koyukuk National Wild River

Location: Northcentral Alaska, in
  Gates of the Arctic National Park;
  67°45′N 150°50′W
River rating: WW1-2
Popular trip length: 100 mi (160 km)
Best time of year: July–September
Annual high water: July–August

USGS maps: Wiseman C-2, C-3, B-2,
  A-2, A-3; Bettles D-3, D-4;
  (headwaters, Summit Lake to
  Redstar Creek: add Chandler Lake
  A-1; Wiseman D-1, D-2)
Designated as Wild River: 1980
Managed by: National Park Service

A clearwater river surrounded by rugged mountain scenery, the North Fork of the Koyukuk drains south-facing slopes of the central Brooks Range. In its upper reaches, it flows past Doonerak Mountain and through the "Gates of the Arctic," which are Boreal Mountain and Frigid Crags. Take a few days to explore the upper river before beginning the float downstream.

From Redstar Creek lakes to Bettles is about 100 mi (160 km). Boaters have flown into "Summit Lake" at the headwaters of the North Fork, but if you do so, expect a difficult portage and considerable lining well past Doonerak Mountain. The distance from the lake to Redstar Creek is about 60 mi (100 km). After Squaw Rapids, WW2, at the confluence of the Glacier River, the river enters a broad valley with wetlands and rolling low hills. Except at the extreme headwaters, the river valley is forested.

Wildlife is typical of the subarctic tundra and boreal forest: moose, brown (grizzly) bears, black bears, wolves, wolverines, Dall sheep, coyotes, lynx, red foxes, snowshoe hares, porcupines, beavers and other furbearers. Caribou migrate through the valley between their winter and summer ranges.

Camp and build campfires on gravel bars to avoid any chance of starting a forest fire. Since northern wood grows so slowly, the use of camping stoves is preferred. Expect large populations of mosquitoes and other biting insects from June through mid-August. Fishing, firearms, fixed-wing aircraft and powerboats are permitted;

MEANDER FACTOR: MAP DISTANCE x 1.4 = RIVER DISTANCE

Old mail-stop cabin on the North Fork. (National Park Service photo by Pat Pourchot)

hunting is not. This is a remote area that requires careful planning and experience in wilderness travel.

Although the subarctic continental climate normally brings warm dry summers, expect cooler temperatures and more rain in the mountains. (See the Wiseman weather table.) Winds, generally light, can be strong through "The Gates." Daylight on June 21 is 24 hours, on December 22, ½ hour. Prominent peaks: Doonerak Mountain, elevation 7457 ft (2273 m); Boreal Mountain, elevation 6666 ft (2032 m); Frigid Crags, elevation 5550 ft (1692 m).

To reach the river, take an air taxi from Bettles (Evansville) to "Summit Lake" (A), elevation 3500 ft (1100 m), or Redstar Creek lakes (B), elevation 1500 ft (460 m). Park service personnel suggest hiking from "Summit Lake" through the "Gates of the Arctic," arranging to pick up boats or rafts where river is deep enough to float. End the float trip at Bettles (C), elevation 600 ft (180 m), which has scheduled air service, food, lodging and a general store.

Suggested reading: Robert Marshall, *Alaska Wilderness: Exploring the Central Brooks Range* (Berkeley: University of California Press, 1970; originally published in 1956 as *Arctic Wilderness*).

Nowitna
National Wildlife Refuge
and Wild River

68

Location: Central Alaska, east of
Galena; 64°30′N 154°W
Wild River rating: WW1-FWC
Popular trip length: 310 mi (500 km)
Refuge size: 1,560,000 acres (631 000
hectares)
High point: 2341 ft (714 m)
Low point: 135 ft (41 m)

Best time of year: Foot,
June–September; boat,
June–September; ski, March–April
USGS maps for Refuge: Kantishna,
Medfra, Melozitna, Ruby
USGS maps for Wild River: Medfra
D-4; Ruby A-4, A-3, A-2, B-2, B-3, C-3,
C-4, D-3, D-4, D-5, C-6
Established: 1980
Managed by: U.S. Fish and Wildlife
Service

An Interior Alaska "solar basin," the Refuge contains forested lowlands and excellent wetland habitat for waterfowl and furbearers. A quarter of a million waterfowl each fall leave the Refuge, most following the Central Flyway to the Lower 48, although many canvasbacks travel to the Atlantic Coast, and pintails and widgeons go to California. As many as 200 trumpeter swans, the largest waterfowl in North America, nest in the Refuge. Watch also for moose, black bears, brown (grizzly) bears, caribou, coyotes, red foxes, lynx, wolves, beavers, mink, muskrats and river otters. Major populations of marten and wolverines are found in the Refuge.

The Nowitna National Wild River, an important sheefish spawning stream, flows, broad, clear and deep, into the Yukon River. The rolling hills in the southeastern portion of the refuge drop to lake-dotted wetlands in the Yukon River floodplain, a boreal-forested lowland.

Within the boundaries of this roadless undeveloped refuge, respect private lands and ask permission before trespassing. Camping and campfires are permitted on public lands. Fishing, hunting, powerboats, snowmobiles and fixed-wing aircraft landings are permitted. Expect large populations of mosquitoes and other biting insects during summer months.

River travel: Nowitna National Wild River is reached by air taxi to the vicinity of Clearwater Creek (A), elevation 700 ft (200 m). The confluence with the Yukon River (B) is 270 mi (430 km) away. The town of Ruby (C), elevation 135 ft (41 m), is 41 mi (66 km) farther down the Yukon. An alternate river trip begins at the Sulatna River crossing (D), elevation 350 ft (110 m), 11 mi (18 km) south of Ruby on the Placerville Road. (This road is not connected with the state highway system.) Float the Sulatna to the Nowitna, WW1-FWC, and continue to the Yukon, ending at Ruby, a total distance of 230 mi (370 km).

In a subarctic continental climate, the area enjoys warm, dry summers and cold, dry, severe winters. (See the Galena weather table.) Winds are normally light. Daylight on June 21 is 22 hours, on December 22, 3½ hours.

Ruby, Galena and Tanana all have scheduled air service, general stores and limited lodging; air taxis operate from Galena and Tanana.

Recommended reading: U.S. Department of the Interior, *Proposed Koyukuk National Wildlife Refuge* and *Proposed Yukon-Kuskokwim National Forest*, Final Environmental Impact Statements (Washington, D.C.: U.S. Government Printing Office, 1974).

Nowitna River. (U.S. Fish and Wildlife Service photo by Jo Keller)

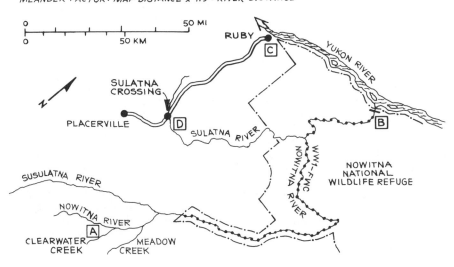

MEANDER FACTOR: MAP DISTANCE x 1.9 = RIVER DISTANCE

Musk-oxen, Nunivak Island. (U.S. Fish and Wildlife Service photo by Jo Keller)

69

Nunivak National Wilderness, Yukon Delta National Wildlife Refuge

Location: Western Alaska, on Nunivak Island; 60°N 166°W
Size: 600,000 acres (243 000 hectares)
High point: 1675 ft (511 m)
Low point: Sea level

Best time of year: Foot, June–August; boat, June–August; ski, February–April
USGS maps: Cape Mendenhall, Nunivak Island
Established: 1929
Managed by: U.S. Fish and Wildlife Service

Once ranging freely across the North American tundra, the musk-ox was an easy target for rifle-wielding explorers and Eskimos; the last survivors in Alaska, a herd of 13, were killed about 1865. In an attempt to re-establish the musk-oxen, 34 animals were brought from Greenland about 1930, studied at the University of Alaska at Fairbanks for five years and then moved to predator-free Nunivak Island. By 1968, the free-roaming herd on this treeless, windswept island had increased to 750, and animals were transplanted to other areas of Alaska: Nelson Island, Barter Island, Kavik River and Cape Thompson. In 1980, the State of Alaska transferred ownership of some of the herds to Oomingmak, an Eskimo cooperative formed to manufacture and distribute luxury handcrafted garments made from qiviut, the extraordinarily soft underhair of the animal. Since the island can support a herd of only about 500 animals, musk-ox hunting, with permits selected by lottery, has continued since 1975.

212

Caribou formerly lived on the island but, according to Eskimo legend, "walked away into the sky" about 1880. Reindeer were brought to the island in 1920 and today number about 4000. The herd is the property of the islanders, supplying meat, hides and antlers for food, clothing and crafts.

A tundra-topped volcanic island with rolling hills, Nunivak has volcanic cones, sand dunes, beaches, sea cliffs, saltwater lagoons, lakes and streams. The Wilderness contains large eelgrass beds—a food source for migrating waterfowl—and extensive seabird rookeries, and is the wintering ground for the rare McKay's snow bunting. Mink, red foxes and arctic foxes are found on the island and sea lions, seals, walruses and whales offshore. The Eskimos of Mekoryuk, on the north side of the island, have a close tie with the Wilderness, whose lands and waters they have hunted for thousands of years; the tradition continues today.

The entire island, except for privately held lands, is included in the Yukon Delta National Wildlife Refuge, with the southern half, 600,000 acres (243 000 hectares), designated as wilderness. There is no recreational development within the Wilderness. Camping is permitted throughout; firewood is scarce. Fishing, hunting, powerboats, snowmobiles and fixed-wing aircraft are permitted.

Hypothermia is a constant danger on this wet, windswept island; prepare for long periods of rain and fog. In the subarctic maritime climate, summers are cooler than in Bethel, foggy and overcast; winters are cold and dry. (See the Nunivak Island weather table.) Winds are strongest from August through October. Frequent, violent and long-lasting storms make boating hazardous in the Bering Sea. Daylight on June 21 is 19 hours, on December 22, 6 hours.

Mekoryuk, the only community on the island, is connected to the mainland by scheduled air service; the nearest air taxi operation is in Bethel. Mekoryuk has a store, but no commercial lodging, although arrangements can be made through the Bering Sea Reindeer Corporation on the island.

Suggested reading: Peter Matthiessen, *Oomingmak: The Expedition to the Musk-Ox Island in the Bering Sea* (New York: Hastings House, 1967); Margaret Rau, *Musk-Oxen: Bearded Ones of the Arctic* (New York: Harper and Row, Publishers, 1976, juvenile); S. H. Reynolds, *Pleistocene Ovibos* (New York: Johnson Reprint Corp., reprint of 1934 edition).

70 Old Sitka State Historic Site

Location: Southeastern Alaska, north of Sitka; 57°07′N 135°23′W
Size: 51 acres (21 hectares)
High point: 50 ft (15 m)
Low point: Sea level

Best time of year; Any time
USGS map: Sitka A-5
Established: 1968
Managed by: Alaska Division of Parks

Originally established in 1799 by Alexander Baranof, manager of the Russian-American Company, and known as St. Michael the Archangel Redoubt, Old Sitka was the first Russian settlement in Southeastern Alaska. It eventually consisted of a two-story barrack, warehouses, a bathhouse, a kitchen, an eight-cornered *kashim*, or communal house, for native workers, a blacksmith shop and a cattle barn. Baranof would have preferred to build the fort where downtown Sitka now stands, but the area was occupied by Tlingit Indians.

During a Tlingit attack in the spring of 1802, all of the buildings in Old Sitka were burned; most of the men were killed and women and children were taken as hostages. Two years later, Baranof was successful in capturing the site of the Tlingit village to the south, and erected a lavish fortified home on a nearby hill. (See Baranof Castle Hill State Historic Site.)

Russian Orthodox cross. (Alaska Division of Parks photo by Robert A. Mitchell)

In 1878, Alaska's first cannery was built on the Old Sitka site, but four years later the machinery was moved to the Kasilof River on the Kenai Peninsula. Local students salvaged lumber from the buildings to build the first structure on the Sheldon Jackson College campus in Sitka.

Old Sitka Site was added to the National Register of Historic Landmarks in 1962. Today the site is marked by a Russian Orthodox cross, an interpretive plaque and a visitors' information center reminiscent of a Russian tea house. Picnic, walk the beach or fish from it, dig clams and watch for bald eagles, ravens and sea mammals. Camping, hunting, use of firearms, snowmobiles and off-road vehicles are not permitted. The Tongass National Forest Starrigavan Campground is just north of the ferry terminal and the Historic Site.

The maritime climate brings cool, wet summers and mild, wet winters. (See the Sitka weather table.) Winds are generally light, stronger on the beach. Daylight on June 21 is 18 hours, on December 22, 7 hours.

Old Sitka, located in a coastal rain forest of tall conifers, is north of the city of Sitka at Mile 6.9, Halibut Point Road, adjacent to the Sitka ferry terminal. Stores, restaurants, lodging, taxicabs, rental cars, scheduled air service, and air and water charters are available in Sitka. Local buses serve the area. Sitka is a port of call for the Southeastern Alaska state ferry and most cruise ships. Sightseeing tours generally include Old Sitka.

Suggested reading: Alaska Geographic, *Sitka and Its Ocean/Island World* (Anchorage: Alaska Northwest Publishing Co., 1982); Hector Chevigny, *Lord of Alaska: Baranov and the Russian Adventure* (Portland, Oreg.: Binford and Mort Publishers, 1970) and *Russian America: The Great Alaskan Venture, 1741-1867* (Portland: Binford and Mort Publishers, 1979); P.A. Tikhmenev, *A History of the Russian-American Company* (Seattle: University of Washington Press, 1978-1979); Keith Wheeler, *The Alaskans* (New York: Time-Life, 1977).

71 Palmer Hay Flats State Game Refuge

Location: Southcentral Alaska, southwest of Palmer; 61°30′N 149°25′W
Size: 25,340 acres (10 250 hectares)
High point: 150 ft (46 m)
Low point: Sea level

Best time of year: Foot, April–October; boat, April–October; ski, January–March
USGS maps: Anchorage, B-7, C-7
Established: 1975
Managed by: Alaska Department of Fish and Game

In this popular waterfowl viewing and hunting area, you can see more than 80 species of birds, including thousands of whistling and trumpeter swans as well as large populations of migratory and nesting Canada geese, pintails and mallards. Consisting entirely of tidal grasslands and mudflats in the Matanuska and Knik river deltas, the Refuge is "rubber boot country." The spring migration occurs in late

Goose watching, Palmer Hay Flats.

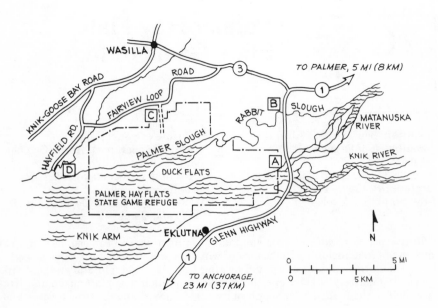

April and early May; the fall migration occurs in September and October, when hunting is permitted.

Swift incoming tides can strand unwary visitors. Sections of tideflats contain spots of quicksand-like mud. Be alert, and always travel with a companion.

Camping is unrestricted in this undeveloped refuge, although few dry sites are available. Campfires, firearms, horses, fixed-wing aircraft, powerboats, off-road vehicles and snowmobiles are permitted.

Expect cool, overcast summers and cold, overcast winters in this subarctic maritime climate. (See the Anchorage weather table.) Winds are normally moderate to strong, frequently blowing dust. Daylight on June 21 is 19½ hours, on December 22, 5½ hours.

The Refuge is accessible by boat from the Knik River Bridge (A), Mile 31, Glenn Highway; by floating Rabbit Slough (B), Mile 33, Glenn Highway (part of the route crosses private property); from Mile 6, Fairview Loop Road (C), where a side road leads south to the Hay Flats; or from Hayfield Road (D), which leaves Fairview Loop Road about Mile 9.4. Rental cars are available in Anchorage; scheduled buses between Anchorage and Palmer or Fairbanks travel the Glenn Highway. Meals and lodging are found at roadside businesses throughout the general area and in Anchorage, Eagle River, Palmer and Wasilla.

72 Petersburg Creek – Duncan Salt Chuck Wilderness, Tongass National Forest

Location: Southeastern Alaska, west of Petersburg; 56°50′N 133°10′W
Size: 46,777 acres (18 930 hectares)
High point: 3577 ft (1090 m)
Low point: Sea level

Best time of year: Foot, May–September; boat, May–September; ski, January–March
USGS maps: Petersburg D-3, D-4, D-5
Established: 1980
Managed by: U.S. Forest Service

Two low U-shaped valleys, richly cloaked in spruce-hemlock rain forest, lie on Kupreanof Island across Wrangell Narrows from Petersburg. With tide flats, a lagoon and a lake, muskeg bogs and rolling uplands, the Wilderness is a popular outdoor recreation area for local residents who come for picnicking, hiking, camping, boating and ski touring. Petersburg Lake National Recreation Trail, 6.5 mi (10 km) long and wet in places, leads from the tidewater mouth of Petersburg Creek to the lake.

Petersburg Creek, a salmon spawning stream, attracts black bears; bald eagles perch and nest on tall snags; and Sitka blacktail deer move quietly through the forest. Also found here are wolves, wolverines and waterfowl, including an occasional swan.

The U.S. Forest Service maintains three public-use recreational cabins (reservations required, fee), two in the Duncan Canal and Salt Chuck area and one at Petersburg Lake. Back-country camping is unrestricted and campfires are allowed, but expect the wood to be wet. Be cautious on the tide flats—don't get caught by the incoming tide. Boaters planning to enter or leave Duncan Salt Chuck should travel at slack high water, to avoid dangerous tidal currents, and watch for shallow submerged rocks in the channel. Fishing, hunting, firearms, fixed-wing aircraft and powerboats are all permitted in the Wilderness.

Cool, wet, overcast summers and mild, wet, overcast winters are typical of this maritime climate. (See the Petersburg weather table.) Winds are generally light. Daylight on June 21 is 18 hours, on December 22, 6½ hours.

The Wilderness is reached by boat or float plane, both available for charter in Petersburg. Restaurants, lodging and a wide variety of stores are also found in this charming fishing town. Petersburg has scheduled air service and is a port of call for the Southeastern Alaska state ferry.

Bird's-eye view of Duncan Salt Chuck. (U.S. Forest Service photo)

73

Potter Point
State Game Refuge

Location: Southcentral Alaska, south
of Anchorage; 61°05'N 149°50'W
Size: 2300 acres (930 hectares)
High point: 15 ft (5 m)
Low point: Sea level

Best time of year: Foot,
April–October; ski, January–March
USGS maps: Anchorage A-8; Tyonek
A-1
Established: 1971
Managed by: Alaska Department of
Fish and Game

Anchorage's backyard refuge contains Potter Marsh, a popular bird-watching area along the Seward Highway south of town. Not so well known are the tide flats and forested strip of Turnagain Arm coastline that lie across the highway northwest of Potter Marsh.

During the spring waterfowl migration in late April and early May, binocular-draped motorists line the Seward Highway, glassing for pintails, widgeon, mallards, green-winged teal, lesser Canada geese and whistling swans. More than 130 species of birds have been identified here. Illustrating the term "gaggle of geese," Canada geese nest within sight of the highway and rear their downy young to the fascination of just about everyone. Horned grebes, red-necked grebes, arctic terns, sandhill cranes and numerous ducks and gulls also nest in the marsh. Watch, too, for moose, coyotes, snowshoe hares, beavers, mink and muskrats. Salmon spawn in Rabbit Creek.

Canada geese with their young.

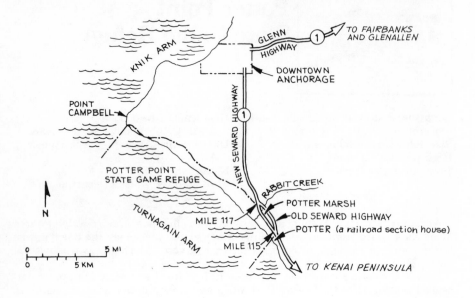

Potter Point State Game Refuge was established to protect waterfowl and enhance their habitat. Several highway pull-offs were constructed to provide safe viewing areas. Stay on the highway shoulders or pull-offs and restrain dogs. To avoid disturbing nesting waterfowl, fishing in Rabbit Creek is prohibited. The area between the New Seward Highway and the Old Seward Highway is closed to hunting. Some types of hunting are permitted in other parts of the Refuge in certain winter months. Since regulations are subject to change, check with the ADF&G before hunting. Only shotguns may be used. Motorized vehicles are allowed for transportation purposes from December 15 through March 31 on that portion of the Refuge seaward of the New Seward Highway. Hovercraft and motorized hang-gliders require a written permit. A public state outdoor rifle range is on the west side of the Seward Highway. Some private lands exist within the Refuge.

When walking on tidal lands, be alert; unvegetated areas can contain spots of quicksand-like silt; don't travel alone. Watch the incoming tide, too, so you won't be stranded.

Summers are cool and frequently overcast, winters cold and overcast, typical of a subarctic maritime climate. (See the Anchorage weather table.) Winds are moderate, occasionally strong. Daylight on June 21 is 19½ hours, on December 22, 5½ hours.

One of the most accessible refuges managed by ADF&G, Potter Point extends along both sides of the Seward Highway from Mile 117 to Mile 115, 10 mi (16 km) south of the Anchorage city center and slightly south of Rabbit Creek Road. Rental cars and taxicabs are available in Anchorage; scheduled buses travel the Seward Highway. The Alaska Railroad, en route from Anchorage to Whittier, parallels the highway through the Refuge but does not stop.

Visitors watching Canada geese, Potter Marsh.

Pribilof Islands

Location: Western Alaska, in the Bering Sea north of the Aleutian Islands; 57°N 170°W
Size: St. Paul Island, 28,160 acres (11 400 hectares); St. George Island, 22,000 acres (8900 hectares)
High point: St. Paul Island, 590 ft (180 m); St. George Island, 946 ft (288 m)

Low point: Sea level
Best time of year: June–August
USGS map: Pribilof Islands
Managed by: St. Paul and St. George community councils, Tanadgusix and Tanaq corporations and U.S. Fish and Wildlife Service

Once the hauling ground for great numbers of fur seals, sea otters, sea lions and walrus, the Pribilof Islands were discovered in 1786 by Russian fur traders who almost completely exterminated the sea otter population and slaughtered large numbers of the fur seals for their valuable furs. The Pribilof Aleut people suffered under Russian rule and, later, under U.S. rule as well, not gaining full rights of citizenship until 1966.

Sitting isolated and treeless in the stormy Bering Sea, St. Paul and St. George islands have villages of the same names, housing the 700 residents. St. Paul is the largest Aleut community in the world.

Common murres, St. Paul Island. (U.S. Fish and Wildlife Service photo by Jo Keller)

The northern fur seal herds, about 28,000 animals, are managed by the National Marine Fisheries, U.S. Department of Commerce, with a harvest each July. Portions of St. Paul and St. George islands and all of nearby tiny Walrus and Otter islands are in the Alaska Maritime National Wildlife Refuge.

Seabirds nest on all four islands, but St. George contains by far the largest populations, including thick-billed murres; least, crested and parakeet auklets; and red-legged kittiwakes—a total of more than 2,500,000 birds. Large numbers of reindeer are grazed on the islands' grasses. Watch also for arctic foxes. Walrus, sea otters, porpoises, dolphins and whales swim offshore.

The islands' weather is normally foggy and overcast; summers are cool, winters are cold in this subarctic maritime climate. (See the St. Paul weather table.) Winds are generally strong with frequent storms. Daylight on June 21 is 18 hours, on December 22, 7 hours.

All visits to St. Paul Island and the fur seals are arranged through Exploration Holidays and Cruises Inc. or through the Tanadgusix and Tanaq corporations (see Pribilof Islands, under Addresses of Parklands in the Appendix) working with Reeve Aleutian Airways. Visitors must arrive on a package tour which includes air fare, a bus tour of the island and lodging at the island's three-story hotel. Prepare for rain and strong winds. Viewing blinds are provided at the rookeries. Camping on St. Paul and St. George islands is limited to designated back-country areas. Sports hunting and firearms are not permitted during summer tour months.

Suggested reading: Alaska Geographic, *Islands of the Seals: The Pribilofs* (Anchorage: Alaska Northwest Publishing Co., 1982); Susan Hackley Johnson, *The Pribilof Islands: A Guide to St. Paul, Alaska* (St. Paul, Alaska: Tanadgusix Corporation, 1978); Dorothy Knee Jones, *A Century of Servitude: Pribilof Aleuts Under U.S. Rule* (Fairbanks: University of Alaska, 1980).

75 Quartz Lake
State Recreation Area

Location: Eastern Alaska, north of
Delta Junction; 64°13′N 145°50′W
Size: 280 acres (110 hectares)
High point: 1269 ft (387 m)
Low point: 75 ft (23 m)

Best time of year: Foot, May–October;
boat, June–September;
ski, February–April
USGS map: Big Delta A-4
Established: 1965
Managed by: Alaska Division of Parks

Set among boreal-forested hills, Quartz Lake, Lost Lake and their marshy and rolling lowlands are popular recreation spots for Fairbanks and Delta Junction residents. The road to Quartz Lake from the Richardson Highway was once part of a dogsled trail used by locals traveling south to Healy and the Tanana River when the area was used for mink farming and fur trapping.

Watch for muskrats in the water, shorebirds and, in the woods, moose, black bears, red foxes, snowshoe hares, lynx, porcupines, grouse, flying squirrels and red squirrels.

Quartz Lake. (Alaska Division of Parks photo by William L. Evans)

Quartz Lake State Recreation Area is an excellent destination for families with children and those who want developed campground facilities. Popular activities include picnicking, swimming, fishing, hiking, boating, ski touring and ice fishing. Hunting is permitted without the use of firearms. Facilities include picnic tables, a boat ramp and toilets. Camping is permitted only in campgrounds (28 units); campfires may be built only in the firepits provided. Power boats are permitted on the lake; snowmobiles, horses, off-road vehicles and aircraft are prohibited. Swimmers may pick up "swimmer's itch" when lake waters are warm.

Expect warm, dry summers with occasional thundershowers and a few cool, overcast, drizzly days. In this subarctic continental climate, winters are cold, dry and severe. (See the Fairbanks weather table.) Winds are light. Daylight on June 21 is 21½ hours, on December 22, 4½ hours. June and July bring large populations of mosquitoes and other biting insects.

The Recreation Area is accessible by automobile or scheduled bus (Fairbanks-Delta Junction route) from Mile 277.9, Richardson Highway, 12 mi (19 km) northwest of Delta Junction. A 2.6-mi (4.2-km) side road leads north to Quartz Lake. Rental cars are available in Fairbanks; restaurants and lodging can be found along the road and in Delta Junction and Fairbanks.

76

Rika's Landing
State Historic Site

Location: Eastern Alaska, near Delta Junction; 64°09′N 145°50′W
Size: 10 acres (4 hectares)
High point/low point: 995 ft (303 m)

Best time of year: Foot, May–October; boat, June–September; ski, February
USGS map: Big Delta A-4
Established: 1977
Managed by: Alaska Division of Parks

After the Tanana Valley gold strike in 1902, a spur to Fairbanks was added to the Valdez-to-Eagle trail. The new route, now part of the Richardson Highway, was a primary access to Interior Alaska. Roadhouses grew up along the trail, providing food and shelter for travelers and acting as freight destinations for nearby residents. One roadhouse—larger than most and the ultimate in functional design and construction—was built sometime between 1909 and 1915 on the southern bank of the Tanana River; a government toll ferry worked nearby. About 1918, Swedish-born

Rika's Roadhouse, circa 1928. (Photo courtesy of Skinner Collection, Alaska Historical Society)

Erika "Rika" Wallen began working at the roadhouse until, in 1925, she was reportedly deeded the property by owner John Hajdukovich in lieu of back wages. That year Rika became the first postmistress of the new Big Delta post office, operated in the east wing of the roadhouse, a position she held for many years. At the time of her death in 1969, at the age of 93, she was living in a nearby cabin. The roadhouse was placed on the National Register of Historic Places in 1976.

Watch for animals typical of the river floodplain—moose, black bears, snowshoe hares, river otters and beavers. You can gaze at the amazing structure of the roadhouse, but until restoration is complete, you won't be allowed to enter—most of the structures are unsafe. Fishing is permitted in the river; the Historic Site is closed to hunting, use of firearms, horses, snowmobiles and off-road vehicles. No recreational development for visitors exists; camping and campfires are not permitted.

The subarctic continental climate brings warm, dry summers and cold, dry, severe winters. (See the Fairbanks weather table.) Winds are light. Daylight on June 21 is 21½ hours, on December 22, 4½ hours. Expect large populations of mosquitoes during June and July.

Rika's Landing is accessible by automobile or scheduled bus (Fairbanks-Delta Junction route) from Mile 275, Richardson Highway, 9 mi (14 km) northwest of Delta Junction. A short side road (signed "Rekas Road") leads north to the roadhouse. Stores, restaurants and lodging are available in Delta Junction and Fairbanks. Automobiles may be rented in Fairbanks.

Suggested reading: Margaret E. Murie, *Two in The Far North* (Anchorage: Alaska Northwest Publishing Co., 1978).

77 Russell Fiord Wilderness, Tongass National Forest

Location: Southeastern Alaska, northwest of Yakutat; 59°45′N 139°20′W
Size: 348,701 acres (141 115 hectares)
High point: 7740 ft (2360 m)
Low point: Sea level

Best time of year: Foot, May–September; boat, April–September; ski, January–April
USGS map: Yakutat
Established: 1980
Managed by: U.S. Forest Service

Densely forested river valleys, tidewater glaciers, a two-armed fjord, alpine meadows and snow-capped peaks combine to create an area of extraordinary beauty. The Wilderness encompasses glacier-carved Russell and Nunatak fjords and portions of the surrounding rugged heavily glaciated mountains. The Fiord was named for Israel Cook Russell, who explored the Yakutat area and discovered the estuary in 1891.

Of great interest to geologists and biologists is the fact that Hubbard Glacier, north of the Wilderness, is advancing and slowly closing off the entrance of Russell Fiord to the ocean. If, as it did in the 1700s, Hubbard Glacier should completely close the mouth of Russell Fiord, the fjord would become a fresh-water lake and drain from its southern end into the Situk River.

Hubbard Glacier terminus and Osier Island, Russell Fiord. (Photo by Gil Mull)

The Yakutat Tlingit Indians have long used the area for subsistence needs. The Russian fur-traders were here, and the U.S. fortified the area during World War II.

Moose, mountain goats, wolves, brown (grizzly) bears and black bears are found in the Wilderness. Seabirds nest on Haenke Island and Cape Enchantment, and sea lions haul out on Knight Island. Watch also for Sitka blacktail deer, bald eagles, seals, sea otters, whales and the rare "blue" glacier bear, a color phase of the black bear. The Gulf of Alaska coastline is a major flyway for migratory birds.

Other than one public-use recreational cabin (reservations required, fee) on Situk Lake, the Wilderness is undeveloped. However, six additional recreational cabins are scattered on the Yakutat Foreland south of the Wilderness. A marked hiking trail from Mile 9, Forest Highway 10, west of Yakutat, leads to Situk Lake and the cabin, 7 mi (11 km) away; a brushy bear trail leads another 1.5 mi (2.4 km) to Mountain Lake. The Situk River and Lake are important spawning waters for all five species of Pacific salmon and for steelhead trout. Fishing is excellent for salmon, trout and Dolly Varden char.

Back-country camping is unrestricted. Campfires, fishing, hunting, firearms, horses, fixed-wing aircraft, powerboats and snowmobiles are all permitted. Prepare for long periods of rain and strong winds, which can delay planned pickups. Storms are most intense in autumn and winter. Travel and camp to avoid meeting or attracting bears, especially near salmon spawning streams. Entering Russell Fiord by boat is hazardous due to icebergs from Hubbard Glacier.

In this maritime climate, expect cool summers and mild winters, with frequent precipitation and overcast. (See the Yakutat weather table.) Winds are moderate, often strong. At high elevations a severe arctic climate prevails. Daylight on June 21 is 19 hours, on December 22, 6 hours. Treeline is about 1500 ft (460 m).

Access to the Wilderness is by foot on the Situk Lake trail or by boat or float plane from Yakutat. Food, lodging and scheduled air service are available in Yakutat.

Suggested reading: Alaska Geographic, *Yakutat: The Turbulent Crescent* (Anchorage: Alaska Northwest Publishing Co., 1975); Frederica de Laguna, *Under Mt. St. Elias: The History and Culture of the Yakutat Tlingit* (Washington, D.C.: Smithsonian Institution Press, 1972).

78  St. Lazaria Refuge, Alaska Maritime National Wildlife Refuge

Location: Southeastern Alaska, southwest of Sitka; 56°59′N 135°42′W
Size: 65 acres (26 hectares)
High point: 281 ft (86 m)
Low point: Sea level

Best time of year: May–September
USGS map: Port Alexander
Established: 1909
Managed by: U.S. Fish and Wildlife Service

A prime breeding habitat for more than a million seabirds, the refuge was originally established by President Teddy Roosevelt to protect an extremely fragile nesting area. One of the state's largest populations of Leach's storm petrels and fork-tailed storm petrels nest in burrows amid the spruce and hemlock roots, emerging only at night to feed in the open ocean. Visitors are requested not to walk on the

St. Lazaria Island. (U.S. Fish and Wildlife Service photo)

island, since the tunnels collapse easily underfoot; special permits are required to land.

Also found in this wilderness refuge are burrowing tufted puffins and rhinoceros auklets and crevice-nesting pigeon guillemots, common murres, glaucous-winged gulls and pelagic cormorants, as well as many other sea and land birds. Both burrowing and cliff-nesting birds leave their nests when disturbed, giving local gulls a chance to feed on the untended eggs and chicks; visitors are asked to view birds from boats without disturbing them.

Originally named "Robin Islands" by the first explorers in 1780, the two volcanic outcroppings are connected by a low tide-washed saddle; steep cliffs ringing the knobs make landing and access difficult. In 1809, the Russians renamed the island St. Lazaria. Designated a Wilderness Area in 1970, the refuge was added to the Alaska Maritime National Wildlife Refuge system in 1980.

As is typical of a maritime climate, the area experiences frequent overcast, with cool, wet summers and mild, wet winters. (See the Sitka weather table.) Winds are normally moderate to strong. Daylight on June 21 is 18 hours, on December 22, 6½ hours.

Sitka, 15 mi (24 km) away, provides stores, restaurants, lodging, air taxis and charter boats. A port of call for the Southeastern Alaska state ferry and most cruise ships, the city is also served by frequent scheduled air service.

Suggested reading: Alaska Geographic, *Sitka and Its Ocean/Island World* (Anchorage: Alaska Northwest Publishing Co., 1982); report reprints, available from Refuge headquarters.

79

Salmon National Wild River

Location: Northwestern Alaska, in
  Kobuk Valley National Park; 67°30′N
  159°45′W
River rating: WW1-FWA
Popular trip length: 140 mi (230 km)
Best time of year: July–September

Annual high water: July–August
USGS maps: Baird Mountains; Baird
  Mountains A-2, A-1, A-3; Selawik D-3
Designated as Wild River: 1980
Managed by: National Park Service

Rising in the rolling tundra-covered Baird Mountains of the western Brooks
Range, the Salmon descends through a poplar-spruce forest to meander finally into
the Kobuk River. In its upper navigable reaches, below Anaktok and Sheep creeks,
this clear small river alternates short shallow pools and riffles. Downriver, the pools
lengthen and the river deepens. Plan to spend some time hiking the tundra country
above the confluence. From Anaktok-Sheep creeks to the village of Kiana is about 90
mi (140 km). The entire length is designated as Wild River.

As might be suspected from its name, the river attracts large numbers of bears
during salmon spawning season. Watch the brown (grizzly) bears, black bears, Dall
sheep, moose, wolves, wolverines, red foxes and lynx. Caribou use the Salmon River
valley during their southward fall migration to winter range in the Kobuk Valley.

Camping is unrestricted, but is generally best on river bars or nearby tundra. On
the latter, select a site with good natural drainage so you don't have to ditch around
the tent and make a scar that will remain for years. Build campfires on river gravel,
not on burnable tundra. Fishing, firearms, fixed-wing aircraft, and powerboats are

*Lining boats through shallows, Salmon River. (National Park Service photo by Pat
Pourchot)*

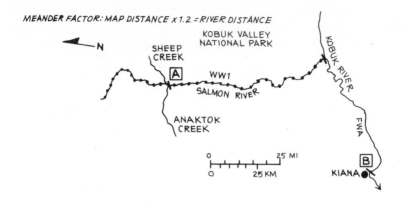

MEANDER FACTOR: MAP DISTANCE x 1.2 = RIVER DISTANCE

all permitted; hunting is not. There are large amounts of private land along the lower river.

Weather tends toward cool summer temperatures, becoming warmer in the lowlands. (See the Kotzebue weather table.) Winds can be strong, making float travel difficult when they blow from downstream. Daylight on June 21 is 24 hours, on December 22, ½ hour.

To get to the river, take an air taxi to gravel bars near the confluence of Anaktok and Sheep creeks (A), elevation 1700 ft (520 m) or higher. Leave the river at the village of Kiana (B), elevation 10 ft (3 m). Air taxis, scheduled air service, food and lodging are available at both Kotzebue and Kiana.

Suggested reading: Alaska Geographic, *The Kotzebue Basin* (Anchorage: Alaska Northwest Publishing Co., 1981); John McPhee, *Coming into the Country* (New York: Farrar, Straus and Giroux, 1977).

80  Selawik National Wildlife Refuge, Wilderness and Wild River

Location: Northwestern Alaska, east of Kotzebue; 66°30′N 159°W
Wild River rating: WW1
Popular trip length: 230 mi (370 km)
Refuge/Wilderness size: 2,150,000 acres (870 100 hectares)
High point: 2021 ft (616 m)
Low point: Sea level

Best time of year: Foot, mid-June–September; boat, July–September; ski, March–April
USGS maps for Refuge/Wilderness: Selawik, Shungnak
USGS maps for Wild River: Shungnak, Selawik
Established: 1980
Managed by: U.S. Fish and Wildlife Service

An extensive system of estuaries, brackish lakes and wetlands along the lower Kobuk and Selawik rivers and the uplands of the Selawik River valley, the delta provides prime feeding and nesting habit for migratory birds from six continents.

Caribou, Selawik Refuge. (U.S. Fish and Wildlife Service photo by Jo Keller)

Snow geese and sandhill cranes stop en route from northern Siberia to winter in California and Mexico; wheatears fly to Africa; other birds travel to China, India and Australia. The Refuge lands are the only recorded North American nesting area for the Asiatic whooper swan. The Eskimo curlew, now thought to be extinct, was once found in the Kobuk-Selawik area; perhaps it still survives somewhere in this remote region. Birds most commonly found in the Refuge are pintails, scaup, cackling Canada geese, lesser Canada geese, white-fronted geese, whistling swans and all four North American loons.

In the uplands, extensive areas of boreal forest with lichen ground cover attract wintering caribou of the Western Arctic herd. Where once the woolly mammoth and the saber-toothed tiger roamed, today's Refuge inhabitants include moose, black bears, brown (grizzly) bears, arctic foxes, red foxes, lynx, wolves, wolverines, beavers, marten, mink, muskrats and river otters.

The Selawik National Wild River, a key habitat for the Alaskan sheefish, rises amid spruce forests in the eastern extension of the Refuge in the Purcell Mountains. Then, meandering slowly through treeless pingo-dotted wetlands, it enters Selawik Lake, an expansive body of water only 5 to 15 ft (2 to 5 m) deep.

Summers in the Refuge are cool and foggy near the coast, but warmer inland, in this subarctic climate that is transitional between maritime and continental. Winters are cold, dry and severe. (See the Kotzebue weather table.) Winds are normally moderate, but can be strong near the coast. Daylight on June 21 is 24 hours, on December 22, 2½ hours.

In this undeveloped Refuge, camping is unrestricted, although campsites are not plentiful in the wetlands. Campfires are permitted, but wood is scarce. Expect large populations of mosquitoes and other biting insects throughout the summer months. Numerous private lands exist within the Refuge boundaries. Fishing, hunting, powerboats, snowmobiles and fixed-wing aircraft are all permitted.

River travel: To float the Selawik National Wild River, take an air taxi to one of the lakes near Shiniliaok Creek (A), elevation 600 ft (180 m). From here it is about 230 mi (370 km) to the village of Selawik (B), at sea level; the lower 70 mi (110 km) are not

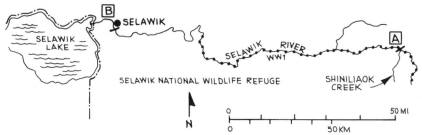

SELAWIK

SELAWIK LAKE

SELAWIK RIVER WW1

SELAWIK NATIONAL WILDLIFE REFUGE

SHINILIAOK CREEK

50 MI

50 KM

N

MEANDER FACTOR: MAP DISTANCE x 2 = RIVER DISTANCE

designated Wild River and are bordered by private lands. The upper third of the River has numerous boulders and sweepers; on the lower 25 mi (40 km), the current is slow, and strong west winds can build waves up to 3 ft (1 m) high.

Access to the Refuge is by air or boat. Air taxis operate from Kiana and Kotzebue; informal boat charters are available at most villages. Kotzebue, Kiana, Noorvik and Selawik have scheduled air service and general stores. Kotzebue, a transportation and distribution center for northwestern Alaska, provides modern lodgings.

Suggested reading: Alaska Geographic, *The Kotzebue Basin* (Anchorage: Alaska Northwest Publishing Co., 1981); J. L. Giddings, *The Arctic Woodland Culture of the Kobuk River* (Philadelphia: University of Philadelphia Museum, 1952) and *Kobuk River People* (College, Alaska: University of Alaska Press and University of Washington, 1961); U.S. Department of the Interior, *Proposed Selawik National Wildlife Refuge*, Final Environmental Impact Statement (Washington, D.C.: U.S. Government Printing Office, 1974).

81

Semidi Refuge, Alaska Maritime National Wildlife Refuge

Location: Southwestern Alaska, southwest of Kodiak Island; 56°10′N 156°40′W
Size: 251,930 acres (101 952 hectares)
High point: 1024 ft (312 m) on Aghiyuk Island

Low point: Sea level
Best time of year: May–August
USGS map: Sutwik A-3
Established: 1932
Managed by: U.S. Fish and Wildlife Service

A group of islands in the stormy Gulf of Alaska, the wilderness refuge is home for millions of pelagic seabirds, some of the largest seabird colonies in North America. Precipitous cliffs up to 200 ft (60 m) high attract murres, kittiwakes, puffins, fulmars and parakeet auklets. The area is also used by sea otters, sea lions, seals, dolphins, porpoises and whales. Consisting of nine major treeless islands, numerous small islets, rocks and submerged lands, the Semidi group was redesignated a part of the Alaska Maritime National Wildlife Refuge in 1980.

Chowiet Island, Semidi Refuge. (U.S. Fish and Wildlife Service photo)

Recreational use of the Refuge is discouraged during nesting periods, since the birds are highly sensitive to disturbance. Visitor restrictions may be in effect, so contact the Refuge Manager before traveling to the islands.

In this maritime climate, the ocean waters are ice-free the entire year, with cool, wet summers and mild, wet winters. (See the Cold Bay weather table.) The area receives three times the precipitation of Cold Bay. Winds are generally strong; frequent severe storms are accompanied by gale-force winds. Daylight on June 21 is 18 hours, on December 22, 7 hours.

Devoid of development, the islands are remote and hard to reach. There are no anchorages or airstrips, and the waters are not well charted. Violent storms make boating hazardous.

Kodiak and Sand Point have stores, restaurants, lodging, scheduled air service and air taxis, and are ports of call for the Southwestern Alaska state ferry.

Suggested reading: report reprints, available from Refuge headquarters.

82

Sheenjek
National Wild River

Location: Northeastern Alaska, in the Arctic National Wildlife Refuge and Wilderness; 68°30′N 143°55′W
River rating: WW2-FWB
Popular trip length: 270 mi (430 km)
Best time of year: July–mid-September

Annual high water: mid-May–June
USGS maps: Table Mountain B-5, B-4, A-4; Coleen D-5, D-6; Coleen; Christian; Fort Yukon D-1, D-2, C-2
Designated as Wild River: 1980
Managed by: U.S. Fish and Wildlife Service

A gentle clearwater river flowing through a broad valley, the Sheenjek skirts some of the highest peaks in the Brooks Range. Providing a long, relatively easy float through some of Alaska's finest wilderness, the river rises on the Arctic Divide and flows south from open tundra through subarctic boreal forest to the Yukon River wetlands. Hiking is excellent in the upper river area.

Extensive overflow ice accumulates in headwater areas in the winter. Since it remains most of the summer, scout ahead to be sure the channel is open all the way through. From Ambresvajun ("Last") Lake to Fort Yukon is 220 mi (350 km), the first 80 mi (130 km) designated Wild River.

In this area rich with wildlife, watch for Dall sheep, caribou, moose, brown (grizzly) bears, black bears, wolves, wolverines, red foxes, lynx and beavers. The lower part of the Sheenjek is in the Yukon Flats National Wildlife Refuge, one of North America's finest migratory waterfowl nesting areas.

Camping is best on river gravel bars, providing some relief from the mosquitoes of the tundra and woods. Build campfires there, too, not in areas with vegetation. Since rainstorms upstream can rapidly raise the river level several feet, choose campsites carefully. Fishing, hunting and fixed-wing aircraft are permitted in the area.

In this subarctic continental climate, warm, dry summers prevail in the lowlands, with cooler weather and more precipitation in the mountains. (See the Wiseman

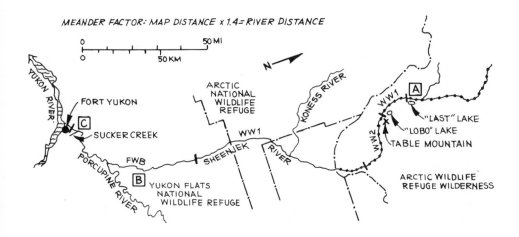

MEANDER FACTOR: MAP DISTANCE x 1.4 = RIVER DISTANCE

Icy portage, Sheenjek River. (U.S. Fish and Wildlife Service photo)

weather table.) Winds are generally light. Daylight on June 21 is 24 hours, on December 22, 0 hours, with several hours of twilight.

The most popular float trip begins at Ambresvajun ("Last") Lake (A), elevation 2400 ft (730 m), Kuirzinjik ("Lobo") Lake, elevation 2200 ft (670 m) or upper river bars, with access by air taxi. Leave the river by air taxi from the lower Sheenjek (B) or the Porcupine River, elevation about 450 ft (140 m), or continue to Fort Yukon. Be sure to beach the boats at Sucker Creek (C), elevation 420 ft (130 m), a tributary of the Porcupine just north of Fort Yukon, where a short road leads to the town. The actual confluence of the Porcupine with the Yukon River is 2 mi (3 km) downstream from Fort Yukon. Air taxis, scheduled air service, food and lodging are available at Fort Yukon.

Suggested reading: John P. Milton, *Nameless Valleys, Shining Mountains* (New York: Walker and Co., 1969); Margaret E. Murie, *Two in the Far North* (Anchorage: Alaska Northwest Publishing Co., 1978); Averill S. Thayer, "Canoeing on the Sheenjek" (*Alaska* magazine, October 1970).

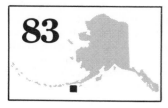

83

Simeonof Refuge, Alaska Maritime National Wildlife Refuge

Location: Southwestern Alaska, in the Shumagin Islands; 54°54′N 159°18′W
Size: 26,046 acres (10 540 hectares)
High point: 1436 ft (438 m)
Low point: Sea level

Best time of year: May–September
USGS map: Simeonof Island
Established: 1958
Managed by: U.S. Fish and Wildlife Service

In the Gulf of Alaska, 58 mi (93 km) south of the Alaska Peninsula, Simeonof was originally established as a wildlife refuge to protect sea otters and the extensive kelp beds that are their habitat. The Shumagin Islands contain the greatest diversity and abundance of seabirds in the entire Alaska Maritime NWR system—as many as three million, especially murres, puffins, auklets, murrelets, kittiwakes, gulls, cormorants and storm petrels.

One of about 30 named islands in the Shumagin Island group, Simeonof was used for cattle and fox ranching from 1896 to 1930, then abandoned. Cattle were reintroduced in 1962 and continue to graze there on leaseholdings. With its gently sloping shores and white sand beaches, Simeonof Island attracts relatively few seabirds. Nearby Murie Inlet, with nesting gulls and Arctic terns, is also included in

Simeonof Island harbor. (U.S. Fish and Wildlife Service photo)

the Refuge; the two islands and nearby tidal waters, along with the rest of the Shumagins, became part of the Alaska Maritime National Wildlife Refuge in 1980.

Arctic and red foxes and river otters, all predatory on seabirds, are found on the islands. So are ground squirrels, ptarmigan and migratory waterfowl, with black brant and emperor geese wintering. Sea otters, seals, sea lions and whales use the Gulf waters. Although the islands were the site of the first contact between Alaska natives and the outside world in 1741, their plant and animal life has only recently been studied.

Simeonof Island has no recreational development. Although it has an excellent harbor with good anchorage, the island is isolated and hard to reach; fog and frequent, long-lasting storms make boating hazardous. Human visitors are requested not to disturb nesting birds. Contact the Refuge Manager before traveling to the islands. Scheduled air service lands at Sand Point, which has air taxis, boat charters, a store, a restaurant and lodging. The Southwestern Alaska state ferry docks at Sand Point occasionally.

Although the weather in the Shumagin Islands is somewhat better than in the Aleutians, the maritime climate brings nearly constant overcast, cool, wet summers and mild, wet winters. (See the Cold Bay weather table.) Ocean waters are ice-free the entire year. Winds are generally strong, with gale-force winds accompanying storms. Daylight on June 21 is 18 hours, on December 22, 7 hours. Many of the islands have rocky precipitous sea cliffs. They are treeless, except where Sitka spruce have been introduced; extensive brush grows below 1000 ft (300 m) elevation.

Suggested reading: Edgar P. Bailey, "Breeding Seabird Distribution and Abundance in the Shumagin Islands, Alaska" (*The Murrelet*, vol. 59 [1978], 82-91); Karl W. Kenyon, *The Sea Otter in the Eastern Pacific Ocean* (New York: Dover Publications, 1975).

84 Sitka National Historical Park

Location: Southeastern Alaska, in Sitka; 57°03′N 135°19′W
Size: 107 acres (43 hectares)
High point: 12 ft (4 m)
Low point: Sea level

Best time of year: Any time
USGS map: Sitka A-4
Established: 1910
Managed by: National Park Service

A raven sits atop a bear that sits atop a beaver at a bend on a pleasant trail. The stately hemlocks nearby seem to have released their spirits in the form of finely carved Tlingit and Haida totem poles. Watch a new pole being carved and visit the restored Russian Bishop's House, a reminder of colonial Russian America.

In 1802, a Tlingit Indian attack destroyed the first Russian settlement in Southeastern Alaska, north of the Park at Old Sitka. (See Old Sitka Historic Site.) Most of the Russian and transplanted Aleut men were killed and the Aleut women and children taken as hostages. Two years later, Alexander Baranof, manager of the fur-trading Russian-American Company, returned with 800 Aleuts, 120 Russians and four ships to confront the Tlingits on this site. The "Battle of Sitka" succeeded in forcing the 700 Tlingit warriors and their families to abandon their fort on the Indian River and their homes at Sitka. This was the last major native act of resis-

Totem pole, Sitka National Historical Park.

tance to white domination in this area. (See also Baranof Castle Hill State Historic Site.)

Picnic tables, cooking grills, a shelter, a visitors' center, interpretive programs and 2 mi (3 km) of trails invite a leisurely visit. Fishing is permitted; camping, hunting and snowmobiles are not. The Park grounds are open from 7 a.m. to 10 p.m. Sundays through Thursdays and from 7 a.m. to 11 p.m. Fridays and Saturdays.

Bordered by Sitka Sound and the Indian River, this flat wooded peninsula has a maritime climate with cool, wet summers and mild, wet winters. (See the Sitka weather table.) Winds are normally light in the forest. Daylight on June 21 is 18 hours, on December 22, 7 hours.

Only 1 mi (1.6 km) from downtown Sitka, the park is within easy walking distance. Follow Lincoln Street east from the center of town to the park. Food, lodging, rental cars, taxis and local buses are available. Guided sightseeing tours coordinate with ferry and cruise ship schedules. The Southeastern Alaska state ferry dock is 7 mi (11 km) north of Sitka.

Suggested reading: Hector Chevigny, *Russian America: The Great Alaskan Venture* (Portland, Oreg.: Binford and Mort Publishers, 1979); James R. Gibson, *Imperial Russia in Frontier America* (New York: Oxford University Press, 1976); Ted Hinckley, *Americanization of Alaska, 1867-1897* (Palo Alto, Calif.: Pacific Book Publishers, 1972); Aurel Krause, *The Tlingit Indians* (Seattle: University of Washington Press, 1956); Hilary Stewart, *Looking at Indian Art of the Northwest Coast* (Seattle: University of Washington Press, 1979).

Coastal rain forest, Baranof Island.

85

South Baranof Wilderness, Tongass National Forest

Location: Southeastern Alaska, south of Sitka; 56°45′N 135°W
Size: 319,568 acres (129 325 hectares)
High point: 4528 ft (1380 m)
Low point: Sea level

Best time of year: Foot, May–October; boat, May–October; ski, December–March
USGS map: Port Alexander
Established: 1980
Managed by: U.S. Forest Service

With precipitous mountains, snowfields and hanging glaciers, high mountain lakes, alpine meadows, waterfalls and long winding fjords, South Baranof Wilderness is a visual delight. Its mountains, the protruding summits of a partially submerged glacier-carved landscape, are cloaked in a dense coastal spruce-hemlock rain forest. Timberline is about 2000 ft (600 m).

The area receives some of the highest precipitation in Southeastern Alaska. Little Port Walter, south of the Wilderness, averages 221 inches (561 cm) a year, while the watershed above Little Port Walter suffers under an estimated 400 inches (1000 cm) a year, making it the wettest location in the state.

The abundant wildlife includes mountain goats, Sitka blacktail deer, brown (grizzly) bears, furbearers, bald eagles and, in the marine waters, sea lions, seals and whales. An exceptionally high density of sea otters is found in the Necker Islands. The Pacific coast is a major flyway for migrating birds.

The U.S. Forest Service maintains four public-use recreational cabins (reservations required, fee), at Avoss Lake, Davidof Lake, North Plotnikof Lake and Rezanof Lake, as well as 6 mi (10 km) of marked hiking trails.

Camping, campfires, fishing, hunting, firearms, fixed-wing aircraft, powerboats and snowmobiles are all permitted. Firewood will be wet. Camp and travel to avoid confrontations with the island's large bear population. Frequent rainstorms and strong winds can delay planned pickup—bring extra food, good rain gear and warm clothes. Swift tidal currents in restricted bays and inlets can make boating hazardous. Because the Wilderness fronts on the open Pacific Ocean, only experienced boaters should attempt to visit the fjords.

This is a maritime climate in the extreme, with much rain and overcast weather. Summers are cool, winters mild. (See the Little Port Walter weather table.) Precipitation decreases radically to the north, where Sitka, just outside the Wilderness, receives 100 inches (250 cm) a year. Winds are variable, but particularly strong off the ocean; during autumn storms they may reach 100 mph (160 kph). Daylight on June 21 is 18 hours, on December 22, 7 hours. Prominent peak: Mount Ada, elevation 4528 ft (1380 m).

The Wilderness is reached by float plane or charter boat from Sitka, which also has food, stores, lodging and scheduled air service and is a port of call for the Southeastern Alaska state ferry.

The island was named in 1805 for Alexander Andreievich Baranof, the first governor of the Russian-American colonies. Baranof was in charge of building the first headquarters of the fur-trading Russian-American Company at Kodiak in 1792, later moving it to Sitka.

Suggested reading: Alaska Geographic, *Sitka and Its Ocean/Island World* (Anchorage: Alaska Northwest Publishing Co., 1982); Alfred Meyer, ed., *Red Salmon, Brown Bear: The Story of an Alaskan Lake* (New York: World Publishing Co., 1971).

86 South Prince of Wales Wilderness, Tongass National Forest

Location: Southeastern Alaska, southwest of Ketchikan; 54°50′N 132°20′W
Size: 90,996 acres (36 825 hectares)
High point: 3580 ft (1091 m)
Low point: Sea level

Best time of year: Foot, May–September; boat, May–September
USGS maps: Craig A-1, A-2; Dixon Entrance D-1, D-2, D-3
Established: 1980
Managed by: U.S. Forest Service

An intricate maze of islands, bays, inlets and lakes, the Wilderness sits on the southwestern corner of Prince of Wales Island and takes in the watershed from Brownson Bay in the south to Klakas Inlet in the north. Trees stunted by the full fury of ocean storms sweeping in from Dixon Entrance cling to rocky promontories. The Wilderness is an inviting, but remote, low-elevation maritime rain forest, with rolling hills, streams, lakes, muskeg meadows and tidal lowlands. The first Haida

Indian village in Southeastern Alaska, now abandoned, was established at Klinkwan in the 19th century.

Wildlife includes Sitka blacktail deer, black bears, wolves and bald eagles. Numerous migratory waterfowl and seabirds winter in the protected bays. Offshore, watch for seals, sea lions, whales and, especially in the Barrier Islands, sea otters.

The regulations of this undeveloped back-country wilderness permit camping, campfires, hunting, fishing, firearms, fixed-wing aircraft and powerboats; off-road vehicles are not permitted. Prepare for long periods of rain and strong winds. Prolonged storms, most intense in autumn and winter, can delay planned pickup. Swift tidal currents in restricted bays and inlets can make boating hazardous.

The maritime climate brings cool, wet, overcast summers and mild, wet, overcast winters. (See the Annette Island weather table.) Winds are constant, often severe. Daylight on June 21 is 17½ hours, on December 22, 7 hours.

Access to the Wilderness is by float plane or boat. Air taxis are based at Ketchikan, charter boats at Hydaburg and Ketchikan. Food is available at Hydaburg, Craig, Ketchikan and Klawock, all of which have scheduled air service. The last three also have lodging. The Southeastern Alaska state ferry stops at Ketchikan.

Barrier Islands. (U.S. Forest Service photo)

Tanana uplands at Twelvemile Summit. The Pinnell Mountain trail climbs dome on left.

87

Steese National Conservation Area

Location: Eastern Alaska, northeast of Fairbanks; 65°30′N 146°W
Size: 1,220,000 (494 000 hectares)
High point: 5580 ft (1700 m)
Low point: 850 ft (260 m)
Best time of year: Foot, June–September; boat, May–September; ski, February–April

USGS maps: Charley River, Circle
Established: 1980
Managed by: Bureau of Land Management

Established to maintain the environmental quality of a portion of the rolling Tanana–Yukon uplands, yet permit multiple use and sustained yields, the Conservation Area permits mineral exploration and development. Several gold mining operations are currently at work. Over the years, miners have unearthed fossil remains of mastodons and other pre-glacial mammals. The public may pan for gold in Birch Creek National Wild River, which is currently muddy from gold-mining activities in its headwaters above the Wild River designation.

In two units straddling the Steese Highway, the Conservation Area contains broad treeless summits, covered by dry alpine tundra above 3500 ft (1100 m), that beckon the hiker, dropping to spruce-birch-aspen forested valleys with clear streams. In this area of discontinuous permafrost, look for ice lenses exposed in unstable soil areas along eroding stream banks. The Pinnell Mountain National Recreation Trail, 24 mi (39 km) long, follows the south border of the northern unit; Birch Creek National Wild River meanders through the southern unit.

243

Watch for wildlife of the uplands: moose, caribou, brown (grizzly) bears, black bears, wolves, coyotes, wolverines, red foxes, lynx, porcupines and beavers. The area contains the highest population of forest grouse in Alaska, including ruffed, sharp-tailed and spruce grouse and willow, rock and white-tailed ptarmigan.

Back-country camping and campfires are permitted, but be particularly careful with fire during dry periods. The Conservation Area is undeveloped except for two small emergency shelters along the Pinnell Mountain Trail. Expect large populations of mosquitoes and other biting insects from June through August. Numerous mining claims exist throughout; you are legally permitted to cross them so long as you do not interfere with mining operations. For your own safety, ask before crossing, if possible, and do not pick up anything from the ground. Fishing, hunting, firearms, horses, fixed-wing aircraft, powerboats and snowmobiles are all permitted.

River travel: Birch Creek National Wild River, WW1-2, see description.

Summers are warm and dry, winters are cold, dry, and severe in this subarctic continental climate. (See the Fairbanks weather table.) Winds are normally light. Snow can fall on the summits in any month. Avoid these peaks and other open areas during summer lightning storms. Although daylight at sea level at this latitude is 21½ hours on June 21, between June 20 and June 22 the midnight sun is visible above 3600 ft (1100 m). On December 22, expect 3 hours of daylight. Prominent peaks are: Mount Prindle, elevation 5286 ft (1611 m); Lime Peak, elevation 5062 ft (1543 m); Pinnell Mountain, elevation 4721 ft (1439 m).

Other than unimproved miners' roads, no public roads penetrate the Conservation Area, but access is easily available from the Pinnell Mountain trailhead, Mile 85.6, Steese Highway, on Twelvemile Summit; at Mile 94, an access road to Birch Creek; on Eagle Summit at the Mile 107 Pinnell Mountain trailhead; and at the Mammoth Creek bridge, Mile 116. Scheduled air service, food and lodging are available at Central, Circle and Circle Hot Springs; air taxis operate from Circle and Circle Hot Springs.

Suggested reading: U.S. Department of the Interior, *Proposed Birch Creek National Wild River*, Final Environmental Impact Statement (Washington, D.C.: U.S. Government Printing Office, 1975).

88 Stikine
– LeConte Wilderness,
Tongass National Forest

Location: Southeastern Alaska, east of Petersburg; 56°45´N 132°10´W
Size: 448,841 acres (181 640 hectares)
High point: 10,023 ft (3055 m)
Low point: Sea level

Best time of year: Foot, April–September; boat, April–September; ski, January–March
USGS maps: Bradfield Canal, Petersburg, Sumdum
Established: 1980
Managed by: U.S. Forest Service

A wilderness of rugged, heavily glaciated mountains dropping steeply to tidewater, granite spires, icefields and glaciers, Stikine–LeConte includes 40-mi- (64-km-) long LeConte Glacier, the southernmost tidewater glacier in North America. The

Stikine-LeConte Wilderness from Limb Island. (U.S. Forest Service photo)

silty, braided Stikine River flows through the Coast Mountains from Canadian uplands, navigable for 158 mi (254 km) from Telegraph Creek, B.C., to tidewater. The area has long been occupied by native peoples who used the river as a major travel corridor. "Stikine" in the Tlingit Indian language translates as "great river." Joseph LeConte was a professor of geology at the University of California in 1887, when the glacier and bay were named for him.

The grasslands, tidal marshes and sandbars of the Stikine River delta are a major staging ground and nesting area for migratory birds. Dense spruce-hemlock rain forests extend from the coastal flatlands to about 2000 ft (600 m) on the mountain slopes. Stands of cottonwoods forest the valley floors. Along the Stikine River, watch for moose, black bears, brown (grizzly) bears, wolves, wolverines, Sitka blacktail deer and bald eagles. Mountain goats, found in the high country in the summer, use winter ranges nearer tidewater—the Horn Cliffs north of LeConte Bay, the Wilkes Range and the slopes of Mt. Stinenia. Seals, sea lions, porpoises, dolphins and whales are found offshore.

An area popular with Petersburg and Wrangell residents, the wilderness has a developed picnic site and 13 public-use recreational cabins (reservations required, fee). An enclosed bathing shelter invites soaking at Chief Shakes Hot Springs on the Stikine River. Back-country camping, mountaineering and campfires are unrestricted, but plan for frequent precipitation. Fishing, hunting, firearms, fixed-wing aircraft and powerboats are all permitted; off-road vehicles are not. Bears are numerous in lowland areas, especially near salmon spawning streams. Severe avalanche hazard can exist in the mountains. Thick brush in the lowlands discourages hiking.

River travel and boating: Stikine River, WW2-FWB, Telegraph Creek to tidewater, 158 mi (254 km). Where freight boats plied the waters in earlier years, recreational boaters now drift. Access to Telegraph Creek is easiest by air taxi from Petersburg or Wrangell. Because you cross international borders, you must report to both Canadian and U.S. customs. In LeConte Bay, keep your distance from the glacier face; waves resulting from calving can swamp floating boats and damage beached craft. Floating and rolling icebergs create similar hazards.

The maritime climate brings cool, wet, overcast summers and mild, wet, overcast winters. (See the Wrangell weather table.) Significantly less precipitation falls inland. Cold, severe arctic weather prevails at high elevations. Winds are moderate to severe. Daylight on June 21 is 18 hours, on December 22, 6½ hours. Prominent peaks: Kates Needle, elevation 10,023 ft (3055 m); Castle Mountain, elevation 7329 ft (2234 m).

The Wilderness is reached by float plane or boat. Petersburg and Wrangell have air taxis, charter boats, food, lodging and scheduled air service, and are ports of call for the Southeastern Alaska state ferry. Telegraph Creek, B.C., is also accessible by automobile via a narrow winding and steep gravel road leaving the Cassiar Highway at Dease Lake.

Suggested reading: Marty Loken, *The Stikine River* (Anchorage: Alaska Geographic, Alaska Northwest Publishing Co., 1979); John Muir, *Travels In Alaska* (1915; reprint ed., New York: AMS Press, 1978).

89 Susitna Flats State Game Refuge

Location: Southcentral Alaska, northwest of Anchorage; 61°20′N 150°30′W
Size: 301,947 acres (122 194 hectares)
High point: 600 ft (200 m)
Low point: Sea level

Best time of year: Foot, April–October; boat, April–October; ski, January–March
USGS map: Tyonek
Established: 1976
Managed by: Alaska Department of Fish and Game

Susitna Flats and Mount Susitna. (U.S. Fish and Wildlife Service photo by Jo Keller)

The extensive wetlands and rolling low hills of the Susitna River delta are prime resting grounds for migrating waterfowl and excellent nesting terrain. Of particular interest are the large populations of Thule white-fronted geese, Canada geese, arctic loons, widgeons and green-winged teal. Trumpeter swans nest in the uplands. The best time for watching migrating birds is late April and early May. Numerous hunters use the area in September.

Camping and campfires are permitted, but dry land and wood are scarce in the tidal grasslands. There is no public recreational development. Hunting cabins, built before the establishment of the Refuge, are private property and should not be disturbed. Firearms, fishing, horses, powerboats, off-road vehicles, snowmobiles and fixed-wing aircraft are permitted. To avoid disturbing nesting waterfowl, airplanes must maintain a minimum altitude of 500 ft (150 m) over the Refuge except when landing or taking off. Tide flats contain treacherous areas of "bottomless" soft silt. Incoming tides can be swift and strand the unwary.

Expect cool, overcast summers and cold, overcast winters in this subarctic maritime climate. (See the Anchorage weather table.) Winds are moderate, often strong. Daylight on June 21 is 19½ hours, on December 22, 5½ hours.

Although the Refuge is only 4 mi (6 km) across Knik Arm from Anchorage International Airport, consider it remote and do not visit it without full survival equipment. Air taxis, stores, restaurants and lodging are available in Anchorage, Chugiak, Eagle River, Palmer and Wasilla.

90

Tebenkof Bay Wilderness, Tongass National Forest

Location: Southeastern Alaska, on
 Kuiu Island southwest of Petersburg;
 56°30′N 134°10′W
Size: 66,839 acres (27 049 hectares)
High point: 3355 ft (1023 m)
Low point: Sea level

Best time of year:
 Foot, May–September;
 boat, May–September
USGS maps: Petersburg B-6, C-6; Port
 Alexander B-1, C-1
Established: 1980
Managed by: U.S. Forest Service

Skunk cabbage.

An intricate many-armed bay opening onto Chatham Strait, Tebenkof has long been used by Alaska natives and local fur farmers. The Wilderness includes the entire watershed of the bay. Rolling uplands of dense rain forest surround the saltwater bay, with muskeg bogs, lakes and streams; alpine vegetation starts at about 2000 ft (600 m).

Watch for Sitka blacktail deer, black bears, wolves, wolverines, bald eagles and trumpeter swans. Chatham Strait is a major migratory route for waterfowl and seabirds that use Tebenkof Bay both summer and winter. Seals, sea lions, porpoises and dolphins use the bay; whales are often spotted in Chatham Strait. Wilderness waters contain cutthroat, rainbow and steelhead trout, Dolly Varden, salmon, crab, shrimp, herring and halibut. The Troller Islands are one of Southeastern Alaska's most important fisheries.

The area is undeveloped and camping is unrestricted. Campfires are permitted, although firewood will probably be wet. Fishing, hunting, firearms, fixed-wing aircraft and powerboats are permitted; off-road vehicles are not. Prepare for long periods of rain. Swift tidal currents in restricted bays and inlets and ocean swells can make boating hazardous.

Cool, wet, overcast summers and mild, wet, overcast winters are typical of this maritime climate. (See the Sitka weather table.) Winds are variable, often severe during autumn storms. Daylight on June 21 is 18 hours, on December 22, 7 hours.

Off the beaten path, the Wilderness is normally reached by boat or float plane. Petersburg and Wrangell have air taxis and, along with Kake, have charter boats, food, lodging and scheduled air service and are ports of call for the Southeastern Alaska state ferry.

Suggested reading: U.S. Forest Service, *Kayaking and Canoeing in Tebenkof Bay* (contact the Wilderness ranger office for a copy).

91 Tetlin National Wildlife Refuge

Location: Eastern Alaska, southeast of Tok; 62°40′N 142°W
Size: 700,000 acres (283 000 hectares)
High point: 8000 ft (2400 m)
Low point: 1650 ft (503 m)

Best time of year: Foot, May–October; boat, June–September; ski, February–April
USGS maps: Nabesna, Tanacross
Established: 1980
Managed by: U.S. Fish and Wildlife Service

Tetlin is one of the coldest areas on the North American continent. Nearby Snag, Yukon Territory, has registered −81°F (−63°C). The Refuge is an excellent example of an Interior Alaska boreal forest ecosystem. Some sections of its highly productive wetlands contain 600 nesting ducks per square mile. Seventeen species of ducks, including ring-necks, redheads and blue-winged teal, nest here, as do large populations of sharp-tailed grouse, ptarmigan and raptors. Up to 300,000 sandhill cranes visit the Refuge during fall migration. Watch also for moose, black bears, brown (grizzly) bears, coyotes, red foxes, lynx, Dall sheep, wolves, wolverines, snowshoe hares, beavers and other furbearers.

Nabesna River basin, Tetlin Refuge. (U.S. Fish and Wildlife Service photo by Jo Keller)

The undulating alluvial plain, with extensive marshes and numerous lakes, was once the bottom of an Ice Age lake. Today, bordered by the Alaska Highway on the north and Canada on the east, the Refuge lowlands rise in the south to rolling uplands and the foothills of the Alaska Range.

The Refuge is undeveloped. Camping and campfires are unrestricted, but be careful with fires, especially during dry periods. Fishing, hunting, horses, powerboats, snowmobiles and fixed-wing aircraft are all permitted; all-terrain vehicles are restricted to designated trails. Expect large populations of mosquitoes and other biting insects from June through August. Avoid disturbing waterfowl during breeding and nesting season.

River travel: Nabesna River, WW2-FWA, from Nabesna to Northway, 66 mi (106 km); Chisana-Nabesna rivers, FW, from Northway Road to about Mile 1280, Alaska Highway, near Bitter's Creek, 20 mi (32 km).

Summers in this subarctic continental climate are warm and dry; winters are cold, dry and severe. (See the Northway weather table.) Winds are generally light. Daylight on June 21 is 20 hours, on December 22, 5 hours.

The Refuge is easily accessible from the Alaska Highway between Mile 1221.3 and Mile 1286.5. Scheduled buses travel the highway frequently, particularly in the summer, en route to Haines or Whitehorse from Tok, Fairbanks and Anchorage. Rental automobiles are available in Fairbanks and Tok; air taxis are based in Northway, Tanacross and Tok. Stores, restaurants and lodging are found at roadside businesses and at Northway and Tok.

Suggested reading: Robert A. McKennan, *The Upper Tanana Indians* (New Haven: Yale University, Department of Anthropology, 1959); U.S. Department of the Interior, *Proposed Wrangell–St. Elias National Park*, Final Environmental Impact Statement (Washington, D.C.: U.S. Government Printing Office, 1974).

92 · Tinayguk National Wild River

Location: Northcentral Alaska, in Gates of the Arctic National Park; 67°45′N 151°30′W
River rating: WW2
Popular trip length: 120 mi (190 km)
Best time of year: July–September
Annual high water: July–August

USGS maps: Wiseman D-4, D-3, C-3 (see North Fork of the Koyukuk National Wild River description for trip-continuation maps)
Designated as Wild River: 1980
Managed by: National Park Service

A small clear river flowing through a glacier-carved alpine valley in the Brooks Range, the Tinayguk has extensive rocky rapids, especially at low water. Heading in the rugged Endicott Mountains and flowing southward from the Arctic Divide, the river drains into the North Fork of the Koyukuk National Wild River. Only a few scattered stands of spruce in the valley bottom dot the sweep of the tundra. The Tinayguk is a remote valley not often visited, and its entire river length is designated as Wild River. From the Savioyok Creek confluence to Bettles (Evansville) is about 120 mi (190 km). About 35 mi (56 km) of this distance is on the Tinayguk.

Wildlife populations are substantially lower here than in valleys like the North Fork that offer good travel routes northward. However, watch for Dall sheep on the peaks, moose, brown (grizzly) bears, caribou, wolves, wolverines and red foxes.

In a valley with little, if any, evidence of man, camp and travel to preserve this quality. Camp on gravel bars, if possible; on tundra, don't ditch around the tent. Use a camping stove for cooking. Avoid burning the precious few trees which grow so slowly in this north country. If you must build campfires, do so on river gravel and bury the blackened rocks. Fishing, firearms, horses, snowmobiles and fixed-wing aircraft are permitted; hunting is not. Expect large numbers of mosquitoes in summer months.

The subarctic continental mountain climate brings cool summers except when the air is quiet and the sun shines. The area can receive snow any time and in general receives more precipitation than Wiseman. (See the Wiseman weather table.) Winds

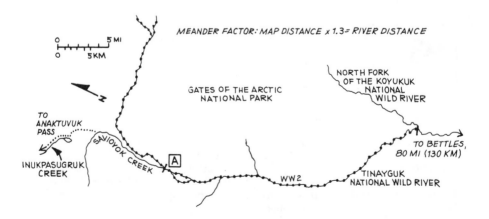

MEANDER FACTOR: MAP DISTANCE x 1.3 = RIVER DISTANCE

Tinayguk River. (National Park Service photo)

are normally light. Daylight on June 21 is 24 hours, on December 22, 0 hours, with 5 hours of twilight.

The river is reached by taking a light plane from Bettles (Evansville) to gravel bars in the vicinity of Savioyok Creek (A), elevation 2000 ft (600 m), or by hiking over Inukpasugruk Creek from Anaktuvuk Pass community, a distance of 16 mi (26 km). End a float trip at Bettles. (See North Fork of the Koyukuk National Wild River description for a map of this part of the trip.) Both communities are served by scheduled air flights and have general stores. Bettles has a restaurant, lodging and air taxi service.

Suggested reading: Robert Marshall, *Alaska Wilderness: Exploring the Central Brooks Range* (Berkeley: University of California Press, 1970; originally published in 1956 as *Arctic Wilderness*).

Tlikakila River

93

Location: Southcentral Alaska, in Lake Clark National Park; 61°40′N 153°30′W

River rating: WW1-4

Popular trip length: 70 mi (110 km)

Best time of year: July–September

Annual high water: July–August

USGS maps: Kenai D-8, C-8; Lake Clark C-1, C-2, B-2, B-3, B-4, A-4

Designated as Wild River: 1980

Managed by: National Park Service

A small glacier-fed river flowing through the deep narrow valley of a major earth fault, the Tlikakila is surrounded by rugged snow-capped peaks, glaciers, waterfalls and sheer rock cliffs. From its alpine headwaters at Summit Lake in the heart of the Chigmit Mountains to its mouth at turquoise Lake Clark, boaters float through some of the most impressive scenery in Alaska. Summit Lake, in Lake Clark Pass where glaciers from all sides almost meet on the valley floor, is the portal to excellent hiking terrain. When you run the Tlikakila, take a few extra days to explore this country.

From Summit Lake, the river drops through a densely forested valley with thick underbrush. Gravel bars of the North Fork invite foot travel, but don't plan extensive hiking from the lower river. Just below the confluence with the North Fork, a short section of WW3-4 rapids can be portaged on the left bank. At high water levels, other WW3-4 rapids appear in the next 3 mi (5 km). The entire 50-mi (80-km) length is designated as Wild River. A ranger station at Port Alsworth on Lake Clark lies 23 mi (37 km) down the lake from the river's mouth.

Watch for Dall sheep on the mountain crags, caribou, moose, black bears, wolves, wolverines and, particularly in the fall at the mouth of the river, brown (grizzly) bears.

Camping and campfires are permitted, as are fishing, powerboats, snowmobiles, fixed-wing aircraft landings and firearms for self-protection. Hunting is prohibited within the Park, but permitted in the Preserve.

In a subarctic climate transitional between maritime and continental, summers

Tlikakila River. (National Park Service photo)

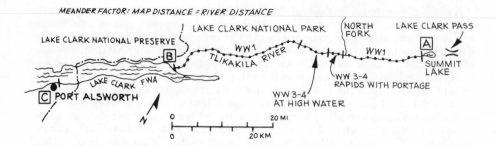

are cool and often overcast. (See the Port Alsworth weather table.) Winds are variable. Daylight on June 21 is 19½ hours, on December 22, 5½ hours.

To reach the river, take a float plane to Summit Lake (A), elevation 1000 ft (300 m). A short portage from the lake to floatable water is necessary. After running the river, take an air taxi from the river's mouth (B) at Lake Clark, elevation 245 ft (75 m), or paddle to Port Alsworth (C). Air taxis are based at Port Alsworth, Anchorage, Homer and Kenai. Lodging and meals are available at wilderness lodges in the Lake Clark area; reservations are generally required.

94

Togiak National Wildlife Refuge and Wilderness

Location: Western Alaska, west of Dillingham; 59°N 160°W

Size: 4,105,000 acres (1 661 000 hectares)

High point: 5500 ft (1700 m)

Low point: Sea level

Best time of year: Foot, June–September; boat, June–September; ski, January–April

USGS maps: Bethel, Dillingham, Goodnews, Hagemeister Island, Nushagak Bay

Established: 1980

Managed by: U.S. Fish and Wildlife Service

Protecting major salmon spawning streams and important seabird nesting areas, the Refuge stretches from restless ocean shores to the treeless tundra uplands of the Ahklun Mountains. The area, which has been occupied for 5000 years by Yupik Eskimos and Aleut Indians, has also seen Captain James Cook, Russian explorers and numerous U.S. miners. Today, residents of the area continue to use the resources of the Refuge for their subsistence needs.

The former Cape Newenham National Wildlife Refuge, established in 1969, is now included in Togiak NWR. Cape Newenham State Game Refuge, established in 1972 to protect the Chagvan Bay waterfowl habitat and now located within Togiak NWR, continues to be administered by the Alaska Department of Fish and Game. The

King Salmon catch, Togiak River. (National Park Service photo by Pat Pourchot)

Subsistence fishing, Tokiak River. (U.S. Fish and Wildlife Service photo by Jo Keller)

northern half of Togiak NWR, 2,270,000 acres (919 000 hectares), has been designated as wilderness.

The largest seabird colonies are found at Cape Newenham and Cape Peirce, where more than a million birds are found offshore in the summer. Waterfowl use the marshy lowlands, lagoons and numerous lakes of the southern part of the Refuge as well as the lowlands along the Togiak River. Common mammals of the Refuge uplands are brown (grizzly) bears, moose, wolves, wolverines and, offshore, sea otters, seals, sea lions, walruses and whales.

Camping is unrestricted and campfires are permitted in this undeveloped roadless refuge; a camping stove is recommended. Avoid attracting or interfering with bears, which are most likely to be found along streams with spawning salmon. Expect large populations of mosquitoes and other biting insects in summer months. Carry extra food since fog, storms or wind often delay planned air pickup. Fishing, hunting, horses, powerboats, snowmobiles and fixed-wing aircraft landings are permitted. Numerous private landholdings exist within the Refuge.

River travel: Kanektok River, WW3-FWC, from Kagati Lake to Quinhagak, 80 mi (130 km); Togiak River, WW2-FWC, from Togiak Lake to Togiak, 60 mi (100 km), WW1-2, from Upper Togiak Lake to Togiak Lake, 10 mi (16 km); Goodnews River, WW3-FWC, from Goodnews Lake to Goodnews Bay, 60 mi (100 km).

Expect cool, foggy summers near the coast, warmer summers inland. Winters are cold, dry and severe in this subarctic maritime continental climate. (See the King Salmon weather table.) Winds are moderate and continuous along the coast, lighter inland. Daylight on June 21 is 18½ hours, on December 22, 6 hours.

The Refuge is reached by air, with scheduled service to Dillingham, Goodnews, Manokotak, Platinum, Quinhagak, Togiak and Twin Hills. Air taxis are available at Dillingham. Manokotak, Quinhagak, Togiak and Dillingham have stores; the latter also has restaurants and lodging.

Suggested reading: Alaska Geographic, *Bristol Bay Basin* (Anchorage: Alaska Northwest Publishing Co., 1978); Margaret Lantis, *Ethnohistory in Southwestern Alaska and the Southern Yukon* (Lexington: University Press of Kentucky, 1970); U.S. Department of the Interior, *Proposed Togiak National Wildlife Refuge*, Final Environmental Impact Statement (U.S. Government Printing Office, 1974).

Tongass National Forest

Location: Southeastern Alaska; 57°N 134°W

Size: 16,578,000 acres (6 708 900 hectares)

High point: 15,300 ft (4663 m)

Low point: Sea level

Best time of year: Foot, May–September; boat, May–September; ski, January–March

USGS maps: Atlin, Bradfield Canal, Craig, Dixon Entrance, Juneau, Ketchikan, Mt. Fairweather, Prince Rupert, Port Alexander, Sitka, Skagway, Sumdum, Taku River, Yakutat

Established: 1907

Managed by: U.S. Forest Service

Forested islands, winding steep-walled fjords, towering snow-capped mountains and massive glaciers—Tongass National Forest covers almost the entire Southeastern Alaska panhandle, making it the largest national forest in the United States. Integrally tied to the economy of the local people, the National Forest provides timber resources, fish spawning grounds, wildlife habitat, recreational lands and tourist attractions.

View from Harbor Mountain near Sitka.

Customs checkpoint, Alaska-Canada border, Tongass National Forest.

Originally established as the Alexander Archipelago Forest Reserve in 1902, the land became the Tongass National Forest in 1907 and has received numerous additions since. In 1980, specific sections were designated by the Alaska National Interest Lands Conservation Act as national monuments and wilderness areas. These lands are treated separately in this book: Admiralty Island National Monument, Misty Fiords National Monument, and 12 additional Wildernesses—Coronation Island, Endicott River, Maurelle Islands, Petersburg Creek–Duncan Salt Chuck, Russell Fiord, South Baranof, South Prince of Wales, Stikine–LeConte, Tebenkof Bay, Tracy Arm–Fords Terror, Warren Island and West Chichagof–Yakobi.

In a region of varied and abundant wildlife, the most visible animals include bald eagles, black bears, brown (grizzly) bears, coyotes, wolves, red foxes, raccoons, marten, weasels, mink, wolverines, river otters, lynx, Sitka blacktail deer, moose, mountain goats, pikas, snowshoe hares, marmots, red squirrels, northern flying squirrels, beavers, muskrats and porcupines. In the coastal waters are found sea otters, sea lions, seals, whales, dolphins and porpoises.

Beachcombing, picnicking, hiking, camping, backpacking, boating, diving, river running, ski touring, mountaineering, snowmobiling, fishing, and hunting in the National Forest are all very much a part of the Southeastern lifestyle. The National Forest contains about 150 public-use recreational cabins (reservations required, fee), eight camping shelters, one ski area, 24 picnic areas, three boat ramps and a visitors' center, offering numerous interpretive programs, at Mendenhall Glacier near Juneau. Other facilities include 10 campgrounds (178 units, fee, no reservations) and more than 400 mi (640 km) of marked trails. Back-country camping is generally unrestricted, although a few sensitive areas may be closed. Campfires, firearms, sport fishing and hunting and fixed-wing aircraft are permitted. Powerboats and snowmobiles may be prohibited in a few environmentally sensitive areas. One of the state's major alpine ski areas, Eaglecrest, is located on Douglas Island near Juneau.

A large number of bears live in the National Forest—camp and travel to avoid confrontations or attracting them. Large sections of private land exist within the National Forest boundaries; respect signs and do not enter private structures.

Boating and river running: Swift tidal currents in restricted bays and inlets or high winds can make boating hazardous. Check tide tables and enter lagoons and areas of swift tidal currents at slack water. River travel: Admiralty Island Canoe Traverse, FWA, between Semour Canal and Mitchell Bay, with portages, 26 mi (42 km); Stikine River, WW2-FWB, from Telegraph Creek, B.C., in Canada, to tidewater in the U.S., 130 mi (210 km); Situk River, WW1, from Nine Mile bridge to Situk Landing (Yakutat area), 15 mi (24 km); Alsek River, WW2-4, from Haines Junction to tidewater, with 10 mi (16 km) portage, 140 mi (230 km).

Weather in the Tongass National Forest is controlled by a maritime climate. Skies are generally overcast; summers are cool, winters mild. Annual precipitation varies from 26 inches (66 cm) at Skagway to more than 220 inches (560 cm) on the south end of Baranof Island. (See the descriptions of individual monuments and wildernesses for specific weather information.) Daylight on June 21 varies from 17½ hours in the south to 19 hours on the northern boundary, on December 22, from 7½ to 6 hours. Prominent peaks: Mount Fairweather, elevation 15,300 ft (4663 m); Mount Root, elevation 12,860 ft (3920 m); Mount Crillon, elevation 12,726 ft (3879 m).

There is no direct land connection with the state or federal highway systems except at Hyder, in Misty Fiords National Monument. Automobiles, trucks and other vehicles, however, can be taken to all major communities via the Southeastern Alaska state ferry system. Highway access points are at Skagway, Haines, Prince Rupert, B.C. and Seattle. The ferry calls at Angoon, Auke Bay, Haines, Hoonah, Hollis, Juneau, Kake, Ketchikan, Metlakatla, Pelican, Petersburg, Sitka, Skagway, Tenakee Springs and Wrangell.

Automobiles may be rented at Haines, Juneau, Ketchikan, Sitka and Skagway, while Craig, Hollis, Juneau, Klawock, Metlakatla, Petersburg, Sitka, Skagway and Wrangell have taxicabs. Scheduled buses serve Haines, Skagway and Prince Rupert on the contiguous highway system, and local buses run between Juneau, Douglas and Auke Bay. The White Pass and Yukon Route railway connects Whitehorse, Y.T., with Skagway.

Scheduled air service stops at Angoon, Annette, Craig, Elfin Cove, Gustavus, Haines, Hoonah, Hydaburg, Juneau, Kake, Ketchikan, Klawock, Pelican, Petersburg, Sitka, Skagway, Stewart, B.C., Wrangell and Yakutat. Air taxis operate from Angoon, Gustavus, Haines, Juneau, Ketchikan, Metlakatla, Petersburg, Sitka, Skagway, Wrangell, and Yakutat. Charter boats, food and lodging are found in most communities.

The lands and waters now within the Tongass National Forest have figured prominently in the history of Alaska, from the arrival of Russian fur traders in 1799 to the transfer of Alaska to the U.S. in 1867 at Sitka to the present day of fishermen, loggers and state legislators.

Suggested reading: Alaska Geographic, *Southeast: Alaska's Panhandle* (Anchorage: Alaska Northwest Publishing Co., 1977); John Muir, *Travels in Alaska* (1915; reprint ed., New York: AMS Press, 1978); Margaret Piggott, *Discover Southeast Alaska With Pack and Paddle* (Seattle: The Mountaineers, 1974); Laurence Rakestraw, *A History of the United States Forest Service in Alaska* (Anchorage: Alaska Historical Commission and U.S. Forest Service, Department of Agriculture, 1981); O.M. Salisbury, *The Customs and Legends of the Thlinget Indians of Alaska* (New York: Bonanza Books, 1962).

Totem pole detail. (Photo by Sandy Rabinowitch)

96

Totem Bight
State Historic Park

Location: Southeastern Alaska, north
of Ketchikan; 55°25′N 131°46′W
Size: 10 acres (4 hectares)
High point: 30 ft (9 m)
Low point: Sea level

Best time of year: Any time
USGS map: Ketchikan B-6
Established: 1972
Managed by: Alaska Division of Parks

In the late 1930s a U.S. Forest Service Civilian Conservation Corps (CCC) program salvaged late 19th-century Tlingit and Haida Indian totem poles. Replicas of decaying poles were carved and a clan house erected. Most of the poles, made of easily worked red cedar, tell a legend or provide a graphic history of an event; they face the sea to greet approaching canoes. The Indians' strong ties with nature are evident in the use of animal symbols; intelligent, bold Raven, creator of the world, frequently stands at the top. Tlingits and Haidas had sophisticated and highly organized tribal structures, among the finest in the Western Hemisphere.

Originally known as Mud Bay, the area was in 1954 given the more euphonious name of Totem Bight, a "bight" being a bay or cove. The site was added to the National Register of Historic Places in 1970.

Picnic, walk the beach along Tongass Narrows, fish from shore and watch for bald eagles, ravens, seals, sea lions, dolphins, porpoises, sea otters and whales. A 0.25-mi (0.4-km) marked foot trail winds through the totem poles; parking area and toilets are provided. Hunting, horses, snowmobiles and camping are not permitted. Several Tongass National Forest campgrounds are nearby.

Expect rain. The maritime climate brings cool, wet summers and mild, wet winters. (See the Ketchikan weather table.) Winds are normally light. Daylight on June 21 is 17½ hours, on December 22, 7½ hours.

Totem Bight is 10 mi (16 km) north of Ketchikan on North Tongass Highway. A port of call for the Southeastern Alaska state ferry and many cruise ships, Ketchikan has stores, restaurants, lodging, car rentals, scheduled air service, charter boats and air taxis.

Suggested reading: Mary G. Balcom, *Ketchikan: Alaska's Totemland* (Ketchikan: Balcom Books, 1980); Viola E. Garfield and Linn A. Forrest, *The Wolf and the Raven: Totem Poles of Southeastern Alaska* (Seattle: University of Washington Press, 1961); Erna Gunther, *Indian Life on the Northwest Coast of North America* (Chicago: University of Chicago Press, 1972); Edward L. Keithahn, *Monuments in Cedar* (Seattle: Superior Publishing Co., 1963).

97  Tracy Arm – Fords Terror Wilderness, Tongass National Forest

Location: Southeastern Alaska, southeast of Juneau; 57°45′N 133°10′W
Size: 653,179 acres (264 332 hectares)
High point: 8526 ft (2599 m)
Low point: Sea level

Best time of year: Foot, June–October; boat, June–October
USGS maps: Sumdum, Taku River
Established: 1980
Managed by: U.S. Forest Service

Sheer rock walls and heavily glaciated mountains surround two narrow glacier-carved fjords, Tracy Arm and Endicott Arm, each more than 30 mi (48 km) long. At the heads of both fjords are active tidewater glaciers that continually calve icebergs into salt water. Large quantities of floating ice create considerable hazard and frequently prevent boat travel to the heads of the fjords. Of the Wilderness land mass, 20% is covered by ice and snowfields.

Fords Terror was reportedly named for the crew member of a naval vessel who, in 1899, rowed into the fjord and was caught in tide rips for six terrifying hours. B. F. Tracy was Secretary of the Navy under President Benjamin Harrison from 1889 to 1893.

Wildlife of the area includes mountain goats, black bears, brown (grizzly) bears, wolves, wolverines, bald eagles and a few Sitka blacktail deer. Holkham Bay, at the

Sawyer Glacier, Tracy Arm. (U.S. Forest Service photo by Kyoko)

junction of the fjords, is a wintering area for migratory waterfowl and seabirds. In the salt water, watch for seals, sea lions, porpoises, dolphins and whales.

No recreational development is provided, making the area attractive to those looking for uncrowded boating and mountaineering. Spruce-hemlock rain forests cover the mountain slopes to about 1500 ft (460 m). Camping and campfires are allowed, but level sites are rare due to the steep terrain; firewood is likely to be wet. Fishing is poor. Hunting, firearms, mountaineering, fixed-wing aircraft and powerboats are all permitted.

This is a remote area, not suitable for casual visits. Prolonged storms can delay planned pickup and make boating dangerous. Floating icebergs can roll without warning. Do not approach active glacier faces closely; waves resulting from calving can swamp floating boats and damage beached boats. Severe avalanche conditions can exist in snow-covered areas.

At low elevations, expect a maritime climate, with cool, wet, overcast summers and mild, wet, overcast winters. (See the Juneau weather table.) High elevations in the Coast Mountains have a severe arctic climate. Winds are variable, frequently extremely strong at high elevations and on exposed headlands. Daylight on June 21 is 18 hours, on December 22, 6½ hours. Prominent peaks: unnamed, elevation 8526 ft (2599 m) and lower; Mount Sumdum, elevation 6666 ft (2032 m).

The Wilderness is most easily reached by air taxi or charter boat, both available in Juneau and Petersburg. Both cities have a wide variety of stores, restaurants and lodging, and are served by scheduled airlines and the Southeastern Alaska state ferry. Neither is accessible from the contiguous highway system.

Suggested reading: John Muir, *Travels in Alaska* (1915; reprint ed., New York: AMS Press, 1978).

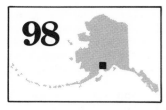

98

Trading Bay
State Game Refuge

Location: Southcentral Alaska,
southwest of Anchorage; 60°55′N
151°40′W
Size: 168,933 acres (68 365 hectares)
High point: 650 ft (200 m)
Low point: Sea level

Best time of year: Foot,
April–October; boat, April–October;
ski, January–March
USGS maps: Kenai, Tyonek
Established: 1976
Managed by: Alaska Department of
Fish and Game

Located at the mouth of the Chakachatna and McArthur rivers, the Refuge
protects prime waterfowl habitat on the shores of Cook Inlet. Of special interest are
large numbers of migrating snow geese, Pacific white-fronted geese and cackling
Canada geese during late April and early May. Watch also for moose, black bears,
brown (grizzly) bears and wolves. The terrain consists of tidelands, salt-grass flats,
river delta wetlands and rolling lowlands.

Spring waterfowl migration begins in late April, fall migration in September,
when numerous hunters use the area. Camping and campfires are permitted, but dry

Oil rig in Cook Inlet, Trading Bay and Mount Spurr in background.

land and wood are scarce in the tidal grasslands. There is no public recreational development. Firearms, horses, powerboats, off-road vehicles, snowmobiles and fixed-wing aircraft are permitted. To avoid disturbing nesting waterfowl, airplanes must maintain a minimum altitude of 500 ft (150 m) over the Refuge, except when landing or taking off. Tide flats contain treacherous areas of "bottomless" soft silt. Incoming tides can be swift, stranding the unwary.

Summers are cool and frequently overcast, winters cold and overcast, typical of a subarctic maritime climate. (See the Anchorage weather table.) Winds are moderate, often strong. Daylight on June 21 is 19½ hours, on December 22, 5½ hours.

A remote area at the foot of the scenic snow- and glacier-covered Chigmit Mountains, the Refuge is rarely visited by anyone other than hunters. It is most easily accessible by air. Air taxis are available at Anchorage, Kenai and Tyonek. Tyonek, Anchorage and Kenai have food; the latter two have lodging as well.

99 Trans-Alaska Pipeline Utility Corridor

Location: Central and Northcentral Alaska, between Fairbanks and Prudhoe Bay; 65°05′N to 69°30′N, 150°W

Size: 3,600,000 acres (1 460 000 hectares)

High point: 7610 ft (2320 m)

Low point: 300 ft (90 km)

Best time of year: Automobile, May–September; foot, mid-May–September; boat, May–September

USGS maps: (South to north) Livengood, Tanana, Bettles, Wiseman, Chandalar, Philip Smith Mountains, Sagavanirktok

Established: 1971

Managed by: Bureau of Land Management

The unpaved Dalton Highway, originally known as the "North Slope Haul Road," penetrates a scenic, hitherto-roadless wilderness as it parallels the Trans-Alaska oil pipeline across the Yukon River and north to Prudhoe Bay on the Arctic Ocean. A strip of land 336 mi (541 km) long and 12 to 24 mi (19 to 39 km) wide was set aside as a utility and transportation corridor for the pipeline and utilities. Traversing the broad scenic valleys of the Yukon, Koyukuk and Dietrich rivers and crossing the crest of the Brooks Range to the North Slope, the corridor protects wildlife habitat and allows low-impact public recreation. The corridor extends from Washington Creek, Mile 18 on the Elliott Highway, north to about Mile 355, Dalton Highway, near Sagwon, 70 mi (110 km) south of Prudhoe Bay—a total road distance within the corridor of 410 mi (660 km). The Dalton Highway north of Mile 211, Dietrich Camp, is closed to public travel.

Boreal forests line river valleys south of the Brooks Range, with trees giving way to tundra on many summits and ridges. From the crest of the Brooks Range north is arctic tundra. The road passes the historic town of Wiseman, on the Middle Fork of the Koyukuk River south of the Brooks Range. Its heyday was about 1910 during the gold rush, but Wiseman today is a quiet sleepy village of fewer than 15 people who like their privacy. Numerous private landholdings and mining claims are in the

Caribou crossing under Trans-Alaska Pipeline.

vicinity of Wiseman, and all buildings are private property; do not trespass.

Wildlife is abundant by northern standards. Watch for moose, black bears, brown (grizzly) bears, caribou, Dall sheep, wolves, wolverines, lynx, coyotes, red foxes, snowshoe hares, marmots, porcupines, red squirrels, northern flying squirrels, arctic ground squirrels, raptors, migratory waterfowl and other birds. Feeding wild animals is a state offense punishable by fine, imprisonment or both. Guard against curious bears–they can be dangerous.

The corridor provides excellent recreational opportunities for hiking, rock-climbing, wildlife observation and river running. Camping is not generally restricted, but designated areas are suggested. Do not camp on the pipeline right of way. Campfires, fishing, hunting, firearms, horses, fixed-wing aircraft landings, powerboats and snowmobiles are all permitted; unauthorized use of off-road vehicles is not permitted.

River travel (listed south to north): Hess Creek, WW1-FWB, from Mile 24, Dalton Highway to Rampart, 70 mi (110 km); Yukon River, FWC; Mile 56, Dalton Highway; Kanuti River, WW1-FWB, from Mile 107, Dalton Highway to Hughes, 240 mi (390 km); Fish Creek, WW2, from Mile 115, Dalton Highway to Allakaket, 120 mi (190 km); Jim River, WW2, from Mile 141, Dalton Highway to Allakaket, 140 mi (230 km); Koyukuk River, South Fork, WW1-2, from Mile 156, Dalton Highway to Allakaket, 140 mi (230 km); Koyukuk River, Middle Fork, WW1, from Mile 207, Dalton Highway to Bettles (Evansville), 120 mi (190 km); Ivishak National Wild River, WW1-FWC, see description.

South of the Brooks Range, the subarctic continental climate brings warm dry summers, with cooler temperatures and more rain in the mountains. Winters are cold, dry and severe. (See the Wiseman weather table.) Winds are generally light. North of the Brooks Range the summers are cool and drier. (See the Galbraith weather table.) Winds on the open tundra are moderate to light. Daylight on June 21 is 22 to 24 hours, on December 22, 3½ to 0 hours, depending upon latitude. Prominent peaks: Table Mountain, elevation 6425 ft (1958 m); Snowden Mountain, elevation 6400 ft (2000 m); Sukapak Mountain, elevation 4200 ft (1300 m); Slope Mountain, elevation 4010 ft (1222 m).

The Dalton Highway is a remote gravel road, with gas, tire repair, wrecker service, emergency communications, food and toilets at the Yukon River bridge and Coldfoot. A public boat launch is on the north bank of the river at the bridge. The road was only recently opened to the public and will undoubtedly have additional services in the future. Clouds of dust and flying rocks from large tractor-trailers traveling at high speeds make this a hazardous road for the family car. Stop only at turnouts, drive with headlights on at all times and carry adequate food, water, fuel and extra spare tires. For your safety and comfort, contact the Alaska State Troopers or the Alaska Department of Transportation in Fairbanks for current conditions before driving the road.

The highway is open as far as the Yukon River year-round. North of the Yukon, the public may travel to Dietrich Camp, Mile 211, from June 1 to September 1. At other times—or to continue to Prudhoe Bay—travel is by permit only, and permits are difficult to obtain for non-commercial vehicles. Contact the Department of Transportation office in Fairbanks.

Scheduled air service lands at Allakaket, Bettles (Evansville), Deadhorse and Wiseman; air taxis operate from Bettles. Food is available at Bettles, Coldfoot, Deadhorse, Livengood and the Yukon River crossing. Lodging can be obtained at Bettles, Coldfoot, Deadhorse and the Yukon crossing.

Suggested reading: Kenneth Andrasko, *Alaska Crude* (Boston: Little, Brown, 1977); Robert Marshall, *Alaska Wilderness: Exploring the Central Brooks Range* (Berkeley: University of California Press, 1970; originally published in 1956 as *Arctic Wilderness*) and *Arctic Village* (New York: Smith and Haas, 1933); James P. Roscow, *800 Miles to Valdez: The Building of the Alaska Pipeline* (Englewood Cliffs, N.J.: Prentice-Hall, Inc., 1977).

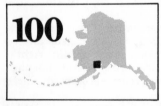

100 Tuxedni Refuge, Alaska Maritime National Wildlife Refuge

Location: Southcentral Alaska, northwest of Homer; 60°08′N 152°35′W

Size: 6445 acres (2608 hectares)

High point: 2674 ft (815 m), on Chisik Island

Low point: Sea level

Best time of year: May–September

USGS maps: Kenai A-7, A-8

Established: 1909

Managed by: U.S. Fish and Wildlife Service

Chisik Island, Tuxedni Refuge. (National Park Service photo by C. Gilbert)

Two islands, Chisik and Duck, at the mouth of Tuxedni Bay, protect major seabird colonies, bald eagles and peregrine falcons. Chisik Island rises ramp-like from Cook Inlet, with a cannery and sandy beaches on the south end and 400-ft (100-m) sea cliffs on the north. A nearly impenetrable jungle of alder, salmonberry and other brush cloaks the lower slopes and fills spruce-forest clearings; summit areas are alpine tundra. Duck Island is a 6-acre (2-hectare) rocky islet with little vegetation. The view of the nearby volcanoes Iliamna and Redoubt from the Refuge is outstanding.

Recreational development is limited to one public-use cabin, for which reservations are required. Camping, campfires and fishing are permitted; hunting is not. Access to the Refuge is by air or water, although the use of small boats on the treacherous waters of Cook Inlet is not recommended because of sudden winds, large waves and strong tides. Air taxis, stores, restaurants and lodging are available in Homer, Kenai and Soldotna.

The Refuge enjoys a maritime climate, with cool, overcast summers and mild, overcast winters. (See the Homer weather table.) Winds are generally light. Daylight on June 21 is 19 hours, on December 22, 6 hours.

101 Unalakleet National Wild River

Location: Western Alaska, east of Unalakleet; 63°55′N 160°20′W
River rating: WW2-FWB
Popular trip length: 70 mi (110 km)
Best time of year: June–September
Annual high water: Late May

USGS maps: Norton Bay A-2; Unalakleet D-2, D-3, D-4
Designated as Wild River: 1980
Managed by: Bureau of Land Management

A clearwater river, the Unalakleet flows through a broad valley in the rolling tundra-covered Nulato Hills and Kaltag Mountains to empty into the Bering Sea. Scattered stands of spruce, birch and poplar dot the valley.

The river and its surrounding lands are used extensively by local Eskimos for subsistence fishing and hunting. The old Kaltag Trail, a gold rush sled trail now part of the present Iditarod National Historic Trail, parallels the river from headwaters to Unalakleet. From the Tenmile Creek confluence to the village of Unalakleet is about 70 river miles (110 km).

Numerous brown (grizzly) bears fish the river for salmon from mid-June to mid-July. Other wildlife of the valley includes moose, caribou, black bears, wolves, wolverines, red foxes, arctic foxes, lynx and many species of migratory birds.

Camping is unrestricted; campfires, hunting, firearms, snowmobiles, fixed-wing aircraft and powerboats are permitted. Fishing is excellent for salmon, grayling and

Unalakleet River. (Bureau of Land Management photo by David Kelley)

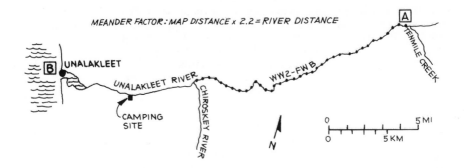

char. Expect large populations of mosquitoes and other biting insects in summer months. Most lands below the Chiroskey River confluence are private. A 1-acre (0.4-hectare) overnight camping site is planned for river travelers between the Chiroskey and Unalakleet.

Summers are cool, foggy and overcast near the coast, warmer and drier inland in this subarctic maritime climate. (See the Nome weather table.) Winds are generally moderate. Daylight on June 21 is 21½ hours, on December 22, 4 hours.

Begin your trip by taking a charter boat from Unalakleet to the upper limit of navigation, which is usually at about Tenmile Creek (A), elevation 300 ft (90 m). Float back down to Unalakleet (B), at sea level, which has scheduled air service, food and lodging.

Suggested reading: Emily Ivanoff Brown (Ticasuk), *The Roots of Tikasuk: An Eskimo Woman's Family Story* (Anchorage: Alaska Northwest Publishing Co., 1981); Muktuk Marston, *Men of the Tundra: Alaska Eskimos at War* (New York: October House, 1969).

102

Walrus Islands State Game Sanctuary

Location: Western Alaska, in Bristol Bay south of Togiak; 58°43′N 160°15′W
Size: 1200 acres (490 hectares)
High point: 1400 ft (430 m)
Low point: Sea level

Best time of year: June–August
USGS maps: Hagemeister Island C-1, C-2, D-1; Nushagak Bay
Established: 1960
Managed by: Alaska Department of Fish and Game

When the pack ice retreats north in the spring, Alaska's migratory wildlife returns home from wintering farther south. Seabirds, of course, return to the Walrus Islands' rocky cliffs, but the most spectacular sight is the 15,000 Pacific walruses who haul out on Round Island. Meanwhile, sea lions sun on the southern tip of the island and red foxes den on the grassy slopes.

A seven-island sanctuary that includes Round, High, Crooked and Summit islands, the refuge was established to protect the last major walrus hauling grounds in the southern Bering Sea. In efforts to learn more about the animals, Fish and Game personnel have marked a few with colored tusk bands and radio transmitters. Black-legged kittiwakes and common murres are the largest seabird populations. Watch the waters of Bristol Bay for dolphins, porpoises, seals and whales.

The treeless islands are steep, with many sea cliffs. Round Island, focal point for most visitors, has no shelter but abundant fresh water. Camping is restricted to specific areas. Fishing, hunting and firearms are prohibited; use of fixed-wing aircraft and boats is restricted.

Violent storms with winds up to 75 mph (120 kph) hit the islands during the summer. Be sure your equipment and clothing are strong, warm and waterproof. Many shredded tents have been hauled from the island. A good rain parka, pants and waterproof boots are a necessity; bring clothes that are warm even when wet. Hypothermia is a serious danger here. Bring a minimum of four days' extra food; storms have delayed pickup for up to two weeks. Visitors must be strong, in good health and prepared for a rugged wilderness experience.

In this subarctic maritime climate, summers are normally cool, foggy and overcast; winters are cold, foggy and overcast. (See the King Salmon weather table.) Daylight on June 21 is 18½ hours, on December 22, 6 hours.

The islands are extremely isolated and hard to reach. There are no good anchorages. Most visitors arrive by air taxi from Dillingham or by charter boat from Togiak. Both towns have scheduled air service and food. Dillingham, a transportation hub, has lodging and a larger selection of stores and services.

Permits are required to visit Round Island and adjacent waters between May 15 and September 15. They set conditions by which visitors must abide to ensure that

Walruses —sunbathing on Round Island. (U.S. Fish and Wildlife Service photo by Dave Cline)

Walruses — taking a dip. (U.S. Fish and Wildlife Service photo by Dave Cline)

walrus will not abandon haul-out sites. Permits are obtainable from Department offices in Dillingham, Anchorage and King Salmon; specify dates desired. The 10-day permits are not limited in number and may be renewed. Department personnel on the island maintain radio contact with the Dillingham office.

Suggested reading: Alaska Geographic, *Bristol Bay Basin* (Anchorage: Alaska Northwest Publishing Co., 1978); Tony Dawson, "Plan a Walrus Adventure" (*Alaska* magazine, February 1982); G. Carleton Ray, "Learning the Ways of the Walrus" (*National Geographic*, October 1979); Victor B. Scheffer, *Seals, Sea Lions and Walruses* (Stanford, Calif.: Stanford University Press, 1969).

103 Warren Island Wilderness, Tongass National Forest

Location: Southeastern Alaska, south of Sitka; 55°53′N 133°53′W
Size: 11,181 acres (4525 hectares)
High point: 2329 ft (710 m)
Low point: Sea level

Best time of year: April–August
USGS map: Craig D-6
Established: 1980
Managed by: U.S. Forest Service

An exposed island fronting on the Pacific Ocean, Warren Island was discovered in 1793 by Captain Joseph Whidbey; Captain George Vancouver named it later in honor of Sir John Borlase Warren, a rear admiral in the British Navy, later ambassador to Russia.

Richly forested, with rocky shorelines, sea cliffs and rocky shoals, the island is a seabird nesting and perching area. Sea otters, sea lions, seals and whales use the

Warren Island. (U.S. Forest Service photo)

waters; Sitka blacktail deer, black bears, wolves and bald eagles are found on shore.

Undeveloped, the island offers primitive camping, fishing and hunting, but prepare for long periods of rain and strong winds. Prolonged storms can delay planned air or water pickup and make boating hazardous. Often inaccessible due to winds and seas, the island has a few protected coves on the leeward side. Only experienced boaters should attempt to visit the island. Carry a camping stove, since wood in this rain forest is normally wet.

The maritime climate brings overcast and rain year-round, with cool summers and mild winters. (See the Sitka weather table.) Winds, prevailing from the southeast, are constant and often extremely strong, especially during autumn storms. Daylight on June 21 is 17½ hours, on December 22, 7 hours. Prominent peaks: Warren Peak, elevation 2329 ft (710 m); Bald Peak, elevation 2212 ft (674 m).

Access to the island is by float plane or boat. Air taxis operate from Ketchikan, Petersburg, Sitka and Wrangell. The nearest communities having scheduled air service, Craig and Klawock, also have charter boats, food and lodging.

104  West Chichagof –Yakobi Wilderness, Tongass National Forest

Location: Southeastern Alaska, northwest of Sitka; 57°55′N 136°20′W
Size: 264,747 acres (107 140 hectares)
High point: 3613 ft (1101 m)
Low point: Sea level

Best time of year: Foot, May–October; boat, May–October; ski, December–March
USGS maps: Mt. Fairweather, Sitka
Established: 1980
Managed by: U.S. Forest Service

A mountainous island wilderness with a rugged 65-mi (105-km) coastline fronting on the Pacific Ocean, West Chichagof–Yakobi also includes many exposed offshore islands, islets and rocks. Intricate bays, lagoons, tidal meadows and estuaries offer well-protected anchorages. Along the outer coast, savannas spread invitingly among open spruce forests. Timberline is about 1500 ft (460 m).

The area, rich in wildlife, has long been occupied by Tlingit Indians. The islands also contain mineral wealth: mines on Chichagof Island have produced almost a million ounces of gold.

Wildlife is varied and abundant, including Sitka blacktail deer, brown (grizzly) bears, furbearers, seals, sea lions, porpoises and dolphins. The waters south of Herbert Graves Island support a large population of sea otters. The Pacific coasts of Chichagof and Yakobi islands lie along a major migratory waterfowl and seabird route.

The Forest Service maintains two public-use recreational cabins (reservations required, fee) and 11 mi (18 km) of marked trails. Back-country camping is unrestricted and campfires are permitted, but expect the wood to be wet. Travel and camp to avoid disturbing the numerous bears, particularly along streams draining into Peril Strait. Hypothermia is a constant danger; prepare for long periods of rain and

Sea otters. (Alaska Department of Fish and Game photo)

273

strong winds. Fishing, hunting, firearms, fixed-wing aircraft and powerboats are permitted; off-road vehicles are not. Swift tidal currents in restricted bays and inlets can make boating hazardous.

A maritime climate brings summers that are cool, wet and overcast, winters that are mild, wet and overcast. (See the Sitka weather table.) Winds are constant, severe during autumn storms. Daylight on June 21 is 18 hours, on December 22, 6½ hours. Prominent peaks: Apex Mountain, elevation 3613 ft (1101 m); El Nido, elevation 3358 ft (1024 m); Mount Lydonia, elevation 3262 ft (994 m).

Access to the Wilderness is by boat or float plane. Air taxis are based at Sitka, charter boats at Sitka and sometimes at Pelican. Both Sitka and Pelican have food and scheduled air service and are ports of call for the Southeastern Alaska state ferry. Lodging is available in Sitka.

Yakobi Island was named in 1804 for Russian general Ivan Yakobi. Admiral Vasili Yakov Chichagov explored Arctic regions in 1765 and 1766; the island was named for him in 1805.

Suggested reading: Alaska Geographic, *Sitka and Its Ocean/Island World* (Anchorage: Alaska Northwest Publishing Co., 1982).

105  White Mountains National Recreation Area

Location: Eastern Alaska, north of Fairbanks; 65°30′N 147°W
Size: 1,000,000 acres (405 000 hectares)
High point: 5286 ft (1611 m)
Low point: 800 ft (200 m)

Best time of year: Foot, June–September; boat, May–September; ski, February–April
USGS maps: Circle, Livengood
Established: 1980
Managed by: Bureau of Land Management

Spectacular white limestone pinnacles and rolling, gentle mountains characterize the White Mountains, a part of the Tanana–Yukon uplands. The summits above 3500 ft (1100 m) are inviting dry tundra, with easy walking. Forested valleys are punctuated by treeless subarctic bogs. In this area of discontinuous permafrost, erosion along stream banks occasionally exposes ice lenses, blocks of ice embedded in the frozen ground. Beaver Creek National Wild River is the principal drainage. Commercial mining is permitted within the Recreation Area.

Watch for moose, caribou, brown (grizzly) bears, black bears, wolves, coyotes, wolverines, red foxes, lynx, porcupines, beavers, grouse and ptarmigan.

The Recreation Area contains 32 mi (51 km) of hiking trails and an 18-mi (29-km) ski touring and snowmobile trail. A public-use recreational cabin, the Borealis–LeFevre cabin (reservations necessary, fee), is accessible via the White Mountain Trail. The cabin is on the far (north) bank of Beaver Creek, which can be too deep and swift to ford on foot in spring and early summer or during periods of wet weather. Back-country camping, campfires, fishing, hunting, firearms, horses, fixed-wing aircraft, powerboats and snowmobiles are all permitted throughout the Recreation

Limestone outcroppings, White Mountains. (U.S. Fish and Wildlife Service photo by Dave Spencer)

Area. Expect large populations of mosquitoes and other biting insects in summer months. Although you are legally permitted to cross the numerous mining claims, do not interfere with mining operations or pick up anything from the ground. If possible, ask before crossing.

River travel: Beaver Creek National Wild River, WW1-FWB, see description.

The climate is a subarctic continental one; summers are usually warm and dry, although temperatures can drop and snow can fall on summits. Avoid peaks and other open areas during summer lightning storms. Winters are cold, dry and severe. (See the Fairbanks weather table.) Winds are normally light. From June 20 to June 22, the midnight sun is visible above 3600 ft (1100 m) at this latitude; daylight at sea level is 22 hours. On December 22, expect 3 hours of daylight. Prominent peaks: Mount Prindle, elevation 5286 ft (1611 m); Lime Peak, elevation 5062 ft (1543 m); Cache Mountain, elevation 4772 ft (1455 m); Wickersham Dome, elevation 3207 ft (977 m). A panoramic view from the summit of Wickersham Dome is only 3 mi (5 km) from the highway.

Although no maintained roads enter the Recreation Area, it is accessible from both the Elliott and Steese highways by trail or primitive road. Access to Nome Creek tributary of Beaver Creek is via two unimproved gravel mining roads leaving the Steese Highway, one 15 mi (24 km) long, at Mile 42 near Belle Creek, and one 7 mi (11 km) long, at U.S. Creek, Mile 58. From the Elliott Highway, Mile 23.5, the White

Mountain winter trail leads to Beaver Creek and the Borealis–LeFevre cabin, 18 mi (29 km) away. The White Mountain summer trail, 19 mi (31 km) long, leads to the same point from the shoulder of Wickersham Dome at Mile 28. From Mile 74.7, Elliott Highway, a 25-mi (40-km) primitive trail leads to Colorado Creek. Food is available at Fox and Livengood. Food, lodging, rental cars and air taxis can be found in Fairbanks.

Suggested reading: U.S. Department of the Interior, *Proposed Beaver Creek National Wild River*, Final Environmental Impact Statement (Washington, D.C.: U.S. Government Printing Office, 1975).

106  Wind National Wild River

Location: Northeastern Alaska, in the Arctic National Wildlife Refuge; 168°00′N 147°00′W
River rating: WW1-3
Popular trip length: 180 mi (290 km)

Best time of year: July–mid-September
Annual high water: May
USGS maps: Philip Smith Mountains B-1, A-1; Arctic; Christian; Chandalar
Designated as Wild River: 1980
Managed by: U.S. Fish and Wildlife Service

A swift, challenging, scenic river with headwaters on the Continental Divide in the rugged heart of the Brooks Range, the Wind flows south through a U-shaped valley to meet the broad forested floodplain of the Chandalar River. The open tundra and glaciated mountains of the upper river invite exploring on foot before heading downriver. The entire length of the Wind is designated as Wild River. Check the water level of the Wind before waving goodbye to the air taxi—the river rating was determined at high water conditions.

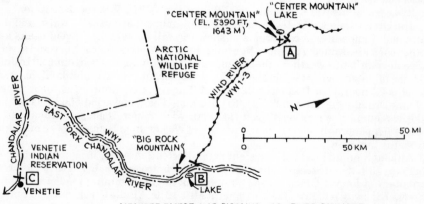

MEANDER FACTOR: MAP DISTANCE x 1.3 = RIVER DISTANCE

Wind River. (National Park Service photo)

Most paddlers continue down the East Fork of the Chandalar River to Venetie. Below the Wind, the East Fork is primarily WW1, with the possibility of some WW2 at low water levels, and may require lining around boulders. Private lands of the Venetie Indian Reservation lie east of the East Fork, with the river as the boundary. From "Center Mountain" lake (A) to "Big Rock Mountain" lake (B) is 80 mi (130 km), and on to Venetie (C) another 100 mi (160 km).

On the Wind River, watch for Dall sheep, caribou, moose, brown (grizzly) bears, wolves, wolverines and red foxes. Black bears, lynx and beavers inhabit the forested regions.

Camping is best on the soft tundra above treeline, but build campfires on river gravel bars; better yet, use a camping stove. In the forested regions, camp on river bars for fewer mosquitoes, but select your campsite carefully, since rainstorms upriver can rapidly raise the water level several feet. Fishing, hunting, horses, snowmobiles and fixed-wing aircraft are permitted.

Although the mountain weather can be cool and wet, the lowlands normally experience warm, dry summers in this subarctic continental climate. (See the Wiseman weather table.) Winds are generally light, stronger on exposed ridges and on open tundra areas. Daylight on June 21 is 24 hours, on December 22, 0 hours, with several hours of twilight.

To reach the river, take a float plane to the lake (A), elevation 2800 ft (850 m), near "Center Mountain" ("summit 5390," at 68°15′N 147°22′W). The trip can end with an air taxi pickup on the lake (B), elevation 1600 ft (490 m), northeast of Big Rock Mountain on the East Fork, or it can continue to Venetie (C), elevation 300 ft (90 m), which has scheduled air service. Air taxis are based at Fort Yukon, which also has scheduled air service, food and lodging.

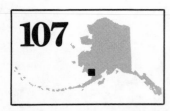

107

Wood–Tikchik State Park

Location: Western Alaska, north of Dillingham; 60°N 159°W
Size: 1,428,329 acres (578 027 hectares)
High point: 5026 ft (1532 m)
Low point: 40 ft (12 m)

Best time of year: Foot, mid-June–September; boat, mid-June–September; ski, February–April
USGS maps: Bethel, Dillingham, Goodnews, Taylor Mountains
Established: 1978
Managed by: Alaska Division of Parks

Spectacular glacier-carved lakes interconnect among tundra-covered craggy mountains. The Park takes in six principal lakes, with Lake Nerka the largest, 29 mi (47 km) long, and Lake Nuyakuk the deepest, 930 ft (280 m). Both lake systems are important salmon spawning areas for the Bristol Bay salmon fishery. Although the Wood River and Tikchik Lakes area has long been used by local Eskimos for fishing, hunting and trapping, its first contact with the outside world was in 1818, when Russian fur traders established a trading post near present-day Dillingham.

In addition to the five species of Pacific salmon, wildlife common to the area includes moose, black bears, brown (grizzly) bears (especially along the Tikchik

Rafting on Peace River at Lake Beverly, Wood-Tikchik State Park. (National Park Service photo by P. Steucke)

River), caribou, beavers, muskrats, river otters, red foxes, wolverines, marmots, golden eagles, ptarmigan and numerous migratory waterfowl species.

An undeveloped wilderness park, Wood-Tikchik attracts hikers and backpackers, kayakers, lake boaters, river runners, ski tourers, fishermen and hunters. Camping and the use of powerboats and snowmobiles are permitted; off-road vehicles are not. Fixed-wing aircraft may land only at designated locations. Expect large populations of mosquitoes and other biting insects in summer months. Boaters should be alert for sudden winds that can whip up large waves on the lakes. Private lands exist within the Park and should be respected.

River travel: Nuyakuk River, WW2-FWB, from Tikchik Lake to Koliganek, 56 mi (90 km) (portage around the waterfall); Tikchik River, WW1-FWC, Nishlik Lake to Tikchik Lake, 60 mi (97 km); Wood River, WW2-FWB, Lake Kulik to Aleknagik, 86 mi (138 km).

Cool overcast summers and cold overcast winters are typical of this subarctic climate, transitional between the maritime and continental. (See the King Salmon weather table, although King Salmon's climate is somewhat more maritime.) Winds are generally moderate, occasionally strong. Daylight on June 21 is 19 hours, on December 22, 6 hours. The terrain is generally brushy to about 1100 ft (330 m); trees seldom extend beyond 900 ft (300 m) elevation. Prominent peak: Mount Waskey, elevation 5026 ft (1532 m).

The Park is most easily reached by air taxi from Dillingham or chartered boat from Aleknagik. Both towns have scheduled air service. They are also connected by road, but not to the contiguous state highway system. Meals, lodging and a variety of stores are available in Dillingham. Wilderness fishing and hunting lodges in the area offer comfortable accommodations, but require reservations.

Suggested reading: Alaska Geographic, *Bristol Bay Basin* (Anchorage: Alaska Northwest Publishing Co., 1978).

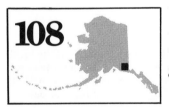

108 Wrangell–St. Elias National Park and Preserve

Location: Eastern Alaska, east of
  Glennallen and Valdez; 61°N 143°W
Size: 12,400,000 acres (5 020 000
  hectares)
High point: 18,008 ft (5489 m)
Low point: Sea level

Best time of year: Foot,
  May–September; boat,
  June–September; ski,
  February–April (low elevations)
USGS maps: Bering Glacier, Cordova,
  Gulkana, Icy Bay, McCarthy, Mt. St.
  Elias, Nabesna, Valdez, Yakutat
Established: 1980
Managed by: National Park Service

Alaska's most extensive and rugged glaciated wilderness, Wrangell–St. Elias is country you write home about. Some of North America's highest peaks are here, topped by regal Mount St. Elias. The massive Bagley Icefield, 90 mi (140 km) long, is reportedly 4000 ft (1200 m) thick. The spectacular Malaspina Glacier, a piedmont glacier, is almost 50% larger than the state of Delaware. Through every valley,

Barnard Glacier, Wrangell-St. Elias National Preserve.

turbulent braided rivers carry their loads of glacial silt to the lowlands. Of the total, 8,700,000 acres (3 520 000 hectares) is designated as Wilderness. The southeastern section of the Park adjoins Canada's similarly rugged Kluane National Park, with its peaks, icefields and glaciers, which contains Mount Logan, second-highest peak in North America.

The sighting of Mount St. Elias by Vitus Bering on July 16, 1741, is the first record of northwestern America in Russian archives. Bering named Cape St. Elias on Kayak Island on the day of that saint, July 20, and the name was later applied to the mountain. The peak was first climbed in 1897.

From a backbone of heavily glaciated volcanoes and peaks, the terrain drops to tundra and boreal-forested uplands in the north. To the south, the mountain slopes spill massive spreading piedmont glaciers nearly to tidewater in the Gulf of Alaska. The Chitina River bisects the Range. Prominent peaks in the Park are: Mount St. Elias, elevation 18,008 ft (5489 m); Mount Bona, elevation 16,421 ft (5005 m); Mount Blackburn, elevation 16,390 ft (4996 m); Mount Sanford, elevation 16,237 ft (4949 m); Mount Wrangell, elevation 14,163 ft (4317 m); Mount Drum, elevation 12,010 ft (3661 m).

The geology of the region is diverse and fascinating. Its mineral wealth attracted attention when the Kennecott Copper Company was formed in the early 1900s to mine the rich copper deposits high in the Chitina River drainage above the Kennicott

Glacier. A railroad was built from Cordova to the mines—an exciting story immortalized in Rex Beach's novel *The Iron Trail*. After the mines closed in 1938, Kennecott and nearby McCarthy became ghost towns. Today the mine buildings are visitor attractions—but please remember that all structures in both towns are privately owned, and many are occupied.

The Park and Preserve contain a diversity of wildlife habitats. While Dall sheep stay mostly on mountainsides inland, mountain goats are attracted to the coastal mountains with their deeper winter snow cover. Caribou roam on the rolling uplands of the north to western plateaus. Bison, introduced in the Copper River drainage, can frequently be seen near Chitina. Moose, black bears, brown (grizzly) bears, wolves, wolverines, beavers, coyotes, red foxes and marmots are common throughout the forests and tundra lands.

Wrangell–St. Elias offers excellent wilderness backpacking, mountaineering, river running, beachcombing and ski touring. Several historic horsepacking trails cross the Park, but dangerous large braided rivers prevent following them all the way on foot. Air taxis can provide access to remote portions. Administrative offices and a visitor center are at Mile 105.5, Richardson Highway, near Copper Center, while ranger stations are located at Chitina, Gulkana airport, Slana and Yakutat. In this undeveloped park with extremely remote areas, only those experienced and prepared should undertake back-country travel. Camping and campfires are permitted on public lands. Please respect the numerous private lands within the boundaries and do not use old structures for firewood. Fishing is generally permitted, as are firearms, horses, fixed-wing aircraft, powerboats and snowmobiles; off-road vehicles are not. Sports hunting is permitted in the Preserve but not in the Park. Expect large populations of mosquitoes and other biting insects in the lowlands in summer months. Do not venture onto glaciers without experience and proper equipment. In winter and after summer snows, avalanche hazard can be severe in the mountains.

River travel: Chitina River, WW2-FWC, McCarthy to Chitina, 60 mi (100 km); Copper River, WW2-FWB, Slana to Copper River Highway near Cordova, 250 mi (400 km); Nabesna River, WW2-FWA, Nabesna to Northway, 66 mi (110 km).

Inland, the subarctic continental climate brings warm dry summers and cold, dry severe winters at low elevations; expect more precipitation in the mountains any time of year. Lowland winds are generally light. (See the McCarthy weather table.) Along the coast, a mild maritime climate prevails, with cool, wet summers and mild, wet winters; winds are moderate. At high elevations, expect a cold, severe arctic climate with frequent storms and high winds. Daylight on June 21 is 19½ hours, on December 22, 5½ hours.

When the weather is clear, the views of the volcanic peaks Sanford, Wrangell and Drum are spectacular from the Richardson, Glenn and Edgerton highways. Although no visitor facilities have as yet been developed, two primitive gravel roads penetrate the Preserve. One, 52 mi (84 km) long, leads from the Glenn Highway (Tok Cutoff) at Slana to long-standing mining interests in the northern Preserve. The other, 63 mi (101 km) long, begins at Chitina on the Edgerton Highway and follows the reworked bed of the historic Copper River and Northwestern Railroad leading to the Kennecott mines, but stops short at the Kennicott River. At press time, two spans of a small hand-operated tramway are the only transportation across the raging waters, still 5 mi (8 km) from Kennecott. An improved river-crossing is planned.

The remainder of the Park and Preserve are primarily accessible by air taxi, with operations based at Cordova, Gulkana, Glennallen, Northway, Valdez and Yakutat. Scheduled air service is available to Cordova and Yakutat; McCarthy's mail plane, leaving from the Gulkana Airport, can often carry a passenger or two. Food and lodging are available at roadside restaurants and motels and at wilderness lodges (reservations required) within the parkland and at Chitina (sometimes), Copper Center, Gakona, Glennallen, McCarthy (hostel) and Yakutat.

Suggested reading: Alaska Geographic, *Wrangell–St. Elias: International Mountain Wilderness* (Anchorage: Alaska Northwest Publishing Co., 1981); Donald C. Defenderfer and Robert B. Walkinshaw, *One Long Summer Day in Alaska: A Documentation of Perspectives in the Wrangell Mountains* (Santa Cruz: University of California, 1981); Lone E. Janson, *The Copper Spike* (Anchorage: Alaska Northwest Publishing Co., 1975); Richard L. Powers, *Yakutat: The Turbulent Crescent* (Anchorage: Alaska Geographic, Alaska Northwest Publishing Co., 1975); U.S. Department of the Interior, *Proposed Wrangell Mountains National Forest* and *Proposed Wrangell–St. Elias National Park*, Final Environmental Impact Statements (Washington, D.C.: U.S. Government Printing Office, 1974).

Jubilant climber, Wrangell-St. Elias National Park.

Yukon–Charley Rivers National Preserve

109

Location: Eastern Alaska, east of
Fairbanks; 65°N 143°W
River rating: WW4-FWC
Popular trip length: 140 mi (230 km)
Preserve size: 2,260,000 acres (915 000
hectares)
High point: 6435 ft (1961 m)
Low point: 600 ft (180 m)

Best time of year: Foot,
June–September; boat (Yukon
River), June–September, (Charley
River), June–August; ski,
February–April
USGS maps for Preserve: Big Delta,
Charley River, Circle, Eagle
USGS maps for Wild River: Eagle
D-5, D-6; Charley River A-5, A-4, B-4;
(Yukon River to Circle) B-5, B-6, C-6;
Circle C-1, D-1
Established: 1978
Managed by: National Park Service

A pleasant, undisturbed wilderness watershed of low mountains and clearwater rivers, the Preserve straddles the placid Yukon River. The Yukon was historically, and still is, an important transportation route, summer and winter, in a region only occasionally penetrated by roads. The nearby small towns of Eagle and Circle, on the south bank, were prominent centers of activity during the heyday of the Klondike and Nome gold rushes. Decaying cabins from that era can still be found among the

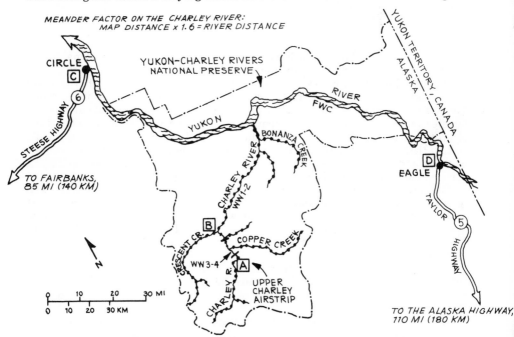

Calico Cliffs on the Yukon River.

tall magenta fireweed lining the banks. Originally established as a National Monument, the area was designated a Preserve with a Wild River in 1980.

Although the Yukon's banks abound with history and artifacts, the Charley River basin was not of particular interest to gold-seekers because it produced little "color." The many branches of the Charley, flowing from open tundra upland through forested valleys, have seldom been visited. Even today, access is limited. One of the clearest streams in Alaska, it has shallow, braided upper reaches and a middle section that skirts steep rock bluffs in a spruce-birch-aspen forest to tumble over boulders and through pools. The lower river meanders through muskeg and black spruce woods. The entire river and its tributaries are designated as Wild River.

Wildlife is typical of the boreal forest and includes moose, lynx, black bears, brown (grizzly) bears, wolves, wolverines and beavers. The entire Charley River area is part of the range of the Fortymile caribou herd, which uses the headwaters as a calving area. The hillsides and bluffs along the Charley are Dall sheep range. Watch for nesting peregrine falcons on the bluffs above the Yukon, but don't disturb this endangered species.

Expect warm, dry summers interspersed with periods of rain and drizzle in this subarctic continental climate. Winters are cold, dry, and severe. (See the Eagle weather table.) Winds are generally light. Daylight on June 21 is 22 hours, on December 22, 3½ hours.

Camping and campfires are permitted throughout this undeveloped Preserve, but be careful where you camp on the Charley; rainstorms in the headwaters can rapidly raise the water level downriver without warning. Prepare for large numbers of mosquitoes and other biting insects in summer months. Fishing, hunting, firearms, horses, fixed-wing aircraft, helicopters (by permit), powerboats and snowmobiles are all permitted; off-road vehicles are not. Private lands and cabins line the Yukon River. Do not disturb them, or fish nets, fish wheels or other private equipment— local residents depend upon subsistence foods for survival.

River travel: To float the Charley River, take an air taxi to the upper Charley airstrip (A), elevation 2400 ft (730 m), on the main river about 20 mi (32 km) above Crescent Creek. The WW3-4 rapids between the airstrip and Crescent Creek may have to be lined or portaged, especially at high water during spring runoff or at low water. An alternate access point is at the Crescent Creek confluence (B), elevation 1900 ft (580 m), via helicopter from Circle. From the airstrip to the Yukon River, elevation 700 ft (210 m), is about 88 mi (140 km); Circle (C), elevation 597 ft (182 m), is another 63 mi (100 km) down the Yukon.

An easier boat trip is a float down the Yukon, FWC, from Eagle (D), elevation 865 ft (264 m), to Circle, a distance of about 150 mi (240 km). Take time to explore up side rivers and hike a bit. Be alert for williwaws—sudden violent winds spilling over mountains onto the river—that can raise whitecaps and large waves capable of capsizing canoes.

Both Eagle, at Mile 161, Taylor Highway, and Circle, Mile 162, Steese Highway, are accessible by automobile from about March 15 to October 15. Neither road is maintained in winter. Both towns have scheduled air service, air taxis, charter boats, food and lodging. Charter helicopters are available in Circle.

Suggested reading: Harold Dinkins, "High Roller on the Charley" (*Alaska* magazine, July 1981); John McPhee, *Coming Into the Country* (New York: Farrar, Straus and Giroux, 1977); U.S. Department of the Interior, *Proposed Yukon-Charley National Rivers*, Final Environmental Impact Statement (Washington, D.C.: U.S. Government Printing Office, 1974).

110  Yukon Delta National Wildlife Refuge

Location: Western Alaska, surrounding Bethel; 61°N 164°W
Size: 19,624,000 acres (7 941 600 hectares)
High point: 4550 ft (1387 m)
Low point: Sea level
Best time of year: Foot, late May–September; boat, late May–September; ski, February–April

USGS maps: Baird Inlet, Bethel, Black, Cape Mendenhall, Goodnews, Holy Cross, Hooper Bay, Kuskokwim Bay, Kwiguk, Marshall, Nunivak Island, Russian Mission, St. Michael, Unalakleet
Established: 1980
Managed by: U.S. Fish and Wildlife Service

Formed by the Yukon and Kuskokwim rivers as they empty into the Bering Sea, this delta, largest in the United States, is one of the most important waterfowl breeding areas in North America, used by more than 200 million migratory birds. In the wetlands nest 90% of the white-fronted geese of the Pacific flyway, all of the world's cackling Canada geese, 90% of the world's bristle-thighed curlews, 80% of the continent's whistling swans, 80% of the world's emperor geese and half of the continent's Pacific black brant.

At least 170 species of birds and 43 species of mammals are found regularly in the Refuge, particularly noteworthy being the large populations of furbearers—beavers, red foxes, arctic foxes, marten, mink, muskrats, river otters, weasels. Wolves, wolverines and moose are found throughout the eastern portion of the Refuge; musk-oxen have been established on Nunivak and Nelson islands. The waterways of the delta are spawning areas for a major salmon fishery.

Containing extensive wet-tundra flatlands, lakes and ponds, the Refuge rises to

Wet-tundra flatlands, Yukon Delta Refuge. (U.S. Fish and Wildlife Service photo by David Marshall)

rolling uplands in the northern and southeastern portions. It is primarily treeless, though forested areas are found inland. Most of the Refuge is underlain by continuous permafrost; the coastal areas flood annually.

Three previously established national wildlife refuges are included in the Yukon Delta NWR: Clarence Rhode NWR, established in 1960, Hazen Bay NWR, established in 1937, and Nunivak NWR, established in 1929. The Nunivak NWR area was designated as Wilderness within the Yukon Delta NWR in 1980, as was a new area, Andreafsky Wilderness. These wildernesses are treated separately in this book; see #69 and #8 respectively.

The center of today's Yupik culture, the Yukon-Kuskokwim delta contains the largest concentration of Eskimos in Alaska. Living within the heart of the Refuge, they continue to use the lands and rivers for subsistence fishing, hunting and trapping—a centuries-old tradition. Extensive private lands exist within the Refuge boundaries, especially along rivers and near villages.

Near the coast, weather is typical of the subarctic maritime climate with cool, foggy summers and cold, dry, severe winters. Further inland, continental forces take effect, with warmer, sunnier summers; winters are severely cold. (See the Bethel weather table.) Winds, constant and generally moderate near the coast, are lighter inland. Daylight on June 21 is 19½ hours, on December 22, 5½ hours.

The Refuge has no development for recreational visitors. Camping is unrestricted on public lands, but the traveler has the responsibility of identifying which lands are public. Assume that most land along navigable waterways and near villages is private. Ask where you may camp. Do not disturb cabins, fish camps or equipment. Although the area is treeless, sufficient driftwood for campfires lines the shores of major rivers and the coast. Dry land for campsites and fire pits may be difficult to find in many areas. Fishing, hunting, powerboats, snowmobiles and aircraft are permitted on public lands. Expect hungry mosquitoes and other biting insects during summer months.

River travel: Andreafsky National Wild River, WW3-FWB, see description; Aniak River, WW2-FWB, from Aniak Lake to Aniak, 110 mi (180 km); Kisaralik River, WW3-FWC, from Kisaralik Lake to Bethel, 160 mi (260 km); Yukon and Kuskokwim rivers, FW in the Refuge, a gradient less than 0.35 ft/mi (0.062 m/km).

Access to the Refuge is by air, with most communities having scheduled air service at least once a week and some daily. The following communities are served by commercial airline: Akiachak, Akiak (NV), Alakanuk, Aniak, Atmautluak (NV), Bethel, Cape Romanzof, Chefornak (NV), Chevak, Eek, Emmonak, Kalskag, Kasigluk, Kipnuk, Kongiganak, Kotlik (NV), Kwethluk (NV), Kwigillingok, Marshall, Mekoryuk, Mountain Village, Napakiak, Napaskiak, Newtok, Nightmute, Nunapitchuk, Russian Mission, St. Marys, Scammon Bay, Stebbins, Toksook Bay, Tuluksak, Tuntutuliak, Tununak. ("NV" indicates that the villagers have indicated they prefer not to have tourists.) In many cases, the plane will be small, with limited passenger space. Air taxis operate from Aniak, Bethel, Emmonak, Hooper Bay and St. Marys. Most of the villages have stores; the larger ones may have a cafe and lodging. (See Table I, "Access and Services," Appendix.) Bethel and St. Marys are transportation hubs for the area, with modern visitor facilities.

Suggested reading: Eugene Cantin, *Yukon Summer* (San Francisco: Chronicle Books, 1973); Margaret Lantis, *Ethnohistory in Southwestern Alaska and the Southern Yukon* (Lexington: University Press of Kentucky, 1970); Lael Morgan, *And the Land Provides: Alaska Natives in a Year of Transition* (New York: Anchor Press, 1974); Jim Rearden, *Yukon-Kuskokwim Delta* (Anchorage: Alaska Northwest Publishing Co., Alaska Geographic, 1979); Lavrentii A. Zagoskin, *Lt. Zagoskin's Travels in Russian America, 1842-44: The First Ethnographic and Geographic Investigations in the Yukon and Kuskokwim Valleys of Alaska* (Toronto: University of Toronto Press, 1967).

111

Yukon Flats
National Wildlife Refuge

Location: Eastern Alaska, surrounding Fort Yukon; 66°30′N 146°W

Size: 8,630,000 acres (3 490 000 hectares)

High point: 4177 ft (1273 m)

Low point: 300 ft (90 m)

Best time of year: Foot, late May–September; boat, late May–September; ski, February–April

USGS maps: Beaver, Bettles, Black River, Chandalar, Charley River, Christian, Circle, Fort Yukon, Livengood

Established: 1980

Managed by: U.S. Fish and Wildlife Service

Here on the Arctic Circle the early-summer sun circles the horizon, giving the Flats 24 hours of sunlight daily. In this "solar basin," summer temperatures often soar above 90°F (32°C), but a record low of −75°F (−59°C) has occurred in January. The Refuge takes in part of the vast floodplain of the Yukon River and its associated lowlands, with extensive wetlands, marshes, 40,000 lakes and 25,000 miles (40 000 km) of rivers, and also includes the surrounding gentle forested mountains. More than 200 mi (320 km) of the Yukon River flows through the Refuge at a gradient of 1 ft/mi (0.2 m/km). Fort Yukon, 1 mi (2 km) above the Arctic Circle, was established by the Hudson's Bay Company in 1847 to compete with the Russians for the lucrative fur trade; today the town is the largest settlement in northeastern Alaska.

One of North America's most productive wildlife habitats, the area has the greatest overall nesting density of ducks in Alaska, more than two million birds. Most abundant are widgeons and scaup; 25% of the continent's canvasback ducks breed here. Watch for caribou in the uplands, and, throughout, moose, black bears, brown (grizzly) bears, coyotes, wolves, wolverines, red foxes, snowshoe hares, marten, mink, muskrats, beavers and river otters.

The roadless Refuge has no recreational development for visitors. Camping is unrestricted on public lands, but since extensive private lands line the rivers, especially near villages, try to ask before using an area. Campfires are normally permitted, although restrictions may be in effect during dry periods. Fishing, hunting, powerboats, fixed-wing aircraft and snowmobiles are permitted. Expect large populations of mosquitoes and other biting insects during summer months.

River travel: Beaver Creek National Wild River, WW1-FWB, see description; Birch Creek, FWC within Refuge (see Birch Creek National Wild River for upper river description); Black River, WW1-FWA, from lakes near Grayling Fork to Fort Yukon, 290 mi (470 km); Chandalar River, North Fork, WW3-FWA, from Chandalar Lake to Venetie, 130 mi (210 km); Chandalar River, East Fork, WW2-FWA, from Arctic Village to Venetie, 170 mi (270 km); Porcupine River, WW1-FWB, from upper Porcupine River or Summit Lake on Bell River, Yukon Territory, to Fort Yukon, 300 mi (480 km) (you must contact both U.S. and Canadian customs offices for clearance prior to your trip—see "Information Sources" in the Appendix for addresses); Sheenjek River, WW2-FWB, see Sheenjek National Wild River; Yukon River, FWC, from Circle to the Dalton Highway bridge, 240 mi (390 km).

In this subarctic continental climate, expect warm, dry summers, and cold, dry,

The Yukon River, Yukon Flats Refuge. (U.S. Fish and Wildlife Service photo by Elaine Rhode)

severe winters. Fort Yukon holds the state's high temperature record of 100°F (38°C). (See the Fort Yukon weather table.) Winds are normally light. Daylight on June 21 is 24 hours, on December 22, 2½ hours.

The southwestern section of the Refuge is accessible from the Dalton Highway (North Slope Haul Road) near the Yukon River bridge; a public boat ramp is at Mile 56.6, at the north end of the bridge. Boaters may also reach the Refuge via the Yukon River from Circle, at the north end of the Steese Highway. Scheduled air service stops at Beaver, Birch Creek, Chalkyitsik, Fort Yukon, Stevens Village and Venetie. Air taxis, boat charters, restaurants and lodging are available in Fort Yukon; most of the villages have general stores.

Suggested reading: Eugene Cantin, *Yukon Summer* (San Francisco: Chronicle Books, 1973); Richard Nelson, *Hunters of the Northern Forest* (Chicago: University of Chicago Press, 1980); Evelyn Bergland Shore, *Born on Snowshoes* (Boston: Houghton, Mifflin, 1954); Hudson Stuck, *Voyages on the Yukon and Its Tributaries* (1917; reprint ed., New York: Charles Scribner's Sons, 1975); U.S. Department of the Interior, *Proposed Yukon Flats National Wildlife Refuge*, Final Environmental Impact Statement (Washington, D.C.: U.S. Government Printing Office, 1974).

Additional Areas of Interest, managed by Alaska Department of Fish and Game

Cinder River Critical Habitat Area, Southwestern Alaska

Location: 57°20′N 158°15′W
Established: 1972

Size: 25,280 acres (10 231 hectares)
USGS maps: Bristol Bay A-1, A-2

Tidal and submerged lands to protect waterfowl habitat.

Clam Gulch Critical Habitat Area, Southcentral Alaska

Location: 60°09′N 151°30′W
Established: 1976

Size: 30,080 acres (12 173 hectares)
USGS maps: Kenai A-4, A-5, B-4; Seldovia D-5

Tidal and submerged lands to protect shellfish habitat.

Copper River Delta Critical Habitat Area, Southcentral Alaska

Location: 60°20′N 145°20′W
Established: 1978

Size: 458,240 acres (185 443 hectares)
USGS map: Cordova

Public, tidal and submerged lands and waters to protect shorebird and waterfowl migration and staging area (part of Chugach National Forest).

Egegik Critical Habitat Area, Southwestern Alaska

Location: 58°10′N 157°35′W
Established: 1972

Size: 8320 acres (3367 hectares)
USGS map: Naknek A-5

Tidal and submerged lands to protect waterfowl habitat.

Biologist recording number of banded goose. (U.S. Fish and Wildlife Service photo by W.N. Ladd, Jr.)

Fox River Flats Critical Habitat area, Southcentral Alaska

Location: 59°48′N 151°00′W
Established: 1972

Size: 6720 acres (2720 hectares)
USGS map: Seldovia D-3

Tidal and submerged lands to protect shorebird and waterfowl habitat.

Kachemak Bay Critical Habitat Area, Southcentral Alaska

Location: 59°30′N 151°30′W
Established: 1974

Size: 215,000 acres
(87 010 hectares)
USGS maps: Seldovia

Tidal and submerged lands to protect seabirds, shellfish, crab and fish.

Kalgin Island Critical Habitat Area, Southcentral Alaska

Location: 60°23′N 151°58′W
Established: 1972

Size: 2880 acres (1166 hectares)
USGS maps: Kenai B-6

Tidal and submerged lands to protect waterfowl and big game habitat.

Pilot Point Critical Habitat Area, Southwestern Alaska

Location: 57°33 'N 157°42 'W

Established: 1972

Size: 46,720 acres (18 908 hectares)

USGS maps: Ugashik B-5, B-6, C-5, C-6

Tidal and submerged lands to protect waterfowl habitat.

Port Heiden Critical Habitat Area, Southwestern Alaska

Location: 56°47 'N 159°00 'W

Established: 1972

Size: 55,560 acres (22 485 hectares)

USGS maps: Chignik D-2, D-3, D-4

Tidal and submerged lands to protect waterfowl habitat.

Port Moller Critical Habitat Area, Southwestern Alaska

Location: 55°52 'N 160°40 'W

Established: 1972

Size: 123,520 acres (49 988 hectares)

USGS map: Port Moller D-2, D-3

Tidal and submerged lands to protect waterfowl habitat (parts included in Alaska Peninsula National Wildlife Refuge).

APPENDIX

Public Campgrounds Along the Alaska State Highway System*

Alaska Highway, from the Canadian border to Delta Junction (mileposts begin at
Dawson Creek, B.C.):
Tok area: Mile 1246.6, Gardiner Creek (ADP); Mile 1249.4, Deadman Lake (ADP)
via 2-mi (3-km) side road; Mile 1256.7, Lakeview (ADP); Mile 1309.3, Tok
River (ADP); Mile 1331.9, Moon Lake (ADP).
Delta Junction area: Mile 1414.8, Clearwater (ADP) via 8-mi (13-km) side road.

Dalton Highway, from Mile 73.5, Elliott Highway to Prudhoe Bay (mileposts
begin at the Elliott Highway): Mile 178.9, Marion Creek; Mile 210.8, road
north may be traveled by permit only.

Denali Highway, from Paxson to Cantwell (mileposts begin at Paxson): Mile 21.5,
Denali (BLM); Mile 21.7, Upper Tangle Lakes (BLM); Mile 104.3, Brushkana
(BLM).

Edgerton Highway, from Mile 82.6, Richardson Highway to Chitina (mileposts
begin at the Richardson Highway): Mile 25, Liberty Falls (BLM).

Elliott Highway, from Mile 11.5, Steese Highway at Fox to Manley Hot Springs
(mileposts begin at the Steese Highway): Mile 57, Tolovana River (BLM);
Mile 152, Manley Hot Springs (local).

Glenn Highway, from Anchorage to Tok (mileposts from Anchorage to Glennallen
begin at Anchorage; mileposts from Glennallen to Gakona Junction are part
of the Richardson Highway; mileposts from Gakona Junction to Tok begin at
Gakona Junction):
Anchorage area: Mile 5, Centennial (municipal); Mile 11.9, Eagle River, Chugach
State Park (ADP), via 2-mi (3-km) side road; Mile 20.9, Peters Creek (ADP);
Mile 26.2, Eklutna Lake, Chugach State Park (ADP), via 10-mi (16-km) side
road.
Palmer area: Mile 42, Palmer (municipal); Mile 42, Finger Lake (ADP), on
Bogard Road, 7 mi (11 km) from Glenn Highway; Mile 54.7, Moose Creek
(ADP); Mile 76.1, King Mountain (ADP); Mile 83.3, Bonnie Lake (ADP), via
3-mi (5-km) side road, too steep for trailers; Mile 85.3, Long Lake (ADP);
Mile 101, Matanuska Glacier (ADP).
Glennallen area: Mile 137.5, Little Nelchina (ADP); Mile 159.8, Lake Louise
(ADP) via 19-mi (31-km) side road; Mile 172.5, Tolsona Creek (ADP); Mile
118, Richardson Highway, Dry Creek (ADP).
Tok area: Mile 64.2, Porcupine Creek (ADP); Mile 109.3, Eagle Trail (ADP).

Haines Highway, from Haines to the Canadian border (mileposts begin at state
ferry terminal; subtract 4.5 from milepost number to determine distance
from Haines): Mile 0, Ferry terminal (for vehicles waiting for the ferry),
4.5 mi (7.2 km) from Haines at Mile 6.4, Lutak Road; Mile 0, Chilkoot Lake
(ADP), at Mile 9.7, Lutak Road; Mile 4.5, Portage Cove (ADP), at Mile 2,
Beach Road; Mile 4.5, Chilkat State Park (ADP) at Mile 5.7, Mud Bay Road;
Mile 31.8, Mosquito Lake (ADP) via 3-mi (5-km) side road.

---

*Campgrounds marked ADP are administered by the Alaska Division of Parks, BLM by the
Bureau of Land Management, NPS by the National Park Service, USFS by the U.S. Forest
Service, and USFW by the U.S. Fish and Wildlife Service.

Klondike Highway 2, from Skagway to the Canadian border (kilometerposts begin at Skagway): Mile 0, Hanousk (municipal), on Fourteenth Avenue; Mile 0, Chilkoot Trail (ADP), Mile 6.8, Dyea Road; Mile 2.6, Liarsville (ADP).

Parks Highway, from Mile 35.3, Glenn Highway to Fairbanks (mileposts begin at Anchorage):
Wasilla area: Mile 35.6, Finger Lake (ADP) on Bogard Road via Trunk Road, 6 mi (10 km) from Parks Highway; Mile 52.3, Rocky Lake (ADP) via 4-mi (6-km) side road; Mile 52.3, Big Lake East (ADP) via 6-mi (10-km) side road; Mile 52.3, Big Lake South (ADP) via 7-mi (11-km) side road; Mile 57.3, Houston (municipal).
Willow area: Mile 66.5, Nancy Lake (ADP); Mile 67.2, South Rolly Lake, Nancy Lake State Recreation Area (ADP), via 7-mi (11-km) side road; Mile 71.2, Willow Creek (ADP), 1-mi (1.6-km) side road; Mile 121.6, Chulitna (ADP); Mile 147, Byers Lake, Denali State Park (ADP); Mile 185.7, East Fork (ADP).
Denali National Park area: Mile 237.3, Denali National Park (NPS), side road to campgrounds. Obtain permit at Riley Creek Visitor Center.

Richardson Highway, from Valdez to Fairbanks (mileposts begin at old Valdez; add 4 to milepost number to determine distance from new Valdez):
Valdez area: Mile 0, Valdez Glacier (municipal) via 2-mi (3-km) side road; Mile 24.1, Blueberry Lake (ADP); Mile 29.4, Worthington Glacier (ADP).
Glennallen area: Mile 65.2, Little Tonsina (ADP); Mile 79.4, Squirrel Creek (ADP); Mile 118, Dry Creek (ADP); Mile 147.4, Sourdough Creek (ADP).
Paxson area: Mile 175, Paxson Lake (BLM) via 1.5-mi (2.4-km) side road; Mile 179.4, Paxson Lake (ADP); Mile 200.5, Fielding Lake (BLM) via 1.5-mi (2.4-km) side road.
Delta Junction area: Mile 237.9, Donnelly Creek (ADP); Mile 267.1, Delta (BLM); Mile 268.4, Clearwater (ADP) via 11-mi (17-km) side road; Mile 277.9, Quartz Lake State Recreation Area (ADP) via 2.6-mi (4.2-km) side road; Mile 321.5, Harding Lake State Recreation Area (ADP) via 1-mi (2-km) side road.
North Pole area: Mile 323.3, Salcha River (ADP); Mile 349, North Pole (municipal).

Seward Highway, from Seward to Anchorage (mileposts begin at Seward):
Seward area: Mile 2.4, Forrest Acres (municipal).
Moose Pass area: Mile 17.2, Primrose Landing, Chugach National Forest (USFS); Mile 23.1, Ptarmigan Creek, Chugach National Forest (USFS); Mile 24.1, Trail River, Chugach National Forest (USFS) via 1.5-mi (2.4-km) side road; Mile 37, Tern Lake, Chugach National Forest (USFS), entrance via Sterling Highway; Mile 46.1, Tenderfoot Creek, Chugach National Forest (USFS).
Turnagain Arm area: Mile 56.4, Porcupine Creek, Chugach National Forest (USFS), 17.5 mi (28.2 km) on Hope Road; Mile 63, Granite Creek, Chugach National Forest (USFS); Mile 65.5, Bertha Creek, Chugach National Forest (USFS); Mile 79.8, Beaver Pond, Black Bear and Williwaw campgrounds, Chugach National Forest (USFS), along 5-mi (8-km) Portage Glacier Road; Mile 101.2, Bird Creek, Chugach State Park (ADP).

Steese Highway, from Fairbanks to Circle (mileposts begin at Fairbanks): Mile 39, Upper Chatanika (ADP); Mile 60, Cripple Creek (BLM); Mile 119.2, Bedrock Creek (BLM).

Sterling Highway, from Mile 37, Seward Highway to Homer (mileposts begin at Seward):
Kenai Lake area: Mile 37.7, Tern Lake, Chugach National Forest (USFS); Mile

45, Quartz Creek, Chugach National Forest (USFS); Mile 45, Crescent Creek, Chugach National Forest (USFS), via 3-mi (5-km) side road; Mile 50.5, Cooper Creek, Chugach National Forest (USFS); Mile 52.8, Russian River, Chugach National Forest (USFS), via 2-mi (3-km) side road; Mile 55, Kenai–Russian River, Kenai National Wildlife Refuge (USFW).

Soldotna area: Mile 57.8, access to Hidden Lake, Upper Skilak Lake, Lower Ohmer Lake, Engineer Lake and Lower Skilak Lake campgrounds, Kenai National Wildlife Refuge (USFW), along 18-mi (30-km) Skilak Lake Loop Road; Mile 59.8, Jean Lake, Kenai National Wildlife Refuge (USFW); Mile 68.5, Kelly Lake and Peterson Lake campgrounds, Kenai National Wildlife Refuge (USFW); Mile 70.8, Watson Lake, Kenai National Wildlife Refuge (USFW); Mile 75.3, alternate access to campgrounds along Skilak Lake Loop Road; Mile 82, Isaak Walton (ADP); Mile 94, Swift Water (municipal); Mile 96, Alaska Purchase Centennial (municipal); Mile 94.5, Bernice Lake (ADP), access from Mile 21.4, Kenai Spur Road; Mile 109.6, Kasilof River (ADP); Mile 111.3, Johnson Lake (ADP).

Ninilchik area: Mile 117.4, Clam Gulch (ADP); Mile 135.4, Ninilchik (ADP); Mile 137.3, Deep Creek (ADP).

Homer area: Mile 151.9, Staraski Creek (ADP); Mile 156.9, Silver King (ADP) via 2-mi (3-km) side road; Mile 161.5, Anchor River (ADP); Mile 173, Homer (municipal).

Taylor Highway, from Tetlin Junction to Eagle (mileposts begin at Tetlin Junction): Mile 49.1, West fork (BLM); Mile 82, Walker Fork (BLM); Mile 131.5, Liberty Creek (BLM); Mile 159.6, Eagle (BLM).

Public Campgrounds Along the State Ferry Systems

SOUTHEAST ALASKA SYSTEM

Haines: See listing for Haines Highway.

Juneau: Glacier Highway, Mile 9, Mendenhall Lake, Tongass National Forest (USFS), at Mile 3.7, Mendenhall Loop Road; Glacier Highway, Mile 15.8, Auke Village, Tongass National Forest (USFS); Douglas Highway, Mile 2.5, Sandy Beach (municipal), obtain permit from Juneau Police Department.

Ketchikan: North Tongass Highway, Mile 6.8, access to Signal Creek, Three C's and Last Chance campgrounds, Tongass National Forest (USFS), along 3-mi- (5-km-) long Ward Lake Road; North Tongass Highway, Mile 18.2, Settlers Cove, Tongass National Forest (USFS).

Klawock: Klawock (municipal).

Petersburg: Tent City (municipal), on Haugen Drive; Mitkof Highway, Mile 21.8, Ohmer Creek, Tongass National Forest (USFS).

Sitka: Sawmill Creek Road, Mile 5.4, Sawmill Creek, Tongass National Forest (USFS), at Mile 1.4, Blue Lake Road; Halibut Point Road, Mile 7.8, Starrigavan, Tongass National Forest (USFS).

Skagway: See listings for Klondike Highway 2.

Thorne Bay: Thorne Bay Road, Mile 4, Gravelly Creek, Tongass National Forest (USFS).

Wrangell: Zimovia Highway, Mile 1.9, City Park (municipal); Zimovia Highway, Mile 11.2, Pats Creek (ADP).

SOUTHWEST ALASKA SYSTEM

Cordova: Copper River Highway, Mile 12.1, Cabin Lake (Eyak Native Corporation), via 3-mi (5-km) side road; Copper River Highway, Mile 17, Alagnak Slough, Chugach National Forest (USFS), via 3-mi (5-km) side road.

Kodiak: Rezanof Road, Mile 3.9, Fort Abercrombie State Historic Park (ADP); Chiniak Road, Mile 4.5, Buskin River (ADP); Chiniak Road, Mile 30.3, Pasagshak (ADP), at Mile 9, Pasagshak Bay Road.

Addresses of Parklands

Admiralty Island National Monument, Tongass National Forest, U.S. Forest Service, P.O. Box 2097, Juneau (99803). Phone: (907) 789-3111

Alagnak National Wild River (See Katmai National Park)

Alaska Chilkat Bald Eagle Preserve, Alaska Division of Parks and Outdoor Recreation, 400 Willoughby, Juneau (99801). Phone: (907) 465-4563

Alaska Maritime National Wildlife Refuge, U.S. Fish and Wildlife Service, 202 Pioneer Ave., Homer (99603). Phone: (907) 235-6546

Alaska Peninsula National Wildlife Refuge, U.S. Fish and Wildlife Service, P.O. Box 277, King Salmon (99603). Phone: (907) 246-3339

Alatna National Wild River (See Gates of the Arctic National Park)

Aleutian Islands Refuge (See Alaska Maritime National Wildlife Refuge)

Andreafsky National Wilderness and Wild River (See Yukon Delta National Wildlife Refuge)

Aniakchak National Monument and Wild River, National Park Service, P.O. Box 7, King Salmon (99613). Phone: (907) 246-3305

Ann Stevens –Cape Lisburne Refuge (See Alaska Maritime National Wildlife Refuge)

Arctic National Wildlife Refuge, U.S. Fish and Wildlife Service, P.O. Box 20, Federal Building, 101 12th St., Fairbanks (99701). Phone: (907) 456-0250

Baranof Castle Hill State Historic Site, Alaska Division of Parks and Outdoor Recreation, 400 Willoughby, Juneau (99801). Phone: (907) 465-4563

Beaver Creek National Wild River (See White Mountains National Recreation Area)

Becharof National Wildlife Refuge, U.S. Fish and Wildlife Service, P.O. Box 277, King Salmon (99603). Phone: (907) 246-3339

Bering Land Bridge National Preserve, National Park Service, P.O. Box 220, Nome (99762). Phone: (907) 443-2522

Bering Sea Refuge (See Alaska Maritime National Wildlife Refuge)

Birch Creek National Wild River (See Steese National Conservation Area)

Bogoslof Refuge (See Alaska Maritime National Wildlife Refuge)

Caines Head State Recreation Area, Alaska Division of Parks and Outdoor Recreation, P.O. Box 1247, Soldotna (99669). Phone: (907) 262-5581

Cape Krusenstern National Monument, National Park Service, P.O. Box 287, Kotzebue (99752). Phone: (907) 442-3890

Captain Cook State Recreation Area, Alaska Division of Parks and Outdoor Recreation, P.O. Box 1247, Soldotna (99669). Phone: (907) 262-5581

Chamisso Refuge (See Alaska Maritime National Wildlife Refuge)

Chena River State Recreation Area, Alaska Division of Parks and Outdoor Recreation, 4418 Airport Way, Fairbanks (99701). Phone: (907) 479-4114

Chilikadrotna National Wild River (See Lake Clark National Park)

Chilkat State Park, Alaska Division of Parks and Outdoor Recreation, 400 Willoughby, Juneau (99801). Phone: (907) 465-4563

Chugach National Forest, U.S. Forest Service, 201 E. 9th Ave., Suite 206, Anchorage (99501). Phone: (907) 261-2500
Branch offices in Cordova and Seward.
Recreation information: (907) 261-2599
Cabin reservations may be made through any Forest Service office in the state or at the Anchorage office, 201 E. 9th Ave., Suite 100, Anchorage (99501). Phone: (907) 261-2599
Recreation information recording: (907) 261-2507
Avalanche and mountain weather forecast recording: (907) 271-4500

Chugach State Park, Alaska Division of Parks and Outdoor Recreation, 2601 Commercial Dr., Anchorage (99501). Phone: (907) 279-3413
Recreation information recording: (907) 274-6713
Avalanche and mountain weather forecast recording: (907) 271-4500

Coronation Island Wilderness, Tongass National Forest, U.S. Forest Service, P.O. Box 8438, Ketchikan (99901). Phone: (907) 225-3101

Creamer's Field Migratory Waterfowl Refuge, Alaska Department of Fish and Game, 1300 College Rd., Fairbanks (99701). Phone: (907) 452-1531

Delta National Wild and Scenic River, Bureau of Land Management, P.O. Box 147, Glennallen (99588). Phone: (907) 822-3218

Denali National Park, National Park Service, P.O. Box 9, Denali National Park (99755). Phone: (907) 683-2294

Denali State Park, Alaska Division of Parks and Outdoor Recreation, SR Box 6706, Wasilla (99687). Phone: (907) 745-3975

Endicott River Wilderness, Tongass National Forest, U.S. Forest Service, 204 Siginaka Way, Sitka (99835). Phone: (907) 747-6671

Forrester Island Refuge (See Alaska Maritime National Wildlife Refuge)

Fort Abercrombie State Historic Park, Alaska Division of Parks and Outdoor Recreation, P.O. Box 3800, Kodiak (99615). Phone: (907) 486-6339

Fortymile National Wild, Scenic and Recreational River, Bureau of Land Management, P.O. Box 307, Tok (99780). Phone: (907) 883-5121

Gates of the Arctic National Park, National Park Service, P.O. Box 74680, Fairbanks (99707). Phone: (907) 456-0281

Glacier Bay National Park, National Park Service, Bartlett Cove, Gustavus (99826). Phone: (907) 697-2232

Goose Bay State Game Refuge, Alaska Department of Fish and Game, 333 Raspberry Rd., Anchorage (99502). Phone: (907) 344-0541

Gulkana National Wild River, Bureau of Land Management, P.O. Box 147, Glennallen (99588). Phone: (907) 822-3218

Harding Lake State Recreation Area, Alaska Division of Parks and Outdoor Recreation, 4418 Airport Way, Fairbanks (99701). Phone: (907) 479-4114

Hazy Island Refuge (See Alaska Maritime National Wildlife Refuge)

Iditarod National Historic Trail, Alaska Division of Parks and Outdoor Recreation, Pouch 7-001, Anchorage (99510). Phone: (907) 762-4504

Independence Mine State Historic Park, Alaska Division of Parks and Outdoor Recreation, SR Box 6706, Wasilla (99687). Phone: (907) 745-3975

Innoko National Wildlife Refuge, U.S. Fish and Wildlife Service, P.O. Box 69, McGrath (99627). Phone: (907) 524-3251

Ivishak National Wild River (See Arctic National Wildlife Refuge)

Izembek National Wildlife Refuge, U.S. Fish and Wildlife Service, Pouch 2, Cold Bay (99571). Phone: (907) 532-2445

John National Wild River (See Gates of the Arctic National Park)

Kachemak Bay State Park, Alaska Division of Parks and Outdoor Recreation, P.O. Box 1247, Soldotna (99669). Phone: (907) 262-5581

Kanuti National Wildlife Refuge, U.S. Fish and Wildlife Service, P.O. Box 20, Federal Building, 101 12th Ave., Fairbanks (99701). Phone: (907) 456-0331

Katmai National Park, National Park Service, P.O. Box 7, King Salmon (99613). Phone: (907) 246-3305

Kenai Fjords National Park, National Park Service, P.O. Box 1727, Seward (99664). Phone: (907) 224-3874

Kenai National Wildlife Refuge, U.S. Fish and Wildlife Service, P.O. Box 2139, Soldotna (99669). Phone: (907) 262-7021

Klondike Gold Rush National Historic Park, National Park Service, P.O. Box 517, Skagway (99840). Phone: (907) 983-2921
Seattle Unit: 117 S. Main St., Seattle, WA 98104. Phone: (206) 442-7220

Kobuk National Wild River (See Gates of the Arctic National Park)

Kobuk Valley National Park, National Park Service, P.O. Box 287, Kotzebue (99752). Phone: (907) 442-3890

Kodiak National Wildlife Refuge, U.S. Fish and Wildlife Service, P.O. Box 825, Kodiak (99615). Phone: (907) 487-2600

Koyukuk National Wildlife Refuge, U.S. Fish and Wildlife Service, P.O. Box 287, Galena (99741). Phone: (907) 656-1231

Lake Clark National Park, National Park Service, P.O. Box 61, 701 C St., Anchorage (99513). Phone: (907) 271-3751

Maurelle Islands Wilderness, Tongass National Forest, U.S. Forest Service, P.O. Box 8438, Ketchikan (99901). Phone: (907) 225-3101

McNeil River State Game Sanctuary, Alaska Department of Fish and Game, P.O. Box 37, King Salmon (99613). Phone: (907) 246-3340

Mendenhall Wetlands State Game Refuge, Alaska Division of Fish and Game, 230 South Franklin Street, Juneau (99801). Phone: (907) 465-4265

Misty Fiords National Monument, Tongass National Forest, U.S. Forest Service, Federal Building, Ketchikan (99901). Phone: (907) 225-2148

Mulchatna National Wild River (See Lake Clark National Park)

Nancy Lake State Recreation Area, Alaska Division of Parks and Outdoor Recreation, SR Box 6706, Wasilla (99687). Phone: (907) 745-3975

Noatak National Preserve and Wild River, National Park Service, P.O. Box 287, Kotzebue (99752). Phone: (907) 442-3890

North Fork, Koyukuk National Wild River (See Gates of the Arctic National Park)

Nowitna National Wildlife Refuge, U.S. Fish and Wildlife Service, P.O. Box 287, Galena (99741). Phone: (907) 656-1231

Nunivak National Wildlife Refuge, U.S. Fish and Wildlife Service, P.O. Box 346, Bethel (99559). Phone: (907) 543-3151

Old Sitka State Historic Site, Alaska Division of Parks and Outdoor Recreation, 400 Willoughby, Juneau (99801). Phone: (907) 456-4563

Palmer Hay Flats State Game Refuge, Alaska Department of Fish and Game, 333 Raspberry Rd., Anchorage (99502). Phone: (907) 344-0541

Petersburg Creek-Duncan Salt Chuck Wilderness, Tongass National Forest, U.S. Forest Service, P.O. Box 1328, Petersburg (99833). Phone: (907) 772-3871

Potter Point State Game Refuge, Alaska Department of Fish and Game, 333 Raspberry Rd., Anchorage (99502). Phone: (907) 344-0541

Pribilof Islands, Tanadgusix and Tanaq Corporations, St. Paul (99660). Phone: (907) 546-3212
Exploration Holidays and Cruises, Inc., 1500 Metropolitan Park Plaza Bldg., Olive Way at Boren, Seattle (98101). Phone: (800) 426-0600

Quartz Lake State Recreation Area, Alaska Division of Parks and Outdoor Recreation, 4418 Airport Way, Fairbanks (99701). Phone: (907) 479-4114

Rika's Landing State Historic Site, Alaska Division of Parks and Outdoor Recreation, 4418 Airport Way, Fairbanks (99701). Phone: (907) 479-4114

Russell Fiord Wilderness, Tongass National Forest, U.S. Forest Service, 204 Siginaka Way, Sitka (99835). Phone: (907) 747-6671

St. Lazaria Refuge (See Alaska Maritime National Wildlife Refuge)

Salmon National Wild River (See Kobuk Valley National Park)

Selawik National Wildlife Refuge and Wild River, U.S. Fish and Wildlife Service, P.O. Box 270, Kotzebue (99752). Phone: (907) 442-3799

Semidi Refuge (See Alaska Maritime National Wildlife Refuge)

Sheenjek National Wild River (See Arctic National Wildlife Refuge)

Simeonof Refuge (See Alaska Maritime National Wildlife Refuge)

Sitka National Historical Park, National Park Service, P.O. Box 738, Sitka (99835). Phone: (907) 747-6281

South Baranof Wilderness, Tongass National Forest, U.S. Forest Service, 204 Siginaka Way, Sitka (99835). Phone: (907) 747-6671

South Prince of Wales Wilderness, Tongass National Forest, U.S. Forest Service, P.O. Box 145, Craig (99921). Phone: (907) 826-3271

Steese National Conservation Area, Bureau of Land Management, 1541 Gaffney Rd., Fairbanks (99703). Phone: (907) 356-2025

Stikine-LeConte Wilderness, Tongass National Forest, U.S. Forest Service, P.O. Box 51, Wrangell (99929). Phone: (907) 874-2323

Susitna Flats State Game Refuge, Alaska Department of Fish and Game, 333 Raspberry Rd., Anchorage (99502). Phone: (907) 344-0541

Tebenkof Bay Wilderness, Tongass National Forest, U.S. Forest Service, P.O. Box 1328, Petersburg (99833). Phone: (907) 772-3871

Tetlin National Wildlife Refuge, U.S. Fish and Wildlife Service, P.O. Box 155, Tok (99780). Phone: (907) 883-5312

Tinayguk National Wild River (See Gates of the Arctic National Park)

Tlikakila National Wild River (See Lake Clark National Park)

Togiak National Wildlife Refuge, U.S. Fish and Wildlife Service, P.O. Box 10201, Dillingham (99576). Phone: (907) 842-1063

Tongass National Forest, U.S. Forest Service, Alaska Regional Office, P.O. Box 1628, Juneau (99802). Phone: (907) 586-8806
  Avalanche advisory recording. Phone: (907) 586-7669
  Cabin reservations may be made through any Forest Service office in the state or at the Centennial Hall Information Center on Egan Dr., P.O. Box 2097, Juneau (99803). Phone: (907) 586-7151
  Chatham Area office: 204 Siginaka Way, Sitka (99835). Phone: (907) 747-6671 Branch offices in Hoonah, Juneau and Yakutat.
  Ketchikan Area office: Federal Building, Ketchikan (99901). Phone: (907) 225-3101
  Branch office in Craig.
  Stikine Area office: P.O. Box 309, Petersburg (99833). Phone: (907) 772-3841 Branch office in Wrangell.

Totem Bight State Historic Park, Alaska Division of Parks and Outdoor Recreation, 400 Willoughby, Juneau (99801). Phone: (907) 465-4563

Tracy Arm-Fords Terror Wilderness, Tongass National Forest, U.S. Forest Service, 204 Siginaka Way, Sitka (99835). Phone: (907) 747-6671

Trading Bay State Game Refuge, Alaska Department of Fish and Game, 333 Raspberry Rd., Anchorage (99502). Phone: (907) 344-0541

Trans-Alaska Pipeline Utility Corridor, Bureau of Land Management, 1541 Gaffney Rd., Fairbanks (99703). Phone: (907) 356-2025

Tuxedni Refuge (See Alaska Maritime National Wildlife Refuge)

Unalakleet National Wild River, McGrath Resource Area, Bureau of Land Management, 4700 E. 72nd Ave., Anchorage (99507). Phone: (907) 267-1200

Walrus Islands State Game Sanctuary, Alaska Department of Fish and Game, P.O. Box 199, Dillingham (99576). Phone: (907) 842-5925

Warren Island Wilderness, Tongass National Forest, U.S. Forest Service, Federal Building, Ketchikan (99901). Phone: (907) 225-3101

West Chichagof-Yakobi Wilderness, Tongass National Forest, U.S. Forest Service, 204 Siginaka Way, Sitka (99835). Phone: (907) 747-6671

White Mountains National Recreation Area, Bureau of Land Management, 1541 Gaffney Rd., Fairbanks (99703). Phone: (907) 356-2025

Wind National Wild River (See Arctic National Wildlife Refuge)

Wood-Tikchik Park, Alaska Division of Parks and Outdoor Recreation, General Delivery, Dillingham (99576). Phone: (907) 842-2375

Wrangell-St. Elias National Park, National Park Service, P.O. Box 29, Glennallen (99588). Phone: (907) 822-5235

Yukon-Charley Rivers National Preserve, National Park Service, P.O. Box 64, Eagle (99738). Phone: (907) 547-2233

Yukon Delta National Wildlife Refuge, U.S. Fish and Wildlife Service, P.O. Box 346, Bethel (99559). Phone: (907) 543-3151

Yukon Flats National Wildlife Refuge, U.S. Fish and Wildlife Service, P.O. Box 20, Federal Building, 101 12th Ave., Fairbanks (99701). Phone: (907) 456-0250

Land Managers

In order to make sense from the overwhelming diversity of rules and regulations, let's look briefly at each of the land managing agencies and the philosophies behind their decisions.

The **Alaska Department of Fish and Game** oversees the state's wildlife resources, from research to the establishment of harvest levels to the enforcement of fishing, hunting and trapping regulations. Parklands managed by other governmental agencies may have more restrictive hunting, fishing and trapping laws, but in the absence of such restrictions, ADF&G regulations apply. A number of land areas are under more restrictive regulations by the ADF&G to protect wildlife and wildlife habitat. *State game refuges* and *state critical habitat areas* permit sports fishing, hunting, trapping and the use of firearms, horses, powerboats, fixed-wing aircraft, snowmobiles and, to a limited extent, off-road vehicles when wildlife and habitat are not adversely affected. *State game sanctuaries* protect extremely critical wildlife populations or habitats, prohibit hunting and severely restrict human activities.

The **Alaska Division of Parks** manages its land units to provide for public recreational opportunities. *State parks* are relatively large areas managed to protect the resources of the land while providing for a wide range of recreational opportunities. Sports fishing, hunting, trapping and the use of firearms, horses, powerboats, fixed-wing aircraft and snowmobiles are often permitted. For public safety or because of the impact on specific lands, wildlife or recreational values, some activities may be restricted or limited to specific areas. In a few parks, for instance, hunting is permitted but firearms may not be used. *State historic parks* and *state historic sites* preserve, interpret or commemorate a part of Alaska's history or prehistory. Historic parks are larger units; historic sites are smaller units. Hunting, trapping and the use of horses or motorized vehicles are usually not permitted. *State recreation areas* and *state recreation sites* have developed facilities to encourage public use, providing picnic areas, campgrounds, trails, boat ramps and interpretive activities and displays. Suitability of fishing, hunting, trapping and the use of horses and motorized vehicles is determined area by area.

The **Bureau of Land Management**'s objective is to provide maximum public benefits from the land through multiple use by many interest groups. Wildlife resources are managed by the Alaska Department of Fish and Game, while BLM oversees the land, maintaining federal land records and fighting forest and tundra fires statewide. Federal public lands not contained within another specific management unit are under the care of BLM. Two classifications have been created to protect land and recreational values beyond the usual BLM guidelines: *national conserva-*

tion areas and *national recreation areas.* Sports fishing, hunting, trapping and the use of firearms, horses, powerboats, fixed-wing aircraft, snowmobiles and, with limitations, off-road vehicles are permitted within the units. The difference lies with mining. In both classifications, valid mining claims in existence when a unit was established are honored. Lands are withdrawn from further mineral entry in national recreation areas, whereas within a conservation area, additional mineral entry can occur at some future time.

The **National Park Service** is charged with the protection and preservation of the land, its resources and its cultural values so that they may be passed on undisturbed to future generations. At the same time, the lands are to be used by people for recreation and enjoyment. In a departure from earlier National Park Service policy, most of their parklands created in 1980 provide for subsistence use by rural Alaskans for the gathering of food and firewood and the use of rural transportation forms—powerboats, airplanes and snowmobiles. In general, these *national parks, national wildernesses* and *national monuments* permit the recreational visitor to fish, carry firearms and use horses, powerboats, fixed-wing aircraft and snowmobiles; hunting, trapping and off-road vehicles are not permitted. Exceptions are the National Park Service units established prior to 1980, which retain their original regulations. *National preserves* permit recreational hunting and trapping in addition to the uses listed above.

The **U.S. Fish and Wildlife Service'**s function is to protect wildlife and its habitat. Other activities may be permitted if they are compatible with wildlife management. In general, *national wildlife refuge* regulations permit sports fishing, hunting and trapping and the use of firearms, horses, powerboats, fixed-wing aircraft and snowmobiles; off-road vehicles are restricted to specific areas. Regulations in *refuge wilderness* areas are similar, but occasionally more restrictive.

The **U.S. Forest Service** manages the *national forests* for multiple use. Sports fishing, hunting, trapping, firearms, horses, powerboats, fixed-wing aircraft, snowmobiles and off-road vehicles are all permitted, but where user values conflict, lands are zoned for or against a specific use. To protect outstanding scenic lands and wildlife habitats, a number of *wildernesses, monuments* and *monument wildernesses* have been established. The recreational visitor will find essentially no additional use restrictions on these lands. The designations, instead, limit development of recreational facilities and commercial use of the land's resources.

Addresses

Alaska Department of Fish and Game, State of Alaska

Alaska State Headquarters, P.O. Box 3-2000, Juneau (99802). Phone: (907) 465-4180 (Fish), (907) 465-4190 (Game)

Anchorage Regional Office, 333 Raspberry Rd., Anchorage (99502). Phone: (907) 344-0541

Branch offices in Barrow, Bethel, Cold Bay, Cooper Landing, Cordova, Delta Junction, Dillingham, Dutch Harbor, Fairbanks, Galena, Glennallen, Homer, King Salmon, Kodiak, Kotzebue, McGrath, Nome, Palmer, Sand Point, Seward, Soldotna, Tok and Unalaska.

Juneau Regional Office, Island Center Building, P.O. Box 20, Douglas (99824-0020). Phone: (907) 465-4293

Branch offices in Haines, Ketchikan, Petersburg, Sitka, Wrangell and Yakutat.

Alaska Division of Parks and Outdoor Recreation, State of Alaska, Department of Natural Resources

Alaska State Office, P.O. Box 7001, Anchorage (99510). Phone: (907) 561-2020

Branch offices in Fairbanks, Juneau, Haines, Kodiak, Palmer and Soldotna.

Bureau of Land Management, U.S. Department of the Interior
  Alaska State Office, 701 C St., P.O. Box 13, Anchorage (99513)
    Land Office, 701 C St., Anchorage. Phone: (907) 271-5960
  Anchorage District Office, 4700 E. 72nd Ave., Anchorage (99507). Phone: (907) 276-1200
    Branch office in Glennallen.
  Fairbanks District Office, 1541 Gaffney Rd., Fairbanks (99703). Phone: (907) 356-2025
    Branch office in Tok.

Forest Service, U.S. Department of Agriculture
  Alaska Regional Office, P.O. Box 1628, Juneau (99802). Phone: (907) 586-8806
  Chugach National Forest, 201 E. 9th Ave., Suite 206, Anchorage (99501). Phone: (907) 261-2500
    Branch offices in Cordova and Seward.
  Tongass National Forest, Chatham Area, 204 Siginaka Way, Sitka (99835). Phone: (907) 747-6671
    Branch offices in Hoonah, Juneau and Yakutat.
  Tongass National Forest, Ketchikan Area, Federal Bldg., Ketchikan (99901). Phone: (907) 225-3101
    Branch office in Craig.
  Tongass National Forest, Stikine Area, P.O. Box 309, Petersburg (99833). Phone: (907) 772-3841
    Branch office in Wrangell.

National Park Service, U.S. Department of the Interior
  Alaska Regional Office, 2525 Gambell St., Anchorage (99503). Phone: (907) 261-2643
    Branch offices in Eagle, Fairbanks, Glennallen, Gustavus, Juneau, King Salmon, Kotzebue, Denali National Park, Nome, Seward, Sitka and Skagway.

U.S. Fish and Wildlife Service, U.S. Department of the Interior
  Alaska Area Office, 1011 E. Tudor Rd., Anchorage (99503). Phone: (907) 786-3487
    Branch offices in Adak, Bethel, Cold Bay, Dillingham, Fairbanks, Galena, Homer, Juneau, King Salmon, Kodiak, Kotzebue, McGrath, Soldotna and Tok.

Information Sources

Parklands

Public Lands Information Centers

    Anchorage: 605 W. 4th Ave. (99501). Opens in late 1986; until then contact Parks and Forests Information Center, 2525 Gambell St., (99503). Phone: (907) 261-2643

    Fairbanks: 250 Cushman St., Suite 1A (99701). Phone: (907) 451-7352

    Juneau: Centennial Hall Information Center, 101 Egan Dr., (99801). Phone: (907) 586-7151

    Tok: Tok Information Center, P.O. Box 335 (99780). Phone: (907) 883-5667

General

Alaska Division of Tourism, Pouch E, Juneau (99811) (Ask for the "Alaska Travel Planner.") Phone: (907) 465-2010

Federal Information Center, 701 C St., Box 33, Anchorage (99513) (For referral to proper federal office.) Phone: (907) 271-3650

Boating

U.S. Coast Guard, Boating Safety Branch, P.O. Box 3-5000, Juneau (99802). Phone: (907) 586-7467

Rescue Coordination Center. Phone: 586-7340 or Zenith 5555 (toll free) (Call via "Operator." Also report to this number information concerning water pollution, missing or inoperative marine navigational aids or suspected violations of U.S. fisheries laws and gear conflicts.)

Guide services, hunting

Alaska Department of Commerce, Division of Occupational Licensing, Pouch D, Juneau (99811). Phone: (907) 465-2542

Guide services, mountaineering and wilderness

Alaska Wilderness Guides Association (originally known as the Alaska Association of Mountain and Wilderness Guides), P.O. Box 141061, Anchorage (99514). Phone: (907) 276-6634

Youth hostels

Alaska Council, American Youth Hostels, Inc., P.O. Box 41226, Anchorage (99509). Phone: (907) 276-3635

    Locations of hostels include Anchorage*, Delta Junction, Fairbanks, Girdwood*, Haines, Juneau*, Ketchikan, Sitka, Soldotna*, Tok and Willow*. (Starred locations are open year-round.)

Other offices listed in text of book

Cooperative Extension Service

    Anchorage: 2651 Providence Dr., (Mail only. Call for new office location.) (99501). Phone: (907) 786-1080

    Fairbanks: University of Alaska, Fairbanks (99775). Phone: (907) 474-7268

    Juneau: Rm. 137 Federal Building, P.O. Box 109, (99802). Phone: (907) 586-7102

Federal Aviation Administration

    Alaska Regional Headquarters, 701 C Street, Box 14, Anchorage (99513). Phone: (907) 272-8812

    Flight Standards Division. Phone: (907) 271-5514

Navigability Project, Alaska Department of Natural Resources, Division of Research and Development, 555 Cordova St., Anchorage (99510). Phone: (907) 276-2653

Weather records: Arctic Environmental Information and Data Center, 707 A Street, Anchorage (99501). Phone: (907) 279-4523

Travelers information

Avalanche advisory, Anchorage area phone: (907) 271-4500; Juneau area phone:
(907) 586-7669

Highway and road conditions, Alaska Department of Transportation, Maintenance
and Operations Division

Anchorage: P.O. Box 196900 (99519-6900). Phone: (907) 266-1450; 243-7675
(recording)

Fairbanks: 2301 Peger Rd. (99701). Phone: (907) 452-1911; 452-ROAD (recording)

Juneau: P.O. Box 3-1000 (99802). Phone: (907) 789-6245

Nome: P.O. Box 1048 (99762). Phone: (907) 443-5266

Valdez: P.O. Box 507 (99686). Phone: (907) 835-4322

Inter-city buslines

Alaska Sightseeing, 349 Wrangell Ave., Anchorage (99501). Phone: (907) 276-1305
or 276-7141.
(Serves Anchorage, Denali National Park, Fairbanks, Glennallen, Haines,
Tok, Whittier and Valdez.)

Norline Tours, Box 4326, Whitehorse, Yukon Territory, Canada Y1A 3T3. Phone:
(403) 668-3355

Seward Buslines, P.O. Box 1668, Seward (99664). Phone: (907) 224-3608 (Seward);
562-0712 (Anchorage). (Serves Anchorage and Seward.)

Valdez-Anchorage Bus Line, 421 E. 45th Ave., Anchorage (99503). Phone: (907)
561-5806.
(Serves Anchorage, Palmer, Glennallen and Valdez.)

White Pass & Yukon Motorcoaches, 300 Elliott Ave. W., Seattle, WA (98119). Phone:
1-800-544-2206 (toll free); (907) 279-0761 (Anchorage). (Serves Anchorage,
Glennallen, Haines, Skagway and Tok in Alaska; Beaver Creek, Carcross,
Dezadeash, Haines Junction, Log Cabin [Chilkoot Trail access] and
Whitehorse in Canada.)

Yukon Stage Lines (Alaska), 213 W. Clay, Fairbanks (99701). Phone: (907)
452-3038. (Service between Fairbanks and Beaver Creek Y.T.; connects with
Norline to serve Whitehorse and Dawson City, Y.T.)

Alaska State Ferry System

Department of Transportation

Main Office (for all reservations): Pouch R, Juneau (99811). Phone: (within
Alaska) 1-800-551-7185; (Outside Alaska) 1-800-544-2251. Telex 45-312.

Local office telephones:

Anchorage, (907) 272-4482	Seattle, Washington, (206) 623-1149
Cordova, (907) 424-7333	(recording; remain on the line)
Haines, (907) 766-2111	Seldovia, (907) 234-7868
Homer, (907) 235-8449	Seward, (907) 224-5485
Juneau, (907) 465-3941	Sitka, (907) 747-8737
Ketchikan, (907) 225-6181	Skagway, (907) 983-2941
Kodiak, (907) 486-3800	Valdez, (907) 835-4436
Petersburg, (907) 772-3855	Wrangell, (907) 874-3711
Prince Rupert, Canada, (604) 627-1744	

British Columbia Ferries

British Columbia Ferry Corporation, 818 Broughton Street, Victoria, B.C.
V8W 1E4

Railroads

Alaska Railroad

Anchorage: (main office) P.O. Box 72111 (99510) Alaska Railroad Depot. Phone:
(907) 265-2494 or 265-2623

Fairbanks: 218 N. Cushman St. (99701). Phone: (907) 456-4155

White Pass and Yukon Route
Not operating.

Airlines
See your travel agent.

Maps and Charts
Alaska topographic maps
By mail:
  Fairbanks: Alaska Distribution Section. U.S. Geological Survey, New Federal Building, Box 12, 101 12th Ave., Fairbanks (99701). Phone: (907) 456-0244.
  Denver: Branch of Distribution, U.S. Geological Survey, Box 25286, Denver Federal Center, Denver, CO 80225. Phone: (303) 236-7477
Over the counter in Alaska:
  Anchorage: Public Inquiries Office, U.S. Geological Survey, 4230 University Dr., Room 101, (99508-4664). Phone: (907) 561-5555. Or: Public Inquiries Office, U.S. Geological Survey, Federal Building Branch, 701 C St., Room E146, Box 53 (99513). Phone: (907) 271-4307
  Fairbanks: See mailing address above.
Alaska marine and aeronautical charts
Available from chart agents in many Alaskan communities; tide tables, Coast Pilots, tidal current tables and charts. Ask for the "Nautical Chart Catalog 3: United States, Alaska, Including the Aleutian Islands."
  Anchorage: Chart Sales Office, National Ocean Service, Federal Building, 701 C Street, Box 38, Anchorage (99513). Phone: (907) 271-5040
  Seattle: Pacific Marine Center, National Ocean Service, 1801 Fairview Ave. E., Seattle, WA (98102). Phone: (206) 442-7657
Aerial photographs
Photogrammetry Branch, N/CG 2314, Nautical Charting Division, National Ocean Service/NOAA, Rockville, MD (20852). Phone: (301) 443-8601.
Canadian topographic maps
  Fairbanks: McCauley's Reprographics, Inc., 721 Gaffney Rd., Fairbanks (99701) Selected inventory. Phone: (907) 452-8141
  Ottawa: Canada Map Office Surveys and Mapping, Energy, Mines and Resources, Canada, 615 Booth St., Ottawa, Ontario K1A 0E9. Phone: (613) 995-4510

United States Customs Service
Main Office: 620 E. 10th Ave., Suite 101, Anchorage(99501). Phone (907) 271-4043
Alcan Office: Mile 1221.8, Alaska Highway, Tok (99780). Phone: (907) 774-2252
Dalton Cache Office: P.O. Box 509, Haines (99827). Phone: (907) 766-2374
Eagle Office: Customs Office, Eagle (99738). Phone: (907) 459-8001
Ketchikan Office: P.O. Box 7080, Ketchikan (99901). Phone: (907) 225-2254
Poker Creek Office: c/o Boundary, Alaska 99790. On Taylor Highway; summer only. Phone: None
  Additional offices at Fairbanks, Fort Yukon, Juneau, Kaktovik, Northway, Sitka, Skagway, Valdez and Wrangell.

Canadian Customs and Excise
Main Office, Connaught Building, Sussex Dr., Ottawa, Ontario K1A OL5. Phone: (613) 993-0534
Dawson City Office, Customs Office, Dawson City, Yukon Territory Y0B 1G0. Phone: (403) 993-5455
Whitehorse Office, P.O. Box 4520, Whitehorse, Yukon Territory Y1A 2R8. Phone: (403) 667-6471

Alaska State Troopers, Department of Public Safety
Emergency: 911 (Not operational in many communities. Call "Information" or check local phone directory.)

Anchorage Office: 5700 E. Tudor Rd., Anchorage (99507). Phone: (907) 269-5511
Fairbanks Office: 1979 Peger Road, Fairbanks (99701). Phone: (907) 452-2114
Juneau Office: 2760 Sherwood Lane, Juneau (99801). Phone: (907) 789-2161
U.S. Border: P.O. Box 335, Tok (99780). Phone: (907) 883-5111
> Additional offices in Bethel, Cantwell, Cooper Landing, Cordova, Craig, Delta Junction, Dillingham, Galena, Glennallen, Haines, Healy, Homer, Ketchikan, King Salmon, Kodiak, Kotzebue, McGrath, Nenana, Ninilchik, Nome, Palmer, Petersburg, St. Marys, St. Paul, Seward, Soldotna, Talkeetna, Tok, Unalakleet, Valdez and Yakutat.

Royal Canadian Mounted Police
Alcan Office, Beaver Creek, Yukon Territory. Phone: (403) 862-7300
Prince Rupert, British Columbia. Phone: (604) 624-2136
Whitehorse, Yukon Territory. Phone: (403) 667-5555
Dawson City, Yukon Territory. Phone: (403) 993-5444

Search and rescue
Alaska Mountain Rescue Group, Fast Action Response Team, 8101 White Drive, Anchorage (99516). Phone: (907) 276-4331
Civil Air Patrol, Polaris Senior Squadron, P.O. Box 1008, Anchorage (99504). Phone: (907) 272-0731 or 277-7913

Alaska Natives
Alaska Federation of Natives, Inc., 411 W. 4th Ave., Suite 301, Anchorage (99501). Phone: (907) 274-3611

Native regional corporations:
Ahtna, Inc., Drawer G, Copper Center (99573). Phone: (907) 822-3476
Aleut Corporation, 4000 Old Seward Hwy., Anchorage (99503). Phone: (907) 561-4300
Arctic Slope Regional Corporation, P.O. Box 129, Barrow (99723). Phone: (907) 852-8633
Bering Straits Native Corporation, P.O. Box 1008, Nome (99762). Phone: (907) 443-5252
Bristol Bay Native Corporation, P.O. Box 100220, Anchorage (99501). Phone: (907) 278-3602
Calista Corporation, 516 Denali St., Anchorage (99501). Phone: (907) 279-5516
Chugach Alaska Corp., 3000 A St., Suite 400, Anchorage (99503). Phone: (907) 563-8866
Cook Inlet Region, Inc., P.O. Box 4N, Anchorage (99509). Phone: (907) 274-8638
Doyon, Limited, 201 1st Ave., Fairbanks (99507). Phone: (907) 452-4755
Koniag, Inc., P.O. Box 746, Kodiak (99615). Phone: (907) 486-4147
NANA Regional Corporation, Inc., P.O. Box 49, Kotzebue (99752). Phone: (907) 442-3301
Sealaska Corporation, One Sealaska Plaza, Suite 200, Juneau (99801). Phone: (907) 586-1512

Museums
Adak: Adak Community Museum
Anchorage: Alaska Historical Museum
  Anchorage Historical and Fine Arts Museum
  Elmendorf Air Force Base Wildlife Museum
  Fort Richardson Army Base Wildlife Museum
Barrow: Naval Arctic Research Laboratory Museum
Bethel: Yugtarvik Regional Museum
Cordova: Cordova Historical Society and Museum
Delta Junction: Delta Historical Society and Museum
Denali Park: Denali National Park Museum

Dillingham: Dillingham Heritage Museum
Fairbanks: Alaskaland Museum
University of Alaska Museum
Pioneer Park Memorial Museum
Fort Yukon: Dinjii Zhuu Enjit Museum
Haines: Sheldon Museum and Cultural Center, Chilkat Historical Society
Homer: Pratt Museum, Homer Museum of Natural History
Juneau: Alaska State Museum
Juneau Mining Museum
Kenai: Kenai Historical Society and Museum
Ketchikan: Ketchikan Indian Museum
Tongass Historical Society and Museum
Totem Heritage Center
Kodiak: Baranof Museum and Kodiak Historical Society
Kotzebue: Museum of the Arctic
Kotzebue Museum
McCarthy: Kennecott Historical Museum
Metlakatla: Duncan Cottage Museum
Naknek: Bristol Bay Regional Museum
Nome: Carrie McLain Memorial Museum
Palmer: Matanuska Valley Historical Society and Museum
Transportation Museum of Alaska, Inc.
Petersburg: Clausen Memorial Museum
Sitka: Sheldon Jackson Museum
Sitka Historical Society and Museum
Sitka National Historical Park
Skagway: Trail of '98 Museum
Soldotna: Damon Memorial Historical Museum
Talkeetna: Talkeetna Historical Society and Museum
Tok: Tok Visitor Information Center
Valdez: Valdez Heritage Center
Whittier: Whittier Historical Society and Fine Arts Museum
Wrangell: Wrangell Historical Society and Museum

Selected clubs

These organizations will also be able to help you contact similar groups elsewhere in the state. Refer to the current Anchorage Directory of Clubs and Organizations, available at any city library branch, for phone numbers or address changes.

Alaska Bicycle Association, Box 4-1153, Anchorage (99509)
Alaska Bowhunters Association, Box 6629, Anchorage (99502)
Alaska Fly Fishers, Box 4-11, Anchorage (99509)
Alaska Motormushers (snowmobiles), 1213 E. 26th Ave., Anchorage (99504)
Alaska Prospector's Society, 3000 E. 33rd Ave., #3, Anchorage (99503)
Alaska Sled Dog Racing Association, P.O. Box 10-569, Anchorage (99511)
Alaska Sport Divers, 715 Pearl Dr., Anchorage (99502)
Alaska Sport Fishing Association, 3605 Arctic Blvd., Suite 800, Anchorage (99502)
Anchorage Powerboat Association, SRA Box 157, Anchorage (99502)
Chugach Gem and Mineral Society, 3300 Knik St., Anchorage (99503)
Knik Kanoers and Kayakers, 3850 Westminster Way, Anchorage (99504)
Mountaineering Club of Alaska, Box 2037, Anchorage (99510)
Nordic Ski Club of Anchorage, P.O. Box 3504, Anchorage (99510)
Sailing Club of Alaska, Box 4-2554, Anchorage (99509)
U.S. Ski Association, Alaska Division, Box 4-2126, Anchorage (99509)

Table 1: Access and Services, Selected Villages and Cities

Population of Alaska: 401,851[1]

Village	Zip	Popu-lation[1]	On road system[2]	Car rental	Taxi cab	Scheduled bus service[3]	Railroad access[3]	Scheduled air service[3]	Air taxi base[4]	Ferry port[3]	Boat charter service[5]	Store	Meals	Lodging	Campground	Hospital or clinic	Visitors welcome
Adak	98791	3315						•				(Military clearance required)					
Akhiok	99615	105						•									
Akiachak	99551	438						•				•	N	N	N		
Akiak	99552	198						•				•	N	N	N		No
Akutan	99553	169						•			•	•	N	N	•		
Alakanuk	99554	522						•				•	N	N			
Aleknagik	99555	154						•			•	N	N	N	N		
Allakaket	99720	163						•				•					
Ambler	99786	192						•	•			•	N	N			
Anaktuvuk Pass	99721	203						•				•					
Anchorage area	99502	174,431	•	•	•	[6]	•	•	•		•	•	•	•	•	•	•
Anchor Point	99556	226	•									•	•	•	•		
Angoon	99820	465						•	•	•	•	•	•	•	•	N	
Aniak	99557	341						•	•		•	•	•	•	•		
Annette	99920	139						•									
Anvik	99558	114						•	•		•	•	•	•	•		
Arctic Village	99722	111						•			•	•	•				
Atka	99502	93						•									
Atmautluak	99559	219						•			•	•	N	N	N		No
Attu	99695	29															
Auke Bay	99821	(See Juneau)				•		•	•	•	•	•	•	•	•		
Barrow	99723	2207				• [7]		•	•			•	•	•		•	
Barter Island	99747	(See Kaktovik)															
Beaver	99724	66						•				•					
Bethel	99559	3576		•		• [7]		•	•			•	•	•	•	•	
Bettles (Evansville)	99726	94						•	•			•	•	•	•		
Big Lake	99687	410	•				•		•			•	•	•	•		
Birch Creek	99790	32						•									
Bird Creek/Indian	99540	322	•			•						•	•	•	•		
Boundary	99780	9	•														

• = Reported available   N = Reported not available
[1] 1980 Census figures.
[2] See road map in Getting Around, Part I.
[3] See Public transportation map in Getting Around
[4] From Federal Aviation Administration (FAA) certification records. See also Air Taxis in Getting Around.
[5] Blanks indicate that no information has been received. Services may or may not exist. Use village population figures as a guide to probable services. See also Villages in Part I.
[6] Both intra-city and inter-city service.
[7] Intra-city service only.
[8] Service to Glacier Bay National Park.

			TRANSPORTATION									SERVICES[5]					
Village	Zip	Population[1]	On road system[2]	Car rental	Taxi cab	Scheduled bus service[3]	Railroad access[3]	Scheduled air service[3]	Air taxi base[4]	Ferry port[3]	Boat charter service[5]	Store	Meals	Lodging	Campground	Hospital or clinic	Visitors welcome
Brevig Mission	99785	138							•								
Buckland	99727	177							•			•					
Cantwell	99729	89	•			•	•		•			•	•	•	•		
Cape Lisburne	99790	36							•			(military site)					
Central	99730	36	•						•			•	•	•	•		
Chalkyitsik	99788	100							•			•					
Chefornak	99561	230							•			•					No
Chevak	99563	466							•		•	•	•	•	N	•	
Chicken	99732	37	•														
Chignik	99564	178									•						
Chitina	99566	42	•						•		•	•	•	•	•		
Chuathbaluk	99557	105										•	N	N	N		
Chugiak	99567	2851	•			•			•			•	•	•	•		
Circle	99733	81	•					•	•			•	•	•	•		
Circle Hot Springs	99730	21	•					•	•				•	•	•		
Clam Gulch	99568	50	•									•	•	•	•		
Cold Bay	99571	228						•	•	•		•	•	•			
Cooper Landing	99572	116	•			•			•		•	•	•	•	•		
Copper Center	99573	213	•			•						•	•	•	•		
Cordova	99574	1879		•	•			•	•	•	•	•	•	•	•	•	
Craig	99921	527			•				•		•	•	•	•		•	
Crooked Creek	99575	108							•			•					
Deadhorse	99701	64	•						•			•					
Deering	99736	150							•			•					
Delta Junction	99737	1230	•			•			•			•	•	•	•	•	
Denali National Park	99755	32	•	•		•	•	•	•			•	•	•	•	•	
Dillingham	99576	1563			•			•	•		•	•	•	•		•	
Douglas	99824	(See Juneau)				[7]						•	•	•			
Dutch Harbor	99692	(See Unalaska)															
Eagle	99738	164	•					•	•			•	•	•	•		
Eagle River	99577	3257	•			•			•			•	•	•	•		
Eek	99578	228							•			•					
Egegik	99579	75							•			N	N	N	N		No
Ekwok	99580	77							•								
Elfin Cove	99825	28							•				•	•			
Elim	99739	211							•								
Emmonak	99581	567						•	•			•	•	•	N		
English Bay	99697	124							•			•					
Ester	99725	149	•			•						•	•				
Fairbanks/College	99701	26,688	•	•	•	[6]	•	•	•			•	•	•	•	•	
False Pass	99583	70							•								
Flat	99584	9							•			•					
Fortuna Ledge	99585	262							•			•					
Fort Yukon	99740	619							•	•		•	•	•	•		
Fox	99790	123	•									•	•				

311

Village	Zip	Population[1]	On road system[2]	Car rental	Taxi cab	Scheduled bus service[3]	Railroad access[3]	Scheduled air service[3]	Air taxi base[4]	Ferry port[3]	Boat charter service[5]	Store	Meals	Lodging	Campground	Hospital or clinic	Visitors welcome
Gakona	99586	87	•			•			•			•	•	•	•		
Galena	99741	765						•	•			•	•	•		•	
Gambell	99742	445						•									
Girdwood	99587	562	•	•	•	•						•	•	•			
Glennallen	99588	511	•		•	•			•			•	•	•	•	•	
Golovin	99762	87						•	•			•					
Goodnews Bay	99589	168						•			•	•	N	N	•		
Grayling	99590	209						•	•			•					
Gulkana	99695	104	•			•			•			•					
Gustavus	99826	98				8		•	•		•	•	•	•	•		
Haines	99827	993	•	•	•	•		•	•	•	•	•	•	•	•	•	
Healy	99743	334	•			•	•					•	•	•	•		
Hollis	99950	N			•					•		N	N	N			
Holy Cross	99602	241						•	•			•	•	•			
Homer area	99603	2914	•	•	•			•	•	•	•	•	•	•	•	•	
Hoonah	99829	680			•			•	•			•	•	•	•		
Hooper Bay	99604	627						•	•			•	N	N	•		
Hope	99605	103	•									•	•		•		
Hughes	99745	73						•			•	•	N	N	•		No
Huslia	99746	188						•				•	N	•	N		No
Hydaburg	99922	298						•		•	•	•	•	N	N		
Hyder	99923	77	•									•	•				
Igiugig	99695	33						•									
Iliamna	99606	94						•	•			•	•	•			
Juneau area	99801	19,528		•	•	7		•	•	•	•	•	•	•	•	•	•
Kake	99830	555						•	•			•	•	•		•	
Kaktovik/Barter Is.	99747	165						•	•			•	•		N		
Kalskag, Upper & Lower	99626	375						•				•					
Kaltag	99748	247						•				•					
Karluk	99608	96						•									
Kasigluk	99609	342									•	•	N	N	•		
Kasilof	99610	201	•								•	•	•				
Kenai city area	99611	5767	•	•	•	•		•	•			•	•	•	•		
Ketchikan area	99901	11,316		•				•	•	•	•	•	•	•	•	•	
Kiana	99749	345						•	•			•					
King Cove	99612	460						•	•	•		•	N	N	N		
King Salmon	99613	545						•	•		•	•	•	•		•	
Kipnuk	99614	371						•				•	N	N			
Kivalina	99750	241						•				•					
Klawock	99925	318			•			•			•	•	•	•	•		
Kobuk	99751	62						•				•					
Kodiak city	99615	4756		•	•			•	•	•	•	•	•	•	•	•	
Kokhanok	99606	83										•	•				
Koliganek	99576	117						•				•					
Kongiganak	99559	239						•			•	•	N	N	N		

Village	Zip	Popu-lation[1]	On road system[2]	Car rental	Taxi cab	Scheduled bus service[3]	Railroad access[3]	Scheduled air service[3]	Air taxi base[4]	Ferry port[3]	Boat charter service[5]	Store	Meals	Lodging	Campground	Hospital or clinic	Visitors welcome
Kotlik	99620	293						•			•	•	N	N	N		No
Kotzebue	99752	2054			•			•	•			•	•	•		•	
Koyuk	99753	188						•									
Koyukuk	99754	98						•	N			N	N	N	N		No
Kwethluk	99621	454						•	•			•	N	•	N		No
Kwigillingok	99622	354						•				•	N	N			
Kwinhagak	(See Quinhagak)							•									
Lake Minchumina	99623	22						•									
Larsen Bay	99624	168						•	•								
Levelok	99625	79						•				•	N	N			
Livengood	99790	14	•										•				
Lower Kalskag	99626	246										•	N	N			
Manley Hot Springs	99756	61	•					•	•			•	•	•	•		
Manokotak	99628	294						•				•					
Marshall	(See Fortuna Ledge)																
McCarthy	99588	23	•											•			
McGrath	99627	355						•	•			•	•	•	•		
Medfra	99629	15						•	•			•					
Meshik	(See Port Heiden)																
Mekoryuk	99630	160						•				•		•			
Metlakatla	99926	1056				•			•	•	•	•	•	•			
Minto	99758	153						•									
Moose Pass	99631	76	•			•			•			•	•	•	•		
Mountain Village	99632	586						•				•					
Naknek	99633	463						•	•		•	•	•	•			
Napakiak	99634	262						•			•	•	N	N	N		
Napaskiak	99559	244						•				•	N				
Nenana	99760	470	•			•	•	•				•	•	•	•	•	
New Stuyahok	99636	331						•				•					
Newtok	99559	131						•				•					
Nightmute	99690	119						•				•					
Nikolai	99691	91											N	N			
Nikolski	99638	50						•				•	N	N	N		
Ninilchik	99639	341	•									•	•	•	•		
Noatak	99761	273						•				•	•	•			
Nome	99762	2301			•			•	•			•	•	•		•	
Nondalton	99640	173						•				•	•	•	N		
Noorvik	99763	492						•				•					
North Pole	99705	724	•			•						•	•	•	•		
Northway	99764	185	•			•			•			•	•	•	•	•	
Nuiqsut	99723	208						•				•					
Nulato	99765	350						•			•	•	N	N	•		No
Nunapitchuk	99641	299						•				•	N	N			
Old Harbor	99643	340						•				•					
Ouzinkie	99644	173						•				•		N			

Village	Zip	Population[1]	On road system[2]	Car rental	Taxi cab	Scheduled bus service[3]	Railroad access[3]	Scheduled air service[3]	Air taxi base[4]	Ferry port[3]	Boat charter service[5]	Store	Meals	Lodging	Campground	Hospital or clinic	Visitors welcome
Palmer area	99645	2141	•		•	•			•			•	•	•	•	•	
Paxson	99737	30	•			•			•				•	•	•		
Pelican	99832	180						•		•							
Petersburg	99833	2821			•			•	•	•	•	•	•	•	•	•	
Pilot Point	99649	66						•	•				N	•			
Pilot Station	99650	325						•				•					
Platinum	99651	55						•				N	N	N			
Point Hope	99766	464						•				•		•			
Point Alsworth	99653	N							•		•	•	•	•			
Port Graham	99603	162										•					
Port Heiden	99549	92						•				•					
Port Lions	99550	215						•		•		•	•	•			
Prudhoe Bay	99701	50										(See Deadhorse)					
Quinhagak	99655	412						•	•			•	N	N			
Rampart	99767	50						•									
Red Devil	99656	39						•	•			•					
Ruby	99768	197						•	•			•	•	•			
Russian Mission	99657	169						•				•					
St. George Island	99660	158						•				•					
St. Marys	99658	382						•	•		•	•	•	•	N		
St. Michael	99659	239						•				•	•				
St. Paul	99660	551						•				•	•	•	N		
Sand Point	99661	625						•	•	•		•	N	•	N		
Savoonga	99769	491						•				•	•	•			
Scammon Bay	99662	250						•			•	•	•		•		
Selawik	99770	361						•				•					
Seldovia	99663	479								•	•	•	•	•	•	•	•
Seward	99664	1843	•	•	•	•		•		•	•	•	•	•	•	•	•
Shageluk	99665	131						•	•		•	•		N	N	N	
Shaktoolik	99771	164						•									
Sheldon Point	99666	103						•									
Shemya	99695	600						•				(military clearance required)					
Shishmaref	99772	394						•			•	•	•	N	•	•	
Shungnak	99773	202						•			•	•	N	•	•		
Sitka	99835	7803		•	•			•	•	•	•	•	•	•	•	•	•
Skagway	99840	814	•	•	•	•	•	•	•	•	•	•	•	•	•	•	•
Skwentna	99667	22						•	•								
Slana	99586	49	•														
Sleetmute	99665	107						•	•			•	N	N			
Soldotna	99669	2320	•		•				•		•	•	•	•	•	•	•
Stebbins	99671	331						•				•					
Sterling	99672	919	•		•						•	•		•	•		
Stevens Village	99774	96						•				•					
Stony River	99557	62						•				•			•		
Sutton	99674	182	•		•												

	TRANSPORTATION									SERVICES[5]					
Village · Zip · Popu-lation[1]	On road system[2]	Car rental	Taxi cab	Scheduled bus service[3]	Railroad access[3]	Scheduled air service[3]	Air taxi base[4]	Ferry port[3]	Boat charter service[5]	Store	Meals	Lodging	Campground	Hospital or clinic	Visitors welcome
Takotna 99675 48						•	•			N	N	N			
Talkeetna 99676 264	•				•		•		•	•	•	•	•		
Tanacross 99776 117	•			•			•								
Tanana 99777 388						•	•			•	•	•		•	
Tatitlek 99677 68						•				N	N	N			
Teller 99778 212						•	•			•					
Tenakee Springs 99841 138						•		•	•						
Tetlin 99779 107	•			•			•								
Thorne Bay 99950 320										•	•	N			
Togiak 99678 470						•			•	•					
Tok 99780 589	•	•		•			•			•	•	•	•	•	
Toksook Bay 99637 333						•				•					
Trapper Creek 99688 N	•			•			•			•	•	•	•		
Tuluksak 99679 236						•				•					
Tuntutuliak 99680 216						•				•					
Tununak 99681 298						•				•					
Twin Hills 99576 70						•									
Tyonek 99682 239							•			•					
Unalakleet 99684 623						•	•			•	•	•			
Unalaska/Dutch Hbr. 99685 1322			•	[7]		•	•			•	•	•	N	•	
Usibelli area 99787 109	•			[7]											
Valdez 99686 3079	•	•	•	•		•	•	•	•	•	•	•	•	•	
Venetie 99781 132						•				•					
Wainwright 99782 405						•				•	•				
Wales 99783 133						•			•	•		•	•		
Wasilla 99687 1559	•			•	•		•			•	•	•			
White Mountain 99784 125						•									
Whittier 99693 198					•			•	•	•	•	•	•		
Willow 99688 139	•			•	•		•			•	•	•	•		
Wiseman 99790 8	•					•									
Wrangell 99929 2184			•			•	•	•	•	•	•	•	•	•	•
Yakutat 99689 449		•	•			•	•		•	•	•	•	•	•	•

CANADA

Village · Popu-lation[1]	On road system[2]	Car rental	Taxi cab	Scheduled bus service[3]	Railroad access[3]	Scheduled air service[3]	Air taxi base[4]	Ferry port[3]	Boat charter service[5]	Store	Meals	Lodging	Campground	Hospital or clinic	Visitors welcome
Carcross, Y.T. 180	•			•	•		•	•		•	•	•			
Stewart, B.C. 1400	•		•	•			•	•		•	•	•	•	•	•
Telegraph Ck., B.C. 300										•	N	N		•	
Whitehorse, Y.T. 16,000	•	•	•	•	•	•	•			•	•	•	•	•	

315

Table 2: Parklands—Access, Special Interests and Recreational Use

Managed by	Automobile	Scheduled bus	Railroad	Scheduled air service	Air taxi	Ferry or scheduled boat service	Charter boat	Sightseeing tours or cruise ship	Guided wilderness trips	Canoe, kayak or raft trips	Good for children or casual visits	Fishing[1]	Hunting[1]	Trapping[1]	Firearms for self-protection	Horses	Fixed-wing Aircraft[2]	Powerboats	Snowmobiles[3]	Off-road Vehicles[4]
1. Admiralty Island Monument USFS					•	•	•	•	•	•		P	P	P	P	NR	P	Z	N	N
2. Alagnak River NPS					•					•		P	P	P	P	P	P	P	N	N
3. Alaska Chilkat Bald Eagle Pres. ADP	•	•			•					•	•	P	P	P	P	N	NA	NA	Z	N
4. Alaska Maritime Refuge USFW					•	•	•	•	•			P	Z	Z	P	P	NA	NA	Z	7
5. Alaska Peninsula Refuge USFW				•	•	•	•	•	•			P	P	P	P	P	P	Z	P	N
6. Alatna River NPS					•				•	•		P	N	N	P	P	P	Z	P	7
7. Aleutian Islands Refuge USFW				•	•			•	•			P	Z	Z	P	P	P	Z	Z	7
8. Andreafsky Wilderness USFW					•				•	•		P	P	N	P	P	P	P	P	N
9. Aniakchak Monument NPS					•				•	•		P	N	N	P	P	P	Z	Z	N
" Preserve NPS					•				•	•		P	P	N	P	P	Z	P	P	N
10. Ann Stevens– Cape Lisburne Refuge USFW				•	•							P	P	P	P	P	P	P	P	7
11. Arctic Refuge USFW					•				•	•		P	P	P	P	P	P	P	P	7
" Wilderness USFW					•				•	•		P	P	P	P	P	N	P	Z	7
12. Baranof Castle Hill ADP	•	•		•	•	•		•			•	N	N	N	N	P	N	P	N	N

Column groups: **HOW TO GET THERE** (Automobile – Canoe, kayak or raft trips); **SPECIAL INTERESTS** (Good for children or casual visits); **RECREATIONAL USE** (Fishing – Off-road Vehicles).

[1] State of Alaska regulations apply wherever not specifically restricted
[2] Federal Aviation Administration (FAA) regulations and restrictions apply
[3] Permitted only at times with adequate snow cover
[4] Includes trail bikes, all-terrain vehicles, Hovercraft and the like
[5] See entry number 112.
[6] Hunting is permitted, but without the use of firearms
[7] By special use permit only

P   Permitted
N   Not permitted
NA Not applicable
NR Not recommended
Z   Zoned; specific areas closed, or other restrictions

ADFG   Alaska Dept. of Fish and Game
ADP   Alaska Division of Parks
BLM   Bureau of Land Management
NPS   National Park Service
TDX   Tanadgusix Corporation
USFS   U.S. Forest Service
USFW   U.S. Fish and Wildlife Service

	Managed by	Automobile	Scheduled bus	Railroad	Scheduled air service	Air taxi	Ferry or scheduled boat service	Charter boat	Sightseeing tours or cruise ship	Guided wilderness trips	Canoe, kayak or raft trips	Good for children or casual visits	Fishing[1]	Hunting[1]	Trapping[1]	Firearms for self-protection	Horses	Fixed-wing Aircraft[2]	Powerboats	Snowmobiles[3]	Off-road Vehicles[4]
						HOW TO GET THERE →				SPECIAL INTERESTS →			RECREATIONAL USE →								
13. Beaver Creek	BLM	•			•	•					•		P	P	P	P	P	P	P	P	N
14. Becharof Refuge	USFW		•		•	•				•	•		P	P	P	P	P	P	P	P	7
" Wilderness	USFW					•				•	•		P	P	P	P	P	P	P	P	7
15. Bering Land Bridge Preserve	NPS												P	N	P	P	P	P	P	P	N
16. Bering Sea Refuge	USFW												P	P	P	P	P	P	P	P	N
17. Birch Creek	BLM	•									•		P	P	P	P	P	P	P	P	N
18. Bogoslof Refuge	USFW					•							P	P	P	P	NR	N	P	P	N
19. Caines Head Recreation Area	ADP					•		•					P	N	N	P	N	N	P	N	N
20. Cape Krusenstern Monument	NPS					•		•		•			P	N	N	P	NR	P	P	P	N
21. Captain Cook Rec. Area	ADP	•									•	•	P	P	P	N	N	N	P	N	N
22. Chamisso Refuge	USFW					•		•					P	N	P	P	NR	N	P	P	N
23. Chena River Recreation Area	ADP	•									•	•	P	P	P	P	Z	N	P	Z	N
24. Chilikadrotna River	NPS					•	•		•	•	•	•	P	Z	P	P	N	NA	P	P	N
25. Chilkat Park	ADP	•			•	•	•	•	•	•	•	•	Z	Z	P	P	N	Z	P	Z	N
26. Chugach National Forest[5]	USFS	•	•	•	•	•						•	Z	Z	Z	Z	Z	Z	Z	Z	Z
27. Chugach State Park	ADP	•	•										P	Z	Z	Z	Z	P	Z	P	Z
28. Coronation Island Wilderness	USFS					•		•					P	P	P	NR	NR	P	P	NR	N
29. Creamer's Field	ADFG	•										•	P	Z	P	NR	N	N	NA	NR	N
30. Delta River	BLM	•								•	•		P	P	P	P	P	Z	Z	P	N
31. Denali National Park	NPS	•	•	•	•	•			•	•	•	•	P	N	N	P	P	P	P	P	N
" " Preserve	NPS					•				•			P	P	P	P	P	P	P	P	N
" " Wilderness	NPS	•	•	•	•	•			•	•			P	N	N	N	N	N	N	N	N
32. Denali State Park	ADP	•	•	•							•	•	P	P	P	P	Z	P	P	P	N

Page 318

Name	Managed by	Automobile	Scheduled bus	Railroad	Scheduled air service	Air taxi	Ferry or scheduled boat service	Charter boat	Sightseeing tours or cruise ship	Guided wilderness trips	Canoe, kayak or raft trips	Good for children or casual visits	Fishing[1]	Hunting[1]	Trapping[1]	Firearms for self-protection	Horses	Fixed-wing Aircraft[2]	Powerboats	Snowmobiles[3]	Off-road Vehicles[4]
33. Endicott River Wilderness	USFS					●		●					P	P	P	P	NR	P	P	NR	N
34. Forrester Island Refuge	USFW					●		●						N	P	P	NR	P	P	NR	N
35. Fort Abercrombie Park	ADP	●			●		●		●			●	P	N	N	N	N	N	N	N	N
36. Fortymile River	BLM	●									●		P	P	P	P	N	P	P	P	Z
37. Gates of the Arctic Park	NPS				●	●				●	●		P	N	N	N	P	P	P	P	N
" " " Preserve	NPS	●			●	●				●	●		P	P	P	P	P	P	P	P	N
38. Glacier Bay Park	NPS	●				●		●		●	●	●		N	N	N	N	Z	Z	N	N
" Preserve	NPS							●			●	●	P	P	N	N	P	P	P	P	N
39. Goose Bay Refuge	ADFG	●											P	P	N	P	N	P	P	P	P
40. Gulkana River	BLM	●	●			●				●	●	●	P	P	P	N	N	P	P	P	P
41. Harding Lake Rec. Area	ADP	●	●										P	N	Z	N	NR	N	P	N	N
42. Hazy Islands Refuge	USFW												Z	N	N	P	NR	P	P	NR	N
43. Iditarod Trail	ADP	●	●										N	Z	P	N	Z	P	P	N	Z
44. Independence Mine Park	ADP	●			●			●					NA	N	N	N	N	NA	NA	N	N
45. Innoko Refuge	USFW										●		P	P	P	P	P	P	P	P	N
" Wilderness	USFW					●		●	●	●	●	●	P	P	P	P	P	P	P	N	Z
46. Ivishak River	USFW				●	●		●			●		P	P	P	P	P	P	NR	N	Z
47. Izembek Refuge	USFW				●		●				●		P	P	P	P	P	Z	P	N	Z
" Wilderness	USFW				●		●				●		P	P	P	P	P	Z	P	N	Z
48. John River	NPS				●	●				●	●		P	N	N	P	P	Z	P	P	Z
49. Kachemak Bay Park	ADP	●								●			P	P	P	N	N	P	P	P	Z
50. Kanuti Refuge	USFW				●	●		●			●		P	Z	P	P	P	P	Z	N	Z
51. Katmai Park	NPS				●	●		●	●	●	●	●	P	N	N	N	P	Z	Z	N	N

	Managed by	Automobile	Scheduled bus	Railroad	Scheduled air service	Air taxi	Ferry or scheduled boat service	Charter boat	Sightseeing tours or cruise ship	Guided wilderness trips	Canoe, kayak or raft trips	Good for children or casual visits	Fishing[1]	Hunting[1]	Trapping[1]	Firearms for self-protection	Horses	Fixed-wing[2] Aircraft	Powerboats	Snowmobiles[3]	Off-road Vehicles[4]
Katmai Preserve	NPS				•			•	•	•	•	•	P	P	P	P	P	P	P	P	N
52. Kenai Fjords Park	NPS	•	•			•	•	•	•	•	•	•	P	N	N	P	P	P	P	P	N
53. Kenai Refuge[5]	USFW	•	•			•	•	•	•	•	•	•	P	P	P	P	P	N	P	P	N
" Wilderness	USFW	•				•	•	•			•	•	P	P	P	P	P	N	N	N	N
54. Klondike Gold Rush Park	NPS	•	•	•	•		•		•	•	•	•	P	N	N	N	N	NA	NA	N	N
55. Kobuk River	NPS										•	•	P	N	N	P	P	P	P	P	N
56. Kobuk Valley Park	NPS					•					•		P	N	N	P	P	P	P	P	N
57. Kodiak Refuge	USFW				•	•		•			•		P	P	P	P	P	P	P	P	N
58. Koyukuk Refuge	USFW				•	•		•			•		P	N	P	P	P	N	P	P	7
" Wilderness	USFW					•		•			•		P	P	N	P	P	N	P	N	7
59. Lake Clark Park	NPS				•	•					•	•	P	N	P	P	P	P	P	P	N
" " Preserve	NPS				•	•				•	•		P	P	P	P	P	P	P	P	N
60. Maurelle Islands Wilderness	USFS							•	•		•		P	P	N	P	NR	P	P	NR	N
61. McNeil River Sanctuary	ADFG					•		•	•			•	P	N	N	P	NR	N	P	P	N
62. Mendenhall Wetlands Refuge	ADFG	•	•		•		•			•			P	N	P	P	P	P	N	N	N
63. Misty Fiords Monument	USFS					•		•	•				P	N	P	P	P	P	P	N	N
64. Mulchatna River	NPS					•		•					P	P	N	P	P	N	P	P	N
65. Nancy Lake Rec. Area	ADP	•	•									•	P	6	N	P	P	N	N	N	N
66. Noatak Preserve	NPS					•		•			•		P	P	P	P	P	P	P	P	N
67. North Fork, Koyukuk River	NPS					•		•			•		P	N	N	P	P	P	N	P	N
68. Nowitna Refuge	USFW					•		•			•		P	P	P	P	P	P	P	P	7
69. Nunivak Refuge	USFW				•	•			•	•	•		P	P	P	P	P	P	P	P	N
" Wilderness	USFW				•	•			•	•	•		P	P	P	P	P	P	P	P	N

# / Name	Managed by	Automobile	Scheduled bus	Railroad	Scheduled air service	Air taxi	Ferry or scheduled boat service	Charter boat	Sightseeing tours or cruise ship	Guided wilderness trips	Canoe, kayak or raft trips	Good for children or casual visits	Fishing[1]	Hunting[1]	Trapping[1]	Firearms for self-protection	Horses	Fixed-wing[2] Aircraft	Powerboats	Snowmobiles[3]	Off-road Vehicles[4]
70. Old Sitka	ADP	•	•				•		•			•	P	N	N	N	N	NA	P	N	N
71. Palmer Hay Flats Refuge	ADFG	•										•	P	P	P	P	P	P	P	P	N
72. Petersburg Creek Wilderness	USFS					•						•	P	P	P	P	NR	P	P	NR	N
73. Potter Point Refuge	ADFG	•	•		•							•	N	N	N	P	P	P	N	N	N
74. Pribilof Islands	TDX, USFW				•				•			•	P	N	N	(ask locally for information)			N	N	
75. Quartz Lake Rec. Area	ADP	•										•	P	N	P	P	N	N	P	P	N
76. Rika's Landing	ADP	•	•										P	N	N	N	N	N	N	N	N
77. Russell Fiord Wilderness	USFS				•	•		•		•			P	P	P	P	NR	P	P	NR	N
78. St. Lazaria Refuge	USFW					•		•			•		P	N	P	P	NR	NR	P	NR	N
79. Salmon River	NPS					•				•			P	N	N	P	P	P	N	P	N
80. Selawik Refuge	USFW				•	•		•			•		P	P	P	P	P	P	P	P	N
" Wilderness	USFW												P	P	P	P	P	P	P	N	N
81. Semidi Refuge	USFW					•		•					P	N	N	P	NR	P	N	N	N
82. Sheenjek River	USFW					•		•		•	•		P	P	P	P	P	P	N	P	N
83. Simeonof Refuge	USFW					•		•					P	P	P	P	NR	P	N	P	N
84. Sitka Historical Park	NPS	•					•			•			P	N	N	N	N	N	N	N	N
85. South Baranof Wilderness	USFS					•		•		•	•		P	P	P	P	NR	P	P	NR	N
86. South Prince of Wales Wild.	USFS					•		•			•		P	P	P	P	NR	P	P	NR	N
87. Steese Conservation Area	BLM	•				•							P	P	P	P	P	P	P	P	N
88. Stikine-LeConte Wilderness	USFS					•		•		•	•		P	P	P	P	NR	P	P	NR	N
89. Susitna Flats Refuge	ADFG					•							P	P	P	P	NR	P	P	N	N
90. Tebenkof Bay Wilderness	USFS	•				•		•					P	P	P	P	NR	P	P	NR	N
91. Tetlin Refuge	USFW	•	•							•	•	•	P	P	P	P	P	P	P	P	N

Legend — recreational use codes: P = permitted/available, N = not permitted, NR = not recommended, NA = not available.

No. / Name	Managed by	Automobile	Scheduled bus	Railroad	Scheduled air service	Air taxi	Ferry or scheduled boat service	Charter boat	Sightseeing tours or cruise ship	Guided wilderness trips	Canoe, kayak or raft trips	Good for children or casual visits	Fishing[1]	Hunting[1]	Trapping[1]	Firearms for self-protection	Horses	Fixed-wing Aircraft[2]	Powerboats	Snowmobiles[3]	Off-road Vehicles[4]
92. Tinayguk River	NPS					•					•		P	N	N	P	P	P	P	P	N
93. Tlikakila River	NPS				•	•					•		P	N	N	P	P	P	P	P	N
94. Togiak Refuge	USFW				•	•		•			•		P	P	P	P	NR	P	P	P	7
" Wilderness	USFW					•				•	•	•	P	P	P	P	NR	P	P	P	7
95. Tongass National Forest	USFS	•			•	•	•	•	•	•	•	•	P	N	N	P	NR	NA	N	N	N
96. Totem Bight Park	ADP	•	•						•			•	P	N	N	N	N	NA	NA	N	N
97. Tracy Arm–Fords Terror Wilderness	USFS					•	•	•	•	•			P	P	P	P	NR	P	P	NR	N
98. Trading Bay Refuge	ADFG				•	•							P	P	P	P	P	P	P	P	P
99. Trans–Alaska Pipeline Corr.	BLM	•							•		•		P	N	P	P	N	N	P	N	N
100. Tuxedni Refuge	USFW												P	N	N	P	P	P	P	P	N
101. Unalakleet River	BLM					•					•		P	P	P	P	P	P	N	P	N
102. Walrus Islands Sanctuary	ADFG					•		•		•			N	N	N	N	N	N	N	N	N
103. Warren Island Wilderness	USFS					•		•		•	•		P	P	P	P	P	NR	P	NR	N
104. West Chichagof	USFS					•		•			•		P	P	P	P	NR	P	P	NR	N
105. White Mountains Rec. Area.	BLM	•				•				•	•	•	P	P	P	P	P	P	P	P	N
106. Wind River	USFW					•					•		P	P	P	P	N	P	N	P	7
107. Wood–Tikchik Park	ADP					•				•	•		P	N	N	P	N	P	P	N	N
108. Wrangell–St. Elias Park	NPS	•			•	•		•		•	•		P	N	N	P	P	P	P	P	7
" " Preserve	NPS	•				•		•			•	•	P	P	P	P	P	P	P	P	7
109. Yukon–Charley R. Preserve	NPS					•		•			•		P	P	P	P	P	P	P	P	7
110. Yukon Delta Refuge	USFW				•	•		•			•		P	P	P	P	NR	P	P	P	7
111. Yukon Flats Refuge	USFW				•	•					•		P	N	P	P	P	P	P	P	7
112. Kenai River Special Management Area	ADP	•				•					•	•	P	N	N	P	N	N	N	N	N

Hours of Daylight at Sea Level

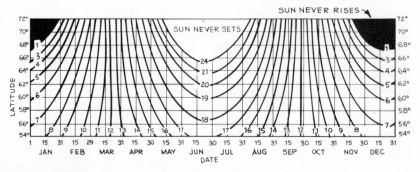

To determine the hours of daylight on any day of the year within Alaska: On a map, find the latitude of the region. Follow the corresponding line on this graph to a point above the date. Read the hours from the nearest curved line, interpolating if the point falls between lines. Example: At a latitude of 62° on April 20, the sun will be above the horizon for about 15 hours.

Weather Tables

For the following weather tables, four months have been chosen as providing the most useful information: January frequently is the coldest month; April is popular for winter sports; July often is the warmest month; October is the wettest month in maritime areas. The tables also include figures for the year (annual). Tabulated are:

- both mean and record high and low temperatures;
- precipitation, with snowfall recorded in water equivalent;
- mean snowfall, measured as it falls, storm by storm, and expressed in snow depth;
- maximum snow accumulation on the ground, expressed in snow depth;
- number of days with measurable precipitation (0.01 inch [0.025 cm] or more), known as "precipitation days."

Weather records were obtained from the Arctic Environmental Information and Data Center (address in Information Sources, Appendix) and are available to the public.

Anchorage

		Temperatures, °F		Precip. inches.	Snowfall, inches.			Precip. days
		High	Low		Mean	Max. on grnd.		
JAN	Mean	20	6	0.8	8	47		3
	Rec.	50	−34					
APR	Mean	42	28	0.7	7	19		2
	Rec.	65	2					
JUL	Mean	65	51	2	0	0		6
	Rec.	81	36					
OCT	Mean	41	28	2	7	13		5
	Rec.	61	−5					
ANN	Mean	42	28	15	71	47		49
	Rec.	85	−34					

Angoon

		Temperatures, °F		Precip. inches.	Snowfall, inches.			Precip. days
		High	Low		Mean	Max. on grnd.		
JAN	Mean	32	23	3	17	43		11
	Rec.	57	−10					
APR	Mean	47	34	2	2	29		8
	Rec.	64	20					
JUL	Mean	61	49	3	0	0		8
	Rec.	82	36					
OCT	Mean	48	39	7	0.3	2		17
	Rec.	68	23					
ANN	Mean	47	43	40	67	43		136
	Rec.	82	−10					

Annette Island

		Temperatures, °F High	Low	Precip. inches.	Snowfall, inches. Mean	Max. on grnd.	Precip. days
JAN	Mean	37	28	10	16	42	15
	Rec.	61	2				
APR	Mean	49	36	8	4	3	14
	Rec.	82	21				
JUL	Mean	64	51	5	0	0	10
	Rec.	86	40				
OCT	Mean	52	42	17	0.3	2	21
	Rec.	71	25				
ANN	Mean	51	40	115	61	42	178
	Rec.	90	1				

Bethel

		Temperatures, °F High	Low	Precip. inches.	Snowfall, inches. Mean	Max. on grnd.	Precip. days
JAN	Mean	12	−2	0.8	7	45	3
	Rec.	48	−46				
APR	Mean	41	15	0.6	6	34	4
	Rec.	58	−31				
JUL	Mean	68	47	2	0	0	8
	Rec.	86	31				
OCT	Mean	43	24	1	4	6	5
	Rec.	65	−5				
ANN	Mean	36	21	17	51	45	63
	Rec.	86	−46				

Atka

		Temperatures, °F High	Low	Precip. inches.	Snowfall, inches. Mean	Max. on grnd.	Precip. days
JAN	Mean	37	29	5	7	6	18
	Rec.	50	14				
APR	Mean	42	33	4	6	2	16
	Rec.	59	24				
JUL	Mean	53	44	4	0	0	20
	Rec.	72	37				
OCT	Mean	46	37	6	1	0	28
	Rec.	57	24				
ANN	Mean	44	36	60	61	6	246
	Rec.	77	12				

Bettles

		Temperatures, °F High	Low	Precip. inches.	Snowfall, inches. Mean	Max. on grnd.	Precip. days
JAN	Mean	−6	−22	0.8	11	71	3
	Rec.	42	−70				
APR	Mean	32	9	0.6	7	86	2
	Rec.	56	−25				
JUL	Mean	69	48	2	0	0	5
	Rec.	92	29				
OCT	Mean	25	12	1	11	19	5
	Rec.	53	−32				
ANN	Mean	30	12	14	77	86	48
	Rec.	92	−70				

Barrow

		Temperatures, °F High	Low	Precip. inches.	Snowfall, inches. Mean	Max. on grnd.	Precip. days
JAN	Mean	−8	−20	0.2	2	22	1
	Rec.	36	−53				
APR	Mean	6	−9	0.2	2	30	1
	Rec.	38	−33				
JUL	Mean	45	33	0.8	0.3	1	4
	Rec.	75	26				
OCT	Mean	19	10	0.6	6	12	3
	Rec.	43	−32				
ANN	Mean	15	4	5	25	30	25
	Rec.	76	−54				

Cold Bay

		Temperatures, °F High	Low	Precip. inches.	Snowfall, inches. Mean	Max. on grnd.	Precip. days
JAN	Mean	33	24	3	9	17	9
	Rec.	50	−55				
APR	Mean	38	28	2	6	9	6
	Rec.	58	4				
JUL	Mean	55	46	2	0	0	8
	Rec.	77	36				
OCT	Mean	44	35	4	4	13	12
	Rec.	69	10				
ANN	Mean	42	33	35	55	18	106
	Rec.	77	−13				

Denali National Park

		Temperatures, °F		Precip. inches.	Snowfall, inches.		Precip. days
		High	Low		Mean	Max. on grnd.	
JAN	Mean	11	−7	0.8	12	51	3
	Rec.	51	−51				
APR	Mean	38	16	0.6	6	43	2
	Rec.	65	−25				
JUL	Mean	66	43	3	0	0	9
	Rec.	87	23				
OCT	Mean	34	16	1	13	17	4
	Rec.	69	−24				
ANN	Mean	37	17	15	80	51	52
	Rec.	90	−52				

Fort Yukon

		Temperatures, °F		Precip. inches.	Snowfall, inches.		Precip. days
		High	Low		Mean	Max. on grnd.	
JAN	Mean	−11	−28	0.4	7	36	4
	Rec.	40	−69				
APR	Mean	34	8	0.2	2	48	2
	Rec.	65	−41				
JUL	Mean	72	51	0.9	0	0	3
	Rec.	97	25				
OCT	Mean	28	13	0.6	7	17	5
	Rec.	61	−37				
ANN	Mean	31	10	7	44	48	42
	Rec.	97	−71				

Eagle

		Temperatures, °F		Precip. inches.	Snowfall, inches.		Precip. days
		High	Low		Mean	Max. on grnd.	
JAN	Mean	−4	−13	0.5	8	39	2
	Rec.	47	−71				
APR	Mean	40	14	0.4	4	42	2
	Rec.	71	−37				
JUL	Mean	73	46	2	0	0	8
	Rec.	95	28				
OCT	Mean	34	17	0.9	9	14	5
	Rec.	66	−28				
ANN	Mean	36	13	11	50	42	51
	Rec.	95	−71				

Galbraith

		Temperatures, °F		Precip. inches.	Snowfall, inches.		Precip. days
		High	Low		Mean	Max. on grnd.	
JAN	Mean	2	−7	0.4	2	13	2
	Rec.	35	−60				
APR	Mean	18	−6	0.2	2	18	1
	Rec.	50	−38				
JUL	Mean	61	40	0.9	0.5	0	4
	Rec.	76	28				
OCT	Mean	16	−3	1	9	9	4
	Rec.	47	−34				
ANN	Mean	23	3	8	48	23	30
	Rec.	82	−61				

Fairbanks

		Temperatures, °F		Precip. inches.	Snowfall, inches.		Precip. days
		High	Low		Mean	Max. on grnd.	
JAN	Mean	−4	−21	0.6	10	40	3
	Rec.	47	−61				
APR	Mean	41	19	0.3	3	37	1
	Rec.	74	−21				
JUL	Mean	72	51	2	0	0	6
	Rec.	94	35				
OCT	Mean	32	17	0.7	10	13	3
	Rec.	65	−27				
ANN	Mean	36	16	10	65	52	40
	Rec.	96	−62				

Galena

		Temperatures, °F		Precip. inches.	Snowfall, inches.		Precip. days
		High	Low		Mean	Max. on grnd.	
JAN	Mean	−3	−20	0.7	7	32	3
	Rec.	45	−64				
APR	Mean	32	13	0.6	6	42	3
	Rec.	64	−35				
JUL	Mean	68	52	2	0	0	7
	Rec.	89	36				
OCT	Mean	29	18	1	8	16	4
	Rec.	56	−29				
ANN	Mean	32	15	13	59	42	55
	Rec.	92	−64				

Glacier Bay

		Temperatures, °F High	Low	Precip. inches	Snowfall, inches Mean	Max. on grnd.	Precip. days
JAN	Mean	28	20	6	36	61	12
	Rec.	44	−11				
APR	Mean	44	33	3	3	62	9
	Rec.	59	19				
JUL	Mean	62	47	4	0	0	11
	Rec.	77	40				
OCT	Mean	46	38	12	2	9	20
	Rec.	58	19				
ANN	Mean	46	35	71	122	74	153
	Rec.	77	−11				

Juneau

		Temperatures, °F High	Low	Precip. inches	Snowfall, inches Mean	Max. on grnd.	Precip. days
JAN	Mean	27	16	4	26	38	11
	Rec.	57	−22				
APR	Mean	47	31	3	5	33	10
	Rec.	71	6				
JUL	Mean	64	47	4	0	0	11
	Rec.	90	36				
OCT	Mean	47	36	7	2	10	18
	Rec.	61	12				
ANN	Mean	47	33	52	109	40	149
	Rec.	90	−22				

Haines

		Temperatures, °F High	Low	Precip. inches	Snowfall, inches Mean	Max. on grnd.	Precip. days
JAN	Mean	29	18	4	39	48	10
	Rec.	47	−10				
APR	Mean	50	34	2	0	4	5
	Rec.	74	19				
JUL	Mean	67	48	2	0	0	5
	Rec.	98	40				
OCT	Mean	48	36	10	3	19	15
	Rec.	60	10				
ANN	Mean	49	34	47	148	50	99
	Rec.	98	−14				

Kenai

		Temperatures, °F High	Low	Precip. inches	Snowfall, inches Mean	Max. on grnd.	Precip. days
JAN	Mean	20	2	1	11	53	5
	Rec.	48	−47				
APR	Mean	41	24	1	6	35	3
	Rec.	63	−22				
JUL	Mean	62	46	2	0	0	7
	Rec.	85	32				
OCT	Mean	43	28	2	4	15	8
	Rec.	62	−11				
ANN	Mean	42	24	19	63	54	70
	Rec.	93	−48				

Homer

		Temperatures, °F High	Low	Precip. inches	Snowfall, inches Mean	Max. on grnd.	Precip. days
JAN	Mean	28	15	2	9	26	6
	Rec.	51	−18				
APR	Mean	42	28	1	4	23	5
	Rec.	63	−9				
JUL	Mean	61	45	2	0	0	6
	Rec.	79	34				
OCT	Mean	44	31	3	2	3	10
	Rec.	64	2				
ANN	Mean	44	30	24	58	35	80
	Rec.	80	−21				

Ketchikan

		Temperatures, °F High	Low	Precip. inches	Snowfall, inches Mean	Max. on grnd.	Precip. days
JAN	Mean	39	29	14	14	62	16
	Rec.	62	−4				
APR	Mean	53	36	12	0.4	6	16
	Rec.	75	16				
JUL	Mean	65	50	8	0	0	12
	Rec.	88	39				
OCT	Mean	53	41	23	0.1	0	22
	Rec.	72	21				
ANN	Mean	52	39	156	41	62	193
	Rec.	90	−4				

King Salmon

		Temperatures, °F High	Low	Precip. inches	Snowfall, inches Mean	Max. on grnd.	Precip. days
JAN	Mean	21	6	1	6	18	4
	Rec.	53	−46				
APR	Mean	38	23	1	5	13	4
	Rec.	65	−19				
JUL	Mean	63	46	2	0	0	7
	Rec.	86	33				
OCT	Mean	40	25	2	3	10	6
	Rec.	62	−11				
ANN	Mean	41	25	19	44	19	62
	Rec.	86	−46				

Little Port Walter

		Temperatures, °F High	Low	Precip. inches	Snowfall, inches Mean	Max. on grnd.	Precip. days
JAN	Mean	36	28	20	34	79	18
	Rec.	52	0				
APR	Mean	45	34	14	6	72	17
	Rec.	62	18				
JUL	Mean	61	48	9	0	0	11
	Rec.	78	37				
OCT	Mean	49	40	36	0.2	1	24
	Rec.	61	25				
ANN	Mean	48	38	224	133	117	207
	Rec.	78	0				

Kodiak

		Temperatures, °F High	Low	Precip. inches	Snowfall, inches Mean	Max. on grnd.	Precip. days
JAN	Mean	34	25	5	15	21	12
	Rec.	54	−5				
APR	Mean	41	32	4	7	25	9
	Rec.	64	10				
JUL	Mean	59	49	4	0	0	10
	Rec.	82	37				
OCT	Mean	45	36	6	4	9	12
	Rec.	61	14				
ANN	Mean	42	36	57	75	35	136
	Rec.	86	−12				

McCarthy

		Temperatures, °F High	Low	Precip. inches	Snowfall, inches Mean	Max. on grnd.	Precip. days
JAN	Mean	−5	−23	0.6	8	42	2
	Rec.	39	−58				
APR	Mean	44	20	0.7	5	36	1
	Rec.	58	−19				
JUL	Mean	71	41	2	0	0	7
	Rec.	83	30				
OCT	Mean	38	20	3	17	18	7
	Rec.	69	−18				
ANN	Mean	39	15	17	73	50	51
	Rec.	87	−58				

Kotzebue

		Temperatures, °F High	Low	Precip. inches	Snowfall, inches Mean	Max. on grnd.	Precip. days
JAN	Mean	4	−9	0.4	6	36	2
	Rec.	39	−47				
APR	Mean	21	3	0.3	5	53	2
	Rec.	46	−31				
JUL	Mean	59	48	1	0	0	5
	Rec.	85	30				
OCT	Mean	28	18	0.6	6	11	3
	Rec.	51	−19				
ANN	Mean	28	15	9	47	53	36
	Rec.	85	−52				

Moose Pass

		Temperatures, °F High	Low	Precip. inches	Snowfall, inches Mean	Max. on grnd.	Precip. days
JAN	Mean	15	−4	0.8	10	32	3
	Rec.	48	−43				
APR	Mean	42	24	1	7	46	4
	Rec.	63	−8				
JUL	Mean	66	44	1	0	0	5
	Rec.	86	29				
OCT	Mean	42	27	5	5	18	10
	Rec.	66	0				
ANN	Mean	42	24	27	94	67	77
	Rec.	86	−43				

Nome

		High	Low	Precip. inches.	Snowfall, inches. Mean	Snowfall, inches. Max. on grnd.	Precip. days
JAN	Mean	14	−2	0.9	9	57	4
	Rec.	43	−40				
APR	Mean	26	10	0.7	6	69	3
	Rec.	51	−30				
JUL	Mean	56	44	2	0	0	7
	Rec.	86	31				
OCT	Mean	34	22	1	4	9	5
	Rec.	59	−10				
ANN	Mean	32	18	16	53	74	60
	Rec.	86	−46				

Nunivak Island

		High	Low	Precip. inches.	Snowfall, inches. Mean	Snowfall, inches. Max. on grnd.	Precip. days
JAN	Mean	18	5	0.9	10	31	5
	Rec.	41	−35				
APR	Mean	29	17	0.8	3	48	4
	Rec.	48	−12				
JUL	Mean	54	43	1	0	0	7
	Rec.	76	28				
OCT	Mean	39	30	2	6	10	9
	Rec.	55	9				
ANN	Mean	35	24	15	57	48	75
	Rec.	76	−48				

North Dutch Group*

		High	Low	Precip. inches.	Snowfall, inches. Mean	Snowfall, inches. Max. on grnd.	Precip. days
JAN	Mean	33	26	10	40	56	14
	Rec.	48	4				
APR	Mean	41	32	7	11	71	13
	Rec.	53	8				
JUL	Mean	61	50	7	0	0	14
	Rec.	75	36				
OCT	Mean	44	37	17	2	4	19
	Rec.	57	26				
ANN	Mean	45	37	121	144	74	183
	Rec.	79	0				

*Located near Perry Island, the weather at North Dutch Group is more typical of Prince William Sound than other weather stations in the area. Data was collected 1934-57. Whittier, on the west side of the Sound is the wettest station; it receives an average annual precipitation of 175 inches.

Petersburg

		High	Low	Precip. inches.	Snowfall, inches. Mean	Snowfall, inches. Max. on grnd.	Precip. days
JAN	Mean	32	22	9	29	61	16
	Rec.	60	−14				
APR	Mean	48	32	7	2	37	16
	Rec.	72	10				
JUL	Mean	64	48	5	0	0	13
	Rec.	84	37				
OCT	Mean	49	38	17	0.9	8	22
	Rec.	72	12				
ANN	Mean	49	35	106	106	83	196
	Rec.	84	−14				

Northway

		High	Low	Precip. inches.	Snowfall, inches. Mean	Snowfall, inches. Max. on grnd.	Precip. days
JAN	Mean	−13	−30	0.3	5	52	2
	Rec.	34	−72				
APR	Mean	40	14	0.2	2	30	1
	Rec.	70	−31				
JUL	Mean	69	48	2	0	0	7
	Rec.	88	34				
OCT	Mean	29	21	0.5	6	21	2
	Rec.	58	−36				
ANN	Mean	32	11	10	31	52	38
	Rec.	91	−72				

Port Alsworth

		High	Low	Precip. inches.	Snowfall, inches. Mean	Snowfall, inches. Max. on grnd.	Precip. days
JAN	Mean	22	1	0.8	14	23	3
	Rec.	54	−53				
APR	Mean	42	21	0.7	4	24	3
	Rec.	63	−18				
JUL	Mean	68	44	2	0	0	7
	Rec.	86	25				
OCT	Mean	42	25	2	2	12	6
	Rec.	66	−7				
ANN	Mean	44	22	17	68	24	54
	Rec.	86	−55				

St. Paul

		Temperatures, °F High	Temperatures, °F Low	Precip. inches	Snowfall, inches Mean	Snowfall, inches Max. on grnd.	Precip. days
JAN	Mean	30	22	2	10	25	8
	Rec.	49	−14				
APR	Mean	32	23	1	6	27	6
	Rec.	45	−8				
JUL	Mean	49	42	2	0	0	8
	Rec.	63	28				
OCT	Mean	42	34	3	3	11	11
	Rec.	58	13				
ANN	Mean	38	30	23	56	32	94
	Rec.	63	−19				

Skagway

		Temperatures, °F High	Temperatures, °F Low	Precip. inches	Snowfall, inches Mean	Snowfall, inches Max. on grnd.	Precip. days
JAN	Mean	29	19	3	9	10	8
	Rec.	50	−20				
APR	Mean	49	32	1	2	3	2
	Rec.	76	7				
JUL	Mean	67	49	1	0	0	5
	Rec.	88	35				
OCT	Mean	49	36	5	1	8	6
	Rec.	68	9				
ANN	Mean	49	34	28	36	10	54
	Rec.	92	−24				

Seward

		Temperatures, °F High	Temperatures, °F Low	Precip. inches	Snowfall, inches Mean	Snowfall, inches Max. on grnd.	Precip. days
JAN	Mean	29	18	5	16	31	9
	Rec.	51	−10				
APR	Mean	44	31	4	8	37	8
	Rec.	65	−1				
JUL	Mean	63	49	3	0	0	7
	Rec.	85	36				
OCT	Mean	46	34	10	3	15	14
	Rec.	64	8				
ANN	Mean	46	33	66	87	41	117
	Rec.	85	−19				

Talkeetna

		Temperatures, °F High	Temperatures, °F Low	Precip. inches	Snowfall, inches Mean	Snowfall, inches Max. on grnd.	Precip. days
JAN	Mean	19	−1	2	19	97	5
	Rec.	45	−48				
APR	Mean	44	22	1	10	76	4
	Rec.	69	−37				
JUL	Mean	69	47	3	0	0	10
	Rec.	90	26				
OCT	Mean	41	24	3	10	19	8
	Rec.	68	−21				
ANN	Mean	44	22	29	115	98	80
	Rec.	91	−53				

Sitka

		Temperatures, °F High	Temperatures, °F Low	Precip. inches	Snowfall, inches Mean	Snowfall, inches Max. on grnd.	Precip. days
JAN	Mean	37	26	8	12	31	15
	Rec.	60	−8				
APR	Mean	48	33	6	3	15	13
	Rec.	79	6				
JUL	Mean	61	48	5	0	0	13
	Rec.	87	38				
OCT	Mean	52	39	15	0.3	5	22
	Rec.	70	16				
ANN	Mean	50	37	95	56	39	183
	Rec.	87	−8				

Wiseman*

		Temperatures, °F High	Temperatures, °F Low	Precip. inches	Snowfall, inches Mean	Snowfall, inches Max. on grnd.	Precip. days
JAN	Mean	−1	−10	0.6	13	38	7
	Rec.	35	−65				
APR	Mean	33	7	0.4	6	46	6
	Rec.	59	−39				
JUL	Mean	69	46	2	0	0	13
	Rec.	89	31				
OCT	Mean	30	14	1	15	9	7
	Rec.	56	−36				
ANN	Mean	32	12	12	85	48	95
	Rec.	89	−65				

*Data collected 1936-52. Records have not been kept since; these are the only figures applicable to the area.

Wrangell

		Temperatures, °F		Precip. inches.	Snowfall, inches.		Precip. days
		High	Low		Mean	Max. on grnd.	
JAN	Mean	34	23	7	20	38	14
	Rec.	62	−10				
APR	Mean	49	35	5	2	3	14
	Rec.	76	16				
JUL	Mean	65	49	5	0	0	13
	Rec.	92	32				
OCT	Mean	50	38	13	0.2	3	22
	Rec.	72	18				
ANN	Mean	50	36	82	70	38	182
	Rec.	92	−10				

Yakutat

		Temperatures, °F		Precip. inches.	Snowfall, inches.		Precip. days
		High	Low		Mean	Max. on grnd.	
JAN	Mean	28	16	9	40	83	14
	Rec.	49	−27				
APR	Mean	43	28	8	20	86	13
	Rec.	68	3				
JUL	Mean	59	47	8	0	0	13
	Rec.	84	35				
OCT	Mean	47	34	20	7	26	22
	Rec.	63	6				
ANN	Mean	45	32	133	225	100	185
	Rec.	86	−24				

Temperature Conversions, Fahrenheit–Celsius

General formula:
$$(°F - 32)(0.556) = °C$$
$$(°C)(1.8) + 32 = °F$$

°F	°C		°F	°C
100	38		10	−12
95	35		5	−15
90	32		0	−18
85	29		−5	−21
80	27		−10	−23
75	24		−15	−26
70	21		−20	−29
65	18		−25	−32
60	16		−30	−34
55	13		−35	−37
50	10		−40	−40
45	7		−45	−43
40	4		−50	−46
35	2		−55	−48
32	0		−60	−51
30	−1		−65	−54
25	−4		−70	−57
20	−7		−75	−59
15	−9		−80	−62

Additional Reading About Alaska

Natural history and parklands

Akasofu, S.-I. *Aurora Borealis: The Amazing Northern Lights*. Anchorage: Alaska Geographic, Alaska Northwest Publishing Co., 1979.

Alaska Geographic. *Alaska's Glaciers*. Anchorage: Alaska Northwest Publishing Co., 1982.

_____. *Alaska Whales and Whaling*. Anchorage: Alaska Northwest Publishing Co., 1978.

_____. *A Photographic Geography of Alaska*. Anchorage: Alaska Northwest Publishing Co., 1980.

Anderson, Jacob Peter. *Flora of Alaska and Adjacent Parts of Canada*. Edited by Stanley Welsh. Provo, Utah: Brigham Young University Press, 1974.

Armstrong, Robert H. *A Guide to the Birds of Alaska*. Anchorage: Alaska Northwest Publishing Co., 1980.

Brown, William, ed. *Alaska National Parklands: This Last Treasure*. Anchorage: Alaska Natural History Association, 1982.

Browning, Robert J. *Fisheries of the North Pacific: History, Species, Gear and Processes*. Anchorage: Alaska Northwest Publishing Co., 1980.

Dyson, James L. *The World of Ice*. New York: Alfred A. Knopf, 1963.

Fuller, William A. and Holmes, John C. *The Life of the Far North*. New York: McGraw-Hill, Inc., 1972.

Gabrielson, Ira N. and Lincoln, Frederick C. *The Birds of Alaska*. Harrisburg, Penn.: The Stackpole Co. and Washington, D.C.: The Wildlife Management Institute, 1959.

Gotshall, Daniel W. and Laurent, Laurence L. *Pacific Coast Subtidal Marine Invertebrates: A Fishwatchers' Guide*. Los Osos, Calif.: Sea Challengers, 1979.

Graham, Ada and Frank. *Birds of the Northern Seas*. Garden City, N.Y.: Doubleday and Co., 1981.

Guild, Ben. *The Alaskan Mushroom Hunter's Guide*. Anchorage: Alaska Northwest Publishing Co., 1977.

Heller, Christine A. *Wild Edible and Poisonous Plants of Alaska*. Anchorage: Cooperative Extension Service, University of Alaska, 1966.

Hodge, Robert Parker. *Amphibians and Reptiles in Alaska, the Yukon and Northwest Territories*. Anchorage: Alaska Northwest Publishing Co., 1976.

Hulten, Eric. *Flora of Alaska and Neighboring Territories: A Manual of the Vascular Plants*. Stanford, Calif.: Stanford University Press, 1968.

Hunter, Celia and Wood, Ginny. *Alaska National Interest Lands*. Anchorage: Alaska Geographic, Alaska Northwest Publishing Co., 1981.

Mark Anthony, Leo and Tunley, A. Tom. *Introductory Geography and Geology of Alaska*. Anchorage: Polar Publishing Co., 1976.

Morrow, James E. *The Freshwater Fishes of Alaska*. Anchorage: Alaska Northwest Publishing Co., 1980.

Murie, Adolph. *The Grizzlies of Mount McKinley.* Washington, D.C.: U.S. Government Printing Office, 1981.

_____. *Wolves of Mount McKinley.* Washington, D.C.: U.S. Government Printing Office, 1971 (reprint of 1944 edition).

Péwé, Troy Lewis. *Permafrost and Its Effects on Life in the North.* Corvallis: Oregon State University Press, 1970.

Pruitt, William O., Jr. *Animals of the North.* New York: Harper and Row, 1967.

Rearden, Jim, ed. *Alaska Mammals.* Anchorage: Alaska Geographic, Alaska Northwest Publishing Co., 1981.

Ricketts, Edward R. and Calvin, Jack. *Between Pacific Tides.* Stanford, Calif.: Stanford University Press, 1968.

Stonehouse, Bernard. *Animals of the Arctic: The Ecology of the Far North.* New York: Holt, Rinehart and Winston, 1971.

Viereck, Leslie A. and Little, Elbert L., Jr. *Alaska Trees and Shrubs.* Forest Service, U.S. Department of Agriculture, Handbook No. 410. Washington, D.C.: U.S. Government Printing Office, 1972.

Wahrhaftig, Clyde. *Physiographic Divisions of Alaska.* U.S. Geological Survey Professional Paper No. 482. Washington, D.C.: U.S. Government Printing Office, 1965.

White, Helen A. *The Alaska–Yukon Wild Flower Guide.* Anchorage: Alaska Northwest Publishing Co., 1974.

Williams, Howel. *Landscapes of Alaska: Their Geologic Evolution.* Berkeley: University of California Press, 1958.

Alaska's history and people

Alaska Geographic. *Alaska's Oil/Gas and Minerals Industry.* Anchorage: Alaska Northwest Publishing Co., 1982

Arnold, Robert D. *Alaska Native Land Claims.* Anchorage: Alaska Native Foundation, 1978.

Balcom, Mary Gilmore. *Ghost Towns of Alaska.* Ketchikan, Alaska: Balcom Books, 1979.

Greiner, James. *Wager with the Wind: The Don Sheldon Story.* New York: Rand McNally, 1974.

Gunther, Erna. *Indian Life on the Northwest Coast of North America.* Chicago: University of Chicago Press, 1972.

Hanrahan, John and Gruenstein, Peter. *Lost Frontier: The Marketing of Alaska.* New York: W. W. Norton and Co., 1977.

Haycox, Steven W. and Betty J. *Melvin Ricks' Alaska Bibliography: An Introductory Guide to Alaskan Historical Literature.* Portland, Oreg.: Binford and Mort, Publishers, 1977.

Hippler, Arthur E. and Wood, John R. *The Alaskan Eskimoes: A Selected Annotated Bibliography.* Fairbanks: Institute of Social, Economic and Government Research, University of Alaska, 1977.

_____. *The Subarctic Athabascans: A Selected Annotated Bibliography.* Fairbanks: Institute of Social, Economic and Government Research, University of Alaska, 1974.

Hulley, Clarence. *Alaska: Past and Present.* Westport, Conn.: Greenwood Press, 1981. (Originally published in 1953 as *Alaska, 1741-1953.*)

Hunt, William R. *Alaska: A Bicentennial History.* New York: W. W. Norton and Co., 1976.

_____. *North of 53°: The Wild Days of the Alaska–Yukon Mining Frontier, 1870-1914.* New York: Macmillan, 1974.

Johnson, Hugh A. and Jorgenson, Harold T. *The Land Resources of Alaska.* Fairbanks: University of Alaska Press, 1977.

Jones, Dorothy M. and Wood, John R. *An Aleut Bibliography.* Fairbanks: Institute of Social, Economic and Government Research, University of Alaska, 1974.

Krause, Aurel. *The Tlingit Indians.* Seattle: University of Washington Press, 1956. Translated by Erna Gunther.

Kresge, David J.; Morehouse, Thomas A.; and Rogers, George W. *Issues in Alaska Development.* Seattle: University of Washington Press, 1978.

Morgan, Lael. *Alaska's Native People.* Anchorage: Alaska Geographic, Alaska Northwest Publishing Co., 1979.

_____. *And the Land Provides: Alaska Natives in a Year of Transition.* New York: Anchor Press, 1974.

Naske, Claus-M. *An Interpretative History of Alaskan Statehood.* Anchorage: Alaska Northwest Publishing Co., 1973.

Shalkop, Antoinette, ed. *Exploration in Alaska, A Bibliography.* Anchorage: Cook Inlet Historical Society, 1980.

Sherwood, Morgan, ed. *The Cook Inlet Collection: Two Hundred Years of Selected Alaskan History.* Anchorage: Alaska Northwest Publishing Co., 1974.

Weeden, Robert B. *Alaska: Promises to Keep.* Boston: Houghton Mifflin Co., 1978.

Recreation, travel and safety

The Milepost: Mile-By-Mile Logs of the Alaska Highway, All Highways in Alaska and Major Travel Routes Through Western Canada. Anchorage: Alaska Northwest Publishing Co., revised annually.

Bureau of Land Management. *Alaska's River Trails: Northern Region.* Anchorage (Brochure).

_____. *Alaska's River Trails: Southern Region.* Anchorage (Brochure).

Carter, Marilyn. *Floating Alaskan Rivers.* Palmer, Alaska: Aladdin Publishing Co., P.O. Box 364, 1982.

Gray, William, *et al. Alaska: High Roads to Adventure.* Washington, D.C.: National Geographic Society, 1976.

HCRS (Heritage Conservation and Recreation Service). *Alaska Float Trips: North of the Arctic Circle.* Anchorage: National Park Service.

_____. *Alaska Float Trips: Southwest Region.* Anchorage: National Park Service.

LaChapelle, Edward R. *The ABC of Avalanche Safety.* Seattle: The Mountaineers, 1978.

Lake, Larry. *Alaska Travel Guide.* Salt Lake City, Utah: P.O. Box 21038, revised annually.

Mitchell, Dick. *Mountaineering First Aid: A Guide to Accident Response and First Aid Care.* Seattle: The Mountaineers, 1975.

Mosby, Jack and Dapkus, David. *Alaska Paddling Guide.* Anchorage: I & R Enterprises, 1982.

Pacific Boating Almanac. Ventura, Calif.: Western Marine Enterprises, revised annually.

Perla, Ronald I. and Martinelli, M., Jr. *Avalanche Handbook.* Washington, D.C.: U.S. Government Printing Office, 1976.

Rearden, Jim. *Alaska Hunting Guide.* Anchorage: Alaska Northwest Publishing Co., 1979.

Stefansson, Vlhjalmur. *Arctic Manual.* Westport, Conn.: Greenwood Press, 1974 (reprint of 1944 edition).

Wayburn, Peggy. *Adventuring in Alaska.* San Francisco: Sierra Club Books, 1982.

Miscellaneous

Alaska. Anchorage: Alaska Northwest Publishing Co. (monthly periodical).

Alaska Almanac: Facts About Alaska. Anchorage: Alaska Northwest Publishing Co., revised annually.

Alaska Shippers Guide. Anchorage: Alaska Northwest Publishing Co., revised annually.

Arctic Institute of North America. *Arctic Bibliography.* Washington, D.C.: U.S. Government Printing Office, from 1953.

Kantola, Kristi. *Environmental Education Resources Directory for Alaska.* Juneau: U.S. Department of Agriculture, Forest Service, 1979.

Orth, Donald J. *Dictionary of Alaska Place Names.* U.S. Geological Survey Professional Paper 567. Washington, D.C.: U.S. Government Printing Office, 1967.

INDEX